PROPHETIC FIGURES IN LATE
SECOND TEMPLE JEWISH PALESTINE

Prophetic Figures in Late Second Temple Jewish Palestine

The Evidence from Josephus

REBECCA GRAY

New York   Oxford

OXFORD UNIVERSITY PRESS

1993

Oxford University Press

Oxford   New York   Toronto
Delhi   Bombay   Calcutta   Madras   Karachi
Kuala Lumpur   Singapore   Hong Kong   Tokyo
Nairobi   Dar es Salaam   Cape Town
Melbourne   Auckland   Madrid

and associated companies in
Berlin   Ibadan

Copyright © 1993 by Rebecca Gray

Published by Oxford University Press, Inc.
200 Madison Avenue, New York, New York 10016

Oxford is a registered trademark of Oxford University Press, Inc.

Library of Congress Cataloging-in-Publication Data
Gray, Rebecca, 1959–
Prophetic figures in late second temple Jewish Palestine : the evidence
from Josephus / Rebecca Gray.
p.   cm.   Includes bibliographical references and index.
ISBN 0-19-507615-X
1. Josephus, Flavius—Views on prophets.   2. Prophets—Palestine—Historiography.
3. Jews—History—168 B.C.–135 A.D.—Historiography.   I. Title.
DS115.9.J6G73   1993   933′.05′0922—dc20   92-22896

2 4 6 8 9 7 5 3 1
Printed in the United States of America
on acid-free paper

*To my parents,
Edwina Taker and Louis Gray,
with love and affection*

Acknowledgments

This book is a revised version of a doctoral dissertation submitted to the Faculty of Theology at Oxford University in August 1990. Many people assisted in the preparation of the original study and in its revision. Ed Sanders supervised my graduate work at Oxford, read several drafts of most of the material included here, and provided helpful advice throughout the various stages of the project. At least as important as his careful direction were his enthusiasm and encouragement, and the splendid example provided by his own work. John Barton read and commented on portions of the dissertation at an early stage, acted as my interim supervisor for two terms when Professor Sanders was on leave, and ultimately served as one of the examiners of the thesis. His work on prophecy has been an important stimulus to my own, and I greatly appreciate the interest he has shown and the support he has given over the years. Tessa Rajak, the other examiner of the dissertation, made numerous helpful suggestions. Fergus Millar and Martin Goodman read and commented on sections of the thesis and in other ways promoted my work at Oxford, for which I am very grateful. David Levene and the late Leslie Styler provided valuable assistance with the translation of several difficult passages in Josephus.

Scholars in the United States have also contributed to this book. David Aune helped me locate some important secondary material and recommended me to Louis Feldman. Professor Feldman generously permitted me to read a draft of his article on "Prophets and Prophecy in Josephus" (since published in *JTS* 41 [1990]: 386–422). A fruitful correspondence followed. The revision of the dissertation was undertaken at Yale University, where I was a Luce Post-Doctoral Fellow from 1990 to 1992. I am especially grateful to Steven Fraade, Susan Garrett, and Wayne Meeks, who carefully read the manuscript and made many helpful suggestions. Any errors that remain are, of course, my own.

I would like to thank Dr. Robin Fletcher, former Warden of Rhodes House, and the Trustees of the Rhodes Scholarship Trust for agreeing to extend funding for an additional year beyond the completion of my bachelor's degree. I am also indebted to the Trustees of the Hall-Houghton Fund, who provided generous financial support from 1986 to 1988. The dissertation was completed during my tenure as Edward White Bate Junior Research Fellow at Brasenose College, Oxford. I am grateful to Sir John Smith of the Manifold Trust for funding that fellowship, and to my colleagues in the Senior Common Room at Brasenose for making my time there both stimulating and enjoyable. Thanks are due also to the Henry R. Luce Foundation, which funded the fellowship at Yale that allowed me to revise the work at my leisure.

Davidson, N.C.   R. G.
August 1992

Contents

A Note on Translation

When quoting individual words, brief phrases, or short passages from Josephus, I have either given my own translation, quoted the translation of the Loeb Classical Library (LCL) edition, or given a slightly modified version of the LCL translation. Longer passages are quoted from the LCL translation unless otherwise noted. The Loeb text and translation are reprinted by permission of the publishers and the Loeb Classical Library from *Josephus,* in ten volumes, translated by H. St. J. Thackeray, R. Marcus, A. Wikgren, and L. H. Feldman (Cambridge, Mass.: Harvard University Press, 1926–65). Passages from the Hebrew Bible and the New Testament are ordinarily quoted from the Revised Standard Version. When citing texts from the Dead Sea Scrolls, I have selected from and occasionally amalgamated the translations of G. Vermes, M. Knibb, and A. Dupont-Sommer. For passages from the Mishnah and the Babylonian Talmud, I have used the translations of H. Danby and the Soncino edition (ed. I. Epstein), respectively. See the bibliography for details of all these works.

Abbreviations

ANRW	*Aufstieg und Niedergang der römischen Welt*, ed. H. Temporini and W. Haase
Ant.	Josephus, *Jewish Antiquities*
ASTI	*Annual of the Swedish Institute*
b	Babylonian Talmud
BZAW	Beihefte zur *Zeitschrift für die alttestamentliche Wissenschaft*
BZNW	Beihefte zur *Zeitschrift für die neutestamentliche Wissenschaft*
CBQ	*Catholic Biblical Quarterly*
CRINT	Compendia Rerum Iudaicarum ad Novum Testamentum
Enc. Jud.	*Encyclopaedia Judaica*, ed. Cecil Roth
ET	English translation
HTR	*Harvard Theological Review*
HUCA	*Hebrew Union College Annual*
IEJ	*Israel Exploration Journal*
JBL	*Journal of Biblical Literature*
JE	*The Jewish Encyclopedia*, ed. Isidore Singer
JJS	*Journal of Jewish Studies*
JQR	*Jewish Quarterly Review*
JSJ	*Journal for the Study of Judaism*
JSNT	*Journal for the Study of the New Testament*

JSNTS	*Journal for the Study of the New Testament,* Supplement Series
JSOT	*Journal for the Study of the Old Testament*
JSOTS	*Journal for the Study of the Old Testament,* Supplement Series
JSPS	*Journal for the Study of the Pseudepigrapha,* Supplement Series
JTS	*Journal of Theological Studies*
LCL	Loeb Classical Library
Lewis and Short	Charlton Lewis and Charles Short, *A Latin Dictionary*
Liddell and Scott	Henry George Liddell and Robert Scott, *A Greek-English Lexicon*
LXX	Septuagint
MT	Masoretic text
Naber	Samuel A. Naber, ed., *Flavii Josephi opera omnia*
Niese	Benedict Niese, ed., *Flavii Josephi opera*
NovT	*Novum Testamentum*
NovTS	*Novum Testamentum,* Supplement Series
NTS	*New Testament Studies*
OS	*Oudtestamentische Studiën*
R.	Rabbi, Rab, or Rabban
RE	Pauly-Wissowa, *Realencyclopädie der classischen Altertumswissenschaft*
Rengstorf	K. H. Rengstorf, ed., *A Complete Concordance to Flavius Josephus*
RQ	*Revue de Qumran*
SBL	Society of Biblical Literature
SJLA	Studies in Judaism in Late Antiquity
SNTSMS	Society for New Testament Studies Monograph Series
TDNT	*Theological Dictionary of the New Testament,* ed. Gerhard Kittel and Gerhard Friedrich

TU	Texte und Untersuchungen
VT	*Vetus Testamentum*
VTS	*Vetus Testamentum,* Supplement Series
War	Josephus, *Jewish War*
WUNT	Wissenschaftliche Untersuchungen zum Neuen Testament
y	Jerusalem Talmud
ZAW	*Zeitschrift für die alttestamentliche Wissenschaft*

PROPHETIC FIGURES IN LATE
SECOND TEMPLE JEWISH PALESTINE

Introduction

In recent years there has been renewed interest in the question of how Jesus of Nazareth should be classified in terms of religious or social type. Should he be described primarily as a teacher, prophet, miracle worker, magician, Galilean charismatic, or militant revolutionary? The list of possibilities could be extended. These types are not mutually exclusive, and it is possible—indeed likely—that a given individual would have combined different roles. But it is still worth asking which single type best describes Jesus.

There is no real consensus among New Testament scholars on this question, but many would agree that the best single category in which to place Jesus is that of prophet. Most studies of Jesus' role as prophet, however, have relied on models based on the classical prophets of the Hebrew Bible—figures like Amos, Isaiah, and Jeremiah—as these figures have been understood by modern critical scholars. Only recently have attempts been made to compare Jesus with contemporary Jewish prophets, and to determine what prophecy might have meant in a specifically first-century context.[1]

The present work is intended as a contribution toward a better understanding of Jewish prophecy around the time of Jesus. It examines the evidence from Josephus for prophetic figures in Jewish Palestine in the late Second Temple period. There are good reasons for beginning a study of early Jewish prophecy with Josephus. His works are, without question, the richest and most important source of information about events in Palestine during this period. They contain a great deal of material about prophets and prophecy, much of which has gone unnoticed by scholars. Also, in comparison with the other literary sources for the study of early Jewish prophecy—sources that include apocalyptic texts and other apocryphal and pseudepigraphical works, rabbinic literature, the Dead Sea Scrolls, and the gospels—Josephus' works present relatively few problems of interpretation. We at least know when they were written, where, and by whom; we also know quite a lot about the career and interests of their author. The interpretation of this material remains a complicated

matter, but it is made easier by general agreement on the most important
introductory questions.

Biographical Sketch

Josephus was born in Jerusalem in 37 C.E. to aristocratic parents of
priestly and royal pedigree: on his father's side, the family traced its
descent back to the daughter of the Hasmonean high priest Jonathan
(161–143/2 B.C.E.).[2] At the age of nineteen, after a trial investigation of
all three major Jewish religious parties—Pharisees, Sadducees, and
Essenes—and a period spent in the wilderness with an ascetic teacher,
Josephus entered public life and decided to "follow the party of the Pharisees."[3] When the revolt against Rome broke out in 66 C.E., he was sent
to Galilee by the revolutionary government to organize the Jewish war
effort in the region. Less than a year later, in the spring of 67, he and his
troops were besieged by the Romans in the Galilean city of Jotapata. The
city fell after forty-seven days, and Josephus himself surrendered to the
enemy. He was brought before the Roman general Vespasian, where he
made a bold prediction: Vespasian was destined to become emperor.
Though he had originally planned to send Josephus to Nero in Rome,
Vespasian decided, after the prediction, to keep the Jewish general as a
prisoner in his own camp. Two years later, in the summer of 69, Josephus' prediction was fulfilled when Vespasian was proclaimed emperor
by the Roman legions in Alexandria. He was released from his chains and
spent the remainder of the war in the Roman camp, performing various
services for Vespasian's son Titus, who took over command of the
Roman forces in Palestine after his father's elevation to the imperial
throne. Josephus was present at the final siege of Jerusalem and witnessed
the destruction of the temple and the fall of the city in 70 C.E.

   After the war, Josephus accompanied Titus to Rome, where he was
made a Roman citizen, given a residence in the former house of the
emperor, and assigned a pension. It was in Rome that Josephus composed all four of his literary works: the *Jewish War*, a history of the revolt
and the events leading up to it (completed in the late seventies); the *Jewish Antiquities*, a longer work recounting the history of the Jews from creation to the outbreak of the revolt (completed in 93 or 94 C.E.); the *Life*,
primarily an account of his activities as general in Galilee (probably published in the late nineties); and an apologetic tract known as *Against
Apion* (probably also dating from the late nineties).[4]

The Plan of the Present Work

While isolated passages from Josephus are routinely cited in survey works
on early Jewish prophecy, no full-scale study of this material has so far

been undertaken.[5] In the present work the evidence from Josephus is interpreted in relation to his personal career and his thought and writings as a whole. The study begins with a general topic. Scholars usually suppose that Jews in the late Second Temple period believed that prophecy had ceased at some point in the past. Chapter 1 examines the evidence from Josephus on this matter and outlines a general theory about the nature and status of prophecy in this period. Chapter 2 considers the prophetic claims that Josephus makes for himself and argues that these claims are both more substantial and more important for a proper understanding of Josephus than is usually thought. These first two chapters introduce some of the most significant features of Josephus' general conception of prophecy and provide the framework for interpreting the evidence considered in the remaining chapters of the book. Chapters 3, 4, and 5 examine the most important passages from Josephus concerning prophetic figures from this period and describe the prophetic types that these individuals represent. It will become apparent that the division into types on the basis of characteristic message and behavior corresponds, in part, to a difference in the social position of these figures: some types of prophecy are represented only by individuals who come from the ordinary people (the sign prophets and Jesus son of Ananias), while others are represented only by figures from the more literate strata of Palestinian society (Josephus and the Essenes).[6] One unfortunate effect of the dominance of the model of the prophetic office based on the classical prophets of the Hebrew Bible is that the literate figures are often ignored in, or dismissed from, discussions of early Jewish prophecy.[7] They receive full treatment here.

It will be important throughout this study to consider the literary context of Josephus' reports, both their immediate context and the more general setting provided by the works in which these reports occur. In particular, the purposes and character of Josephus' individual works and the differences among them should be borne in mind. The question of whether Josephus' treatment of a given prophet reflects the influence of a literary source will occasionally have to be raised.

Though my interest in early Jewish prophecy began with Jesus of Nazareth, I shall refer to him only tangentially in this study. The one substantial reference to Jesus in Josephus' works, the so-called *Testimonium Flavianum* (*Ant.* 18.63–64), is notoriously problematic. There is wide agreement that the passage as it now stands has been altered by Christian interpolators, but no agreement on what Josephus originally wrote about Jesus.[8] The interpretation of the evidence from the gospels is even more controversial and would require a full-length study of its own. I have also excluded John the Baptist from consideration here primarily because there is already a sizable body of secondary literature on him which includes discussion of the account in Josephus (*Ant.* 18.116–19). There is an additional reason for excluding both of these figures from the present study: many investigations of early Jewish prophecy are, in my view, too narrowly determined by the writer's interest in illuminating the material about Jesus and John. It is easier to consider the topic in its own right, and in the proper dimensions, if these two figures are omitted from consideration.

The terms "prophet" and "prophecy" are here used in a very broad way. I began my research by adopting the standard definitions of these terms in use among biblical scholars. As I noted earlier, these definitions are based almost exclusively on the classical prophets of the Hebrew Bible. They also reflect the important and relatively recent critical insight that these great prophets were not primarily predictors of the future but rather social, moral, and religious critics and reformers. In the course of my work I have found it necessary to expand, refine, and correct the standard definitions in light of Josephus' use of prophetic terminology. I shall repeatedly draw attention to the differences between the modern-critical understanding of prophecy and the early Jewish view; a great deal is to be gained by temporarily suspending our current assumptions and looking at things through Josephus' eyes. His treatment of the ancient prophets is especially instructive. He does not share the bias of most modern biblical scholars toward the classical prophets of the pre-exilic and exilic periods and so rescues some of the other ancient prophets from obscurity. He also frequently fails to distinguish figures whom we would call "prophets" from others who might be classified as "prognosticators," "apocalyptists," or "mantic wise men." His failure to make these distinctions can help us to see that some of the distinctions we routinely make are really rather artificial. One aim, then, of the present work is to broaden our conception of prophecy beyond the narrow understanding current among biblical scholars.

This study is restricted almost exclusively to the works of Josephus, though other sources are considered at appropriate points (especially in chapter 3). The results of my investigation might serve as a framework for interpreting the other sources of information about early Jewish prophecy. They could provide no more than a framework, since it is impossible to know in advance how representative Josephus' evidence and his views on prophecy are; but at least they could suggest some possible starting points for further investigation and for comparative study of all the sources.

1

Josephus and the Belief that Prophecy Had Ceased

The interpretation of the evidence concerning individual prophetic figures in Jewish Palestine in the late Second Temple period has, to a very large degree, been determined by more general convictions about the nature and status of prophecy in this period. For that reason, this investigation begins with a discussion of these larger issues.

It is often argued or assumed that Jews in this period believed that prophecy had ceased at some point in the past. The text most frequently cited as evidence for such a view is Tosefta Sotah 13.2: "From the death of Haggai, Zechariah and Malachi, the latter prophets, the Holy Spirit ceased from Israel. But in spite of that it was allowed them to hear messages from God by a Bath Qol [lit. "daughter of a voice"]."[1] Other texts from the late Hebrew Bible materials, the apocrypha and pseudepigrapha, Josephus, and the rabbinic literature have been adduced as evidence for the view that prophecy had come to an end.[2]

These passages have been systematically discussed by others, and it is not my intention to review their results here.[3] Most previous discussions of the topic have been concerned chiefly with the question of how widespread belief in the cessation of prophecy was, that is, with the question of which segments of the Jewish community shared this belief. It is normally assumed that, for those who accepted it, the belief that prophecy had ended had the status of an absolute dogma.

I wish to challenge this last assumption. The question raised in this chapter may be put as follows: How was the view that prophecy had ceased actually understood by those who held it? That is, what were the practical implications of such a belief? How did it affect the assessment of contemporary figures who claimed prophetic powers? In particular, did the view that prophecy had ceased entail the belief that there was no longer anything at all like prophecy and no one at all like the prophets?

The passage from the Tosefta quoted above already suggests that this

7

last question ought to be answered in the negative: prophecy had ceased, but God still communicated by means of a Bath Qol, that is, in a way apparently different from, yet analogous to, the way he had communicated in the past through prophets. The evidence from Josephus points in the same direction. In two passages, Josephus indicates that he believed that prophecy of a particular sort had ceased at some point in the past. The first of these passages, *Against Apion* 1.41, is regularly discussed in the secondary literature on this topic; the second, *Antiquities* 3.218, has received less attention. The present chapter begins with an examination of these passages (pp. 8–23). There is, in addition, persuasive evidence that Josephus thought that the whole variegated phenomenon of prophecy had come to an end; this evidence is considered in the next section (pp. 23–26).

In spite of the fact that Josephus seems to have believed that prophecy belonged, in some sense, to the past, it can be demonstrated that he thought that there were still, in his own day, individuals who said and did very much the same sorts of things as the ancient prophets had said and done. In the second part of the chapter this point is illustrated in relation to the important topics of prophetic inspiration (pp. 27–30) and prediction of the future (pp. 30–34).

Finally, if Josephus did believe both that prophecy had ended sometime in the past and that certain of his contemporaries were very much like the ancient prophets, then this fact will affect our general understanding of the belief that prophecy had ceased. The argument made here takes up and develops the suggestion of John Barton that this belief should be understood not as a rigid dogma about the end of prophecy but rather as one expression of a wider nostalgia for the distant past.

Evidence that Josephus Believed that Prophecy Had Ceased

Against Apion *1.41: Prophecy and the Writing of History*

In *Against Apion* 1.39–40 Josephus gives a brief description of the twenty-two "justly accredited" books of the Jews:

> Of these, five are the books of Moses, comprising the laws and the traditional history from the birth of humanity down to his [Moses'] death. This period falls only a little short of three thousand years. From the death of Moses until Artaxerxes, who succeeded Xerxes as king of Persia, the prophets subsequent to Moses wrote the history of the events of their own times in thirteen books. The remaining four books contain hymns to God and precepts for the conduct of human life.[4]

He adds a further comment in 1.41:

> From Artaxerxes to our own time the complete history has been written,
> but has not been deemed worthy of equal credit with the earlier records,
> because of the failure of the exact succession of the prophets.

This last passage is regularly cited as evidence that Josephus believed that prophecy had ceased in Israel sometime during the Persian period.[5] We shall see that this claim needs to be very substantially qualified. Consideration of the context of the passage will show that it concerns only one very limited type of prophecy, namely, the type that resulted in the composition of historical narrative. In addition, we shall see that Josephus' theory that "the exact succession of the prophets" had come to an end after the reign of Artaxerxes is not, in the first instance, a theory about the disappearance of individuals called "prophets," but rather a reflection of a particular view about the limits of the age in which authoritative *writings* were produced.

Against Apion 1.6–56 is the first of a series of arguments that Josephus makes in response to critics of his account of the origin of the Jews in his earlier work, the *Antiquities*. These critics disputed Josephus' claims about the extreme antiquity of the Jewish people and pointed out in support of their position that the Jews are not mentioned in the works of the best-known Greek historians of antiquity (*Against Apion* 1.2). In response, Josephus argues that the Greeks—in contrast to the Egyptians, Babylonians, Phoenicians, and especially the Jews—are not reliable historians of the most ancient period, and thus that their failure to mention the Jews is not really significant. According to him, "the proof of historical veracity is universal agreement in the description, oral or written, of the same events" (1.26). Greek historians of antiquity fail precisely when measured by this most important standard: "More often than not they confute each other in their works, not hesitating to give the most contradictory accounts of the same events" (1.15). Examples of such contradictions are provided in 1.16–18.

In Josephus' view, the primary cause of the inconsistencies and contradictions in the works of the Greek historians of antiquity is the lack of reliable sources for the earliest period of Greek history (1.6–14, 20, 23). The most ancient Greek records, the poems of Homer, were originally transmitted orally and only later collected and committed to writing; as a result, Josephus complains, they contain "numerous inconsistencies" (1.12). The earliest written Greek histories are from a relatively late date (1.13), and the first philosophers who wrote did not produce much material and were in any case dependent on the works of Egyptians and Chaldeans (1.14). Because they are in possession of so few reliable sources for the early period, Josephus considers it "absurd that the Greeks should be so conceited as to think themselves the sole possessors of a knowledge of antiquity and the only accurate reporters of its history" (1.15).

It is in relation to these observations about the sources available to the historians of Greek origins that Josephus' comments about the authorship, preservation, and reliability of Jewish texts in *Against Apion* 1.28–41 must be understood. In defending his own account of Jewish origins in the *Antiquities*, Josephus claims that he has had access to more reliable sources than his Greek counterparts. As he indicates more than once, his sources for the early period were the "sacred books" of the Jews, identical with the twenty-two "justly accredited" books described in *Against Apion* 1.39–40.[6] It should be noted that he regards these books here as historical sources. Also, because the dispute in *Against Apion* concerns the origin and earliest history of the Jews, Josephus' attention is focused on his sources for that period, the five books of Moses; his comments in 1.40 about the works of the successors to Moses and in 1.41 about more recent histories are not fully developed, and their meaning is not entirely clear. In the main argument of *Against Apion* 1.6–56, then, Josephus is comparing his own account of the origin and earliest history of the Jews in the *Antiquities* with the Greek histories referred to in 1.16–18, and the sacred books of the Jews—especially the books of Moses—with the poetry of Homer and the other Greek sources mentioned in 1.12–14.

Josephus' constructive argument about the reliability of the ancient Jewish historical records concerns both the composition of these works and their preservation. He assigns these two tasks, respectively, to prophets and priests. It would be fair to say that Josephus could have indicated this division of labor more clearly. He nowhere says, in so many words, that the prophets wrote the records and then the priests were given charge over them, and he further confuses the issue by lumping prophets and priests together in one passage (1.29) and assigning to them, collectively, the task of preserving the records. But in 1.37 Josephus says explicitly that the prophets alone (μόνων τῶν προφητῶν) wrote the records, and when he describes these records in summary form in 1.39–40, they are all attributed to prophetic authors.[7]

The role of the priests in relation to the sacred books and the prophets who wrote them is more difficult to establish. Commentators are often puzzled by Josephus' inclusion, in 1.30–36, of an argument concerning the keeping of priestly genealogies.[8] He introduces this section by saying that he intends to demonstrate that the ancient Jewish historical records had been preserved down to his own time, and would continue to be preserved in the future, "with scrupulous accuracy" (1.29). The argument he makes is twofold. First, he claims that the ancient records of the Jews were entrusted in the beginning to "men of the highest character, devoted to the service of God" (1.30). The continuation of the passage suggests that he is referring to the priests. This is confirmed by *Antiquities* 4.304, where Josephus reports that Moses, author of the most ancient records, handed over all the books he had written "to the priests" shortly before his death (cf. Deut. 31.9). Chapter 2 will consider further evidence that Josephus assumed that priests were the proper physical guardians of sacred texts; we shall see there that he also believed that priests were specially qualified to interpret the meaning of such texts. Josephus nowhere explains why he supposed that the care and preservation of sacred books should be a specifically priestly responsibility or why priests could be relied upon to preserve such texts "with scrupulous accuracy"; apparently he felt these things were so obvious that they required no explanation.[9]

Josephus, then, assumed that the ancient Jewish historical records would be accurately preserved as long as they remained in the care of legitimate priests. The discussion of priestly genealogies that forms the second part of his argument in *Against Apion* 1.30–36 is intended to assure the reader that the purity of the priestly line had been scrupulously maintained from the beginning down to his own day, and therefore that all those who had been entrusted with the care of the historical records through the ages had been duly qualified for the task.

It is only in 1.37, and there only parenthetically, that Josephus indicates why he thought that the *original* records concerning the history of the Jews could be relied upon to be completely consistent and accurate: these records had all been written by prophets, "obtaining their knowledge of the most remote and ancient history through the inspiration which they owed to God, and committing to writing a clear account of the events of their own time just as they occurred." Josephus here distinguishes between the writing of "the most remote and ancient history" (τὰ . . . ἀνωτάτω καὶ παλαιότατα), and the writing of the history of the events of one's own day (τὰ . . . καθ᾽ αὑτούς).[10] This distinction corresponds to the one he draws between Moses and his successors in 1.39–40: Moses wrote "the traditional history" (παράδοσις) from the creation down to the time of his own death, while the prophets after Moses wrote "the history of the events of their own times" (τὰ κατ᾽ αὑτοὺς πραχθέντα). In 1.37 Josephus states explicitly that the composition of the history of the very earliest period, undertaken by Moses, required divine inspiration (ἡ ἐπίπνοια ἡ ἀπὸ τοῦ θεοῦ), and it is easy to see why he might have thought that this was so: if Moses knew exactly what had happened at the creation of the world and in the earliest period of Israel's history (and Josephus, of course, assumed that he did), this could not be because he had been there to observe and record events, but only because he was granted this knowledge by God. Josephus says nothing at all, in the present passage, about how the successors to Moses obtained their knowledge of the events of their own day, but I think we must suppose that he believed that they, too, were inspired; this much seems to be implied by the fact that he thought of them as prophets.[11] Still, Josephus does make a distinction of sorts between Moses and his successors: while the writing of the history of the events of one's own day was a prophetic task, requiring inspiration, the writing of ancient history required a special, more extraordinary sort of inspiration, which had been enjoyed only by Moses.[12]

In 1.41 Josephus goes on to make a further distinction, this time between all the historical books of ancient origin (those written by Moses and his successors) and more recent works, including, presumably, his own history of the Jewish revolt against Rome. He acknowledges that the more recent works have not been as highly regarded as the ancient ones, and he explains this fact as a result of "the failure of the exact succession of the prophets" (τὸ μὴ γενέσθαι τὴν τῶν προφητῶν ἀκριβῆ διαδοχήν). In the remainder of this section I shall try to determine what Josephus meant, in this context, when he spoke of "the exact succession of the prophets," and why he thought that this succession had come to an end after the reign of the Persian ruler Artaxerxes I (fifth century B.C.E.).

Apart from the passage in *Against Apion* which we have been considering, there is no evidence that Josephus had a well-developed notion of a continuous prophetic "succession" (διαδοχή) stretching from the time of Moses into the Persian period. He knew from scripture that Joshua had been the successor to Moses and that Elisha had succeeded Elijah, but he does not emphasize or elaborate on these relationships in the *Antiquities*, and he does not develop a general theory of the succession of the prophets in that work.[13] The idea of a continuous prophetic succession, as expressed in *Against Apion* 1.37–41, appears to be directly related to the existence of a set of writings which were believed to record, with complete accuracy, the history of the entire period from Moses to Artaxerxes. In fact, the theory of a continuous prophetic succession seems to be *derived from* the existence of such a set of writings, in something like the following way: Josephus believed that only prophets, inspired by God, were capable of writing perfectly accurate history; there existed what he regarded as perfectly accurate histories for each successive period from Moses to Artaxerxes; therefore, he concluded, there must have been a prophet in each successive generation throughout this period who recorded the history of his own day.

This way of putting things is, of course, rather artificial. I do not suppose that Josephus' thought consciously followed the steps just outlined, or that he would have stated his view in this way if he had been asked about it directly. Nevertheless, I believe that the summary given here correctly describes the actual direction of the logic underlying his position. Josephus' theory that a continuous prophetic succession had existed in the period from Moses to Artaxerxes is, in my view, inferred from the existence of a set of writings, regarded as authoritative, which chronicled the history of the Jews throughout this same period.

Similarly, I would argue that Josephus' conviction that "the exact succession of the prophets" had come to an end after the reign of Artaxerxes is primarily a reflection of certain facts about the written sources that were available to him when he was composing the *Antiquities* and not, in the first instance at least, a theory about the disappearance of individuals called "prophets." Two things seem to have shaped his view. First, there was the simple fact that the historical sources for the period after Arta-xerxes were not very abundant; and second, even the sources that did exist for this period were not as highly regarded as the sources for the ear-lier period: as Josephus writes in *Against Apion* 1.41, the histories written after Artaxerxes had "not been deemed worthy of equal credit with the earlier records." These two points require further consideration.

It can be seen from the *Antiquities* that Josephus arranged the five books of Moses and the thirteen books written by the prophets after Moses in what he thought was their chronological order, beginning with Genesis and ending with the book of Esther, which he believed had been written during the reign of Artaxerxes I.[14] For the entire period between Esther (and Artaxerxes) and the outbreak of the Maccabean revolt, Jose-phus had as source material mainly some popular legends about Alex-ander the Great, the story of the Tobiads, and the Letter of Aristeas. He follows 1 Maccabees for the early Maccabean period, but then runs out of written Jewish sources completely.[15] I suggest that, by the kind of log-ical process described above, the discontinuous nature of his sources for the period after Artaxerxes led Josephus to conclude that there had no longer been, in this period, a continuous succession of prophets of the history-writing sort.

It might be objected that Josephus does not actually say, in *Against Apion* 1.41, that historical sources were lacking for the period from Arta-xerxes to his own day; on the contrary, he says that "the complete his-tory" of this period had been written. Two points can be made in response. First, the Loeb Classical Library (LCL) translation, quoted here, may be misleading. The phrase γέγραπται ... ἕκαστα may not mean "the complete history has been written" in the sense that every sin-gle event had been recorded, but rather in the sense that every single period of history had been recorded.[16] That is, the phrase may describe the actual state of Josephus' sources for the later period: there was enough material to string together a story, but not enough to write a completely comprehensive history of the period. It must be admitted, however, that the LCL translation is the more natural of the two. But—and this is my second point—even if Josephus does claim in this passage that a complete account existed of all the events from the time of Artaxerxes down to his own day, examination of the *Antiquities* shows that this was not the case. I have suggested that it was partly the scarcity of sources for this period that led him to conclude that the exact succession of the prophets had come to an end.

The second factor that seems to have shaped Josephus' view has to do with the relative status of ancient and modern histories in his day. In *Against Apion* 1.41 Josephus says that it was *because of* the failure of the exact succession of the prophets that historical works from the period after Artaxerxes were not as highly regarded as earlier histories, but I would suggest, once again, that the logic underlying his position may actually have run in the opposite direction. That is, it may be that the ancient historical works Josephus describes in *Against Apion* 1.39–40 had in fact come to be more highly regarded in his day than more recent histories,[17] and that he concluded from this that there were no longer prophets of the sort who produced historical works worthy of the highest regard.

In reality, the relationship between the idea that prophecy of the history-writing sort had ceased at some time in the past and the idea that ancient historical works were more reliable than modern ones was more complicated than this description suggests. I have argued that the conviction that there were no longer completely reliable history books, as there had been in the past, led Josephus to the conclusion that there were no longer prophets of the sort who wrote completely reliable history; but it is clear that this conclusion, once arrived at, would itself have served to reinforce the original conviction that modern history books were not as reliable as ancient ones—how could they be, if there were no more prophets to write them? The reasoning is thus slightly circular, but I would still maintain that Josephus' theory that the exact succession of the prophets had ceased after the reign of Artaxerxes is primarily a reflection of prior convictions about the relative status of the twenty-two "justly accredited" books described in *Against Apion* 1.39–40, on the one hand, and more modern writings on the other.

Before leaving this topic, I must correct a mistaken impression that my argument so far may have created. I have written in some instances as if Josephus' views about the authority and reliability of the twenty-two books described in *Against Apion* 1.39–40 were his own private opinions, but it is clear that he believed that these views were commonly held by Jews. The twenty-two books are, he says, "justly accredited," that is, by Jews as a whole. Similarly, in 1.41 he reports it as a matter of general consensus that more recent works are not as reliable as the histories written by Moses and his successors.[18] In 1.42–43 he claims that all Jews regarded these latter books as the decrees of God and were even willing to die for them. There is no reason to doubt that most Jews of Josephus' day did share his views about the authority and reliability of the twenty-two books described in *Against Apion* 1.39–40, though a lengthy argument would probably be required to prove the point. Similarly, the beliefs that I have described as being derived from these views—namely, that these books had been written by prophets and that the exact succession of such prophets had ceased in the distant past—appear to have been widespread.[19]

One final question needs to be raised. Granted that Josephus believed that the exact succession of the prophets had come to an end after the reign of Artaxerxes, does this mean that he thought there were no more prophets *at all* who were capable of writing reliable history, and that it was impossible that such a prophet should appear, or only that there was no longer an *exact succession* of such prophets?[20]

One passage in the *Antiquities* might suggest that the latter interpretation is correct, and that Josephus did think that the occasional prophet-historian might still appear in the period after Artaxerxes. In *Antiquities* 1.240–41 Josephus quotes the first-century B.C.E. Greek historian Alexander Polyhistor, who, in turn, refers to a history of the Jews written by "Cleodemus the prophet [ὁ προφήτης], also called Malchus" (1.240). Very little is known about this Cleodemus.[21] The passage that refers to him is quoted by Josephus in support of an anonymous tradition according to which the land of Africa was named after a descendant of Abraham who had shared in the conquest of Libya.[22] The designation of Cleodemus as "the prophet" is part of the quotation from his source, however, and for that reason it is difficult to know whether Josephus himself attached any real significance to the term in this instance.

We might get a better idea of precisely how Josephus understood the "failure of the exact succession of the prophets" if we could establish how he saw his own role as a historian in relation to the ancient prophet-historians, Moses and his successors. Did he think that in writing the history of the events of his own day he was performing a prophetic task?

It is quite difficult to answer this question satisfactorily. In the introduction to the *War*, Josephus explains that he does not intend to describe events from the earliest period of Jewish history, since these events had already been recorded by prophets in scripture and translated into Greek by earlier historians (*War* 1.17).[23] He will begin his own work "where the historians of these events and our prophets conclude" (1.18).[24] This statement can be (and has been) interpreted in two opposing ways: either Josephus is claiming to continue the work of the prophets who wrote scripture, or he is implicitly acknowledging that his own work does *not* continue theirs. It is impossible, on the basis of this passage alone, to decide between the two alternatives. We must look for other evidence of how Josephus understood his role as a historian.

In this connection, it is significant that Josephus never defends the accuracy of his history of the Jewish revolt by referring to his credentials as a prophet. His most spirited defense of the *War* occurs in *Against Apion* 1.47–56, at the close of the argument about Jewish and non-Jewish historical works that has been considered in this section. In this passage, Josephus defends the accuracy of his history of the revolt in a perfectly ordinary way by reminding his readers that he was an eyewitness to most of the events he describes, kept careful notes, and had access to information that was inaccessible to other historians of the war. He makes no suggestion that he was inspired by God or that his account of events was in any way supernaturally guaranteed. His failure to make such claims is all the more significant since he did not hesitate to make prophetic claims for himself in other contexts, as we shall see in chapter 2.

It therefore seems that Josephus did not claim to be a prophet-historian of the same stature as Moses or even of the same stature as the successors to Moses who wrote before the time of Artaxerxes. This, in turn, would suggest that he understood "the failure of the exact succession of the prophets" in the stronger of the two senses defined above. Josephus seems to have believed that there were no more prophets at all of the sort who could write absolutely authoritative history and that it was impossible that such a prophet should appear in his own day.

Antiquities *3.218: John Hyrcanus and* the End of Priestly Divination

In a little-noticed passage in *Antiquities* 3, Josephus states that one particular sort of divination, which involved the use of some of the vestments worn by the high priest, had ceased to be practiced at a definite point in the past. We shall see that Josephus considered such divination a form of prophecy and believed that its last practitioner had been the Hasmonean high priest John Hyrcanus. I shall suggest several reasons why Josephus might have associated this kind of prophecy with Hyrcanus. Finally, I shall ask whether anything can be learned about Josephus' more general views on the cessation of prophecy from his convictions about the end of priestly divination.

In *Antiquities* 3.102–87 Josephus describes the construction and provisioning of the original Mosaic tabernacle. The passage includes a description of the vestments worn by the ordinary priests (3.151–58), as well as a description of the four items of apparel peculiar to the high priest: the blue tunic (3.159–61), the ephod (3.162), the breastplate or ἐσσήν[25] (3.163–71), and the headdress (3.172–78). After a brief explanation of the symbolic significance of the tabernacle, its furnishings, and the priestly vestments (3.179–87), Josephus resumes the main narrative in 3.188. He soon digresses again, however, in order to provide some additional information about the ephod and breastplate worn by the high priest. I quote the relevant passage in full:

> However, I would here record a detail which I omitted concerning the vestments of the high-priest. For Moses left no possible opening for the malpractices of prophets, should there in fact be any capable of abusing the divine prerogative, but left to God supreme authority whether to attend the sacred rites, when it so pleased Him, or to absent himself; and this he wished to be made manifest not to Hebrews only but also to any strangers who chanced to be present. Well, of those stones which, as I said before, the high-priest wore upon his shoulders—they were sardonyxes, and I deem it superfluous to indicate the nature of jewels familiar to all—it came about, whenever God assisted at the sacred ceremonies, that the one that was buckled on the right shoulder began to shine, a light glancing from it, visible to the most distant, of which the stone had before betrayed no trace. That alone should be marvel enough for such as have not cultivated a superior wisdom to disparage all religious things; but I have yet a greater marvel to record.

By means of the twelve stones, which the high-priest wore upon his breast stitched into the breastplate, God foreshowed victory to those on the eve of battle. For so brilliant a light flashed out from them, ere the army was yet in motion, that it was evident to the whole host that God had come to their aid. Hence it is that those Greeks who revere our practices, because they can in no way gainsay them, call the breastplate *logion* [oracle]. Howbeit, breastplate and sardonyx alike ceased to shine two hundred years before I composed this work, because of God's displeasure at the transgression of the laws. (*Ant.* 3.214–18)[26]

This passage requires some explanation. In ancient Israel, priests practiced various sorts of divination, the most important being divination by means of the Urim and Thummim. The precise nature of these objects and the method of their operation are unknown, but it is generally agreed that they were sacred lots of some sort that were used to obtain oracular responses from God. They were stored in a pocket in the breastplate worn by the high priest, which was attached to the ephod, a kind of overgarment worn by the high priest on the upper body.[27] Apparently because of their association with the Urim and Thummim, the ephod and breastplate eventually came to be regarded as divinatory instruments themselves.[28]

Josephus never mentions the Urim and Thummim, probably because he himself did not know what these objects were or how they had been used to secure oracular responses. He does, however, attribute oracular powers to both the ephod and the breastplate. In the passage just quoted, he provides an explanation of how these two oracles worked. Both functioned by the flashing of lights: the sardonyx on the right side of the ephod would shine whenever God was in attendance at the temple, and the stones on the breastplate would light up before battle if victory were assured. This explanation may still reflect the early association of the ephod and breastplate with the Urim and Thummim, for it appears to be related to a traditional etymology according to which the word "Urim" signified "light" or "enlightenment." The same etymology associated "Thummim" with the notion of "perfection" or "fulfillment," and it may be that there was some connection between this second half of the etymology and Josephus' view that divination performed with the aid of the ephod and breastplate was superior to advice given by prophets. More on this later.[29]

Judging from the terminology that he uses to describe it, Josephus believed that priestly divination of the sort being considered here was a form of prophecy. There are eight accounts in the *Antiquities* that describe oracular consultation with the high priest.[30] Only two of these specify the use of the priestly vestments (6.115, 359–60), but all eight accounts are so similar in terms of the situation and procedure they describe that it is reasonable to conclude that it was assumed that the vestments were used even where they are not explicitly mentioned. Josephus regularly uses the verb προφητεύω in these passages to describe the giving of oracular responses by the high priest.[31] In addition, he once refers to the sort of oracle that could be obtained through the high priest as a "prophecy" (προφητεία, 7.72). Finally, in one passage (6.271) it would seem that Josephus actually refers to the reigning high priest as "the prophet" (ὁ προφήτης), though this is not certain.[32]

Although Josephus' use of προφητεύω and related terms in this context is sometimes dismissed as insignificant,[33] it seems to me to be very significant indeed. There is only one account of oracular consultation with the high priest in the *Antiquities* in which there is no prophetic terminology at all (6.122–23), and the absence of such terminology in this passage is easily explained: in this case, no response was given to the question put to the high priest—that is, no prophecy was made—because of some sin on the part of the Israelites. Josephus himself seems to be responsible for the introduction of prophetic terminology into the other seven accounts: there is nothing corresponding to this terminology in the biblical passages on which the accounts are based, at least not in the Hebrew or LXX texts known to us. Josephus' use of προφητεύω and related terms in this context is thus both consistent and, it appears, deliberate, and his usage indicates that he considered divination performed by the high priest with the aid of the priestly vestments to be a form of prophecy.

There are no reports in scripture of the practice of divination by the high priest after the time of David. The role of giving oracles seems to have been taken over by prophets in the later period: in narratives describing events in the time after David, prophets are often sought out for an oracle in situations in which the high priest would once have been consulted.[34]

There was speculation in later periods about precisely when divination by the high priest had come to an end. A range of opinions is expressed in bSotah 48b, where the topic of debate is the date at which the Urim and Thummim had ceased to give oracular responses.[35] One view was that the use of the Urim and Thummim had ended after the time of Samuel, David, and Solomon.[36] Another was that their use had continued at least until the days of King Uzziah of Judah and the priest Zechariah (2 Chron. 26.5) in the eighth century B.C.E.[37] A passage from the anonymous work, the Lives of the Prophets, associates the end of priestly divination with the murder of a different Zechariah, a priest who was active during the ninth-century B.C.E. reign of Joash, king of Judah (2 Chron. 24.20–22): "From that time visible portents occurred in the Temple, and the priests were not able to see a vision of angels of God or to give oracles from the Holy of Holies, or to inquire by the Ephod, or to answer the people through Urim as formerly" (Lives of the Prophets 23.2).[38] A third view recorded in bSotah 48b is that the Urim and Thummim had ceased when the first temple was destroyed.[39] Tosefta Sotah 13.2

expresses the same opinion, and bYoma 21b includes the Urim and Thummim in a list of five things that were in the first temple but not in the second. Finally, bSotah 48b attributes to R. Nahman the view that the Urim and Thummim had ceased before the days of Haggai, Zechariah, and Malachi, but after all the other prophets—that is, sometime after the destruction of the first temple, but before the return under Cyrus. In bShebuoth 16a, R. Nahman, R. Huna, and Abba Saul are all credited with the assumption that there were no longer Urim and Thummim when the exiles returned to Jerusalem under Ezra.[40] In summary, later opinions ranged from the view that high-priestly divination by means of the Urim and Thummim had ended after Solomon, that is, while the first temple was still standing, to the view that it had ceased with the destruction of the first temple or shortly afterward, in any case, by the time of the return from exile under Ezra.

There is nothing in the narrative portions of the *Antiquities* to lead one to believe that Josephus' views about the relative merits of priestly divination and prophetic oracles, or his views on the question of when priestly divination had ceased, were in any way remarkable. He duplicates without comment and without significant alteration the scriptural pattern described above: he does not record any instances of divination by the high priest after the time of David, and he portrays later prophets acting in situations in which the high priest would once have been consulted.[41] In the editorial passage from *Antiquities* 3 quoted at the beginning of this section, however, Josephus expresses what seems to be his own view on these matters: he indicates clearly that he believed that high-priestly divination was superior to consultation with a prophet, and that such divination had ceased not at the time of the return from exile or earlier, but after the reign of John Hyrcanus in the second century B.C.E. Let us consider each of these points in turn.

In *Antiquities* 3.214 Josephus writes that Moses, by designing the ephod and breastplate of the high priest in such a way that they could be used for the purpose of divination, had "left no possible opening for the malpractices of prophets, should there in fact be any capable of abusing the divine prerogative." This statement suggests that Josephus believed that the sort of divination practiced by the high priest with the aid of the ephod and breastplate was superior to consultation with a prophet: whereas prophets could deceive and "abuse the divine prerogative," the responses provided by the high priest were completely reliable.[42] A similar conviction about the superiority of priestly divination to the oracular responses of prophets is expressed in bYoma 73b: "Although the decree of a prophet could be revoked, the decree of the Urim and Thummim could not be revoked, as it is said: 'By the judgment of the Urim' [Num. 27:21]."[43] As I noted earlier, the view that priestly divination was superior to the oracles of prophets may be related to a traditional etymology which connected the word "Thummim" with the notions of "perfection" and "fulfillment." It is possible that Josephus was familiar with, and influenced by, such etymological speculation. Even if this was the case, however, it is likely that he himself held the view expressed in *Antiquities* 3.214. As we shall see at numerous points in later chapters, Josephus had an extraordinarily high estimation of the priestly office and of priestly varieties of prophecy.[44]

In *Antiquities* 3.218 Josephus explains that the stones on the breastplate and the sardonyx on the right side of the ephod had both "ceased to shine two hundred years before I composed this work." The *Antiquities* was completed in 93 or 94 C.E.[45] The figure of two hundred years, then, if interpreted precisely, would suggest a date sometime during the reign of John Hyrcanus.[46] It is likely, however, that Josephus used two hundred as a round number, and that he believed that priestly divination of the sort he describes in *Antiquities* 3.214–18 had ceased at the conclusion of John's reign.

The end of this sort of prophecy is nowhere else connected with John Hyrcanus. The traditions surveyed above all propose a much earlier date for its demise—at the very latest, the time of the return from exile. Apparently, then, the statement in *Antiquities* 3.218 represents Josephus' own view on the matter. It is worth asking why he associated this form of prophecy with John Hyrcanus and why he thought it had ended after John's reign.

As we have seen, Josephus highly esteemed the sort of divination that was practiced with the aid of the high-priestly ephod and breastplate and valued it as a superior form of prophecy. He knew that such divination had ceased at some point in the past, and that it was not known precisely when this had happened. I believe that Josephus associated this kind of divination with John Hyrcanus because he idealized John as the last great military leader, high priest, and prophet in Israel.

Josephus knew, of course, that Hyrcanus had been a successful military leader who had been able to expand considerably the territory ruled by the Jews in Palestine. It is worth noting, in this connection, that priestly divination of the kind considered here was closely associated with the conduct of war in ancient Israel.[47] Before taking the field against an enemy, the leader of the Israelites would consult Yahweh through the high priest to determine whether or not the proposed battle should be fought, and sometimes to obtain instructions on when and how it should be fought.[48] Josephus also associated high-priestly divination with the conduct of war. In the passage from *Antiquities* 3 quoted at the beginning of this section, he states that, through the stones on the high priest's breastplate, "God foreshowed victory to those on the eve of battle" (3.216). Elsewhere Josephus writes that Moses taught the people "how the troops when taking the field should consult the oracular stones" (*Ant.* 4.311).[49] Moreover, all eight passages in the *Antiquities* that describe oracular consultation with the high priest concern the conduct of war.[50] While he never actually describes John Hyrcanus using the breastplate to consult God before embarking on a military campaign, Josephus may have made some sort of connection between John's military success and his own preferred method of obtaining military advice, namely consultation with the high priest.[51]

Along with a preference for priestly forms of prophecy, Josephus also had a preference for priestly forms of government. In *Against Apion* 2.185 he asks rhetorically: "Could there be a finer or more equitable polity than one which sets God at the head of the universe, which assigns the administration of its highest affairs to the whole body of priests, and entrusts to the supreme high-priest the direction of the other priests?" In an earlier passage in the same work, he coins a word to describe this form of government, calling it a "theocracy" (θεοκρατία) in order to emphasize the fact that, under such a constitution, "all sovereignty and authority" were "in the hands of God" (2.165). What this meant in practical terms, as the passage quoted above suggests, was that the nation was to be ruled by priests, under the direction of the high priest. Josephus claimed that this theocratic constitution had been ordained by God through Moses, and he himself seems to have preferred it, in particular, to the rule of kings.[52]

In *Antiquities* 11.111–13 Josephus offers a brief survey of the various political constitutions under which the Jews had lived from the time of Moses through the Hasmonean period. A similar review is outlined and extended into the Roman period as part of the history of the high priesthood recorded in *Antiquities* 20.224–51. John Hyrcanus occupies a very important place in this schematization of Jewish political history. According to Josephus, John was the most illustrious and also the last of a long line of theocratic rulers stretching back to the time of the return from exile. Immediately after his death, the fortunes of the Hasmoneans and of the Jews in Palestine began to decline. His son, Aristobulus I, seized power unlawfully and assumed the title of king in addition to that of high priest, thereby bringing theocratic rule, as Josephus understood it, to an end.[53] Aristobulus was guilty of other crimes as well: he put his mother in prison, where she starved to death; he also imprisoned his brothers, except for Antigonus, whom he later murdered. Aristobulus was succeeded in office by his brother, Alexander Jannaeus, whose long reign (103–76 B.C.E.) was marked by almost continual war, including a bloody civil war. Josephus relates with horror how, at the conclusion of the civil war, Jannaeus had eight hundred of his Jewish opponents crucified and their wives and children slaughtered, "while he looked on, drinking, with his concubines reclining beside him" (*War* 1.97; cf. *Ant.* 13.380). The reign of Salome Alexandra (76–67 B.C.E.), who succeeded her husband as head of state, was relatively peaceful, but it was followed by the bitter and protracted civil war between Aristobulus II and Hyrcanus II which finally led to the intervention of Rome. Josephus is probably referring to this entire period of decline when he writes, in *Antiquities* 3.218, that the high-priestly ephod and breastplate had ceased to function after the reign of John Hyrcanus "because of God's displeasure at the transgression of the laws."

There was a brief revival of theocratic government when Pompey conquered Palestine and appointed Hyrcanus II high priest in 63 B.C.E. and again when the Romans took over direct control of Judaea in the year 6 C.E. But Hyrcanus II and the high priests who served under the prefects and procurators were theocratic leaders of the nation in a very limited sense, since their powers were restricted by the Roman administrators and officials to whom they were responsible; certainly their achievements could in no way compare with the fabulous successes of John Hyrcanus. John thus looms large in Josephus' overall interpretation of Jewish history as the last great, independent high priest to preside over a theocratic government of the sort ordained by God.

Finally, Josephus was familiar with traditions that attributed prophetic powers to John Hyrcanus. In *Antiquities* 13.322–23 he describes a dream by means of which John discovered which of his two elder sons would succeed him. We shall see later that Josephus often associated such revelatory dreams with prophecy. Another story about John's prophetic experiences is related in conjunction with the account of a war involving the forces of Antiochus Cyzicenus:

> Now about the high priest Hyrcanus an extraordinary story is told how the Deity communicated with him, for they say that on the very day on which his sons fought with Cyzicenus, Hyrcanus, who was alone in the temple, burning incense as high priest, heard a voice saying that his sons had just defeated Antiochus. And on coming out of the temple he revealed this to the entire multitude, and so it actually happened. (*Ant.* 13.282–83)

Josephus concludes his account of John's reign with the following remark:

> Now he [Hyrcanus] was accounted by God worthy of three of the greatest privileges, the rule of the nation, the office of high-priest, and the gift of prophecy [προφητεία]; for the Deity was with him and enabled him to foresee and foretell the future; so, for example, he foretold of his two elder sons that they would not remain masters of the state. (*Ant.* 13.299–300; cf. *War* 1.68–69)

Most of this material about John's prophetic abilities and experiences appears to be traditional.[54] There are rabbinic parallels to the story of Hyrcanus and the voice in the temple,[55] and, while there are no parallels elsewhere in Jewish literature to the story of Hyrcanus' dream in *Antiquities* 13.322–23, Josephus introduces the account with the word λέγεται ("it is said," 13.321), which he often uses to introduce anonymous traditions.[56] The association of John Hyrcanus with the threefold office of prophet, priest, and ruler may also be traditional, though this is less certain.[57] Even if all this material is traditional, it is nevertheless significant that Josephus takes it up and incorporates it into his account of John's reign. He evidently accepted the stories about John's prophetic experiences and idealized John as a great leader who combined in his person the three authoritative types of Israelite history: prophet, priest, and ruler.[58]

None of the traditions surveyed here connects John Hyrcanus specifically with the high-priestly breastplate; I am suggesting a more indirect association. Josephus admired John as the last great military leader of Israel, the last larger-than-life high priest, and a renowned prophet; he highly esteemed the sort of divination that was practiced with the aid of the high-priestly breastplate and considered it a superior form of prophecy; he knew of the tradition that it had ended at some point in the past, and he attached this tradition to John. I shall return to consider the implications of all of this for Josephus' general views about the cessation of prophecy.

Josephus' Use of Προφήτης and Related Terms

We have so far considered evidence that Josephus believed that two particular types of prophecy had ceased at some point in the past. This does not yet prove that he believed that prophecy of every sort had come to an end. There is, however, one reliable indication that this was his view: he uses the word προφήτης and related terms almost exclusively in connection with figures from the past and does not ordinarily apply this language to himself or to others of his own day.

It is important to be precise in describing Josephus' usage. It is not strictly correct, for example, to say that he applies the word προφήτης *exclusively* to figures from the distant past. On one occasion, Josephus refers to certain of his own contemporaries as προφῆται. In *War* 6.283–84 he describes the fate of six thousand Jews who perished in the final battle for Jerusalem when the Romans set fire to the portico of the temple on which they had taken refuge. According to Josephus, "they owed their destruction to a false prophet [ψευδοπροφήτης], who had on that day proclaimed to the people in the city that God commanded them to go up to the temple, to receive there the signs of deliverance" (6.285).[59] He adds the following comment: "At that time, many prophets [προφῆται] were planted among the people by the tyrants to announce that they should wait for help from God, in order that desertions might be lessened and hope might encourage those who were beyond fear and precaution" (6.286).[60]

It is not clear to whom the word προφῆται refers in this last passage. It is probably a collective reference to figures Josephus mentions elsewhere, who, like the ψευδοπροφήτης of *War* 6.285, are said to have promised their followers deliverance or freedom and a display of signs and wonders. We know that some of these figures explicitly claimed to be prophets. According to Josephus, Theudas, who appeared during the procuratorship of Fadus (44–?46 C.E.), "stated that he was a prophet" (προφήτης . . . ἔλεγεν εἶναι, *Ant*. 20.97); a few years later an Egyptian Jew likewise "declared that he was a prophet" (προφήτης εἶναι λέγων, *Ant*. 20.169). As we shall see in chapter 4, Josephus rejects the prophetic claims of Theudas, the Egyptian, and others like them, calling them "false prophets," "impostors," and "deceivers." It is clear that he also condemns the actions of the προφῆται mentioned in *War* 6.286: he associates them with the "false prophet" responsible for the deaths of the six thousand and suggests that they acted in concert with the "tyrants," that is, with the leaders of what was left of the armed resistance to Rome; in *War* 6.288 he evidently includes them among the "deceivers and those who misrepresented God" by whom the Jews were misled. Yet, strangely, he does call them προφῆται in *War* 6.286.[61]

Josephus' usage in this passage is exceptional, and apart from this one instance it is perfectly correct to say that he restricts the application of προφήτης and related terms to figures from the distant past. Even here, however, we must be careful about the language we use. It is often said that Josephus uses προφήτης-terminology only of "biblical," "canonical," or even "Old Testament" figures, but the use of such canon-related terms is inaccurate and should be avoided.[62] As we have seen, Josephus uses explicitly prophetic language of two postbiblical figures from the past, Cleodemus the historian and the Hasmonean high priest John Hyrcanus. We saw that it was possible that Josephus had taken over the designation of Cleodemus as "the prophet" from his source, Alexander Polyhistor, and for that reason not much weight can be placed on the passage. The fact that Josephus ascribes prophetic powers to John Hyrcanus is much more significant. We have seen that he believed that John had been a prophet, indeed a prophet of some distinction. Terms related to the canon are thus, strictly speaking, inaccurate if employed to describe Josephus' use of prophetic language; for the period in which prophets were still active included, according to him, the time of John Hyrcanus, and hence does not coincide exactly with any period that might be labeled "biblical" or "canonical."

There is another reason for objecting to the use of canon-related terms in this context: this usage often derives from and reinforces the view that the belief that prophecy had ceased arose in the first place because of, or as a result of, the canonization of scripture. Though this view is widespread, I believe it to be mistaken. The problem is a large and difficult one that cannot be explored in detail here; but I have already touched on the question in the discussion of *Against Apion* 1.41 at the beginning of this chapter, and shall comment here at somewhat greater length on the evidence from Josephus.

It is not clear that *Against Apion* 1.37–41 constitutes evidence for the existence of a canon of scripture, if by "canon" we mean a closed set of books, officially regarded as authoritative. The passage is usually read in this way, but a convincing argument against this interpretation has been made by Barton.[63] For the moment, however, let us assume that there was, already in Josephus' day, a canon of scripture in the strict sense, and that the passage from *Against Apion* describes its contents. Did the existence of this canon of scripture lead Josephus (and other Jews of his day) to the conclusion that prophecy had ceased?

It may seem that I have already suggested that it did. I argued above that Josephus' view that the exact succession of the prophets had come to an end after the reign of Artaxerxes should be understood primarily as a reflection of prior convictions about the status of the ancient books written by Moses and his successors in comparison with more recent works. It must be emphasized again, however, that *Against Apion* 1.37–41 concerns only the type of prophecy that resulted in the composition of historical narrative. This category might be expanded to "the type of prophecy that resulted in the composition of authoritative (or canonical) books of various sorts," since it seems likely that Josephus regarded the twenty-two books described in the passage as especially authoritative in other respects as well.[64] Even so defined, however, this category does not begin to exhaust the meaning of prophecy. Although Josephus' views about the authority and scope of the justly accredited books of the Jews may have led him to conclude that there were no more prophets of the sort who wrote canonical books, there is no reason to believe that the same views led him to conclude that there were no more prophets of any sort whatsoever. We shall see that his belief that prophecy of the canonical book-writing sort had ceased was stronger and more dogmatic than were his views about the cessation of other types of prophecy.

I shall not argue the point here, but it seems to me unlikely that there was any direct causal connection between the canonization of scripture and the rise of the general view that prophecy of every sort had ceased. This latter view, as I shall suggest in the conclusion to this chapter, is best regarded as an expression of a rather vague nostalgia that conceived of the distant past as a golden age in which there had been truly great prophets, and in which people in general had been holier and closer to God. The canonization of scripture, far from *producing* the belief that prophecy had ceased, was itself most likely a *result* of the same kind of nostalgic view of the past. Ancient books, that is, were probably considered more authoritative than modern ones for exactly the same reason that ancient prophets were believed to be superior to their modern counterparts: *because they were ancient.*[65]

For several reasons, then, canon-related terms should not be used to delimit the period in the past in which Josephus believed that there had been individuals truly worthy of being called prophets. There is really no reason to suppose that he defined the limits of this golden prophetic age very precisely. He gives a definite cutoff point in *Against Apion* 1.41, but that is because his theory that the exact succession of the prophets had ended after the reign of Artaxerxes is closely connected with his views about the twenty-two justly accredited books of the Jews; he can thus say, precisely, that the sort of prophecy he has in mind ended after the production of the last of these writings, the book of Esther. His treatment of John Hyrcanus shows more clearly that the limits of the prophetic age were flexible. The rabbis disagreed about precisely when high-priestly divination had ceased: was it during the First Temple period, or when the temple was destroyed, or at the time of the return from exile? Josephus was able to extend the golden age of the great prophets to include his own personal hero, John Hyrcanus.

The Continuation of Prophecy After
Its Supposed Cessation

The fact that Josephus applies the word προφήτης and related terms almost exclusively to figures from the past does seem to be significant. He evidently intends by this usage to make some sort of distinction between his own age and the age when the great prophets had lived, but the precise nature and significance of this distinction need to be established. Let us return to the question raised in the introduction to this chapter: did Josephus believe that there was no longer anything at all like prophecy and no one at all like the prophets?

Although he does not call them προφῆται, Josephus mentions with approval a number of contemporary figures whom he depicts as saying and doing the very sorts of things that, in his view, the ancient prophets had said and done. Even those individuals whose prophetic claims he rejects are sometimes depicted in terms reminiscent of the ancient prophets. Perhaps most significantly, Josephus portrays his own role in the events of his day fairly comprehensively in prophetic terms.

The extent of the similarity between the ancient prophets and more recent figures, as Josephus depicts them, has not generally been appreciated by commentators. This has been due primarily to a failure to recognize that there are vast differences between Josephus' understanding of the ancient prophets and modern-critical perceptions of these figures. The fact that such differences exist can be seen most readily in connection with the terminology we use to classify various religious types. Barton has shown that Josephus and other Jews of his day generally fail to distinguish clearly between figures whom we would call "prophets," on the one hand, and others whom we might classify as "seers," "apocalyptists," or "practitioners of mantic wisdom."[66] For certain purposes, of course, it is necessary and desirable to make the kinds of distinctions that our modern categories allow. But in order to evaluate the evidence from Josephus correctly, it is essential to begin by asking what sort of distinctions *he* makes between various sorts of figures, and by trying to adopt his mentality as completely as possible. We are greatly aided in this task by the existence of a collection of material from which Josephus' views on prophets and prophecy may be reliably inferred, namely his version of the ancient history of the Jews in the early books of the *Antiquities*.

In the two sections that follow, I shall consider Josephus' understanding of prophetic inspiration and predictive prophecy. It can be shown in relation to these important topics that, often when we suppose that Josephus means to distinguish figures of his own day from the ancient prophets, his intention is in fact precisely the opposite. The treatment of Josephus and other figures from his time will necessarily be anticipatory and somewhat sketchy here, and will have to be confirmed and filled in by the more detailed discussion of these figures in later chapters.

Dreams and Prophetic Inspiration

In *Life* 208–10 Josephus describes "a marvelous dream" that served to encourage him early in the revolt, when his opponents in Jerusalem were seeking to oust him from his position as general in Galilee. He also claims that it was on the basis of certain dreams, interpreted in relation to "the prophecies of the sacred books," that he later made his famous prediction that Vespasian would become emperor (*War* 3.351–54, 399–408).[67] Apparently other Jews of Josephus' day could interpret dreams; for example, he records that an Essene named Simon correctly interpreted a dream for Archelaus, the ethnarch of Judaea, shortly before the latter was banished to Gaul by Augustus in 6 C.E. (*War* 2.112–13; *Ant.* 17.345–48).

Modern students of late Second Temple Judaism usually consider dreams to be a less direct means of revelation than the visions and auditions traditionally associated with the ancient Israelite prophets.[68] The increased frequency with which dreams are mentioned in postbiblical literature is generally thought to be one of the features that distinguish this literature from earlier, genuinely prophetic texts. Because we think in these terms, we do not suppose that Josephus' remarks about revelatory dreams and their interpretation in his own day have anything to do with prophecy.

When we review his reports in the *Antiquities*, however, it becomes clear that Josephus believed that the *ancient* prophets had received many of their revelations in dreams. He sometimes adds a reference to a dream where there is none in his scriptural source,[69] and it is likely that his extraordinarily high estimation of Daniel is based in large part on that prophet's ability to interpret dreams. Josephus writes of this ability as if it were something marvelous and God-given. As an interpreter of dreams, Daniel was "fully able to discover things which were not within the understanding of others" (*Ant.* 10.239); he was "a wise man and skilful in discovering things beyond human power and known only to God" (10.237); because of his abilities, it was believed that "the divine spirit . . . attended him" (τὸ θεῖον αὐτῷ πνεῦμα συμπάρεστι, 10.239).

The fact that Josephus supposed that the ancient prophets had received so many of their revelations in dreams requires explanation. There are, of course, reports of revelatory dreams in scripture, and there was the outstanding example of Daniel. But dreams are not frequently mentioned in scripture in connection with the ancient prophets, and there was an established tradition, which must have been known to Josephus, that was critical of dreams as a means of revelation.[70] It seems that Josephus has read his own experience of revelation back into ancient times: convinced that he himself had received messages from God in the form of dreams, he naturally supposed that God had communicated with the ancients in the same way.[71]

If this analysis is correct, it suggests that Josephus and others of his day experienced what they believed were genuine divine revelations in the form of dreams. It also suggests that when they claimed to have had such dreams, or claimed to be able to interpret them, they did not intend thereby to distinguish themselves from the ancient prophets, but on the contrary to suggest that they were, in these respects, like the ancient prophets.[72]

If we consider some of the other evidence concerning prophetic inspiration from Josephus' works, it becomes even clearer that he believed that individuals in his own day could have very much the same kinds of experiences as the ancient prophets had had. It is sometimes thought to be significant that Josephus never speaks of the "spirit of God" in relation to contemporary figures.[73] It is true that he uses this phrase almost exclusively in relation to prophecy,[74] and also that he uses it only with reference to figures from the past. But he very rarely uses the expression at all, and most of the time he writes about prophets, prophecy, and prophesying without any reference to the spirit of God.[75]

Indeed, Josephus uses a variety of expressions to describe prophetic inspiration and its effects on the ancient prophets, and he does not seem to use these expressions in a very systematic way or to attach particular significance to any one of them. Most importantly from our point of view, he also uses some of the same expressions to describe his own experiences and those of his contemporaries.

Let us consider an example. In *Antiquities* 6.56 Josephus uses the phrase γενόμενος ἔνθεος to describe what happened to Saul when he encountered an assembly of prophets at Gibeath-elohim. Samuel predicts to Saul: "On coming thence to Gabatha, you will meet an assembly of prophets and, divinely inspired [γενόμενος ἔνθεος], you will prophesy [προφητεύσεις] with them."[76] From the report of a second, similar encounter in *Antiquities* 6.221–23, we can infer that the inspiration mentioned in this passage produced very extraordinary, irrational behavior. Josephus describes its effects on Saul: "Saul, losing his reason under the impulse of that mighty spirit, stripped off his clothes and lay prostrate on the ground for a whole day and night in the sight of Samuel and David" (6.223).[77] This second account, incidentally, does speak of the "spirit of

God" as the means of inspiration (τὸ θεῖον πνεῦμα, 6.222; cf. 6.223), and it is very unlikely that Josephus intended to distinguish the kind of inspiration described in this passage from that described in the earlier account by the phrase γενόμενος ἔνθεος.

The sort of inspiration that enabled the ancient prophets to perform superhuman deeds is sometimes described by this same phrase. Saul was "divinely inspired" (ἔνθεος γενόμενος, *Ant.* 6.76) when he dismembered a team of oxen in order to rally the Israelites to war against the Ammonites,[78] and it was because he was "divinely inspired" (ἔνθεος γενόμενος, 8.346) that Elijah was able to outrun Ahab's chariot from Mount Carmel to Jezreel.[79]

The same phrase is also used once of a type of inspiration that involved some sort of trance that issued in the giving of an intelligible oracle. When the kings of Israel, Judah, and Edom came to consult Elisha, Josephus reports, the prophet called for a musician, and upon hearing the music became "divinely inspired" (ἔνθεος γενόμενος, *Ant.* 9.35) and was able to give the kings the advice they sought.[80]

Josephus thus uses the phrase ἔνθεος γενόμενος in connection with a number of ancient prophets, but he does not use it consistently of a single type of inspired behavior, and he sometimes uses other phrases to describe what appear to be similar sorts of experiences—we saw, for example, that he speaks of the "spirit of God" (τὸ θεῖον πνεῦμα) in *Antiquities* 6.222–23. It remains only to be pointed out that Josephus also uses the expression ἔνθεος γενόμενος with reference to himself on one very important occasion. Describing the experience that led him to predict that Vespasian would become emperor, Josephus states that he was "divinely inspired" (ἔνθους γενόμενος) to understand the meaning of his recent dreams (*War* 3.353). The implication of this usage is that Josephus believed himself to be inspired by God in the same way that he imagined Saul, Elijah, and Elisha had been.

Even where there are no precise terminological parallels, Josephus' descriptions of the behavior of his contemporaries sometimes suggest that he thought they were inspired in much the same way that the ancient prophets had been. Again, let us consider an example, this time Josephus' report concerning Jesus son of Ananias (*War* 6.300–309). According to this report, Jesus appeared in Jerusalem four years before the beginning of the war against Rome, proclaiming a message of doom against Jerusalem and the temple:

> A voice from the east,
> a voice from the west,
> a voice from the four winds;

> a voice against Jerusalem and the sanctuary,
> a voice against the bridegroom and the bride,
> a voice against all the people. (6.301)

He repeated this warning day and night without ceasing, and was arrested and punished by "some of the leading citizens" (6.302) as a result. When this did not silence him, he was sent to the Roman governor:

> There, although flayed to the bone with scourges, he neither sued for mercy nor shed a tear, but, merely introducing the most mournful of variations into his ejaculation, responded to each stroke with "Woe to Jerusalem!" When Albinus, the governor, asked him who and whence he was and why he uttered these cries, he answered him never a word, but unceasingly reiterated his dirge over the city, until Albinus pronounced him a maniac [καταγνοὺς μανίαν] and let him go. (6.304–5)

Upon his release, Jesus took up his message again, "his voice never flagging nor his strength exhausted" (6.308), and repeated it until he was struck and killed by a Roman missile.

What stands out in Josephus' account is the compulsive way in which Jesus repeated his message of doom, even in the face of punishment. It was apparently this compulsive behavior that led Albinus to conclude that he was insane. Behavior of a similar sort—though less intensely compulsive—is attributed by Josephus to the prophet Jeremiah.[81] Like Jesus, Jeremiah predicted that Jerusalem would be captured and the temple destroyed,[82] and his fixation on these predictions caused many to conclude that he was "out of his mind" (ἐξεστηκὼς τῶν φρενῶν, *Ant.* 10.114). He was also punished by the magistrates and imprisoned: "The prophet Jeremiah, however, who was in prison, did not remain quiet but cried his message aloud and urged the people to open the gates and admit the Babylonian king; for, he said, if they did so, they would be saved together with their families, but if not, they would be destroyed" (10.117). This behavior prompted the Jewish leaders to ask the king to put Jeremiah to death "as a madman" (ὡς μεμηνότα, 10.119).

I shall return to Josephus' account of Jesus son of Ananias in chapter 5. For the present, my point is that the similarities between his portrayal of Jesus and his portrayal of Jeremiah suggest that Josephus thought that the two men were similarly inspired by God.

Fortunately we know, even apart from the parallels with Jeremiah, that Josephus believed that Jesus was inspired. In *War* 6.303 he writes that Jesus' failure to respond to punishment led the Jewish magistrates to conclude that "the man was under some supernatural impulse" (δαιμονιώτερον τὸ κίνημα τἀνδρός); Josephus adds his own opinion that this "was indeed the case" (ὅπερ ἦ).[83]

Prophecy as Prediction

Josephus claims to have made other predictions in addition to the one concerning Vespasian. According to *War* 3.405–7, he predicted that the city of Jotapata would fall to the Romans after forty-seven days and that he himself would be taken prisoner. After his prophecy to Vespasian was fulfilled, he says, his "power of insight into the future was no longer discredited" (*War* 4.629).

In addition, Josephus narrates stories about three Essenes, each of whom made a prediction concerning a prominent public figure. I have already mentioned Simon, who interpreted the dream of Archelaus and predicted that his reign was about to end (*War* 2.112–13; *Ant.* 17.345–48). Josephus claims that Herod the Great was favorably disposed to the Essenes because one of their number, Menahem, had predicted to him, when he was still a boy, that he would become king of the Jews (*Ant.* 15.373–79). According to Josephus, Menahem possessed "foreknowledge of the future from God" (πρόγνωσις ἐκ θεοῦ τῶν μελλόντων, 15.373). The murder of Antigonus, the son of John Hyrcanus, was predicted by another Essene, Judas (*War* 1.78–80; *Ant.* 13.311–13). Josephus writes of Judas that "his predictions had never once proved erroneous or false" (*War* 1.78; cf. *Ant.* 13.311). He is pictured surrounded by companions who were with him "for the purpose of receiving instruction in foretelling the future" (διδασκαλίας ἕνεκα τοῦ προλέγειν τὰ μέλλοντα, *Ant.* 13.311). Finally, in one of his discussions of the Jewish "philosophies," Josephus makes the following general comment about the Essenes: "There are some among them who profess to foreknow the future, being educated in sacred books and various purifications and sayings of prophets; and seldom, if ever, do they err in their predictions" (*War* 2.159).[84]

Modern scholars regularly distinguish the prediction of specific events in the public-political sphere from genuine prophecy. Crone, for example, labels Josephus himself and the Essenes mentioned above "seers" and "prognosticators" and concludes: "In neither case [Josephus or the Essenes], however, was this prediction considered prophecy in the literal sense. It was much more in the strict apocalyptic tradition."[85]

Though we might want to distinguish between prophets and apocalyptists and place predictors of the future in the second category, it is essential to realize that Josephus did not do so. Like most of his contemporaries, he realized that the ancient prophets had done many different sorts of things, but he very much emphasizes their role as predictors of the future.[86] In the *Antiquities*, Josephus mentions a number of predictions made by the great prophets of the past. Just before dying, Moses "prophesied to each of the tribes the things that in fact were to come to pass" (4.320). The prophet Nahum predicted the downfall of Nineveh "and many more things beside," and "all the things that had been foretold concerning Nineveh came to pass after a hundred and fifteen years" (9.242). Both Ezekiel and Jeremiah predicted Zedekiah's capture and exile, but the king refused to believe them because their predictions appeared to contradict one another (10.104–7); Josephus is careful to point out that events proved that both predictions were in fact correct

(10.107, 141). This account is very similar to his version of 1 Kings 22 (*Ant.* 8.400–410), according to which Micaiah's prediction that Ahab would die in three days' time was rejected because it appeared to conflict with the prediction of Elijah, "who was better able than Micaiah to foresee the future" (8.407). Once again, Josephus shows that the discrepancy between the two predictions was only apparent (8.417–20). Isaiah predicted the rise of Cyrus (11.5–6), Daniel the rise of Alexander the Great (11.337). John Hyrcanus foretold that his two elder sons would not remain in power (13.300; cf. *War* 1.69). The list could go on.

Josephus believed that the ancient prophets had predicted many of the events of his own day. Jeremiah (*Ant.* 10.79), Ezekiel (10.79), Daniel (10.276), and others had predicted the destruction of the temple and the capture of Jerusalem in 70 C.E. In the course of his narrative concerning the Jewish revolt against Rome, Josephus refers several times to ancient prophecies which he believed were being fulfilled in the events of the time (*War* 4.386–88; 6.108–10, 311–13).

Josephus even believed that the ancient prophets had predicted things that would occur in what was still the future from his own perspective. He declines to explain the significance of the stone "cut out by no human hand" mentioned in Daniel 2.34–35, evidently because he interpreted it as an indication that the Roman empire would one day be overthrown by the God of the Jews:

> And Daniel also revealed to the king the meaning of the stone, but I have not thought it proper to relate this, since I am expected to write of what is past and done and not of what is to be; if, however, there is anyone who has so keen a desire for exact information that he will not stop short of inquiring more closely but wishes to learn about the hidden things that are to come, let him take the trouble to read the Book of Daniel, which he will find among the sacred writings. (*Ant.* 10.210)

Josephus was extraordinarily impressed by this sort of long-range prediction and—in another affront to our modern sensibilities—thought that such predictions were especially impressive if they were detailed and specific. It is once again with reference to Daniel that he writes:

> Now it is fitting to relate certain things about this man which one may greatly wonder at hearing, namely that all things happened to him in a marvellously fortunate way as to one of the greatest prophets, and during his lifetime he received honour and esteem from kings and people, and, since his death, his memory lives on eternally. For the books which he wrote and left behind are still read by us even now, and we are convinced by them that Daniel spoke with God, for he was not only wont to prophesy future things, as did the other prophets, but he also fixed the time at which these would come to pass. (*Ant.* 10.266–67)

We may associate detailed prediction of the distant future with apocalyptists, seers, and prognosticators; but for Josephus it was characteristic of "one of the greatest prophets."[87]

The fact that God made predictions through his spokesmen, the prophets, was evidence, in Josephus' view, of God's providential care for his people, and the fulfillment of such predictions in the past provided a basis for continued trust in God. The following passage is an elaboration of the scriptural account of Solomon's dedication of the temple in 1 Kings 8:

> [Solomon] turned to address the multitude and made clear to them the power and providence of God in that most of the future events which He had revealed to David, his father, had actually come to pass, and the rest would also come about, and how God Himself had given him his name even before he was born, and had foretold what he was to be called and that none but he should build Him a temple, on becoming king after his father's death. And now that they saw the fulfilment of these things in accordance with David's prophecies, he asked them to praise God and not despair of anything He had promised for their happiness, as if it were not to be, but to have faith because of what they had already seen. (*Ant.* 8.109–110)

Josephus' concluding comments on the predictions of Daniel express the same point of view:

> All these things, as God revealed them to him, he left behind in his writings, so that those who read them and observe how they have come to pass must wonder at Daniel's having been so honoured by God, and learn from these facts how mistaken are the Epicureans, who exclude Providence from human life and refuse to believe that God governs its affairs. . . . It therefore seems to me, in view of the things foretold by Daniel, that they are very far from holding a true opinion who declare that God takes no thought for human affairs. For if it were the case that the world goes on by some automatism, we should not have seen all these things happen in accordance with his prophecy. (*Ant.* 10.277–80)

Josephus knew that it was possible to ignore the predictions made by the ancient prophets and so to thwart God's intention to bless his people. In *War* 6.288–315 he lists a whole series of portents that should have alerted the Jews of his own day to the impending destruction of Jerusalem by the Romans. The list includes two oracles from the "sacred scriptures" of the Jews (6.311–13). Josephus makes the following comment on his generation's response to these warnings from God:

> Reflecting on these things, one will find that God cares for human beings, and in all kinds of ways shows His people the way of salvation. . . . For all that, it is impossible for human beings to escape their fate, even though they foresee it. Some of these portents, then, the Jews interpreted to please themselves, others they treated with contempt, until the ruin of their country and their own destruction convinced them of their folly. (*War* 6.310, 314–15)[88]

Included in the list of warnings sent by God in *War* 6.288–315 is Jesus son of Ananias (6.300–309). Apparently, then, Josephus did not believe that it was only through the ancient prophets and the oracles they left behind that God warned his people. The activity of his contemporary, Jesus, is also interpreted as evidence that God "cares for human beings."

Conclusion

With respect to both inspiration and prediction, Josephus seems to have perceived some sort of distinction between the ancient prophets, on the one hand, and himself and other recent figures on the other. He writes of Moses that "in all his utterances one seemed to hear the speech of God Himself" (*Ant.* 4.329); he is convinced that Daniel "spoke with God" (*Ant.* 10.267); and he says of John Hyrcanus that "so closely was he in touch with the Deity, that he was never ignorant of the future" (*War* 1.69). Josephus is not willing to say these sorts of things about Jews in his own generation, nor does he attribute to any of them the kind of long-range predictions that he admires so in the ancient prophets. He evidently thought that these things belonged to an age in the past when the great prophets had lived, and he accordingly restricts the use of the word προφήτης almost exclusively to figures from this golden age.

But Josephus believed that there were still individuals in his own day who did the same sorts of things that the ancient prophets had done, and who were inspired in the same sort of way. He and Simon the Essene could interpret dreams and make predictions; other Essenes made predictions, too. Jesus son of Ananias was "under some supernatural impulse," and those who ignored his message of doom were fools who "disregarded the proclamations of God" (*War* 6.288). Josephus writes of himself that God had "made choice of my spirit to announce the things that are to come" (*War* 3.354); he refers to himself as God's "minister" (διάκονος, *War* 3.354), and even as "a minister of the voice of God" (διάκονος τῆς τοῦ θεοῦ φωνῆς, *War* 4.626). The inspiration and abilities that Josephus claims for himself and for others of his day are not inconsiderable, and they are not different in kind from those he believed had been possessed by the ancient prophets.

The evidence from Josephus thus suggests that Barton is correct when he argues that the belief that prophecy had ceased was not an absolute dogma, but rather one expression of a vague nostalgia that idealized the past as a time when people were, in some indescribable way, closer to God and holier than in the present.[89] We saw from Josephus' treatment of John Hyrcanus that the limits of this golden age were not very clearly defined: it was simply that period in the distant past when the truly great prophets had lived. These giants from the past were thought to have been superior in every way to their modern counterparts; but it was generally believed that modern counterparts did exist. We now proceed to consider the evidence for these latter-day prophets, beginning with Josephus himself.

2

Josephus as Prophet

We have seen that Josephus did not make a claim to prophetic authority in connection with his account of the Jewish revolt against Rome and the events leading up to it. He seems to have been firmly convinced that the sort of prophets who wrote books that contained completely reliable history belonged to the distant past; they were part of a succession that began with Moses and ended, definitively, after the reign of Artaxerxes. In other contexts, however, Josephus was less hesitant about making prophetic claims for himself. This chapter considers the evidence suggesting that he understood himself, and intended to present himself, as a prophet.

The best way to begin the inquiry is by examining Josephus' self-portrayal in those narratives in the *War* in which he reports his surrender to the Romans (3.340–91), his appearance in the Roman camp and interview with Vespasian (3.392–408), and his eventual release after his prediction that Vespasian would become emperor had come true (4.622–29). I shall attempt to show that Josephus presents himself in these narratives as a prophetic servant and messenger of God. Careful attention to the particular language he employs will help to define more precisely how he understood this role. Having considered these accounts in some detail, I shall then examine other evidence that Josephus understood himself as a figure very much like the prophets of old.

The Revelation at Jotapata

The events under consideration here are well known and can be briefly summarized. After a siege of forty-seven days, the Galilean city of Jotapata, where Josephus was commander of the Jewish forces, was captured by the Romans. A general massacre ensued. Josephus himself, however, managed to hide in a cave just before the entry of the Romans; in thus escaping with his life he was, he says, blessed with "some divine assistance" (*War* 3.341). Forty other Jews, described as "persons of distinction" (3.342), hid with him. One member of the party was captured after two days and, when interrogated, told the Romans where they could find Josephus. Vespasian, the commander of the Roman forces, sent two envoys with orders to try to persuade Josephus to give himself up; they were later joined by a third messenger, an old friend of Josephus, a Roman tribune named Nicanor.

Josephus claims to have had a divine revelation while he was trying to decide whether or not to surrender. At that crucial moment, he says, he was reminded of certain dreams he had had, which concerned "the coming misfortunes of the Jews" and "the future events relating to the Roman rulers" (3.351). He was able to understand the meaning of these dreams with the aid of certain "prophecies of the sacred books" (3.352). Josephus' account of this experience of revelation will be examined from several points of view and in considerable detail in a subsequent section of this chapter. For now, it is sufficient to note that it was as a result of this experience that he decided to surrender to the Romans. At least that is how he presents the episode.

Josephus' intention to surrender was opposed by the other Jews hiding with him in the cave. They urged him to commit suicide, and so to die honorably and in accordance with Jewish law (3.355–60). Josephus was not very enthusiastic about this proposal. He tried to persuade his Jewish companions with a speech on the evils of suicide (3.361–82), and when this failed to convince them, he made a proposal that they accepted: they would draw lots, then kill one another in sequence, and the last person would kill himself. Josephus drew the next to the last lot, a fortunate result that he, however, attributed to the providence of God (3.391). Everything proceeded according to plan until it was Josephus' turn to die; he then persuaded the other remaining Jew not to kill him and surrendered to the enemy.

Josephus was conducted to the Roman camp. When he learned that Vespasian intended to send him to Nero, he requested, and was granted, an interview with the Roman general. His report of their meeting includes a short speech in which he predicts to Vespasian that he would become emperor (3.400–402). Vespasian put no store in this prediction at first, suspecting that it was merely "a trick of Josephus to save his life" (3.403). But he became more interested when he discovered that Josephus had made accurate predictions about other matters, including the precise date of the fall of Jotapata and his own capture (3.405–7). In addition, Josephus explains, "God was already rousing in him [Vespasian] thoughts of empire and by other tokens foreshadowing the throne" (3.404). This is a reference to the so-called *omina imperii*, to which I shall return. Vespasian decided not to send Josephus to Nero after all, and kept him instead as a prisoner in his own camp.

Josephus was released from captivity after his prediction to Vespasian had come true (4.622–29). The new emperor was forced to concede that

Josephus' predictions, which he had initially "suspected of being fabrications prompted by fear," had in fact proved to be "divine" (θείας, 4.625). As a result of his fabulous success in this one instance, Josephus' "power of insight into the future was no longer discredited" (4.629).

Josephus does not label himself a προφήτης anywhere in this narrative, probably for reasons of the sort considered in chapter 1. He does, however, present himself very much in prophetic terms. He claims that he was "chosen" (ἐπιλέγομαι, 3.354) and "sent" (προπεμπόμενος, 3.400) by God to act as his "messenger" (ἄγγελος, 3.400) and "minister" (διάκονος, 3.354). In a speech attributed to Vespasian, Josephus describes himself as "a minister of the voice of God" (διάκονος τῆς τοῦ θεοῦ φωνῆς, 4.626). Throughout the narrative, as I shall seek to demonstrate, he portrays himself as one who was called to God's service in a dramatic moment of revelation, who acted in obedience to God's command, and who was saved from danger by God's providence.

The Content of the Revelation

The immediate result of the revelatory experience that Josephus claims to have had in the cave at Jotapata was the prediction to Vespasian that he would become emperor. As we shall see below, Josephus himself, in the narrative describing his surrender to the Romans, emphasizes the importance of delivering this particular message. It is not surprising, then, that most commentators have focused exclusively on this prediction when discussing the Jotapata episode.

From the description that Josephus gives of the experience in *War* 3.351–54, however, it is clear that the revelation at Jotapata involved more than this single prediction. He describes the content of the divine message in quite general terms. In *War* 3.351 he says that his dreams had concerned "the coming misfortunes of the Jews" (τάς τε μελλούσας . . . συμφοράς . . . Ἰουδαίων) and "the future events relating to the Roman rulers" (τὰ περὶ τοὺς Ῥωμαίων βασιλεῖς ἐσόμενα). In the prayer recorded in *War* 3.354, he provides another, slightly fuller, description of the content of the revelation. There, he implies that he learned three things: that God, who had created the Jewish people, had decided to "punish" them;[1] that "fortune" (τύχη) had passed to the Romans; and that God had chosen him, Josephus, "to announce the things that are to come" (τὰ μέλλοντα εἰπεῖν).

Josephus evidently intended that the prediction to Vespasian should be understood as part of this more comprehensive revelation. For that reason, and because the larger dimension of the revelation is so often overlooked by commentators, it deserves a brief examination. In particular, it must be determined what Josephus meant when he wrote that God had decided to punish the Jews, and that fortune had passed to the Romans. As we shall see, both of these ideas, as Josephus develops them,

are distinctively Jewish, although the use of the term "fortune" might at
first glance suggest otherwise. The two ideas are central to the *War*, for it
is primarily with their aid that Josephus seeks in that work to provide an
explanation, at the religious level, for the defeat of the Jews and the
destruction of Jerusalem and the temple by the Romans.[2]

Sin and Punishment

Throughout the *War*, Josephus frequently expresses the conviction that
the disasters suffered by the Jews during the revolt were divine punishment for the sins committed by the rebels. He is not always clear about
precisely what these sins were.[3] He accuses the rebels of transgressions of
practically every kind, but emphasizes the charge that they polluted and
profaned the temple: they abandoned the proper sacrifices, plundered the
sacred treasures, appointed an illegitimate high priest, converted the temple into a fortress and a sepulcher, and stained the holy precincts with
their own blood and that of their countrymen.[4] By contrast, he portrays
the Romans and the moderates among the Jews as defenders of the temple and its sanctity.[5] Because of the sins of the rebels, Josephus suggests,
God abandoned his temple and went over to the side of the Romans; he
was fighting on behalf of the Romans, using them to punish his own people for their sins and to purify his temple.[6] Josephus insists, however, that
the rebels could have repented at any time, up to the very end, and that
God would have forgiven them and abandoned his intention to punish
them.[7]

This interpretive scheme, according to which national disasters were
viewed as divine punishment for sins, has a long history in Israelite religion, reaching back to the deuteronomic historian and the great classical
prophets of the Hebrew Bible;[8] it was also used by other Jewish writers
attempting to come to terms with the events of 70 C.E.[9] Josephus deviates
from the traditional scheme in emphasizing the sins committed during
the war rather than those committed beforehand;[10] also, he focuses on the
sins of a particular group (the rebels) and does not speak of the sins of the
Jewish people as a whole. But apart from these differences, his thought
corresponds to the traditional view.

Τύχη and the Rise of Rome

Alongside this sin-and-punishment scheme, Josephus uses a second idea
to explain the disasters of 70 C.E., the notion that "fortune" (τύχη) had
passed over to the Romans. Josephus attaches a number of different
meanings to the word τύχη, which need not be surveyed here.[11] In the
prayer recorded in 3.354, and in several other passages in the *War*, Josephus attributes the rise of Rome as a world power to the influence of τύχη,
and it is this particular use of the term that is of interest to us.[12]

The notion that τύχη was responsible for the rise of Rome would have been familiar to Josephus' Roman readers from the works of Polybius, and that is probably why he chose to use this terminology in his own work.[13] But Josephus uses the Polybian language of τύχη to express a distinctively Jewish understanding of history and of the rise and fall of empires. According to this view, it is the God of the Jews who establishes and deposes the great rulers of the world in sequence, decreeing the length of time that each shall rule. Such a view is expressed or assumed at several places in the Hebrew Bible and in Jewish works from the postbiblical period.[14] It can be seen especially clearly in Daniel 2.31–45, which records Daniel's interpretation of Nebuchadnezzar's dream about an image made of four metals. In the biblical account, the four metals are said to signify four successive kingdoms, identifiable as the Babylonian, Median, Persian, and Hellenistic empires. It is assumed that these empires and their emperors had been (or, from the point of view of the putative author, would be) established and removed by God, that is, by the God of the Jews (Dan. 2.37–38; see also 2.21). Furthermore, it is asserted that this same God or his agent, represented by the stone "cut out by no human hand," would one day destroy the fourth kingdom and establish his own eternal kingdom on behalf of his chosen people (Dan. 2.34–35, 44–45).

Josephus shared the understanding of the rise and fall of kingdoms expressed in Daniel 2.31–45. He was interested in this passage and interpreted it in relation to the situation in his own day. According to him, the four metals of Nebuchadnezzar's vision represented, respectively, the Babylonian, the Median-Persian, the Hellenistic, and the Roman empires.[15] Thus, in *Antiquities* 10.208, Josephus' Daniel identifies the head of gold with Nebuchadnezzar and the Babylonian kings before him. According to the same passage, the silver hands and shoulders of the image represent two kings who would bring the Babylonian empire to an end; these kings are elsewhere identified as "Cyrus, king of Persia, and Darius, king of Media" (10.232; see also 10.113, 244, 248, 272). The ruler of the third kingdom, represented by the bronze belly and thighs of the image, would come "from the west" (10.209); he is later identified as "a certain king of the Greeks" (10.273). The reference is almost certainly to Alexander the Great.[16] Also included in the third kingdom are the Seleucid rulers who followed Alexander (10.274–76).

Josephus does not explicitly identify the fourth kingdom, but there are several indications that he thought of it as Rome. Without indicating precisely which passage he has in mind, he notes that "Daniel also wrote about the empire of the Romans" (*Ant.* 10.276). In his account of Nebuchadnezzar's dream, he omits the detail that the feet of the image were made of a mixture of iron and clay and, correspondingly, eliminates the scriptural references to the weakness and instability of the fourth kingdom in his version of Daniel's interpretation.[17] Presumably these omissions were made in deference to his Roman readers. Most significantly, Josephus declines to comment on the meaning of the stone "cut out by no human hand" that was expected to crush the fourth kingdom, stating that it was not his business as a historian to speculate on "what is to be" (τὰ μέλλοντα, 10.210). The excuse is not convincing, and Josephus' reluctance to explain the meaning of the stone is understandable only if he identified the fourth kingdom with Rome. In that case, the stone would signify that Roman hegemony was only temporary, and that the God of the Jews would eventually act to reestablish his people—convictions that Josephus would not want to express unambiguously to his Roman readers.[18]

When Josephus explains the rise of Rome by referring to the influence of τύχη, he is expressing essentially the same understanding of the rise and fall of kingdoms as the one expressed in Daniel 2. Τύχη, in this context, is not an autonomous power, as in Polybius, but is under the control of the God of the Jews; indeed, τύχη almost signifies God in his role as establisher of empires.[19] In several passages that concern the rise of Rome or the Roman emperors, Josephus refers to God and τύχη almost interchangeably. In Agrippa's speech in *War* 2.345–401, for example, it is implied three times that the rise of Rome was due to τύχη (2.360, 373, 387); but later in the same speech it is said that God was responsible for the building up of the Roman empire (2.390). In *War* 4.622 Vespasian's rise to power is attributed to τύχη (along with πρόνοια ["providence"] and εἱμαρμένη ["destiny"]); but in 3.6 and 5.2 it is attributed to God. In *War* 6.399–400 a dramatic Roman military victory is attributed both to τύχη and to God. The near equivalence of the two terms in this context can be seen especially clearly in *War* 5.367: "Fortune [τύχη], indeed, had from all quarters passed over to them [the Romans], and God who went the round of the nations, bringing to each in turn the rod of empire, now rested over Italy." As in Daniel 2, it is the God of the Jews who decides who will rule the world and for how long.

The temporal indication "now" (νῦν) in the passage just quoted is of some significance. It suggests that Josephus did not believe that Roman domination would last forever; his remarks about the stone in Daniel 2 suggest the same. Throughout the *War*, however, Josephus consistently maintains that the God of the Jews had determined that the Romans should rule the world for the present time, and that it was sinful to resist the divine purpose in this as in all other matters.[20]

Conclusion

These two explanations—that God was punishing the Jews for the sins of the rebels and that fortune had passed to the Romans—are independent of one another and can be employed independently. Commentators sometimes point out that there is a certain degree of tension between them, in that fortune functions in an inexorable way, whereas the sin-and-punishment scheme presupposes that repentance is possible and would change God's plans.[21] Josephus, however, does not seem to have perceived any tension between the two ideas.[22] Occasionally he connects them, usually by suggesting that God or τύχη promoted the Romans as world rulers because of the sins of the rebels, or in order to punish the Jews.[23]

As I noted earlier, Josephus evidently intended that his prediction to Vespasian should be understood as part of this larger revelation concerning God's purposes. He does not explain precisely where the prediction fits in, but it can be understood perfectly well in relation to both the sin-and-punishment scheme and the τύχη theme. When God punishes his people, he sometimes uses particular individuals to do so; and, as Cohen has written, "the divine authorization of a pagan empire involves the divine authorization of a particular monarch."[24]

The Apologetic Purpose of the Narrative

The purpose of the extended narrative under consideration here is apologetic, in a personal sense. Josephus' account of the revelation in the cave at Jotapata, his surrender to the Romans, his prediction to Vespasian, and his later release is designed to counter accusations of cowardice and treachery that were leveled against him at the time of the events he is depicting, and that were apparently still being made when the *War* was written.[25] These accusations seem to have arisen, in the first instance, as a result of the surrender itself; but they probably also reflect Josephus' later activities and circumstances, as we shall see.

There are clear indications in the *War* that Josephus' decision to surrender gave rise to charges of cowardice and treachery. In *War* 3.432–42 Josephus describes the reaction of the inhabitants of Jerusalem to the news of the fall of Jotapata and his own fate. At first, it was reported that he had been killed—news that, he says, "filled Jerusalem with the profoundest grief" (3.435). But when it was discovered that he was alive and well and living comfortably in the Roman camp, "profoundest grief" turned to outrage:

> But when time revealed the truth and all that had really happened at Jotapata, when the death of Josephus was found to be a fiction, and it became known that he was alive and in Roman hands and being treated by the commanding officers with a respect beyond the common lot of a prisoner, the demonstrations of wrath at his being still alive were as loud as the former expressions of affection when he was believed to be dead. By some he was reproached for cowardice [ἀνανδρία], by others for treason [προδοσία], and throughout the city there was general indignation, and curses were heaped upon his devoted head. (*War* 3.438–39)[26]

There are several echoes of this dual accusation of cowardice and treachery in the narrative under consideration. In the prayer that concludes his
account of the revelation at Jotapata, Josephus calls upon God to witness
that he is surrendering to the Romans "not as a traitor [προδότης], but
as your minister [διάκονος]" (*War* 3.354). When the other Jews hiding
with him realize that he had decided to surrender, they threaten to kill
him; their interpretation of the situation is expressed in the following
way: "If you meet death willingly, you will have died as general of the
Jews; if unwillingly, as a traitor [προδότης]" (3.359). They also accuse
him of "cowardice" (ἀνανδρία, 3.384). Finally, Josephus himself reports
that, when he first made his prediction to Vespasian, the Roman general
believed that he was acting deceitfully out of fear (4.625), and to save himself (3.403).

Later accusations of this sort were almost certainly based on more
than the simple fact that Josephus had surrendered. Much of what followed the surrender would have increased suspicion against him: Josephus was treated rather well by the Romans, even while he was still a prisoner; during the final siege of Jerusalem, he served as Titus' translator and
tried repeatedly to persuade the Jews in the city to surrender; he helped
with the interrogation of Jewish deserters and may have performed other
services in the Roman camp; after the war, in Rome, he lived comfortably
at the expense of the Flavians.[27] All of this would have reinforced the
impression that he had betrayed his people and acted in a cowardly way
in order to preserve his own life.

It is necessary, then, to consider the apologetic function of the Jotapata narrative on two levels, though these levels overlap to some extent.
Most immediately, Josephus is attempting to explain why he decided to
surrender to the Romans rather than kill himself as some Jews believed
he should have done. In the narrative describing the events in the cave
immediately after his moment of inspired insight (*War* 3.355–91), this
seems to be his main concern, and here he focuses quite narrowly on the
prediction to Vespasian. The narrative is difficult to interpret, and I shall
examine it in detail in the next section. I shall argue there that Josephus
claims that he only agreed to surrender because he had been commissioned by God with an important prophetic task that required his survival: to inform Vespasian that he was about to become emperor.

At a more general level, however, Josephus is attempting to explain
not only his decision to surrender, but also his later circumstances and
efforts on behalf of the Romans. He does this by presenting the revelation
at Jotapata as the decisive turning point in his life, as the moment in
which he first came to understand God's plans for his people and the true
significance of the events unfolding around him. We have already seen
what Josephus claims to have learned in this moment: that God was punishing the Jews for the sins of the rebels; that God himself had decreed
that the Romans should, for the present time, be rulers of the world, with

Vespasian as their emperor; and that he (Josephus) had a special role to play in these events as God's messenger. I believe that Josephus intended that the more controversial aspects of his later career should be understood with reference to this one dramatic moment of revelation: as a result of this experience, he knew that he must surrender to the Romans and make his prediction to Vespasian; that he must try to communicate to the Jews what had been revealed to him by God, and persuade them to repent of their sins and submit to Roman rule; that he must do whatever he could to assist the Romans, who had been chosen by God to rule over the Jews and the rest of the world.[28]

Josephus does not explicitly connect any of these later activities with the revelation at Jotapata. He himself appears to have made such a connection, however, and he intended the reader of the *War* to make the connection as well. This can be seen most clearly in the way he presents himself as a preacher of repentance to the rebels in Jerusalem in the final stages of the war. He portrays himself, in this role, as a second Jeremiah, a prophet of God who was called to preach an unpopular message to his people and who was abused and rejected as a result (*War* 5.391–93). In the long speech in which he makes this comparison (5.362–419), he develops precisely those ideas that he claims first came to him in the cave at Jotapata: God was punishing the rebels for their sins (5.392–93); God, or fortune, had gone over to the Romans, and the Jews should therefore submit to their rule (see esp. 5.366–68). The long recital of examples of God's aid in the past (5.375–412) combines these two themes, and is designed to convince the Jews that God had forsaken them because of their sins and had gone over to the Romans (see esp. 5.412). Thus, even though Josephus does not explicitly refer back to the revelation at Jotapata in this speech, the connection is there.[29]

By suggesting that Josephus' account of his revelation, surrender, and prediction to Vespasian should be understood primarily as a defense of his own conduct, I intend to oppose what is still a common interpretation of this important narrative. Josephus' *War* is often understood as a piece of Flavian propaganda. When this view is taken of the work as a whole, it is natural to suppose that Josephus recorded his prediction to Vespasian primarily in order to flatter or glorify the emperor, and at the same time to emphasize the importance of his own prediction in relation to the other *omina imperii* recorded in the tradition.

Tessa Rajak has convincingly argued against this interpretation of the Jotapata narrative, and it is worth reviewing her arguments briefly before examining the passage in greater detail.[30] Josephus' prediction was one of many prophecies and omens recorded by Tacitus, Suetonius, and Cassius Dio, which were believed to have foretold Vespasian's rise to power.[31] As Rajak notes, it is generally advantageous for aspiring rulers to be seen to be marked out by destiny,[32] and it was probably especially important for Vespasian to be so regarded, since he was not a man of distinguished birth. Vespasian seems to have actively encouraged some of the omens and predictions recorded in the tradition in order to boost his claim to the throne.[33] It is possible, then, that Josephus made his prediction knowing that it would be welcomed by Vespasian and hoping that it would save his own life. But by the time the *War* was written, Vespasian was firmly established as emperor; there would have been no reason for him to cultivate the memory of the *omina* any longer, and consequently little to be gained by Josephus from retelling the story of his prophecy.[34] It is important, then, to distinguish between Josephus' motives in making the prediction in the first place and his motives in recording it in the way that he does in the *War*. At the time he made the prediction, he may have wanted to flatter Vespasian in order to save his own skin; but his account of the prediction in the *War* has an apologetic purpose.[35]

In any case, as Rajak has pointed out, Josephus' account of the prediction does not read like a piece of Flavian propaganda.[36] In the preface to the *War* (1.23–24), Josephus promises that the *omina imperii* will be one of the subjects of his history. This might lead the reader to expect a full and independent account of them, but no such account is given. Although Josephus refers to the *omina* twice in the narrative concerning his prediction to Vespasian (3.404 and 4.623), he does so virtually in passing and does not give them separate or sustained attention. Some would see this as evidence that he was trying to play down the importance of the other *omina* in comparison to his own prophecy.[37] There may be something in this, but Josephus does not press the narrative in this direction— certainly this supposed motive does not explain the passage as a whole. Finally, there is nothing in the account to suggest that Josephus' main purpose in composing it was to flatter or glorify Vespasian. The speech in which the prediction is made (3.400–402) includes some praise of Vespasian's might and majesty, but this theme is not emphasized or elaborated upon, either in the speech itself or in the rest of the narrative.

I suggested earlier that the apologetic purpose of the Jotapata narrative needs to be considered on two levels. In the preceding pages, I have examined the more general of these two levels. We have seen how Josephus seeks to justify his surrender and his later circumstances and activities by presenting the revelation in the cave as a dramatic turning point at which he first came to understand God's purposes in the great events unfolding around him. I now turn to the narrower aspect of his apology.

Josephus' Defense of His Decision to Surrender

How does Josephus defend his decision to surrender? This question is more difficult to answer than one might expect. The difficulty is knowing how to interpret the extraordinary account that Josephus gives of events between the moment of revelation and his arrival in the Roman camp, that is, his account of what happened between himself and the other Jews in the cave just before his surrender (*War* 3.355–91).[38] Let us review these events very briefly. When they realized that Josephus intended to surrender, his Jewish comrades, who believed that it was his duty to commit suicide, threatened to kill him (3.355–60). It is at this juncture that Josephus claims to have delivered his speech against suicide (3.361–82). This infuriated the others and they prepared to assault him (3.383–86). Josephus then proposed the lot-drawing scheme, only to renege on the pact when it was his turn to die (3.387–91).

I have described Josephus' account of these events as extraordinary, and I must explain what I mean by that description. The narrative seems to present Josephus himself in an extremely bad light. The speech against suicide and the lot-drawing incident are especially problematic. For reasons that we shall consider more fully below, Josephus' speech against suicide impresses most modern readers as unconvincing and deeply hypocritical.[39] The lot-drawing episode, probably more than anything else, has contributed to Josephus' reputation as a coward and a scoundrel, and this is certainly understandable: his conduct, as he presents it, is deplorable by any standard.

The phrase "as he presents it" is significant. We must remember that it is only from Josephus' account in the *War* that we know anything at all about what went on in the cave at Jotapata. Why does he present the story in a way that reflects so badly on himself? Most commentators seem to believe that Josephus was such a morally bankrupt person that he did not even realize that his conduct was less than completely admirable. While I would not want to defend Josephus' personal character unreservedly or in every instance, I believe that this negative and somewhat cynical evaluation of him is based largely on a misreading of the Jotapata narrative. In what follows, I shall describe the usual interpretation of this passage and then suggest an alternative.

Interpretive difficulties are posed especially by the speech against suicide and the account of the lot-drawing episode. How should these passages be understood? They are usually interpreted in a fairly straightforward way: the speech against suicide is read as a genuine attempt at persuasion, and, similarly, the account of the lot-drawing episode is taken to be Josephus' innocent report of an incident in which he thought he had acted with admirable resourcefulness.

Rajak's interpretation of the Jotapata narrative may be considered as an example of this type of reading, although she is more generous to Josephus than are many commentators. As I have already noted, Rajak argues (correctly, in my view) that the purpose of this narrative is primarily apologetic: Josephus is attempting to defend himself against charges of cowardice and treachery that arose as a result of his decision to surrender rather than commit suicide. Rajak distinguishes three sorts of explanations that Josephus provides for his decision in this narrative.[40]

The first of these explanations she describes as "practical," though "rational" might be a better term. Josephus begins the speech to his compatriots in the cave by arguing that suicide is not the appropriate or most honorable course of action in the circumstances in which he finds himself: while acknowledging that it is honorable to die in war at the hands of the enemy, he argues that it is foolish to kill oneself if the enemy is inclined to spare one (*War* 3.363–64); he agrees that it is honorable to die for liberty, but only if one dies while fighting (3.365); he contends that it is "equally cowardly not to wish to die when one ought to do so, and to wish to die when one ought not" (3.365). He goes on to make other appeals to reason: if it is death that one fears in surrendering to the enemy, then it makes no sense to kill oneself to avoid surrendering (3.366–67); committing suicide to avoid slavery is equally foolish (3.367). Finally, he argues that suicide is not a noble act, as the others contend, but an act of cowardice (3.368).

This last point leads on to the second type of argument Josephus makes against suicide, which Rajak describes as a "moral" argument. In the second part of his speech (*War* 3.369–78), Josephus attempts to prove that suicide is an offense against nature and against God: the will to live is a natural law (3.370); life is a gift from God, not to be spurned (3.371); the soul is "a portion of the Deity" entrusted to human beings (3.372); those whose souls are reclaimed by God enjoy some sort of eternal life, while the souls of those who commit suicide go down into "the darker regions of the nether world" (3.374–75); moreover, their descendants are made to suffer as a result of their impiety (3.375); not only the laws of the Jews, but also the laws of other nations, punish the one who kills himself (3.376–78).

The third explanation Josephus offers for his conduct "relies on supernatural sanction."[41] According to this last explanation, Josephus refused to commit suicide because he had been commanded by God to predict to Vespasian that he would become emperor.

Rajak argues that all three of the explanations Josephus provides for his conduct were aimed at moderate Jews and were intended to be persuasive. In discussing his moral argument against suicide, for example, she notes that, while suicide is not discussed in the Pentateuch, it was later explicitly forbidden by Jews. She suggests, quite reasonably, that the topic was debated in Josephus' day, and that the moral argument he makes in his speech should be understood in relation to this ongoing debate: "Josephus' [moral] argument against suicide is, then, one which could have found a real response in an audience of moderate Jews. It is rhetorical, but not solely rhetoric."[42] Similarly, she regards Josephus' rational and supernatural arguments against suicide as carefully considered arguments intended to be persuasive; together with his moral argument they form "a series of justifications designed to appeal to Jews who were not fanatics."[43] Rajak gives no indication that she regards any one of Josephus' arguments as more significant, or more central to his presentation, than the others, though she expresses some doubt about the sincerity of what she terms his supernatural explanation.[44]

As I noted, Rajak's interpretation of this narrative is fairly representative of the majority view. In what follows, I shall argue for a different interpretation that makes better sense of the narrative as a whole and that takes into account evidence that most interpreters have either overlooked or discounted. I shall argue that Josephus presents his prophetic commissioning (the supernatural explanation, in Rajak's terms) as his primary motivation for not committing suicide, and that the rational and moral arguments he makes in his speech are subsidiary and in some sense not really intended to be persuasive. I shall argue, in addition, that Josephus presents the lot-drawing episode as a deliberate ruse on his part, which would have been inexcusable if he had not had an overwhelming justification for acting in the way that he did. The justification he provides for his conduct is that he had been commissioned by God to perform a prophetic task that required his survival at all costs.

It is important to note that, as Josephus presents the story, the supernatural explanation of his conduct is not revealed to those who are with him in the cave at Jotapata. The speech against suicide employs only the rational and moral arguments summarized above. The fact that he had been called by God to act as his prophetic messenger, and the significance of this fact in determining his behavior in relation to his Jewish comrades, are revealed only to the reader. It is only when Josephus appears before Vespasian that his real motivation is made clear to those around him.

At several points in the narrative recording the dispute with his Jewish companions about whether he should consent to die or surrender, Josephus indicates to the reader the real reason that he refused to commit suicide: he had been called by God to perform an important prophetic task and so had to remain alive. At the beginning of the narrative stands the account of his moment of inspired insight (*War* 3.351–54). It is important to note, once again, that this experience is related only to the reader. The Jews with Josephus perceive that he is wavering and is on the verge of surrendering (3.355), but they do not know that he has had a prophetic revelation, and they do not hear the prayer recorded in 3.354: Josephus expressly says that it "escaped notice" (λελη϶υῖαν, 3.353). But to the reader Josephus presents the incident as the key to all that follows. The reader now knows (or is supposed to know) that Josephus has been commissioned with a prophetic task and is acting not as a traitor, but as God's minister (3.354).

In another important passage, Josephus in effect distinguishes between the real reason he refused to commit suicide and the reasons he supplied to those who were with him at the time. As I have already observed, no mention is made of his prophetic call in the speech in which he marshals his rational and moral arguments against suicide, but the speech is introduced, significantly, in the following way: "Josephus, fearing an assault, and holding that it would be a betrayal of God's commands, should he die before delivering his message, proceeded, in this emergency, to reason philosophically with them" (3.361). Josephus thus presents the speech to the reader as a somewhat desperate ("in this emergency") attempt to save himself. As I noted above, the speech strikes most modern readers as just such a desperate attempt to persuade. Rajak has tried to make Josephus' arguments seem more plausible (and hence less desperate) by placing them in the context of a larger first-century debate concerning the moral and legal status of suicide. But the problem with Josephus' speech is not that the views he expresses in it are implausible in their wider historical context, but rather that they are inconsistent with the views he expresses or implies at other places in the *War*, and that they are explicitly contradicted by a statement he makes later in the Jotapata narrative itself. These two points require some discussion.

As we have seen, Josephus argues in his speech that suicide is not appropriate in his particular situation, and more generally that it is cowardly, unnatural, impious, and against the Jewish law. Other Jews did not share these views. Josephus implies that his companions in the cave believed that suicide was enjoined by the Jewish law (οἱ πάτριοι νόμοι, 3.356) for someone in his situation; they were incensed by his speech (3.384). Elsewhere in the *War*, Josephus records several instances in which Jews chose to commit suicide rather than surrender to their enemies or die at their hands.[45] In no case does he explicitly condemn the act of suicide, and most of the reports seem generally approving.[46]

Josephus' account of the collective suicide of the defenders of Masada (*War* 7.275–406) is a special case that requires separate discussion. As has often been noted, Josephus' attitude toward the Sicarii who occupied the fortress and who decided to commit suicide rather than fall into Roman hands is curiously mixed.[47] On the one hand, he condemns and attacks the Sicarii in this report as he does throughout the *War*. He prefaces his account of the events at Masada with a review of the crimes of the various rebel factions who played a part in the war (7.254–74) and there accuses the Sicarii of cruelty, avarice, and lawlessness (7.256, 262). When describing the siege of the fortress, he suggests that God himself assisted the Romans in battle by changing the direction of the wind at a crucial moment, thereby ensuring that the defensive wall constructed by the Sicarii was burnt down.[48] In the two speeches attributed to him by Josephus, the leader of the Sicarii, Eleazar, is made to acknowledge that God was punishing the Sicarii for their sins, and had himself deprived them of every hope for deliverance (7.329–33, 358, 387).

On the other hand, Josephus presents the suicide itself as an act of astonishing courage and boldness. In the two speeches attributed to him, Eleazar describes the collective suicide he has proposed as a "noble" and "honorable" deed (καλῶς, 7.325, 380; καλός, 7.337, 386; γενναῖος,

7.326), which requires "courage" (εὐτολμία, 7.342), "manliness" (ἀνδρεία, 7.383), "valor" (ἀρετή, 7.342), and a "stout heart" (εὐκαρδίως, 7.358). He promises his listeners that the Romans will feel "astonishment" (ἔκπληξις) at the manner of their death and "amazement" (θαῦμα) at their "daring" (τόλμα, 7.388) if they carry out the plan.[49]

Such language might be (and occasionally is) dismissed as ironic, since it is placed in the mouth of a hated enemy. But similar language is used by Josephus himself in his description of the execution of the suicide plan by the Sicarii (7.389–401), and in his description of the response of the Romans (7.402–6). He reports that the Sicarii were eager to prove their "manliness" (ἀνδρεία, 7.389) by committing suicide without delay; in the end, "not one was found a truant in so daring a deed [τόλμημα]" (7.393). When the Romans discovered what had happened, they were "incredulous of such an amazing act of daring" (τῷ μεγέθει τοῦ τολμήματος ἀπιστοῦντες, 7.405); they admired the "nobility" (γενναιότης) of the resolve of the Sicarii, and were "astonished" (ἐθαύμασαν) by their contempt of death (7.406).

A similar mixture of condemnation and admiration characterizes Josephus' account of the activities of a group of Sicarii refugees in Alexandria after the fall of Masada (*War* 7.409–19). He accuses them of promoting "revolutionary schemes" (καινοτέροις . . . πράγμασι, 7.410) and "revolt" (ἀπόστασις, 7.411), and of murdering a number of prominent Jews (7.411). He refers three times to their "madness" or "desperation" (ἀπόνοια, 7.412, 417). Yet, at the same time, he gives an admiring account of their resistance under torture:

> Nor was there a person who was not amazed at the endurance and—call it which you will—desperation [ἀπόνοια] or strength of purpose [τῆς γνώμης ἰσχύς], displayed by these victims. For under every form of torture and laceration of body, devised for the sole object of making them acknowledge Caesar as lord, not one submitted nor was brought to the verge of utterance; but all kept their resolve, triumphant over constraint, meeting the tortures and the fire with bodies that seemed insensible of pain and souls that wellnigh exulted in it. But most of all were the spectators struck by the children of tender age, not one of whom could be prevailed upon to call Caesar lord. So far did the strength of courage [ἡ τῆς τόλμης ἰσχύς] rise superior to the weakness of their frames. (7.417–19)

At the beginning of this passage, Josephus indicates that the endurance of the Sicarii might be attributable either to "desperation" or "strength of purpose"; but in the concluding sentence he speaks less ambivalently of "strength of courage."[50]

The views Josephus expresses in his Jotapata speech are not only inconsistent with the views implied by passages like these. A further, and more significant, problem is posed by a passage that occurs within the Jotapata narrative itself. According to *War* 3.400, when Josephus appeared before Vespasian he proclaimed himself "a messenger of greater things" and said, "had I not been sent on this errand by God, I knew the law of the Jews [τὸν Ἰουδαίων νόμον] and how it is fitting for soldiers to die." Josephus here admits that he in fact knew that it was his duty, according to Jewish law, to commit suicide rather than surrender to his enemies, an admission that directly contradicts the arguments made in his speech.

The modern reader, then, is fully justified in viewing Josephus' speech against suicide as hypocritical and unconvincing. My point is that Josephus *intends* the speech to be read in this way. The impression that is deliberately created by the introduction to the speech, quoted above, is that he was willing to make whatever arguments were required to convince his opponents. This impression is reinforced by the notice at the conclusion of the speech which suggests that he has recorded only a sample of the arguments he made at the time: "By these *and many similar arguments* Josephus sought to deter his companions from suicide."[51] Moreover, he presents to the reader the real reason that he was not willing to commit suicide: he believed that "it would be a betrayal of God's commands, should he die before delivering his message" (3.361). The message that he had been commanded to deliver, as the sequel reveals, was that God was about to make Vespasian emperor.[52]

If, as I have argued, Josephus presents his speech against suicide as a rather desperate attempt to save himself, the same must be said of his presentation of the lot-drawing episode. There are several indications that he intends it to be understood as a deliberate ruse on his part. In proposing the scheme, he claims to have said to his comrades that "it would be unjust that, when the rest were gone, any should repent and escape" (3.389). This is, of course, precisely what Josephus himself then does. He even heightens the grossness of his deception by reporting how compliant the others were, and how devoted to him: "Each man thus selected presented his throat to his neighbour, in the assurance that his general was forthwith to share his fate; for sweeter to them than life was the thought of death with Josephus" (3.390).[53] An additional point concerns Josephus' use of the language of chance and providence in his account of this episode. It is clear that Josephus viewed his own preservation in this desperate situation as a result of God's providential intervention on his behalf. I noted above that he says, at the beginning of the entire Jotapata narrative, that he found his way safely to the cave "with some divine assistance" (δαιμονίῳ τινὶ συνεργίᾳ χρησάμενος, 3.341). Similarly, he tells the reader that he proposed the lot-drawing scheme "trusting in God's protection" (πιστεύων τῷ κηδεμόνι θεῷ, 3.387). When he recommends the procedure to his Jewish comrades, however, he suggests that the lot operates by fortune (τύχη), understood in this instance as blind chance:

> Since we are resolved to die, come, let us leave the lot to decide the order in which we are to kill ourselves; let him who draws the first lot fall by the hand of him who comes next; fortune [τύχη] will thus take her course through

the whole number, and we shall be spared from taking our lives with our own hands. (3.388–89)

Josephus thus suggests to the other Jews that the outcome of the procedure he has proposed depends on τύχη alone. When he himself draws so as to come next to the last in the succession, he speculates (again, privately to the reader) on whether this was "by fortune" (ὑπὸ τύχης) or "by the providence of God" (ὑπὸ θεοῦ προνοίας, 3.391). There is uncertainty about the text of this passage. In three important manuscripts (P, A, and L) the phrase "should one say by fortune or" (εἴτε ὑπὸ τύχης χρὴ λέγειν, εἴτε) is omitted, so that the passage reads, "He [Josephus], however, was, by the providence of God, left alone with one other." Even if we allow the expanded text to stand, there is no doubt about which of the alternative explanations is being commended to the reader: as we have seen, the way in which Josephus introduces the entire Jotapata narrative (3.341) and this particular episode (3.387) makes it clear that he believed that his preservation was providential, and not the result of chance.[54]

Josephus thus admits that he deliberately misled his companions by suggesting that the lot operated by blind chance, when he himself felt confident that God would save him. The whole episode is presented as a deliberate ruse, deplorable by ordinary standards of morality. Again, we must bear in mind that it is Josephus himself who presents the incident in this way. As Daube has commented, "No one would report such an action of his, and in such a way, unless he were sure that he had an overwhelming justification."[55] The justification that Josephus believed he had, and that he has already presented to the reader, was that he had been called by God to announce to Vespasian that he was about to become emperor.

One point made above is worth emphasizing again. When Josephus appears before Vespasian, he acknowledges that he in fact knew that it was his duty to die rather than surrender, and he explains why he did not do so: "Had I not been sent on this errand by God, I knew the law of the Jews and how it is fitting for soldiers to die" (3.400). This I take to be conclusive proof that the usual reading of the narrative is mistaken. Josephus wishes the reader to recognize that the real reason he did not commit suicide was that he had been called by God to deliver a prophetic message, and that the speech against suicide and the lot-drawing scheme were just desperate attempts to survive.

One final note. We do not know who might still have been accusing Josephus of cowardice and treachery at the time the *War* was written. There are no clearly identifiable opponents, as there are in the later *Life*. But presumably those who made accusations against him in connection with his surrender to the Romans and his later activities on their behalf were Jews and not Romans. If it is correct that Josephus is writing with Jewish accusers in mind, and if it is also correct that he defends himself by claiming that he had been called as God's prophet, then it follows that his portrayal of himself as a prophet in this narrative is one that he thought would appeal to Jewish readers. Let us consider that self-portrayal from a slightly different point of view.

The Revelatory Experience Described in *War* 3.351–54

We have seen that Josephus defends his conduct at Jotapata and afterward by pointing to a dramatic experience in which he suddenly came to understand God's purposes for his people and the true meaning of the events unfolding around him. In what follows, I shall consider more closely the nature and significance of this experience. I begin by giving my own fairly literal translation of Josephus' description of the moment of revelation:

> As Nicanor was urgently pressing his proposals, and Josephus heard the threats of the hostile crowd, there came to him remembrance of the nocturnal dreams through which God forecast to him the coming misfortunes of the Jews and the future events relating to the Roman rulers. With regard to interpretations of dreams, he was able to understand correctly the ambiguous utterances of the Deity; in addition, he was not ignorant of the prophecies of the sacred books, since he himself was a priest and a descendant of priests. At that hour, being divinely inspired by them, and drawing out of himself the horrible images of his recent dreams, he offered to God a silent prayer: "Since," he said, "it seems good to you, the creator, to punish[56] the nation of the Jews, and all fortune has passed to the Romans, and you have chosen my soul to announce the things that are to come, I willingly give my hands to the Romans and live, but I call you to witness that I go not as a traitor, but as your minister." (*War* 3.351–54)

Careful translation does not solve all the problems in this passage, as we shall see, but it does help to clarify a few things:

1. The passage refers to the inspired interpretation of dreams with the aid of scripture, and not to the inspired interpretation of scripture, as is often supposed.[57] In *War* 3.353 Josephus says that he was divinely inspired "by" the prophecies of the sacred books, not that he was inspired "to read their meaning," as the LCL edition translates.[58] The latter translation is not only inaccurate from a grammatical point of view;[59] it also conflicts with what is said in 3.352. There, Josephus claims that he was able to understand the prophecies of the sacred books not because he was inspired but because he was a *priest*. Since this claim is frequently regarded as strange or even incredible by scholars, I shall devote the next section (pp. 53–58) to the topic of priestly expertise in the interpretation of scripture.

2. Josephus provides the following information about his dreams in the passage I am considering:
   a. There were more than one of them.
   b. They were sent by God.
   c. They occurred sometime in the recent past. Apparently Josephus had forgotten them until the moment when he had to decide whether to kill himself or surrender. Probably he attributed their timely recollection to God; at least, this seems to be implied by the passive way in which he describes the experience of remembering them.[60]
   d. The dreams that Josephus recalled consisted of "horrible images" (τὰ φρικώδη ... φαντάσματα, 3.353) whose significance was unclear; the message that God was trying to communicate through these images was "ambiguous" (ἀμφιβόλως, 3.352) and required interpretation.
   e. The dreams concerned events in the future.
   In a later section (see pp. 58–69) I shall consider other reports of revelatory dreams and their interpretation in Josephus with the aim of clarifying the nature and significance of the experience he describes in this passage.
3. I just argued that *War* 3.351–54 refers to the inspired interpretation of dreams with the aid of scripture and not the inspired interpretation of scripture, but the precise role of scripture and inspiration in the dream-interpretive process is unclear. I shall return to the topic (see pp. 69–70).

Priestly Expertise in the Interpretation of Scripture

In the Hebrew Bible the tasks of interpreting, teaching, and applying the law are consistently assigned to the priests.[61] It is widely believed, however, that these tasks were gradually taken over, from the second century B.C.E. on, by lay scribes and Pharisees, who eventually became the recognized experts in the interpretation of scripture.[62] Part of the evidence for the "pharisaic revolution," as this supposed transition from priestly to pharisaic authority is sometimes termed, is taken from the works of Josephus. In several passages, Josephus acknowledges that the Pharisees were regarded as expert interpreters of the law; occasionally, in his later works, he goes even further and suggests that civil and religious institutions in Jewish Palestine in his own day were run in accordance with the pharisaic interpretation of the law.[63]

I shall not discuss these passages here. I wish, instead, to draw attention to a different set of passages which show that Josephus ordinarily assumed that priests were the authorized guardians and interpreters of scripture and that public institutions were run in accordance with their rulings. I make no attempt in what follows to determine which of these two groups of passages—pharisaic or priestly—reflects "what really happened." The question of the role and influence of the Pharisees in relation to the priesthood in this period is a large and fundamental one, which would require detailed discussion of a wide range of evidence. My own view is that the Pharisees probably were widely respected as expert interpreters of the law by Josephus' day, but that this role was still regarded largely as a priestly one; I also think it is unlikely that the Pharisees controlled public life in this period in the way that Josephus sometimes suggests they did.[64] But, to repeat, the present discussion does not directly address these larger historical issues, being restricted for the most part to the question of Josephus' views about the role of priests in relation to scripture.

We have already seen evidence that Josephus thought that the physical care and transmission of sacred texts was a specifically priestly responsibility. In *Against Apion* 1.28–36 he argues that the twenty-two "justly accredited" books of the Jews, originally written by prophets, had been entrusted to priests who had preserved them (the verb used is φυλάσσω) down through the ages "with scrupulous accuracy" (μετὰ πολλῆς ἀκριβείας, 1.29). To the evidence from this passage should be added the many references in Josephus' works to sacred texts that were handed over to priests or deposited in the temple for safekeeping.[65]

There is evidence from the whole range of Josephus' works that he also regarded priests as expert *interpreters* of scripture. One passage from the *War* is of special interest because it is part of the report of a particular incident and not an editorial comment of Josephus. In the summer of 66 C.E., Eleazar, the captain of the temple and a proponent of revolt against Rome, persuaded the priests then serving in the temple to refuse all sacrifices offered by foreigners, including those traditionally offered on behalf of Rome and the emperor (*War* 2.409). The "chief priests" and "notables" tried to persuade Eleazar and the others to lift the ban, but without success (2.410). The same group—now described as "the powerful," "the chief priests," and "the most notable Pharisees" (2.411)—made a second attempt at persuasion, this time bringing in "priestly experts on the traditions" (τοὺς ἐμπείρους τῶν πατρίων ἱερεῖς), who confirmed that the action taken by Eleazar represented an innovation that did not conform to ancestral practice (2.417). Josephus thus thought there were priests who were "experts on the traditions," whose authority was such that they might have been able to persuade the rebels where the other leaders of the people (including "the most notable Pharisees") had failed.

The legal point at issue in this case concerned the proper conduct of worship in the temple. In other passages, however, Josephus makes it clear that he thought that the legal expertise and responsibilities of priests extended beyond the cultic realm into the whole of Jewish life. In *Against Apion* 2.185–87 he provides a summary of the duties of priests according to the theocratic constitution ordained by Moses. First and foremost, the priests were entrusted with the ordering and conduct of "the divine worship" (ἡ περὶ τὸν θεὸν . . . θεραπεία, 2.186); but they also had more general responsibilities: "But this charge further embraced a strict superintendence of the Law [τοῦ νόμου . . . ἀκριβὴς ἐπιμέλεια] and of the pursuits of everyday life; for the appointed duties of the priests included general supervision, the trial of cases of litigation, and the punishment of condemned persons" (2.187). A similar summary description of the duties of priests in a theocratic society is given a few paragraphs later: "The priests are continually engaged in His worship, under the leadership of him who for the time is head of the line. With his colleagues he will sacrifice to God, safeguard the laws [φυλάξει τοὺς νόμους], adjudicate in cases of dispute, punish those convicted of crime" (2.193–94). According to these passages, the priests were responsible for interpreting and applying the law not only as it pertained to the conduct of worship, but over the whole range of the law's jurisdiction, that is to say, over the whole of life.

It might be objected that Josephus is here expressing not his views about the realities of first-century Jewish Palestine, but rather his conception of the ideal polity. But it is important to remember, as we saw in chapter 1, that Josephus believed that the Jews had actually lived under a theocratic constitution at various stages of their history. Moreover, he believed that the Jewish constitution had been a theocracy during the period of direct Roman rule—not a perfect theocracy, since the powers of the ruling high priests had been restricted by the Romans, but a theocracy nonetheless. Thus, the passages just quoted refer to the situation that, according to Josephus, actually obtained in Jewish Palestine before the war.

Another passage needs to be considered here. Early in the war, when Josephus was general in Galilee, a delegation was sent out by the provisional government in Jerusalem to remove him from his post (*Life* 189–98). The delegation comprised four persons "of different classes of society but of equal standing in education" (ἄνδρας κατὰ γένος μὲν διαφέροντας, τῇ παιδείᾳ δ᾽ ὁμοίους, 196). Two of them were "from the ordinary people" (δημοτικοί) and were Pharisees; another was also a Pharisee, but was from a priestly family; the fourth was from a high-priestly family and was not a Pharisee (197). They were "of equal standing in education" in the sense that all of them, like Josephus himself, were experts in the law (198). This passage certainly suggests that Josephus believed that Pharisees were expert interpreters of the law. But it also shows that he thought that such expertise could be routinely expected of aristocratic priests.[66] In spite of their lowly social status, Josephus is saying, the Pharisees on the committee (surprisingly) knew just as much about the law as the upper-class priests (of course) did.

Most of the passages considered so far concern the legal, or halakic, interpretation of scripture. Josephus speaks of his own interpretive expertise in a different context, and here, too, he connects this expertise with priestly status and credentials. In two passages, he claims that his training as a priest specially qualified him to compose the *Antiquities*. In *Against Apion* 1.54 he writes: "In my *Antiquities*, as I said, I have translated the sacred writings, being a priest by descent and having some knowledge of the philosophy which is in those writings."[67] In this passage, being a priest by descent is connected (though there is no explicit causal connection in the Greek) with having a knowledge of the "philosophy" of scripture, which, in turn, is thought to qualify one as a "translator" of scripture.[68]

Closely related to this text is the following passage from the conclusion to the *Antiquities*, which carries on into the *Life*. I quote the passage in full:

> And now I take heart from the consummation of my proposed work to assert that no one else, either Jew or Gentile, would have been equal to the task, however willing to undertake it, of issuing so accurate a treatise as this for the Greek world. For my compatriots admit that in our native learning I far excel them. I have also laboured strenuously to partake of the realm of Greek prose and poetry, after having gained a knowledge of Greek grammar, although the habitual use of my native tongue has prevented my attaining precision in the pronunciation. For our people do not favor those persons who have mastered the speech of many nations, or who adorn their style with smoothness of diction, because they consider that not only is such skill common to ordinary freemen but that even slaves who so choose may acquire it. But they give credit for wisdom to those alone who have a clear knowledge of the laws [τοῖς τὰ νόμιμα σαφῶς ἐπισταμένοις] and who are capable of interpreting the meaning of the sacred writings [τοῖς . . . τὴν τῶν ἱερῶν γραμμάτων δύναμιν ἑρμηνεῦσαι δυναμένοις]. Consequently, though many have laboriously undertaken this training, scarcely two or three have succeeded, and have forthwith reaped the fruit of their labors. (*Ant.* 20.262–65)[69]

In this passage, Josephus emphasizes that the most important qualification for composing a work like the *Antiquities* is expertise in the "native learning" of the Jews. He goes on to specify more closely what such expertise entailed: a clear knowledge of the laws and the ability to interpret the meaning of the sacred writings (20.264). He does not refer to his priestly qualifications in that portion of the text just quoted, but the passage continues: "Perhaps it will not seem to the public invidious or awkward for me to recount briefly my lineage and the events of my life" (20.266). This sentence leads to the opening paragraphs of the *Life*, in which Josephus emphasizes his priestly and royal background and describes his early education:

> Having been educated along with my brother Matthias (for he was my legitimate brother, from both parents), I made great progress in my education, gaining a reputation for an excellent memory and understanding. While still a mere boy, about fourteen years old, I won universal applause for my love of letters; insomuch that the chief priests and the leading men of the city used constantly to come to me for precise information on some particular in our ordinances [περὶ τῶν νομίμων ἀκριβέστερόν τι γνῶναι]. (*Life* 8–9)[70]

Here, the education that Josephus received as the son of an aristocratic priest is said to have resulted in expertise in the precise interpretation of the law, which in turn (remembering the connection with *Ant.* 20.262–66) qualified him to write the *Antiquities*.[71]

None of these passages concerns the sort of esoteric interpretation of scripture that is referred to in *War* 3.351–54. Did Josephus think that priests were also experts in this kind of interpretation? In chapter 1, I briefly referred to evidence that Josephus believed that certain ancient scriptural prophecies were being fulfilled in the events of his own day. This evidence is of two sorts. First, there are passages in the *Antiquities* in which Josephus notes that particular events from this period had been predicted by ancient prophets in the writings they left behind. He believed, for example, that Moses, Jeremiah, Ezekiel, and Daniel had predicted the destruction of the temple and the capture of Jerusalem in 70 C.E.[72] In other passages in the *Antiquities* he expresses the more general view that everything happens in accordance with the predictions of the ancient prophets.[73] Second, Josephus refers several times in the *War* to ancient prophecies that he believed were being fulfilled in events that took place during the revolt.[74]

In all these cases, Josephus himself is claiming (implicitly or explicitly) to be able to interpret scripture in its predictive dimension, that is, to know which of the passages in the books written by the ancient prophets refer to events in his own day and what their meaning is. He never directly connects his expertise in this sort of esoteric interpretation with his status or training as a priest, but in one or two passages he gives some indication of the sort of people who engaged in such interpretation, and of the qualities required for success. In *War* 6.312–13 he mentions an "ambiguous oracle" from the sacred scriptures that indicated that someone from Judaea was about to become ruler of the world. According to Josephus, "many wise men" (πολλοὶ τῶν σοφῶν) misunderstood the oracle, believing that it referred to a Jew; in fact, he explains, it pointed toward Vespasian. This oracle and another one mentioned in *War* 6.311 are both included in the list of portents that preceded and pointed to the destruction of Jerusalem by the Romans (*War* 6.288–315). There was disagreement, at the time, about how these portents should be understood. A mysterious light seen in the temple, for example, was interpreted by "the inexperienced" (τοῖς . . . ἀπείροις) as a good omen, but was correctly regarded by "the sacred scribes" (τοῖς . . . ἱερογραμματεῦσι) as a portent of evil (6.291). Similarly, when the temple gate opened of its own accord, "the unskilled" (τοῖς . . . ἰδιώταις) thought this was "the best of omens," but "the learned" (οἱ λόγιοι) correctly understood it as a sign of coming destruction (6.295). Apparently, then, the interpretation of omens and portents, which in this case included two oracles from scripture, was the province of "sacred scribes" and "the learned."

These last passages underline an important point that is also illustrated by some of the other material considered in this section: in Josephus' view, it was not priestly status or descent as such that made one an expert in the interpretation of scripture, but rather the kind of training and education that were common among priests, at least among priests of his social standing. This kind of education was not restricted exclusively to such persons, and Josephus was fully prepared to acknowledge the existence of nonpriestly experts on scripture. We saw, for example, that he granted that the Pharisees in the delegation sent to recall him from Galilee were as well educated as their high-priestly colleague and himself. We shall see in chapter 3 that he thought that the Essenes—most of whom were not priests—could predict the future partly because they were educated in "sacred books" and "sayings of prophets" (*War* 2.159). Josephus also knew that not all priests were well trained: he condemns Phanni son of Samuel, who was appointed high priest by the Zealots, not only because he was not of high-priestly descent, but also because of his "boorishness" (ἀγροικία, *War* 4.155); he complains that Phanni did not even know what the high priesthood meant, and had to be instructed "how to act in keeping with the occasion" (4.155–56). There is nothing magical, then, about being a priest; Josephus is drawing a more general connection between education and the ability to interpret scripture. He assumes, however, that most priests are well educated, and they provide for him the standard by which others are measured.

Revelatory Dreams and Visions and Their Interpretation in Josephus

The following discussion of revelatory dreams and visions and their interpretation in Josephus is based primarily on his accounts of his own dream experiences (*War* 3.351–54; *Life* 208–10), his description of Simon the Essene's interpretation of the dream of Archelaus (*War* 2.112–13; *Ant.* 17.345–48), and his version of the biblical narratives concerning Joseph (*Ant.* 2.9–200) and Daniel (*Ant.* 10.186–281). The focus on a few selected passages is intended simply to bring some order into a discussion that might otherwise become chaotic. I shall occasionally refer to other accounts and I shall try to indicate any respects in which my choice of dreams and visions is unrepresentative.

Terminology for Dreams and Visions

The terms for dreams and visions used most frequently by Josephus are ὄναρ/ὄνειρος and ὄψις. In the principal passages just listed ὄναρ/ὄνειρος occurs forty-three times[75] and ὄψις twenty-one times.[76] In addition, ἐνύπνιον occurs six times and φάντασμα three times.[77] These terms are fairly evenly distributed throughout the major passages; that is, it is not the case that one term is concentrated in one or two narratives and another term in another narrative.

On the whole, Josephus does not make precise distinctions among the various terms that he uses for dreams and dreamlike experiences. He frequently uses ὄναρ/ὄνειρος and ὄψις interchangeably to denote the same experience.[78] His usage of ἐνύπνιον and φάντασμα is similarly imprecise.[79] A good illustration of the near equivalence of all these terms in Josephus is provided by his account of Pharaoh's dream and its interpretation in *Antiquities* 2.75–86. At the beginning of this passage, he reports that Pharaoh "saw in his dreams two visions" (ὄψεις ἐνυπνίων θεασάμενος δύο) along with their explanations; upon awakening, he remembered the "dreams" (ὀνειράτων), but forgot the explanations (2.75). In 2.80 the expression ὀνειράτων ὄψεις is used with reference to the same experience. Up to this point, Josephus is at least consistent in using ὄψεις to designate the two dream episodes that together constituted the dream experience as a whole; but in 2.82, these two episodes are individually termed ὄψις, φάντασμα, and ὄναρ. I repeat the point: Josephus does not, on the whole, make precise distinctions among the various terms for dreams.

Two features of his usage require further comment. First, as the account of Pharaoh's dream illustrates, Josephus sometimes uses compound phrases that combine two different terms for dreams—we encountered ὄψεις ἐνυπνίων in *Antiquities* 2.75 and ὀνειράτων ὄψεις in 2.80. In *War* 3.353, describing his own experience at Jotapata, he speaks of "the horrible images of his recent dreams" (τὰ φρικώδη τῶν προσφάτων ὀνείρων . . . φαντάσματα). When he uses compound phrases of this sort, Josephus seems to be making a distinction between the individual episodes of a dream or the particular images seen in a dream, on the one hand, and the dream experience as a whole on the other.

Second, it may be worth noting that Josephus does not use ὄναρ/ὄνειρος, his preferred term for dreams, to describe waking visions. He seems to have assumed that revelatory visions ordinarily occurred in sleep, that is, that they took the form of dreams. Most of his accounts of such visions include the observation that the experience occurred while the visionary was sleeping.[80] His biblical source, however, and perhaps some of the other sources he used, preserved accounts of visions that were in many respects like dreams, but were experienced while awake. Accounts of two such waking visions are taken over by Josephus, for example, from the biblical narrative about Daniel: Belshazzar's vision of the hand writing on the wall (Dan. 5 = *Ant.* 10.232–47) and Daniel's vision at Susa (Dan. 8 = *Ant.* 10.269–76). Josephus does not use the term ὄναρ/ὄνειρος to describe visions of this sort, and it may be that he reserved this term specifically for dreams, that is, for revelatory visions experienced while sleeping.

In spite of the fact that Josephus makes this slight terminological distinction between dreams and waking visions, he does not seem to have distinguished the two phenomena more generally. Apart from the obvious difference that one occurred when asleep and the other when awake, he describes the two types of experiences in very much the same way, as we shall see from numerous examples below. According to him, dreams and waking visions have the same general significance and purpose (they are sent by God, they predict the future, etc.) and work in the same way (the dream or vision as a whole, or the images within it, signify certain things); the process of interpretation is the same in both cases, and the same professional interpreters are consulted. Since Josephus did not distinguish carefully between them, experiences of both sorts will be included in the following survey.

General Characteristics of Revelatory Dreams and Visions

First, Josephus distinguishes between ordinary dreams and significant, revelatory dreams. This distinction is assumed throughout his works, but is made explicit, for example, in *Antiquities* 2.11, in which Joseph's first dream is described as "a vision very different from the dreams that ordinarily visit us in sleep." The phrase is an addition to the scriptural account (Gen. 37.5) and emphasizes that revelatory dreams are somehow different from ordinary ones.

Second, Josephus assumes that revelatory dreams and visions come from God and are one means by which he communicates his will and intentions to humans; this is true even when the recipients of dreams are non-Jews. A few examples will suffice. In *Antiquities* 2.13 it is said that "the Deity [τὸ θεῖον] ... sent Joseph a second vision."[81] When the prophet Daniel was called upon to interpret the dream of Nebuchadnezzar, he began by saying that "God wished to reveal to you in your sleep all those who are to reign and sent you the following dream" (*Ant.* 10.205). Similarly, when asked to interpret the meaning of Belshazzar's vision of the hand writing on the wall, Daniel explained that "God had become wrathful with him and was making known beforehand through this writing to what an end he must come" (10.243). Josephus describes the dreams that he himself recalled in the cave at Jotapata as those "through which God had foretold to him the coming misfortunes of the Jews and the future events relating to the Roman rulers" (*War* 3.351). Later in the same passage, referring to his ability to interpret dreams, he boasts that he was able to understand the meaning of "the ambiguous utterances of the Deity" (τὰ ἀμφιβόλως ὑπὸ τοῦ θείου λεγόμενα, 3.352), the assumption being that the contents of revelatory dreams were, in some sense, "utterances of the Deity."

Third, it is possible to distinguish two basic types of revelatory dreams, message dreams and symbolic dreams.[82] Message dreams are those in which the Deity or some other heavenly figure or, less frequently, a person appears and speaks to the dreamer. Symbolic dreams, on the other hand, consist of a series of visual images that may be more or less complex. I shall return to the question of how symbolic dreams were thought to work and how they were interpreted.

Most of the symbolic dreams recorded by Josephus are entirely visual experiences, though one or two include an auditory element. He regularly begins the account of a symbolic dream with phrases such as "he saw in his sleep" or "he thought he saw."[83] It accords with this emphasis on the visual character of symbolic dreams that their contents, or the individual elements of such dreams, are sometimes described as "what was seen" or "the things that were seen."[84] The images that appear in such dreams are often derived from ordinary daily life, though they may appear in strange combinations or sequences; sometimes, however, these images are more fantastic and bizarre. The dreams from the Joseph narrative are of the first sort, while the dreams and visions recorded in the book of Daniel are of the second type. We shall see below that Josephus attached some importance to this distinction.

Message dreams are primarily auditory experiences, though they also include a visual element. In these dreams, a figure appears and speaks to the dreamer. The dream that Josephus himself claims to have experienced in Galilee, early in the war, is of this type (*Life* 208–10). He had decided, under pressure from opponents, to resign his post as commander of the Jewish forces in Galilee, but changed his mind partly as a result of "a marvelous dream." In this dream, a figure appeared to him—whether human or angelic we are not told—and exhorted him to take heart and not to be afraid: he would be promoted to greatness and would enjoy good fortune, and would lead his troops against the Romans.[85] The dream of Glaphyra, the wife of Archelaus, recorded in *War* 2.114–16 and in *Antiquities* 17.349–53 is also a message dream. In this case, the figure who appears in the dream and speaks is a recognizable human figure, Glaphyra's first husband, Alexander, now dead. He reproaches her for taking a third husband and warns that he is going to reclaim her for himself. According to Josephus, she died a few days later.

The selection of dreams on which I have based this study is misleading in that it suggests that accounts of symbolic dreams are more frequent in Josephus than reports of message dreams. Apart from the main passages surveyed here, there is only one other account of a symbolic dream in Josephus (*Ant.* 5.218–22 = Jgs. 7.9–15). Most of the dreams he records are message dreams, while a few are mixed in form.[86]

Fourth, both message dreams and symbolic dreams are described by Josephus as strange and extraordinary experiences. I have already mentioned *Antiquities* 2.11, which distinguishes revelatory dreams from "the dreams that ordinarily visit us in sleep." In other passages, revelatory dreams are described as "wonderful" or "marvelous." The adjective most frequently employed in this context is ϑαυμάσιος or ϑαυμαστός. We have already seen that Josephus describes his own dream of reassurance in Galilee as "a marvelous dream" (ϑαυμάσιον οἶον ὄνειρον, *Life* 208). In *Antiquities* 2.13 Joseph's second dream is described as "far more marvelous [ϑαυμασιωτέραν] than the first." Similarly, Pharaoh's second dream is said to have been "more wondrous" (ϑαυμασιώτερον) than the first (2.82). In 10.195 Nebuchadnezzar's first dream is described as "wonderful" (ϑαυμαστόν). Belshazzar's vision of the hand writing on the wall is described as "wonderful" (ϑαυμάσιον) and "portentous" (τεράστιον, 10.232). Many other examples could be given.

Related to the strange quality of revelatory dreams and visions is the fact that the dreamer or visionary is frequently said to be disturbed or agitated in some way by the dream or vision. Upon awakening from his dreams, Pharaoh felt "oppressed" (ἀχϑόμενος) by what he had seen (*Ant.* 2.75).[87] Belshazzar was "troubled" (ταραχϑείς) by his vision (10.234).[88] Daniel's reaction to the vision at Susa is described in the same way (10.269).[89] Josephus speaks of the "dreadful" (φρικώδη) images of his own dreams (*War* 3.353).

In the case of complex symbolic dreams, much of the unsettling effect of the experience results from the highly symbolic and obscure character of the dreams and from the fact that they often seem to bode ill, though the dreamer does not understand their precise meaning. Relatively simple symbolic dreams do not cause the same sort of anxiety.[90] Message dreams, as we have seen, consist of clear and intelligible speech and not a series of images; they cause either joy or distress, depending on the message they communicate. Before his dream in Galilee, Josephus had decided in despair to quit his post as general; afterward, he says, he was eager to carry on with his mission. Presumably Glaphyra was less cheered by the tidings brought by her dead husband.

Fifth, As many of the examples already considered illustrate, symbolic dreams serve primarily to predict the future. This is true of the dreams that Josephus claims to have remembered in the cave at Jotapata as well as the other symbolic dreams he records. He describes his own dreams as those "through which God forecast [προεσήμανεν] to him the coming misfortunes of the Jews [τάς . . . μελλούσας . . . συμφορὰς . . . Ἰουδαίων] and the future events relating to the Roman rulers [τὰ περὶ τοὺς Ῥωμαίων βασιλεῖς ἐσόμενα]" (*War* 3.351). As a result of this experience, he realized that God had chosen him "to announce the things that are to come" [τὰ μέλλοντα εἰπεῖν, 3.354]. Immediately after his surrender, as we have seen, he predicted to Vespasian that he would become emperor. The content of message dreams is more variable, but all of them include an element of prediction.

Though these dreams and visions all concern events in the future, there is considerable variation both in the timescale involved and in the scope of the events predicted. Some dreams predict events for the immediate future, some for the more distant future, and some for the very distant future. The dream of Pharaoh's butler indicated that he would be released from prison "within three days" (*Ant.* 2.65). Events under Antiochus Epiphanes, on the other hand, had been predicted "many years" in advance by Daniel, on the basis of his visions (10.276). As we saw in chapter 1, Josephus believed that Daniel had predicted events that occurred in the Roman period, and even events that were still to come from his own (Josephus') point of view.

There is also considerable diversity in the scope of the events predicted in dreams. Some concern the personal destinies of individuals, while others relate to the events of history on the grandest scale. The dreams of Josephus himself offer a contrast in this respect. The message dream recorded in *Life* 208–10 concerns his personal fortunes quite narrowly. The dreams that he recalls in the cave at Jotapata, on the other hand, have to do with God's purposes on a vast scale.

Sixth, we saw in chapter 1 that Josephus believed that the fact that God made predictions through his spokesmen, the prophets, was evidence of his providential care for his people. This was also the case when these predictions were believed to have come in the form of dreams. I quoted Josephus' concluding comments on the predictions of Daniel (*Ant.* 10.277–80) near the end of chapter 1, but one or two further examples may be given here. At the conclusion of his account in the *Antiquities* of the dreams of Archelaus and Glaphyra, Josephus makes the following editorial comment:

> I do not consider such stories extraneous to my history, since they concern these royal persons and, in addition, they provide instances of something bearing on the immortality of the soul and of the way in which God's providence [προμήθεια] embraces human affairs; therefore I have thought it well to speak of this. (17.354)[91]

The "immortality of the soul" is demonstrated, it seems, by the fact that a dead person, in this case Alexander, the husband of Glaphyra, can appear in a dream and speak, and God's providential care is shown by the fact that he warns individuals of their fate through dreams.[92]

A passage from the Joseph narrative reveals a similar understanding. After interpreting Pharaoh's dreams to mean that there would be seven years of plenty in Egypt followed by seven years of famine, Joseph encourages Pharaoh to take the practical measures necessary to prevent devastation by famine. He tells the king, "it is not to distress human beings that God foreshows to them that which is to come, but that fore-warned they may use their sagacity to alleviate the trials announced when they befall" (*Ant.* 2.86).

Seventh, and finally, many dreams that concern events in the future also serve to clarify both the past and the present; for that reason, they should not be considered exclusively predictive. The dreams that Jose-phus remembered at Jotapata concerned future events—disasters for the Jews, world rule for the Romans. But, as we saw above, he claims that they also led him to interpret the events of his own day in a new way and to adopt a new role for himself.

As has become evident from the preceding discussion, the dreams that Josephus describes in *War* 3.351–54 fall into the category of symbolic dreams: his report suggests that they consisted of a series of "horrible" images whose meaning was unclear; they had to be interpreted before their significance could be understood. In what follows I shall consider more closely the question of how such dreams were thought to work and how they were interpreted.

How Symbolic Dreams Work

Symbolic dreams as a whole or the individual images within them were believed to signify certain things or events in the real world. The two terms most frequently used by Josephus in this connection are σημαίνω and δηλόω.[93] A review of one or two passages from the *Antiquities* will illustrate the use of these terms and will provide some examples of sym-bolic dreams and their interpretations.

While in prison, Pharaoh's baker had a dream that he reported to Joseph in the following way:

> "I thought," he said, "that I was carrying three baskets on my head, two filled with loaves, and the third with dainties and various meats of the sort that are prepared for kings, when birds flew down and devoured them all, heedless of my efforts to scare them away." (*Ant.* 2.71)[94]

He asked Joseph to explain to him "what the things he had seen might mean" (τί . . . δηλοῦν βούλεται τὰ . . . ὀφθέντα, 2.70). Joseph informed him that the baskets "signified" (σημαίνειν) that he had only two days to live, "and that on the third day he would be crucified and become food for the fowls, utterly powerless to defend himself" (2.72–73).

Nebuchadnezzar's dream is described by Josephus' Daniel in the following way:

> You seemed to see a great image standing up, of which the head was of gold, the shoulders and arms of silver, the belly and thighs of bronze and the legs and feet of iron. Then you saw a stone break off from a mountain and fall upon the image and overthrow it, breaking it to pieces and leaving not one part of it whole, so that the gold and silver and bronze and iron were made finer than flour, and, when the wind blew strongly, they were caught up by its force and scattered abroad; but the stone grew so much larger that the whole earth seemed to be filled with it. (*Ant.* 10.206–7)

The interpretation of the dream reads:

> "This, then, is the dream which you saw; as for its interpretation, it is as follows. The head of gold represents [ἐδήλου] you and the Babylonian kings who were before you. The two hands and shoulders signify [σημαίνουσιν] that your empire will be brought to an end by two kings. But their empire will be destroyed by another king from the west, clad in bronze, and this power will be ended by still another, like iron, that will have dominion for ever through its iron nature," which, he said, is harder than that of gold or silver or bronze. And Daniel also revealed to the king the meaning of the stone, but I have not thought it proper to relate this. (*Ant.* 10.208–10)

In both of these cases, the individual images seen in the dream are understood to point to or signify certain events in the real world. These real events are sometimes referred to as "the things that are signified" by the dream.[95] The task of the dream interpreter is to translate or decode the images presented in the dream, that is, to make the correct correlation between the dream images and the real events that they signify.

The Interpretation of Symbolic Dreams

Josephus does not seem to have taken much of a speculative interest in the question of how symbolic dreams were interpreted, which is rather surprising given his general interest in dreams and their interpretation. He does not expound a theory on the topic, and the terminology he uses to describe dream interpretation is varied and does not point toward any one method or set of methods.[96] Examination of his accounts of the interpretation of symbolic dreams does, however, yield some information that may help us to understand the report of his experience at Jotapata more fully.

The first point to be made is a negative one: apart from the account in *War* 3.351–54, Josephus nowhere refers to the use of scripture to interpret symbolic dreams. It is sometimes suggested that his reports about the Essenes show that he believed that they practiced this sort of dream interpretation. The connection is almost there, but not quite. In *War* 2.159 Josephus says that the Essenes were able to predict the future in part because of their knowledge of "sacred books" and "sayings of prophets"; in another passage, he tells the story of the interpretation of a symbolic dream by Simon the Essene (*War* 2.112–13; *Ant.* 17.345–48); but he does not directly connect scripture and the interpretation of dreams in these passages in the way that he does in *War* 3.351–54. It is sometimes argued that the account concerning Simon itself—that is, even apart from *War* 2.159—describes the interpretation of dreams with the aid of scripture, but this argument cannot be sustained. I shall consider the problem in detail in chapter 3.

A second point arising from a reading of Josephus' accounts of symbolic dreams and their interpretation concerns the role of inspiration in the process of interpreting dreams. Josephus seems to have graded symbolic dreams in terms of their complexity and, correspondingly, to have distinguished the sort of gifts that were required for their interpretation. Even here, he does not systematize, but makes what seem to be intuitive distinctions. In some cases, the meaning of a symbolic dream is self-evident and requires no interpretation. The two dreams of the young Joseph fall into this category (*Ant.* 2.11–16).[97] The correspondence between the images of these dreams and the real events that they signify is so obvious that those to whom Joseph reports the dreams are said to understand their meaning immediately.

Most of the symbolic dreams recorded by Josephus are more complex than this and require expert interpretation before their meaning can be understood. Even within this category, Josephus seems to have distinguished between relatively simple and relatively complex dreams. In more simple symbolic dreams, the images seen by the dreamer are drawn from ordinary life and are relatively easy to understand, at least relatively easy for the expert interpreter to understand. The dreams of Pharaoh's butler (*Ant.* 2.63–69) and baker (2.70–73) and of Pharaoh himself (2.74–86) belong to this category.

Dreams of this sort were interpreted in a fairly straightforward way through what might be described as a process of analogical reasoning. The interpreter considered the sequence of events depicted in the dream, the characteristic properties or associations of the images that were seen, and any information that was known about the character and circumstances of the dreamer; taking all of this into account, he offered an interpretation of the dream. Let us consider an example. In *Antiquities* 2.64 Pharaoh's butler describes a dream in which he saw a vine with three branches full of ripe grapes; he pressed the grapes into a cup and offered the cup to Pharaoh, who received it graciously. Joseph concludes that the dream is a favorable one, since

> the fruit of the vine was given by God to human beings as a blessing, seeing that it is offered in libation to Himself and serves humans as a pledge of fidelity and friendship, terminating feuds, banishing the sufferings and sorrows of those who take it to their lips, and wafting them down into delight. (*Ant.* 2.66)[98]

The fact that Pharaoh accepted the cup graciously is taken to mean that the butler would be released from prison and would return to Pharaoh's service (2.76). The three branches indicate that this would happen within three days (2.76). Josephus has given a fuller account of the interpretation of the dream than is given in the Bible, but the process of interpretation he describes is essentially the same as that suggested by the biblical account (Gen. 40.9–13). Symbolic dreams of this relatively simple type, then, were interpreted in a fairly straightforward, analogical way: the meaning assigned to the persons, objects, or events seen in such a dream was largely determined by the meaning these persons or things had in ordinary life.

Another type of symbolic dream, represented by the dreams and visions of the Daniel narrative, is more complex. In these dreams, the images seen by the dreamer are more fantastic and bizarre, and the correlation between dream-image and real event more obscure. In the case of these more complex dreams, analogical interpretation, as just described, was not possible, since the strange images seen in such dreams had no obvious analogues in the real, everyday world. Some other method of interpretation was required for dreams of this sort. Josephus gives no indication of the precise method or methods that were used in such cases.

According to Josephus, the interpretation of both types of symbolic dreams—relatively simple and complex—required knowledge or wisdom of an esoteric sort. When he introduces the story of Joseph, he says that Jacob favored him above all his other sons partly because he was superior to them in "understanding" (φρόνησις, *Ant.* 2.9).[99] In the rest of the narrative, "understanding," "intelligence" (σύνεσις), and "wisdom" (σοφία) are all connected with the interpretation of dreams.[100] A similar connection is made in the Daniel narrative, though σοφία-terminology predominates there.[101]

It is important to notice that dream interpretation belongs to the sphere of esoteric wisdom rather than practical wisdom. Practical wisdom concerns the conduct and understanding of ordinary human affairs; esoteric wisdom deals with secrets and mysteries, with things that are hidden from view and incomprehensible by normal rational means.[102] According to Josephus, both Joseph and Daniel were experts in this sort of esoteric wisdom. He explains that the name given to Joseph by Pharaoh meant "discoverer of secrets" (κρυπτῶν εὑρετής) and was given to him in view of his "amazing intelligence" (τὸ παραδόξον τῆς συνέσεως, *Ant.* 2.91).[103] In the narrative about Daniel in the *Antiquities* there is a strong and repeated insistence on the fact that the wisdom possessed by Daniel was the sort that enabled him to understand mysteries that were beyond the comprehension of others. To consider just one example, when the professional wise men of the Babylonian court were unable to interpret the vision seen by Belshazzar, the king was urged to summon Daniel, who is described in this context as "a wise man and skilful in discovering things beyond human power and known only to God" (10.237).[104] Of course, practical and esoteric wisdom are not entirely unrelated. Both Joseph and Daniel excelled as practical men of affairs, just as they surpassed their contemporaries in the esoteric arts. Probably anyone who possessed esoteric wisdom would also be expected to be able to advise on practical matters, but the reverse is not the case: esoteric wisdom is more than an abundance of practical wisdom.

As is the case everywhere in Jewish tradition, this kind of esoteric wisdom is regarded by Josephus partly as an acquired skill and partly as a gift from God. On the one hand, it requires special training or education. Daniel and his companions received such an education at the court of Nebuchadnezzar (*Ant.* 10.186–89, 194). According to Josephus, Joseph, too, was educated in Egypt (*Ant.* 2.39), though the Bible (Gen. 39.1–6) says nothing of this. On the other hand, however, esoteric wisdom is not regarded purely or solely as an acquired skill. Especially in Josephus' narrative about Daniel, there is a strong emphasis on the fact that the kind of wisdom required to interpret dreams comes from God.[105]

In general, Josephus' understanding of these matters is close to the views expressed or presupposed in the Bible. On this last point, however, he diverges from scripture in a significant way. In the Bible, both Joseph and Daniel are presented as *inspired* figures, and it is stressed that their ability to interpret dreams is a gift that comes from God.[106] Josephus has retained this emphasis in the case of Daniel, but not in the case of Joseph.[107] In Genesis 40.8 Pharaoh's butler and baker explain to Joseph why they are so downcast: "We have had dreams, and there is no one to interpret them." Joseph invites them to tell him their dreams, adding, "Do not interpretations belong to God?" Similarly, when Pharaoh summons Joseph to interpret his dream, the latter replies, "It is not in me; God will give Pharaoh a favorable answer" (Gen. 41.16). When Joseph successfully interprets the dream and offers practical advice, Pharaoh concludes that God had revealed these things to him (41.39), and that he has the spirit of God in him (41.38).

Josephus has omitted all these statements.[108] The omissions occur in sections of the narrative where he otherwise follows the Bible quite closely and can hardly be accidental.[109] I suggest that he has eliminated the reference to the spirit of God in Genesis 41.38 and the other passages that imply that Joseph's ability to interpret dreams came from God because he believed that the interpretation of relatively simple symbolic dreams like those described in the Joseph narrative required only a low-grade type of esoteric wisdom. Even this, to be sure, was still *esoteric* wisdom, and as such was considered at least partly a gift from God. But it could not compare with the higher gift required to interpret more complex and fantastic dreams like those described in the book of Daniel. Only when the spiritual gift involved is of this higher order does Josephus speak of *inspiration.*[110]

This still does not tell us precisely how Josephus thought that complex symbolic dreams were interpreted, but it does have implications for our understanding of the Jotapata narrative. It is often said that Josephus presents himself in this narrative as a second Joseph, but in light of the present discussion, it might be more accurate to say that he presents himself as a second Daniel, for, as we have seen, he claims to have been "divinely inspired" (ἔνϑους γενόμενος) to understand the meaning of his dreams (*War* 3.353). We can now see more clearly that this is a substantial claim. Josephus is not claiming to possess the kind of esoteric wisdom possessed by Joseph (though that, in itself, would not have been an insubstantial claim), but rather the superior kind of esoteric wisdom possessed by Daniel, a man whom Josephus rated as "one of the greatest prophets" (*Ant.* 10.266).

The Mechanics of Interpretation in War 3.351–54

The preceding review of Josephus' other accounts of revelatory dreams and their interpretation has not provided much information about the role of scripture and inspiration in the interpretation of the dreams referred to in *War* 3.351–54. Let us return to consider more closely what Josephus says in that passage.

In *War* 3.352 Josephus claims that he was able to "interpret," or "understand correctly," the ambiguous messages sent by God in the form of dreams. It seems to be a general claim, which suggests that he had interpreted other dreams before the Jotapata incident. The verb he uses for "interpret" here, συμβάλλω, tells us nothing in itself about which particular method or methods of interpretation he employed.[111] In 3.353 Josephus comes closer to giving a description of the interpretive process, but even this does not take us very far: he was divinely inspired by the prophecies of the sacred books, and "drew out of himself" (σπάσας) the images of his dreams, and (he implies) suddenly understood what God was trying to tell him. This sounds like the kind of decoding process that was necessary before the meaning of a symbolic dream could be determined. In this case, it appears that the individual images of Josephus' dreams (remembering the significance of the compound phrase τὰ τῶν ὀνείρων φαντάσματα) were decoded with the aid of certain prophecies from scripture.

More than this cannot be said with certainty. The precise role of inspiration, in particular, remains unclear. We saw earlier that the passage refers to the inspired interpretation of dreams with the aid of scripture, and not the inspired interpretation of scripture: Josephus says that he was inspired "by" the prophecies of the sacred books, not that he was inspired "to read their meaning," as the LCL translates.[112] He was able to understand the meaning of scripture, he claims, because of his status and training as a priest. It remains unclear, however, what Josephus means, positively, when he says that he was divinely inspired "by" the prophecies in scripture to understand the meaning of his dreams. Otto Betz has suggested that he may have believed that God had directed him, in his hour of need, to just the right texts that would enable him to decipher his dreams.[113] That is as good a suggestion as any and better than most.

More could probably be said if Josephus had reported the contents of his dreams or indicated which prophecies he used to interpret them, but he did neither. The scholarly literature abounds in speculation about the identity of the prophecies referred to in *War* 3.352–53, but no agreement has been reached on the question. It is often suggested or assumed that the text Josephus had in mind was the "ambiguous oracle" mentioned in *War* 6.312–13, according to which someone from Judaea was to become ruler of the world.[114] There is, however, no reason to suppose this was the case.[115] In *War* 3.351–54 Josephus speaks of prophecies in the plural, and he nowhere draws any connection between his experience at Jotapata and the oracle referred to in *War* 6.312–13. It must be remembered that the content of the revelation at Jotapata was extremely broad. The message that came to Josephus in the cave concerned not only Vespasian's rise to power (the subject, according to Josephus, of the oracle in *War* 6.312–13), but also God's plans for the Romans and the Jews on a grand scale. We do not know how these various elements fit together in Josephus' mind. Did he come to believe that God was about to make Vespasian emperor and conclude from this that he was promoting the Romans to world dominance and punishing his own people, the Jews? Or did he begin from the insight that God was punishing the Jews for their sins and infer from this that the Romans and Vespasian were his chosen instruments? Other combinations can be imagined. If we consider the complexity and very general character of the revelation, and remember that Josephus included a wide range of texts under the heading of "prophecy" (recall *Against Apion* 1.37–41), then it will be apparent that a large number of passages from scripture might have served to interpret the dreams he describes in *War* 3.351–54. It is impossible to identify the ones he actually used without knowing a great deal more than we do about the experience.

Typological Correspondences Between Josephus and the Ancient Prophets

There is evidence of a rather different sort that suggests that Josephus thought of himself as a figure very much like the prophets of old. In an article published in 1980, David Daube describes a kind of typological thinking that plays an important role in human understanding generally and that has been especially prominent in parts of the Jewish and Christian religious traditions.[116] He points out that the way in which we understand and respond to a given person, place, thing, or event is always to some extent determined by previous experiences of a similar sort. He provides illustrations of this phenomenon from many different realms of human experience, among them: a man may marry a particular woman because she reminds him of his mother; a historian might describe Stalin as a modern Ivan the Terrible or compare modern Munich with ancient Athens; the parting of the Jordan at the time of the entry into the promised land may be understood as a repetition of the parting of the Red Sea at the time of the exodus from Egypt. The influence of past exemplars may be very great or relatively small in any given case; the comparison may be conscious or completely unconscious; but in every case there is some transfer from the past that affects the interpretation of the present.

The process, moreover, is a circular one, because the transfer from the earlier experience to the later in turn affects the way in which the earlier, model experience is understood: having married a woman who reminds him of his mother, our man will no doubt find that his mother begins to remind him more and more of his wife; once the historian begins to think of Stalin as a modern Ivan, then features of Stalin's personality and career may be retrojected back onto Ivan; and so on. This retroeffect of the original comparison serves to strengthen the link between the two experiences.

Daube cites one relatively trivial example from the religious realm that illustrates the circular nature of this kind of typological thought and the sort of anachronism it sometimes produces.[117] In Matthew 23.2 there is a reference to "the chair of Moses." The rabbis of the tannaitic period (roughly from 20–200 C.E.) thought of themselves as Moses-like figures; he was for them the ideal teacher, and they self-consciously modeled themselves on him. But the influence ran in the opposite direction as well. By the time Matthew 23.2 was written, the most revered teachers of the law evidently sat on a special chair, and, as a result of the kind of retroeffect described above, it was supposed that Moses, too, had had such a chair. The retrofiguration reinforces the original link.

As Daube notes, there is no evidence that Josephus was, in general, any more typological in his thinking than other Jews or other historians of his day. His treatment of his own role, however, forms something of an exception.[118] Daube has noted dozens of typological correspondences between Josephus' description of himself and his description of certain ancient Israelite prophets, in particular Jeremiah, Daniel, Joseph, and Esther-Mordecai.[119] These parallels suggest that Josephus understood himself, or at least wished to present himself, as a figure very much like these ancient heroes. I shall not review all of Daube's evidence here. Instead, I want to focus on the two figures who were the most important models for Josephus, Jeremiah and Daniel. In each case, I shall take up one point that Daube mentions in passing and develop it more fully.

Finally, I shall say a word about Joseph, since it is so often thought that he served as a model for Josephus.

Jeremiah

In the speech that he claims to have delivered to the rebels in Jerusalem late in the revolt (*War* 5.362–419), Josephus cites a series of positive and negative examples from the history of Israel to illustrate the principle that military success does not depend on strength of arms, but on God's bless- ing and assistance.[120] The first of the negative examples comes from the period shortly before the destruction of the first temple:

> When the king of Babylon besieged this city, our king Zedekiah having, contrary to the prophetic warnings of Jeremiah, given him battle, was him- self taken prisoner and saw the town and the temple levelled to the ground. (5.391)

Josephus goes on to argue that the rebels of his own generation have even less reason to hope for success in war than the Jews of Jeremiah's day. His argument implies a comparison between the situation in his own day and that in the time of Jeremiah, and a comparison between himself and the ancient prophet:

> Yet, how much more moderate was that monarch [Zedekiah] than your leaders, and his subjects than you! For, though Jeremiah loudly proclaimed that they were hateful to God for their transgressions against Him, and would be taken captive unless they surrendered the city, neither the king nor the people put him to death. But you—to pass over those scenes within, for it would be beyond me adequately to portray your enormities—you, I say, assail with abuse and missiles me who exhort you to save yourselves, exasperated at being reminded of your sins and intolerant of any mention of those crimes which you actually perpetrate every day. (5.391–93)

The comparison with Jeremiah is not completely ridiculous. There are important biographical parallels between the ancient prophet and Josephus.[121] Both men were priests.[122] Both interpreted the war in which their people were involved as divine punishment for sins; both predicted victory for the foreign enemy and urged their compatriots to surrender.[123] Both were accused of deserting to the enemy, an accusation that was true in Josephus' case, though not in Jeremiah's.[124] Both suffered abuse at the hands of their own people. In the passage just quoted, Josephus says that he was "assailed with abuse and missiles" by the rebels in Jerusalem, and reports elsewhere in the *War* provide examples of such treatment.[125] Jere- miah was accused of breaking down the spirit of the people with his pre- dictions of defeat.[126] He was also imprisoned by his own people more than once, in rather more difficult conditions than those endured by Jose- phus.[127] Both Josephus and Jeremiah, moreover, had to contend with prophets who promised the people deliverance. As we shall see in chapter

4, Josephus describes the so-called sign prophets of his own day in a way reminiscent of his description of the prophetic opponents of Jeremiah, calling them "false prophets" and "deceivers." Finally, as I noted in chapter 1, Josephus believed that Jeremiah had predicted the destruction of Jerusalem by the Romans (*Ant*. 10.79); this was, then, one more thing that, from Josephus' point of view, united them.[128]

In what follows, I wish to draw attention to one way in which Josephus has strengthened the parallels between his own preaching and the message of Jeremiah. This particular case furnishes a good example of what Daube describes as retrofigurement, whereby features of one's own life or activity are transposed back onto an earlier individual.

I have already considered evidence from the *War* that suggests that Josephus had a special concern for the temple and its sanctity: when describing the sins of the rebels, he concentrates especially on their alleged sins against the temple and he portrays the Romans, particularly Titus, as protectors of the temple. This concern for the temple is especially evident in the speech in *War* 5 from which I quoted earlier; that is, precisely in the speech in which Josephus compares himself with Jeremiah.[129]

There is no evidence that the prophet Jeremiah displayed a similarly exaggerated concern for the temple, though the temple does figure in some of his recorded pronouncements.[130] Josephus, however, has introduced specific references to the temple in several places in his account concerning Jeremiah in the *Antiquities*. In Jeremiah 36.2, for example, the scroll written by Baruch at Jeremiah's dictation is said to contain "all the words that I [Jeremiah] have spoken to you against Israel and Judah and all the nations"; according to Josephus, it concerned "the things which were to befall the city and the temple and the people" (*Ant*. 10.93). As we shall see, the collocation of city and temple occurs frequently in the Jeremiah narrative in the *Antiquities*. In Jeremiah 38.17–18, the prophet's advice to Zedekiah is recorded as follows:

> Thus says the Lord, the God of hosts, the God of Israel, if you will surrender to the princes of the king of Babylon, then your life shall be spared, and this city shall not be burned with fire, and you and your house shall live. But if you do not surrender to the princes of the king of Babylon, then this city shall be given into the hand of the Chaldeans, and they shall burn it with fire, and you shall not escape from their hand.

The oracle includes a warning against the city and the royal house, but does not specifically mention the temple. In his version of this passage, Josephus notes that Jeremiah advised Zedekiah to surrender the city, and continues:

> This, he [Jeremiah] said, God prophesied to the king through him, if, indeed, he wished to be saved and to escape the impending danger and not have the city brought down to the ground *and the temple burned*; for, if he

disobeyed this warning he would be the cause of these calamities to the inhabitants of the city and of the disaster to himself and all his house. (*Ant.* 10.126; emphasis mine)

In *Antiquities* 10.128 Josephus summarizes Jeremiah 38.20–23, and once again adds a specific reference to the temple where none exists in scripture:

The prophet, however, bade him [Zedekiah] take courage, and said that his apprehension of punishment was groundless, for he should suffer no harm by surrendering to the Babylonians, neither he himself nor his children nor his wives, *and that the temple, moreover, should remain unharmed.*[131]

In another passage, Josephus adds a reference to the temple to one of Jeremiah's predictions of future restoration. The biblical promise reads:

For thus says the Lord: When seventy years are completed for Babylon, I will visit you, and I will fulfil to you my promise and bring you back to this place. . . . I will restore your fortunes and gather you from all the nations and all the places where I have driven you, says the Lord, and I will bring you back to the place from which I sent you into exile. (Jer. 29.10, 14)

In *Antiquities* 10.113 Josephus gives his version of this promise:

At that time, by overthrowing the Babylonians, the Persians and Medes will free us from servitude to them, and, when we have been sent back by them to this land, *we shall once more build the temple* and restore Jerusalem.[132]

Further examples of this phenomenon could be cited,[133] but the point is already clear: Josephus has strengthened the parallels between himself and Jeremiah by attributing to the ancient prophet his own special concern for the temple and its preservation.

Daniel

We have already seen that Josephus greatly admired the prophet Daniel. A lengthy account of his career is given in *Antiquities* 10.186–281.[134] As with Jeremiah, there are certain biographical parallels between Daniel and Josephus. Both were of royal descent.[135] Both showed early promise.[136] Both were dreamers and interpreters of dreams, who rose to a position of honor under a foreign ruler as a result of their skills. Both predicted the defeat of the Jews by the Romans.[137]

In what follows, I wish to draw attention to a certain pattern that is common to Josephus' portrayal of himself in the *Life* and his portrayal of Daniel in the *Antiquities*. According to this pattern, an innocent and pious hero falls into danger as a result of the calumnies of envious opponents, but is rescued by the providence of God. The pattern is already present to some extent in the book of Daniel, but Josephus has made it clearer by explicitly identifying the motives of Daniel's opponents and by emphasizing Daniel's innocence. As we shall see, he has done this in a way that reinforces the parallels between himself and the ancient prophet.

According to Daniel 6, when Darius conquered Babylon, he appointed Daniel to one of the most important administrative posts in the land and later decided to increase his authority (Dan. 6.1–3). As a result, the other officials of the realm plotted to get rid of Daniel. Failing to find any grounds for complaint as far as his administrative practices were concerned, they concocted a scheme of a different sort for entrapping him (6.4–9). They convinced Darius to pass a decree prohibiting the offering of prayers to any god or man except the king, knowing that Daniel, a pious Jew, would not cease his practice of praying to God three times a day. When Daniel was caught praying in violation of the decree, he was turned in to the king, who reluctantly cast him into the lions' den (6.10–24).

Nothing is said in scripture about the motives of Daniel's opponents, though it is fairly evident that they were envious of his success, power, and favor with the king. Josephus makes this explicit:

> And so Daniel, being held in such great honour and such dazzling favour by Darius and being the only one associated with him in all matters because he was believed to have the divine in him, became a prey to envy [ἐφϑο-νήϑη], for people are jealous [βασκαίνουσι] when they see others held by kings in greater honour than themselves. (*Ant.* 10.250)[138]

The same motives are attributed to Daniel's enemies in *Antiquities* 10.256–57.[139]

It is possible that the attribution of motives of envy and jealousy to Daniel's opponents is simply one example of a general tendency on the part of Josephus to fill in and heighten the psychological aspects of the stories he relates in the *Antiquities*.[140] As I noted above, though nothing is said about the motives of Daniel's opponents in scripture, it is reasonably clear that they acted out of jealousy and envy. It may be that Josephus is simply making explicit what is already implicit in the biblical text, and that no further explanation is required. But I think it is significant that Josephus claims that many of his own personal enemies were motivated by envy and jealousy. As we shall see, the parallels between himself and the Daniel of the *Antiquities* in this respect extend beyond the description of the motives of their enemies into a more general pattern of description.

Josephus frequently claims that his archenemy, John of Gischala, acted against him because he was envious or jealous of his good fortune. According to *Life* 84–85, for example, John tried to persuade the inhabitants of Tiberias to abandon Josephus and ally themselves with him because he was envious of the affection and loyalty that the Galilean population demonstrated for Josephus.[141]

The passage that immediately precedes the account of this particular episode of conflict between Josephus and John is of special interest in this connection. In *Life* 77–79 Josephus describes the measures he took to stabilize the situation in Galilee after the two priests who had been appointed to serve as generals along with him had returned to Jerusalem. Having made it clear that he had the situation well in hand, he remarks: "I was now about thirty years old, at a time of life when, even if one restrains his lawless passions, it is hard, especially in a position of high authority, to escape the calumnies of envy [φϑόνος]" (80). He denies, however, that there was any substance to the charges made against him by envious opponents, and claims that he conducted himself in a perfectly upright way (except in one case, as we shall see). He "preserved every woman's honour" (80) and refrained from punishing John and his Galilean supporters, even though (he says) he had many opportunities to do so (82). The bulk of his denial, however, concerns charges of financial improprieties:

> I scorned all presents offered to me as having no use for them; I even declined to accept from those who brought them the tithes which were due to me as a priest. On the other hand, I did take a portion of the spoils after defeating the Syrian inhabitants of the surrounding cities, and admit to having sent these to my kinsfolk in Jerusalem. (80–81)

This protestation of innocence should be compared with the following passage from Josephus' Daniel narrative. It comes immediately after the passage (*Ant.* 10.250) in which Josephus claims that Daniel's enemies were envious of his privileged relationship with the king:

> But, although those who were resentful of the esteem in which he [Daniel] was held by Darius sought some pretext for slander and accusation against him, he never gave them a single cause, for, being superior to considerations of money and scorning any kind of gain and thinking it most disgraceful to accept anything even if it were given for a proper cause, he did not let those who were envious of him find a single ground for complaint. (*Ant.* 10.251)

The parallel passage in the book of Daniel (6.4) reads as follows:

> Then the presidents and the satraps sought to find a ground for complaint against Daniel with regard to the kingdom; but they could find no ground for complaint or any fault, because he was faithful, and no error or fault was found in him.

Josephus has expanded this passage by adding references to alleged financial improprieties, exactly the sort of charges against which he defends himself in *Life* 80–82. He has also made it explicit, once again, that Daniel's enemies were "resentful of the esteem in which he was held by Darius."

The parallels go on. Josephus claims that, because he conducted himself in the honorable way described in *Life* 80–82, God preserved him through the "numerous perils" that he faced in Galilee (83). Prominent among these perils were those posed by his envious friend, John of Gischala.[142] Daniel, too, was preserved by God when the accusations of his enemies endangered him: he was saved from the lions "through the Deity and His providence" (*Ant.* 10.260).[143]

In another passage in the *Life*, Josephus describes his own situation in a way that parallels his description of Daniel even more closely. In *Life* 422–23 he describes his treatment after the war:

> When Titus had quelled the disturbances in Judaea, conjecturing that the lands which I held at Jerusalem would be unprofitable to me, because a Roman garrison was to be quartered there, he gave me another parcel of ground in the plain. On his departure for Rome, he took me with him on board, treating me with every mark of respect. On our arrival in Rome I met with great consideration from Vespasian. He gave me a lodging in the house which he had occupied before he became Emperor; he honoured me with the privilege of Roman citizenship; and he assigned me a pension. He continued to honour me up to the time of his departure from this life, without any abatement in his kindness towards me.

He continues: "My privileged position excited envy and thereby exposed me to danger" (423). He refers to a particular case, in which he was accused by a certain Jew, Jonathan, of providing arms and money in support of an insurrection in Cyrene.[144] But he indicates that this was not the only case in which accusations were brought against him by envious opponents: "Subsequently, numerous accusations against me were fabricated by persons who envied me my good fortune; but, by the providence of God, I came safe through all" (425).

The parallel with Daniel in this instance is very marked: Josephus' privileged position in relation to a foreign ruler—a position that he owed, ultimately, to his ability to interpret dreams—leads to envy; envy leads to accusations and danger; but God protects him through it all.

Joseph

It is often suggested that Josephus understood himself as a Joseph-like figure, but the evidence in this case is not as convincing as in the cases of Jeremiah and Daniel.[145] There are biographical parallels, most of which also connect Joseph and Daniel. Both Josephus and Joseph were dreamers and interpreters of dreams; both were promoted from the status of prisoner to a position of honor as a result of successful dream interpretations; both served foreign rulers; both were providentially protected by God and promoted to greatness by him.

Josephus does not, however, elaborate on these themes in his treatment of the biblical account in the *Antiquities*. He does make a few editorial adjustments to the story that have the effect of strengthening the connection between Joseph and himself. For example, as we saw above, he claims that Joseph was given "a liberal education" by Potiphar, his Egyptian master, though nothing is said of this in scripture.[146] He also emphasizes that Joseph's brothers acted against him out of envy. According to scripture, his brothers hated him because their father loved him more than any of them and because of his dreams, which portended future greatness for him (Gen. 37.4–5, 8); in one passage, it is said that they were jealous of him (37.11). Josephus explicitly states several times that the brothers were envious or jealous of Joseph, and that it was for this reason that they sought to kill him.[147] But the theme of envy is entirely restricted to the story of Joseph's early relations with his brothers and does not recur in the account of his later political career. It is not nearly as central as in the Daniel narrative. All of this adds support to the suggestion made above that Daniel was a more important model for Josephus than was Joseph.

Conclusion

Josephus presents himself in two different, but overlapping, prophetic roles. He appears, first, as a Jeremiah-like figure, a priest who denounces sin and preaches repentance, whose message is that submission to foreign rule is God's will, who stands fast against the delusions of the false prophets and rebels, and who is concerned, above all, with preserving God's holy temple. He claims to have been called to perform this role in a dramatic moment of revelation in which he appears, secondly, as a Daniel-type figure, an esoteric wise man who can interpret the meaning of even the most difficult dreams and omens, who understands the prophecies of the sacred books, and who knows God's plans for kings and kingdoms; in this portrait, too, I noted a certain priestly element. Like Daniel, Josephus was to rise to a position of prominence under a foreign ruler as a result of his prophetic gifts and would be subject to accusations from envious opponents and rivals.

One question remains: how much of this self-portrait is true? That is, how much of Josephus' portrayal of himself as a prophet reflects what he actually said and did and thought at the time of the events he is depicting, and how much of it is a result of later reflection and literary elaboration?

This is, of course, an extraordinarily difficult question to answer. There is no denying that the picture we now possess of Josephus as a prophet has been refined and developed in various ways. For example, the ideas that he claims first came to him in a moment of prophetic revelation at Jotapata—that God was punishing the Jews for their sins and that fortune had gone over to the Romans—have become major interpretive themes in the *War* as a whole. Josephus also sometimes reinforces the prophetic claims that he makes for himself by subtle changes in his presentation of the ancient prophets. And it is probable that, with the passage of time, Josephus' image of himself as a prophet became clearer in his own mind.

In my view, however, it is extremely unlikely that Josephus created this image out of nothing. It is virtually certain, for one thing, that he actually did predict to Vespasian that he would become emperor. The historicity and the timing of the prediction have been questioned, but as Daube has observed, the rewritings of the incident proposed by critics are less plausible than Josephus' own account.[148] Even if we grant that he could not possibly have foreseen, in the summer of 67 c.e., the political upheavals that would bring Vespasian to power two years later, he clearly had nothing to lose and everything to gain by making the prediction when he did. Coming as it did in a moment of crisis for him personally, this insight may well have been experienced by him as prophetic.

We also know that Josephus joined the revolutionary cause after the defeat of Cestius (if not before) and served as commander of the Jewish forces in Galilee, but that he eventually came to the conclusion that the war was not only hopeless but also against God's will. It is perfectly reasonable to suppose that this insight first came to him when he says it did, after the fall of the city that he and his troops were defending and the collapse of the whole Jewish war effort in Galilee, and at the moment when he himself was faced with the prospect of death or imprisonment at the hands of the enemy. Certainly he has elaborated the account of this moment of insight and strengthened its prophetic character, but the basic account he gives is completely plausible from a psychological point of view.

Finally, we must bear in mind a point that Daube makes in connection with typology. There was a limit to the extent to which Josephus could distort the portrayal of his own role in these events for the simple reason that there were still people around who remembered what he had actually done.[149] This means, for example, that although Josephus may have elaborated the portrait of himself as a Jeremiah-like prophet of repentance, it is very unlikely that he created it out of nothing. He probably really did walk around the walls of Jerusalem trying to persuade the Jews inside that it was God's will that they should surrender. And if he really did this, then I see no reason to doubt his claim that he consciously conceived of himself and presented himself, at the time, as a second Jeremiah; the same comparison might, after all, occur to a Jew or a Christian today who found himself or herself in a similar situation.

3

The Essenes

In *War* 2.159 Josephus makes a general statement about the ability of some of the Essenes to predict the future. Elsewhere in his works, he provides accounts of the activities of three individual Essene prophets: Judas (*War* 1.78–80; *Ant.* 13.311–13), Menahem (*Ant.* 15.373–79), and Simon (*War* 2.112–13; *Ant.* 17.345–48). In this chapter, I shall examine these passages in some detail and outline the general features of the type of prophecy represented by the Essenes, which is similar in many ways to that described in chapter 2 and represented by Josephus himself.

Two preliminary topics require discussion: first, the relationship between the Essenes described by Josephus, Philo, and other classical authors, and the community at Qumran known to us through the Dead Sea Scrolls; and second, the question of the sources of Josephus' reports about the Essenes.

On the first point, I share the view of the majority of commentators that the community at Qumran is to be identified as a branch of the wider Essene movement. The evidence for this view has been described many times and will not be repeated here.[1] Both the Scrolls and the classical sources suggest that there were two basic types of Essenes, a celibate group, whose members lived a separate existence, and another variety, whose representatives married and had children and settled in towns and villages. It is sometimes argued that these two types represent different stages in the development of a unified Essene movement; that is, that the entire party moved, over a period of time, from marrying and having children to practicing celibacy, or vice versa. The evidence is better explained, however, if we suppose that the two types of Essene communities existed at the same time: a celibate group at Qumran and various noncelibate groups dispersed throughout the towns and villages of Jewish Palestine.[2] The archaeological evidence suggests that no more than a few hundred people ever occupied the site at Qumran at any one time.[3] Both Josephus and Philo estimate the total number of Essenes at more than four thousand.[4] If this last figure is even approximately correct, then the vast majority of Essenes lived outside of Qumran in the ordinary settled areas of the country. We do not know precisely what the practical relationship was between the two basic types of communities, but that is not very important for the purposes of this discussion.

In one passage (*War* 2.160) Josephus suggests that the two types of Essenes differed only in their views on marriage, but we know from the wider evidence that they were distinguished by other differences in practice, organization, and belief.[5] In what follows, I shall try to keep the differences between the celibate community at Qumran and other Essenes clearly in mind; this is especially important since the individual Essene prophets mentioned by Josephus were apparently not from Qumran. Among the Scrolls, I shall refer to the Community Rule (1QS) as the chief witness to the practices of the sectarians at Qumran, and to portions of the Damascus Rule (CD) as the main evidence for the practices of Essenes away from Qumran.[6]

Josephus knew that there were both celibate Essenes (*Ant.* 18.21; *War* 2.120–21) and "another order" who married and had children (*War* 2.160–61), but he does not describe the two groups separately, and he does not mention the settlement at Qumran; according to him, Essenes settled "in every city" (*War* 2.124). Some of the statements he makes about the Essenes are paralleled in the Community Rule, some in the Damascus Rule; others have no parallel at all in the Scrolls. Sometimes the practices Josephus describes combine elements that are separately attested by the two major Rules.[7] He states, for example, that the Essenes practiced both community of goods and hospitality: new members were required to turn over all their property to the order (*War* 2.122; cf. *Ant.* 18.20), and in every city one person was appointed to provide visiting members with clothing "and other necessaries" out of a common fund (*War* 2.124–25). From the Scrolls, however, we learn that community of goods was practiced by the sectarians at Qumran and not by those Essenes represented by the Damascus Rule.[8] The latter were required to give at least two days' wages each month to the local overseer and judges, who used this money to assist orphans, the poor, and other needy members of the community (CD 14.12–16). Presumably members visiting from elsewhere were provided for out of the same charitable fund. In this instance, then, the Scrolls allow us to make a distinction that Josephus does not make.

It is not my intention to provide a full discussion of the evidence from the Scrolls in relation to the topics considered here, but rather to use this material to check and supplement the evidence from Josephus in a fairly general way. We have just seen that the Scrolls sometimes enable us to distinguish those statements in Josephus that refer to the celibate branch of the Essenes from those that refer to the marrying group. In other ways, too, the evidence from the Scrolls can be used to clarify and fill in the statements that Josephus makes about the Essenes. I shall occasionally refer to the other classical accounts of the Essenes, but I have made no attempt to integrate these fully into the present discussion.[9]

It is important to bear in mind that there were probably more sub-groups among the Essenes than are represented by the Community Rule and the Damascus Rule. I have already mentioned that some of Josephus' statements about the Essenes are not paralleled in either of these documents. In some or all of these cases, Josephus' information may simply be mistaken; but it is also possible that the unparalleled statements in his accounts describe the practices of a group or groups not represented by any of the Scrolls.[10] For example, the Essenes represented by the Community Rule probably rejected the Jerusalem temple completely and did not participate in any way in the worship conducted there; the Damascus Rule, on the other hand, appears to presuppose more or less normal participation in the temple cult. In *Antiquities* 18.19 Josephus describes a third practice, which falls between these two: he claims that the Essenes sent votive offerings to the temple, but did not sacrifice there because of a disagreement about the purification rites required for entry.[11] It may be that Josephus is simply in error on this point; but it is also possible that he is describing the practice of a group of Essenes otherwise unknown to us. Similarly, neither the Damascus Rule nor any of the other Scrolls speaks for a Jerusalem group; but the evidence from Josephus suggests that there were Essenes who lived in Jerusalem. Finally, the three individual Essene prophets mentioned by Josephus appear to belong neither to the community at Qumran, nor to the type of community represented by the Damascus Rule. This means that the two principal Rules cannot tell us everything we should like to know about these figures; but it also means that the present study may be expected to contribute to our general knowledge of diversity within the Essene movement.

The second preliminary topic that has to be considered is the question of the sources of Josephus' reports about the Essenes, both his general reports and his accounts concerning individual prophets. Josephus claims to have "gone through" (διῆλθον) the sect of the Essenes, as well as the Pharisees and Sadducees, sometime between the ages of sixteen and nineteen (*Life* 10–12). Precisely what this means is unclear, but it seems to imply that he received some kind of training in the central teachings of each of the three parties. Even if we grant some credence to this claim, rather than dismissing it as simply a literary topos, it is difficult to see how such a basic training course could have provided Josephus with the kind of detailed knowledge of Essene practices and beliefs displayed, for example, in *War* 2.119–61; this is especially true when we consider the secrecy surrounding the celibate branch of the sect and the long period of apprenticeship required for full entry. On other grounds, too, I consider it likely that the general account in *War* 2.119–61 is from a literary source: it is replaced in the *Antiquities* by a much shorter account (18.18–22), which was almost certainly taken over from Philo (*Every Good Man Is Free* 75–91) or from a common source.[12]

All three of Josephus' reports concerning individual Essene prophets are well-defined literary units that stand out from their contexts. The source of this material is uncertain. It is often assumed that the accounts were taken over from the work of Nicolaus of Damascus, but the last of them, concerning Simon, occurs after the point at which Nicolaus' narrative is generally thought to have ended (the accession of Archelaus).[13] I consider it most likely that these reports came from Jewish tradition, perhaps even from Essene circles. This is impossible to prove, but it is worth noting that one of the accounts is introduced in the *War* with the expression "they say" (φασίν, 2.112), one of several phrases that Josephus and other historians sometimes used to introduce anonymous traditions.[14]

It is difficult to assess the historical reliability of Josephus' reports about these Essene prophets. The events they describe are less public than those surrounding the sign prophets, for example, whom I shall consider in chapter 4; these events also lay well in the past at the time Josephus was writing. In addition, the reports have been shaped to reflect Josephus' own interests and perceptions. On the other hand, there is nothing outrageously implausible about any of the accounts, and they may very well preserve reminiscences of actual events.

The General Statement in *War* 2.159

Near the end of his longest description of the beliefs and practices of the Essenes (*War* 2.119–61), Josephus writes that "there are some among them who profess to foreknow the future, being educated in sacred books and various purifications and sayings of prophets; and seldom, if ever, do they err in their predictions" (2.159).[15] The passage is placed immediately before the reference to the other order of Essenes who married and had children (2.160–61), and thus seems to refer to the stricter, celibate group. I shall return to the question of the extent to which it might also describe other Essenes.

The Study of "Sacred Books"

According to Josephus, when new recruits were formally admitted to the Essene community, they were required to swear, among other things, "to preserve the books of the sect" (*War* 2.142).[16] The scrolls found at Qumran and excavations of the site have confirmed that the production and study of books were of central importance to the sectaries who lived there. A passage from the Community Rule describing the origins of the group defines it as a community dedicated to the study of the law of Moses, which is understood as the "way" in the wilderness (Isa. 40.3) that the sectarians went out to prepare (1QS 8.12–16). Prospective members were given an initial period of instruction in the correct interpretation of the law, after which they were evaluated on the basis of their understanding and practice (1QS 5.21; 6.18); apparently a similar review of all the sectaries was conducted annually (5.23–24). Every group of ten fully initiated members was to include at least one person who studied the law continually, day and night (6.6–7); moreover, all the members of the community were to meet for a third of every night of the year "to read the book and to study law and to pray together" (6.7–8). In addition to evidence of this sort from the Community Rule, there is also a large number of writings from Qumran that fall into the category of interpretation of sacred books, not only the pesharim (biblical commentaries; sing., pesher) but other works as well.[17] Archaeologists working at the site have unearthed writing tables, inkwells, and ink.[18] All this evidence testifies to the great importance attached to the study of sacred books in the life of the community at Qumran.

Books may be studied for a variety of reasons. The passages from the Community Rule cited above emphasize the halakic, or legal, study of sacred writings. The pesharim and some of the other interpretive works found at Qumran show that the sectaries also studied these writings for other sorts of information; for example, for information about the history of the sect and its future, about the great events expected at the End, and about the identity and mission of the Messiah(s).

Though Josephus presents the Essenes as a scrupulously observant group, he does not mention their practice of studying scripture for guidance on halakic matters. The two passages in which he refers explicitly to the Essenes' preoccupation with books (*War* 2.136 and the passage under examination, 2.159) suggest that their interests were rather more esoteric. In *War* 2.136 Josephus writes of the Essenes:

> They are extraordinarily zealous in the study of the writings of the ancients [τὰ τῶν παλαιῶν συντάγματα], choosing especially those which benefit soul and body; with the help of these, and with a view to the healing of diseases, they investigate medicinal roots and the properties of stones.[19]

Josephus gives an indication of the sort of books that might have been studied for such information in *Antiquities* 8.42–49.[20] In 8.44, following his scriptural source (1 Kgs. 4.32–33), Josephus refers to the vast number of odes, songs, parables, and similitudes composed by King Solomon. The remarks that follow this description have no parallel in scripture:

> There was no form of nature with which he [Solomon] was not acquainted or which he passed over without examining, but he studied them all philosophically and revealed the most complete knowledge of their several properties. And God granted him knowledge of the art used against demons for the benefit and healing of men. He also composed incantations by which illnesses are relieved, and left behind forms of exorcisms with which those possessed by demons drive them out, never to return. (*Ant.* 8.44–45)

All this information, it is implied, was preserved in written form.[21]

Josephus claims that this material was still being studied and used in his own day. He describes an exorcism, which he himself witnessed, that followed the procedures recommended by Solomon. The exorcist, a Jew named Eleazar, performed the cure in the following way:

> He put to the nose of the possessed man a ring which had under its seal one of the roots prescribed by Solomon, and then, as the man smelled it, drew out the demon through his nostrils, and, when the man at once fell down, adjured the demon never to come back into him, speaking Solomon's name and reciting the incantations which he had composed. (*Ant.* 8.47)

The parallels between these passages from *Antiquities* 8 and Josephus' statement about the Essenes in *War* 2.136 should be apparent. In *War* 2.136 Josephus says that the Essenes studied ancient books in order to learn how to use roots and stones to heal diseases; in *Antiquities* 8.44–45 he states that some of the books composed by Solomon concerned the properties of various forms of nature and the way in which they could be used to benefit and heal people; the particular example of healing he provides is an exorcism involving the use of a root (8.47).[22]

No Solomonic books of the sort described in *Antiquities* 8.44–45 have been found at Qumran; I mention them only to illustrate the type of book to which Josephus seems to be referring in *War* 2.136. Several of the works that were included in the library at Qumran confirm that the Essenes who lived there were interested in healing.[23] In this connection, it should be recalled that one of the etymologies proposed for the name "Essenes" connects this term with the Aramaic word for "healers," אסיא.[24]

In *War* 2.159 Josephus connects the study of "sacred books" (βίβλοι ἱεραί) with prediction of the future. There is no reason to restrict the meaning of the phrase "sacred books" in this passage to those works now included in the canon of the Hebrew Bible, though this is often done.[25] Most of the biblical books are represented at Qumran (all of them except Esther), but the library there also included other works attributed to ancient authors. There is evidence that at least some of these works were regarded by the Essenes as sacred and equal in authority to those books that were eventually to become canonical. In CD 16.2–4, for example, the new convert who has committed himself to keeping the law of Moses as interpreted by the sect is referred to the book of Jubilees for an account of "the exact determination of their times," that is, for information about the liturgical calendar followed by the community.[26] One work found at Qumran makes an extraordinary claim to authority: the Temple Scroll (11QTemple) is written in the first person as a direct revelation from God and contains new laws in addition to biblical laws. It was almost certainly regarded as a sacred and authoritative work by the community at Qumran.[27]

Josephus does not say precisely how sacred books were used by the Essenes to predict the future. It is often suggested that pesher exegesis, as practiced at Qumran, provides the key to understanding the process. An evaluation of this suggestion will follow a consideration of Josephus' three accounts concerning individual Essene prophets.

The Meaning of the Phrase "Various Purifications"

The text of *War* 2.159 is sometimes emended by scholars so that the phrase διαφόροις ἀγνείαις, "various purifications," becomes διαφόροις ἁγίαις, which is then translated "holy writings."[28] But, as Beall has pointed out, this emendation is both problematic and unnecessary.[29] There is no textual evidence for the proposed reading and no reason to believe that the text of the passage has been corrupted.[30] Moreover, the word διάφορος occurs sixty-two times in Josephus, but never with the meaning "writing." Finally, as I shall attempt to show in what follows, the "various purifications" practiced by the stricter group of Essenes were a reflection of the especially holy character of their community, which was, in turn, connected (by Josephus, at least) with their ability to predict the future.

According to Josephus, the Essenes observed a number of special purity regulations.[31] They did not use oil to soften their skin, and even washed if they accidentally came into contact with it, considering it "a defilement" (κηλίς, *War* 2.123).[32] They wore linen loincloths for bathing and put on special white clothing for meals and perhaps for other ceremonial occasions.[33] They bathed before meals (2.129), after defecation (2.149), and after contact with an outsider or even a member of the community of inferior rank (2.150).[34] It is likely that the sect's practice of celibacy and their opposition to slavery were also based in part on considerations of purity.[35]

The Community Rule does not mention the avoidance of oil or the wearing of linen loincloths and special white clothing, but it does provide evidence for the practice of ritual bathing by the sectaries at Qumran. There are general references to purificatory baths (1QS 3.4–5, 9), and one passage (5.13) refers specifically to the bath that preceded the Pure Meal of the community.[36] The language of ritual bathing is also used in a figurative way to describe God's cleansing of his people at the final judgment (4.20–21). The literary evidence for bathing at Qumran is supported by archaeological evidence as well. Several large cisterns and two or three smaller pools have been found at the site, and it is generally agreed that at least some of these were used for bathing.[37]

The Essenes' concern for purity and holiness is especially apparent in Josephus' description of their common meal (*War* 2.129–33), which is paralleled at several points by references to the Pure Meal in the Community Rule.[38] This meal was restricted to fully initiated members of the community in good standing.[39] As we have seen, it was preceded by a purificatory bath and the donning of white robes. The diners then assembled in a room and processed to the refectory "as to some sacred shrine" (καθάπερ εἰς ἅγιόν τι τέμενος, *War* 2.129). Before the meal began, the priest who was presiding said a prayer (*War* 2.131; 1QS 6.4–5). According to *Antiquities* 18.22, the food that was served was prepared by priests as well. During the meal, silence was maintained (*War* 2.130, 133). Afterward, the priest said another prayer (*War* 2.131). Before returning to their work, those present removed their robes, laying them aside "as sacred vestments" (ὡς ἱεράς, *War* 2.131).[40]

Josephus' description of this common meal suggests an analogy with the priesthood, and several of the purity practices that he attributes to the Essenes are priestly in character. We shall see that some of these rites would have been observed only by priests officiating in the temple. Others were performed routinely by priests, but were also observed on special occasions by ordinary Jews. Finally, we shall see that one or two of the purity practices mentioned by Josephus were observed by priests and laypersons alike; even these practices, however, suggest that the stricter group of Essenes treated their community, in some respects, as if it were the temple.

Priests on duty in the Jerusalem temple wore linen breeches and, on special occasions, white vestments, also made of linen.[41] The linen loincloths worn by the Essenes may not have been exactly like the breeches worn by priests, but they are similar enough, and unusual enough, to suggest that the Essenes were imitating priestly dress in this respect.[42] It is more difficult to know whether the white garments worn by the Essenes on ceremonial occasions should also be considered priestly. As just noted, priests wore white vestments some of the time, but ordinary Jews apparently also dressed in white on especially sacred or solemn occasions.[43] It is thus possible that the white robes of the Essenes were not specifically priestly, but rather symbolized purity and holiness more generally.

Immersing before meals may be described as a priestly practice, though ordinary people were occasionally required to observe the rite. According to biblical law, purification was required only for the consumption of holy food.[44] This category included the first fruits, tithes, and peace offerings that were eaten at home by priests and their families, as well as the sacrifices that were consumed by priests in the temple. Ordinary people, like priests, had to be pure when they ate holy food, but such occasions were rare.[45] In bathing before meals, then, the Essenes were adopting what was ordinarily a priestly rite, and the practice shows that they regarded the food served at these meals as holy food.

Some of the other purity practices attributed to the Essenes by Josephus may also be described as priestly. Priests on duty in the temple probably immersed immediately after defecation and after contact with semen or any other impure thing or person.[46] We do not know what practices they followed in regard to these matters when away from the temple. It is safe to assume that even off-duty priests were more careful than ordinary Jews, and even Pharisees, about avoiding contact with persons or objects from which secondary impurity could be contracted.[47] There is no evidence, however, that they immersed immediately after such contact when they were not officiating in the temple. It is also unlikely that they immersed immediately after defecation or the emission of semen when they were outside the temple. In these circumstances, they probably relied on a daily immersion before the evening meal to remove all these minor impurities.[48] If the Essenes really did immerse immediately after defecation and immediately after contact with an outsider or an inferior member of the sect, as Josephus implies, then they were adhering to a standard of purity normally kept only by priests in the temple.

Finally, anyone entering the temple was required to abstain from sexual intercourse for a period beforehand, since intercourse rendered both partners unclean until immersion and the setting of the sun.[49] The practice of celibacy by the Essenes at Qumran may reflect this restriction on entry into the temple.[50] If so, the practice is not specifically priestly—even ordinary laypersons had to be free of semen-impurity when entering the temple—but it does suggest that the group at Qumran treated their community, in this respect, as if it were the temple.

The practices attributed to the Essenes by Josephus mark them out as a sect specially concerned with purity and holiness. We have been able to find parallels in the Community Rule for many of these practices, but it is possible that Josephus (or his source) has exaggerated the distinctively priestly character of the Essene rites. Only an independent analysis of the evidence from the Scrolls could decide the matter. It should be noted that Josephus does not actually say that the Essenes were priests. As is well known, the Community Rule sharply distinguishes lay members of the group from the priests and Levites. Holiness and purity, not priestliness, are central.

We saw earlier that Josephus connected the ability of some of the Essenes to predict the future with their training in "sacred books." His mention of "various purifications" in this context shows that he thought that the Essenes' prophetic ability derived not only from their study of scripture but also in part from their practice of special purity rites. Josephus does not directly explain how, in his view, purity and prediction of the future were related; I shall return to the question in the conclusion to this chapter.

In light of the connection drawn by Josephus between the Essenes' ability to predict the future and their practice of special purifications, some of them priestly, it is worth noting that another etymology proposed for the name "Essenes" connects the term with the breastplate of the high priest, the divinatory functions of which were described in chapter 1. Josephus transcribes the Hebrew word for "breastplate," חשן, as ἐσσήν, and it has been suggested that one of the two words he uses for "Essenes," Ἐσσηνοί, is related to this term. But Josephus never mentions the breastplate in connection with the Essenes, or vice versa, and this fact does seem significant: in view of his extraordinarily high opinion of both high-priestly divination and Essene prediction, it seems likely that he would have made the connection between the two explicit if he thought that such a connection existed.[51]

The Study of "Sayings of Prophets"

It is not clear precisely what Josephus is referring to when he states, in *War* 2.159, that the Essenes studied "sayings" or "apophthegms of prophets" (προφητῶν ἀποφθέγματα). The phrase may refer to written sayings attributed to ancient prophets and included among the "sacred books," though it is difficult to see why Josephus would have mentioned them separately in that case.[52] Another possibility is that the phrase refers to a collection or collections of oracles taken from different works attributed to ancient prophets. We know that such collections existed at Qumran: the Florilegium (4Q174) and Testimonia (4Q175) are examples. We should remember, in this connection, that the category of prophetic books was broader for a first-century Jew than it is for us—the texts excerpted in the Florilegium and the Testimonia are not all from the prophetic section of the present Hebrew canon. Finally, I see no reason to rule out the possibility that the phrase "sayings of prophets" refers to oral material of some sort, perhaps even to the sayings or teachings of past or present members of the sect.

Conclusion

We have seen that Josephus connects the ability of some of the Essenes to predict the future with their study of sacred books, their practice of various purifications, and their knowledge of sayings of prophets, the precise identity of which is uncertain. He does not explain how these three things came together to issue in prediction of the future. I have promised to return to the question later in this chapter.

I noted earlier that the placement of *War* 2.159—just before Josephus' reference to the other order of Essenes who married and lived in the towns and cities of Jewish Palestine—suggests that the passage refers primarily to the stricter, celibate variety of Essenes. The comparative evidence already discussed, most of it from the Community Rule, also concerns this group. I now consider the question of whether and to what extent *War* 2.159 might also describe the practice of other Essenes. I begin by asking whether there were significant differences between the Qumran community and those Essenes represented by the Damascus Rule as far as the study of sacred books and the practice of purity are concerned.

First, with regard to purity, we have seen that some of the purity practices attributed to the Essenes by Josephus are also attested in the Community Rule. The general concern for purity was evidently shared by members of the wider Essene movement. The Damascus Rule admonishes its readers to "distinguish between clean and unclean" and to "proclaim the difference between holy and profane" (CD 6.17–18; 12.19–20). Its statutes include food laws,[53] rules about purificatory baths,[54] and other purity regulations.[55]

There is, however, evidence that the Essene communities whose practice is reflected in the Damascus Rule did not observe the same strict purity laws as did the community at Qumran; more precisely, there is evidence that they did not attempt to keep themselves in a (more or less) constant state of purity in the way that the Qumran sectaries did. The differences between these two types of Essenes can be illustrated with reference to two important purity issues: sexual relations and contact with outsiders.

The Essenes who lived in the towns and villages of Jewish Palestine, unlike their counterparts at Qumran, married and had sexual intercourse. It is clear from the sources that they regulated their sexual lives carefully. Josephus emphasizes that "their motive in marrying is not self-indulgence but the procreation of children": only those women who had given proof of their fertility were selected for marriage, and couples abstained from intercourse whenever the ·woman was pregnant (*War* 2.161). The Damascus Rule prohibits sexual intercourse in Jerusalem (CD 12.1–2), thereby treating the entire city as if it were the temple. Though there is no direct evidence, we may assume that married Essenes observed at least the usual purity regimes associated with semen-, menstrual-, and childbirth-impurity. Even if they did so scrupulously, however, they could not have been pure as continuously as the celibates who lived at Qumran. Women were impure when menstruating and after childbirth, and could communicate their impurity to others; couples were impure after intercourse until the next sunset. The Essenes represented by the Damascus Rule were probably stricter with regard to all these matters than were most Jews, but they did not conduct themselves as if their homes or community were the temple.

On the question of relations with outsiders, Josephus states that the Essenes bathed after contact with outsiders (*War* 2.150). The Community Rule does not mention bathing in this connection, but it does include a number of regulations concerning relations with those outside the community. Especially important are the rules laid down in 1QS 5.10–20. According to this passage, the newly admitted member of the community was to undertake "to separate from all the men of falsehood who walk in the way of wickedness" (5.10–11). The rest of the passage spells out in greater detail what this separation entailed. Members were not to consort with outsiders with regard to work or property (5.14–15); they were not to follow them in matters of law or justice (5.15–16); and they were not to eat or drink anything of theirs (5.16). They were to separate themselves from outsiders and all that belonged to them, for "all their deeds are defilement before Him, and all their possessions unclean" (5.19–20). Apparently some commercial contact was permitted, and was probably unavoidable: 1QS 5.16–17 states that members had to pay for anything received from an outsider. But the overall attitude of the sect toward outsiders is well expressed in the many injunctions to hate the sons of darkness or the sons of the Pit, and to separate oneself and all of one's belongings from them.[56]

The situation reflected by the Damascus Rule is rather different. There is one general injunction to the members of the group to separate themselves from the sons of the Pit (6.14–15), and CD 13.14–15, like 1QS 5.16–17, specifies that commercial transactions with outsiders should be conducted on a strictly cash basis. But the only other rules laid down on the subject suggest that contact with outsiders—even with Gentiles—was not as restricted among the Essenes represented by the Damascus Rule as it was at Qumran. In CD 11.14–15 members of the group are commanded not to spend the Sabbath in the vicinity of Gentiles. The implication is that at least some other days could be and were spent in their vicinity. Similarly, 12.8–11, which prohibits the sale of clean animals, grain, wine, and slaves to Gentiles, implies that other items could be and were sold to them. The relatively lenient attitude is what one would expect of a group that, among other things, lived and worked among outsiders, conducted business with them, and visited the temple.

It can be said, then, on the basis of the two examples considered here, that those Essenes whose practice is reflected in the Damascus Rule, while greatly concerned about purity, did not aspire to be continuously in a state of purity such as was demanded for entrance into the temple, as did the Essenes at Qumran.

With regard to the second topic, the study of sacred books, I have already considered the evidence that shows that great importance was attached to the study of sacred books at Qumran. Essene attitudes and practices outside of Qumran are rather difficult to determine. According to the Damascus Rule, the leaders of town-dwelling communities were expected to be well educated: judges were to be learned in the Book of Meditation and in "the constitutions of the Covenant" (CD 10.6); the priest or Levite who presided over a group of ten was to be learned in the Book of Meditation, which here appears to include the law of leprosy (13.2–7); the priest who was the overseer of the many was supposed to be expert in the Book of Meditation and in the interpretation of the law, so that he could pronounce judgments correctly (14.6–8).[57] None of these passages, however, refers to the instruction of ordinary members of the community.

In CD 13.7–8 it is said that the overseer of the camp "shall instruct the congregation in the works of God" and "cause them to consider his mighty deeds," and "shall recount all the happenings of eternity to them." It is unclear whether this instruction was based on sacred books, but it seems likely that it was. A little further along, it is said that the overseer "shall examine every man entering his congregation with regard to his deeds, understanding, strength, ability and possessions, and shall inscribe him in his place according to his rank in the lot of Light" (13.11–12). This sounds like the kind of examination that was made of new members at Qumran, and presumably implies a similar preparatory period of study.[58]

The literary evidence thus suggests that the Essenes represented by the Damascus Rule were given some instruction by their local leaders in the correct interpretation of the law and in the special rules governing community life. There is no evidence, however, for the kind of intensive study of sacred books that produced the pesharim and the other interpretive works found at Qumran, and nothing corresponding to the Qumran requirements that one in every group of ten should study the law continuously, and that the entire membership should devote a third of every evening to study of the law.[59] This, again, is what might be expected on general grounds. The Essenes whose practice is reflected in the Damascus Rule evidently had their own homes, went out to work in the world, raised families, and were generally involved in the duties and pressures of everyday life to a much greater extent than their Qumran counterparts. Presumably they had less time to devote to study.

In conclusion, then, it can be said that the practice of purity and the study of sacred books were important both at Qumran and among those Essenes represented by the Damascus Rule, but that both were given greater emphasis at Qumran. This supports the tentative conclusion I drew from the placement of *War* 2.159 in Josephus' larger account: the passage seems to refer, in the first instance, to the stricter group of Essenes who lived at Qumran. It must be emphasized again, however, that there were probably more subgroups among the Essenes than are represented by the Community Rule and the Damascus Rule. There may have been some groups outside of Qumran that were closer to the sectarians in their purity practices and study habits than were the Essenes represented by the Damascus Rule. We shall see that the individual Essene prophets mentioned by Josephus may represent such a group.

Josephus' Reports Concerning Individual Essene Prophets

In addition to the general statement about the predictive powers of some of the Essenes in *War* 2.159, Josephus provides accounts of three incidents involving individual Essene prophets. The first is set during the brief reign of Aristobulus I (104–103 B.C.E.), eldest son of John Hyrcanus, and concerns an Essene prophet named Judas.

*Judas (*War *1.78–80;* Antiquities *13.311–13)*

According to Josephus, Judas predicted that Antigonus, the brother of Aristobulus, would be murdered on a certain day at a place called Strato's Tower, which he (Judas) evidently understood to mean the coastal town then called by that name.[60] On the day predicted for the murder, however, Judas saw Antigonus in Jerusalem, approximately sixty-five miles away from the town of Strato's Tower.[61] Knowing that Antigonus could not possibly travel so great a distance in what remained of the day, Judas feared that his prediction would be proven false. Later the same day, however, he learned that Antigonus had been murdered in an underground passage in Jerusalem that was also called Strato's Tower. It was the identity of the names, Josephus explains, that confused the seer (*War* 1.80; *Ant.* 13.313). Judas' prediction was thus fulfilled, though not precisely in the way that he himself had anticipated.[62]

Several features of Josephus' brief account are of interest. It is worth noting, first, that the episode involving Judas is set in Jerusalem. The evidence for the presence of Essenes in Jerusalem is rather sparse. The Damascus Rule, which I have been treating as the major witness among the Scrolls for the practice of non-Qumran Essenes, probably was not written for a community resident in Jerusalem since it includes a rule prohibiting sexual intercourse in the city (CD 12.1–2).[63] In fact, none of the documents known to us from Qumran can be said with certainty to represent the point of view of a Jerusalem group.

What little evidence we possess for the presence of Essenes in Jerusalem comes from Josephus. The story about Judas itself constitutes part of the evidence, though it is possible that he and his companions were not resident in the city, but were there as visitors. We shall see that the other two incidents recorded by Josephus in which individual Essene prophets play a role may also be set in Jerusalem, though this is uncertain. Finally, Josephus reports that one of the gates of the city was called "the gate of the Essenes" (*War* 5.145). This gate is not mentioned in any other source, and it is not clear why it was named after the Essenes. It may be that the Essenes in Jerusalem lived near the gate.[64] Yadin has suggested a reason why they might have done so. Judging from Josephus' description, the Essene gate was near a latrine situated outside the city walls.[65] Yadin has proposed that Essenes who lived in Jerusalem or who were visiting the city used this latrine in order to avoid defiling the holy city with their excrement; those who resided permanently in the city would have settled near the gate in order to have ready access to the latrine.[66] In any case, the existence of an Essene gate indicates at the very least that members of the party visited Jerusalem on occasion.

It is somewhat more surprising to find Judas and his companions inside the temple.[67] It is generally agreed that the Essene community at Qumran boycotted the temple completely.[68] Their attitude can be briefly summarized:[69] the temple in Jerusalem was thought to be defiled, its priests wicked, and its liturgical calendar illegitimate; members of the community were not permitted to visit the temple or sacrifice there; they may have continued to send offerings, though this seems unlikely;[70] they looked forward to the day when temple worship would be reorganized in accordance with their own beliefs; in the meantime, they regarded their community as a substitute for the temple, and considered prayer and righteous conduct to be substitutes for the sacrifices that, according to the law, ought to be offered in the temple.

There is, however, reason to believe that other Essenes did not reject the temple cult in the same way, and even some evidence that they continued to participate in sacrificial worship there. The statutes of the Damascus Rule include regulations about gifts and sacrifices to the temple, and appear to assume fairly normal participation in the temple cult. CD 11.17–21, for example, legislates that no sacrifice should be offered on the Sabbath except for the Sabbath burnt offering, and stipulates that anyone taking a burnt offering, cereal offering, incense, or wood to the temple must be ritually clean.[71] We do not know the views of Essenes resident in Jerusalem on the subject, but it is safe to assume that they were at least as liberal as those held by the group represented by the Damascus Rule.

Judas is said to have possessed the ability to predict future events accurately. In the introduction to the account in the *War*, Josephus writes that "[Judas'] predictions had never once proved erroneous or false" (1.78); the parallel in the *Antiquities* states that he "had never been known to speak falsely in his predictions" (13.311).[72] In the particular case that Josephus goes on to describe, the prediction made by Judas concerned a specific event in the public-political sphere: the murder, on a particular day, of the brother of the Hasmonean ruler. It should be noted that Judas himself appears to have had no connection with these public figures—he is not said to have made his prediction to Antigonus, for example. He appears, rather, as an outsider politically.

The narrowness and precision of Judas' prediction distinguish it from the predictions made by the other Essene prophets described by Josephus, as we shall see, and still further from the promises of deliverance made by the sign prophets (to be considered in chapter 4) and the prediction of destruction made by Jesus son of Ananias (chapter 5). All these figures— Judas, the other Essenes, the sign prophets, and Jesus—may be described as "predictors of the future," but it is important to note the differences in the sorts of predictions they made.

Josephus evidently regards Judas' ability to predict the future as something extraordinary. He introduces the account in both the *War* and the *Antiquities* by remarking that the reader may well be "astonished" (θαυμάζω, *War* 1.78; *Ant.* 13.311) by the story he is about to tell. We shall see that he makes similar comments in connection with the other Essene prophets, Menahem and Simon.

In both of Josephus' accounts, Judas is said to be accompanied by others, who are described as γνώριμοι, ἑταῖροι, and μανθάνοντες.[73] The first of these terms, γνώριμοι, can mean simply "acquaintances" or it can mean "pupils"; similarly, ἑταῖροι can mean either "companions" or "pupils" or "disciples."[74] It is clear from the context that both terms have the more specialized meaning "pupils" or "disciples" in the present passages. In *War* 1.78 γνώριμοι is equivalent to μανθάνοντες, and in *Antiquities* 13.311 it is expressly stated that the γνώριμοι and ἑταῖροι of Judas were "with him for the purpose of receiving instruction in foretelling the future" (διδασκαλίας ἕνεκα τοῦ προλέγειν τὰ μέλλοντα παρέμενον). It is difficult to say with any more precision what the relationship between Judas and the others was. Descriptions that suggest that Judas was the head of a formal school are probably overdone,[75] but he is clearly depicted as giving some form of instruction in prediction of the future. According to the *War*, "many" students were present (οὐκ ὀλίγοι, 1.78), but no precise number is given. In light of Essene injunctions against revealing secrets to outsiders, it may be assumed that the students were also Essenes, or at least potential converts.

Prediction of the future is here regarded as a skill that can be taught and learned. Similarly, in *War* 2.159, as we have seen, Josephus connects the Essenes' ability to predict the future with their education in sacred books, purifications, and sayings of prophets. It is difficult to know whether we should go further and conclude that the instruction offered by Judas was of the sort described in *War* 2.159. We saw in the preceding section that that passage refers, in the first instance, to the stricter group of Essenes who lived at Qumran. The married and town-dwelling Essenes represented by the Damascus Rule did not observe the same strict purity regulations that were in force at Qumran, and it is unlikely that they studied sacred books as intensively. The present passage, however, shows that there were those outside of Qumran who devoted at least some of their time to learning the esoteric craft of predicting the future. Perhaps such Essenes represent a separate group whose practices differed both from those of the Qumran sectarians and from those of the communities that followed the Damascus Rule. In any case, we need to be cautious about using the general statement in *War* 2.159 in a direct way to interpret Josephus' statements about Judas and his pupils.

Finally, in both the *War* and the *Antiquities* Judas' prediction of the murder of Antigonus is referred to as τὸ μάντευμα, and Judas himself is called a μάντις.[76] Similar terminology recurs in Josephus' account concerning Simon the Essene. I shall consider the possible significance of Josephus' use of μάντις-terminology in connection with the Essene prophets later in this chapter.

Menahem (Antiquities 15.373–79)

The second of Josephus' narratives concerning individual Essene prophets is set during the lifetime of Herod the Great and is appended to an account of the measures taken by Herod around the year 20 B.C.E. to prevent his Jewish subjects from revolting against him (*Ant.* 15.365–72).[77]

According to Josephus, Herod reduced the usual taxes by one-third, hoping by this gesture to appease "those who were disaffected" (15.365). He also prohibited meetings of any sort, even "walking together or being together" (15.366). An army of spies was dispatched to inform against those who violated these prohibitions and offenders were severely dealt with. Finally, Herod required his subjects to swear an oath of loyalty, "a sworn declaration that they would maintain a friendly attitude to his rule" (15.368).

Josephus reports that two groups of Jews were exempted by Herod from the requirement to swear the oath of loyalty: "Pollion the Pharisee and Samaias and most of their disciples" (15.370) and "those who are called by us Essenes" (15.371). He explains that the former were "shown consideration on Pollion's account" (15.370). Pollion was a Pharisee who had predicted to the members of the Sanhedrin convened by Hyrcanus II that Herod would one day persecute them all if they failed to punish him for his offenses in Galilee; later, when Herod and Sossius were besieging Jerusalem, he urged the inhabitants of the city to open the gates and admit them.[78] The Essenes, according to Josephus, were excused from taking the oath because Herod held them in honor, having "a higher opinion of them than was to be expected given their mortal nature" (15.372). He tells the story of Herod's encounter with the Essene prophet Menahem in order to explain why the king regarded the Essenes so highly (15.372, 378); he notes, incidentally, that the account will also serve to illustrate "what the general opinion of these men was" (15.372).[79]

The story can be briefly summarized. According to Josephus, Menahem once approached Herod when the latter was still a schoolboy and predicted to him that he would become king of the Jews (15.373).[80] When the boy responded in disbelief, Menahem elaborated on the prediction in a speech which, as reported by Josephus, was a mixture of good and bad tidings for the young Herod (15.374–76): he assured him that he had been chosen by God to become king, and that he would be "singled out for such good fortune as no other man has had," and would "enjoy eternal glory"; but he also predicted that Herod would "forget piety and justice," and that God would punish him for this at the end of his life (15.376). He slapped the boy gently on the backside and urged him to remember the blows as a "symbol [σύμβολον] of how one's fortune can change" (15.374).[81]

At the time, Josephus reports, Herod took no notice of Menahem's words, but when he had become king as predicted and was "at the height of his power" (15.377), he sent for Menahem and asked him how long his reign would last. The prophet did not at first reply. When Herod pressed him, he predicted that he would reign for another twenty or thirty years, but refused to specify the number precisely. This rather vague answer satisfied Herod, however, and Josephus reports that he dismissed Menahem "with a friendly gesture," and notes further that "from that time on he [Herod] continued to hold all Essenes in honour" (15.378).

The story cannot, of course, be accepted as an adequate explanation of why Herod decided to excuse the Essenes from the obligation to swear the oath of loyalty to him, if in fact he did excuse them—and it is difficult to see why Josephus would have tried to explain the decision if it had never been made. Josephus (or his source) is here "anecdotalizing" and personalizing what were evidently much more complex historical forces and developments.

We might speculate on the real reasons for Herod's decision. According to Josephus, the Essenes avoided swearing oaths of any kind (*War* 2.135), except for the "awesome oaths" that new members were required to take at the time of their full entry into the community (2.139–42).[82] The Community Rule mentions only the entry oath (1QS 5.8) and thus seems to support Josephus' report. The Damascus Rule permits certain oaths in addition to the oath of entry, but the use of these oaths is significantly restricted in comparison to biblical law.[83] Thus, though there may have been some differences of opinion and practice between the group at Qumran and those Essenes represented by the Damascus Rule, it appears that both groups tried to avoid oaths, and had strict rules about those that were permitted. Herod may have regarded the Essenes as a special case because of their views.[84]

Also, strange as the suggestion may seem at first glance, it is conceivable that Herod and the Essenes were political allies of sorts. They shared a bitter enemy, the Hasmoneans. At least this is the case if we accept the most widely held view of Essene origins.[85] According to this view, the community at Qumran was founded by the Teacher of Righteousness in response to the appointment of the Hasmonean (and non-Zadokite) Jonathan to the office of high priest in 152 B.C.E. It is sometimes suggested that the Teacher himself served as high priest in Jerusalem between the death of Alcimus in 159 B.C.E. and the appointment of Jonathan, but this is uncertain. It is certain, however, that the sect at Qumran was and remained bitterly opposed to the Hasmoneans, whom they regarded as illegitimate usurpers of the high-priestly office. It may be assumed that even those Essenes who did not withdraw to Qumran with the Teacher shared this basic antipathy.

Herod also hated and, more importantly, feared the Hasmoneans. He probably hoped that his marriage in 37 B.C.E. to Mariamme, the granddaughter of both Hyrcanus II and Aristobulus II, would help to associate him, in the eyes of the people, with the illustrious family. But the marriage quite obviously did not calm his fears. When he and Sossius captured Jerusalem later the same year, Antigonus, the reigning Hasmonean king and high priest, was sent to be executed, and Herod then proceeded to eliminate all the remaining Hasmoneans one after the other: first the popular young high priest Aristobulus III; then the aged Hyrcanus II, who was not even eligible to be high priest because of a physical deformity; then Mariamme; her mother, Alexandra; some distant relatives of the Hasmoneans known as the sons of Babas; and, finally, his own two sons by

Mariamme, Alexander and Aristobulus.[86] Herod's obsession with the Hasmoneans continued throughout the whole of his reign: Mariamme's sons were probably executed in 7 B.C.E., just three years before his own death. The Essenes' opposition to the Hasmoneans, combined with their general objections to swearing oaths, probably accounts for Herod's decision to exempt them from the oath of loyalty mentioned above. He evidently regarded them as reliable allies against the Hasmoneans and, for that reason, was willing to make this concession to them. The Essenes, for their part, must have offered him some real support.[87]

It is worth noting, in any case, that the picture Josephus presents of the political relationship between the Herods and the Essene prophets is a mixed one. In the cases of both Menahem and Simon (who is portrayed as a member of the court of Herod's son, Archelaus), cooperation with and approval of the Herods is combined with an element of criticism. This is a perfectly plausible picture.

Once again, several features of Josephus' account deserve comment. Like Judas, Menahem evidently was not a member of the Essene community resident at Qumran. It is impossible to say with certainty where he was from, however, or even where the two encounters with Herod took place. The first of these encounters, as we have seen, is said to have occurred when Herod was still a schoolboy, probably sometime in the sixties B.C.E.[88] There is no indication of where Herod's family lived during this period. His father, Antipater, was an Idumaean by descent and probably governor of Idumaea, but he became involved in Judaean politics at the beginning of the civil war between Hyrcanus II and Aristobulus II in 67 B.C.E.[89] The second meeting between Herod and Menahem is said to have taken place after Herod had been appointed king, when he was "at the height of his power" (*Ant.* 15.377), probably sometime between 23 and 20 B.C.E.[90] Though it is likely that this second meeting took place in Jerusalem, this is not certain: the location is not specified in the text, and Herod had official residences in several different places.[91]

Unlike Judas, who is pictured surrounded by pupils, Menahem is portrayed as a solitary figure. His initial prediction was unsolicited and he appears to have been unknown to Herod at the time he made it. When summoned by Herod years later to a second interview, he was reluctant to answer the king's questions. All of this suggests that Menahem was not an official adviser to Herod or a court figure of any sort.[92] In this respect, there is a contrast between him and the Essene prophet Simon, as we shall see below.

The gift possessed by Menahem is described as "foreknowledge of the future" (πρόγνωσις . . . τῶν μελλόντων); it is a gift that, according to Josephus, came "from God" (ἐκ θεοῦ, *Ant.* 15.373). As was the case with Judas, Menahem's recorded predictions concern events in the public-political realm, in this case the political fortunes of Herod on a fairly broad scale. Once again, nothing is said about the methods by which these predictions were made, and the reservations I have expressed about drawing conclusions about these matters on the basis of the general statement in *War* 2.159 apply in this instance as well. As he did in his account of Judas, Josephus indicates that he considers Menahem's ability to predict the future to be an extraordinary gift. In an editorial comment at the conclusion of the account, he says that he decided to tell the story even though he realized that some would find it "incredible" (παράδοξα, *Ant.* 15.379).

In the speech attributed to Menahem by Josephus, prediction of the future is combined with a certain element of moral exhortation, with special emphasis on "justice" and "piety."[93] This pair of terms is typically used by Josephus to summarize the whole range of religious and moral obligations enjoined by Jewish law, the word "justice" referring to one's obligations to one's fellow human beings, and "piety" to one's obligations toward God.[94] He especially emphasizes that the fate of kings depended on whether they practiced justice and piety, that is, on whether they kept the commandments of the law.[95] One passage from the *Antiquities*, which concerns the Israelite king Baasha and the prophet Jehu, is especially close to the report of Menahem's encounter with Herod, except that Jehu's message contains only bad news for the king, whereas Menahem's speech combines good and bad tidings. According to Josephus, when King Baasha proved to be even more wicked and impious than his predecessor Jeroboam,

> God ... sent to him the prophet Jehu and warned him that He would destroy all his line and would utterly crush them under the same calamities as He had brought upon the house of Jeroboam, because, after having been made king by Him, he had not requited His kindness by justly [δικαίως] and piously [εὐσεβῶς] governing the people—a course which would, in the first place, be of benefit to those who followed it, and then pleasing to God as well—but had imitated Jeroboam, the vilest of men. . . . Therefore, He said, Baasha should justly experience a like ill fate since he had acted in a like manner. (*Ant.* 8.299–300)[96]

As the note to the LCL translation indicates, Josephus has amplified his scriptural source in this passage.[97] In 1 Kings 16.1–4 Baasha is accused by Jehu of "walking in the ways of Jeroboam" and of causing the people to sin, but nothing is said about justice and piety and their benefits to king and people. The latter seem to have been themes of special interest to Josephus.

Josephus also connected justice and piety, in the sense defined above, with "virtue." In *Antiquities* 9.236 he states that King Jotham of Judah "lacked no single virtue [ἀρετή], but was pious toward God [εὐσεβὴς μὲν τὰ πρὸς τὸν θεόν] and just toward men [δίκαιος δὲ τὰ πρὸς ἀνθρώπους]." Once again, this is Josephus' own formulation: 2 Kings 15.34 says simply that Jotham "did what was right in the eyes of the Lord." Virtue is also equated with the practice of justice and piety in Josephus' account of King Josiah (*Ant.* 10.49–77; see esp. 10.49–51). To return to the Essenes, Josephus says that every new member, on admission to the community, was required to swear a twofold oath, "first that he will practise piety towards the Deity [εὐσεβήσειν τὸ θεῖον], next that he will observe justice towards men [τὰ πρὸς ἀνθρώπους δίκαια φυλάξειν]" (*War* 2.139). His description of the group shows that he admired them as especially virtuous Jews.[98]

There is one final link in this chain. In his account of Menahem's encounter with Herod, Josephus claims that the ability of some of the Essenes to predict the future was related to their character as virtuous men. He introduces the figure of Menahem with the remark that his "virtue was attested in his whole conduct of life and especially in his having from God a foreknowledge of the future" (*Ant.* 15.373); he closes the account with the comment that "many of these men [the Essenes] have indeed been vouchsafed a knowledge of divine things because of their virtue" (15.379).[99] It is safe to assume that virtue is here equated, as in the passages already cited, with the practice of justice and piety, which in turn is understood as obedience to the law of Moses.

Finally, two phrases in Josephus' report concerning Menahem suggest that foreknowledge of the future was only part of a wider esoteric knowledge that the Essenes were believed to possess. As we have seen, in the speech attributed to him by Josephus, Menahem urges Herod to be just and pious, but also predicts that he will not do so. He knows this, he says, because he "understands everything" or "the totality" (τὸ πᾶν ἐπιστάμενος, *Ant.* 15.375). Van Unnik has shown that this phrase, τὸ πᾶν ἐπιστάμενος, is one form of an expression that is frequently used in material from widely different ages and circles to describe individuals who enjoyed a special relationship with God or the gods and, as a result, possessed knowledge of "all things."[100] "All things," in this context, refers both to ordinary things and to extraordinary, secret things, but emphasizes the latter: the one who "knows all things" knows especially those things that are unknowable by ordinary means.

Van Unnik cites a passage from Dio Chrysostom that illustrates the range of subjects encompassed by this esoteric knowledge. The text refers to "divine men" (θεῖοι ἄνθρωποι) who

> claim to know all things [πάντα εἰδέναι φασί], and concerning all things to be able to tell how they have been appointed and what their nature is, their repertoire including not only human things and demi-gods, but gods, yes, and even the earth, the sky, the sea, the sun, the moon and the other stars— in fact the entire universe—and also the processes of corruption and generation and ten thousand other things.[101]

In other texts, the meaning of "all things" is specified with the aid of a threefold formula referring to past, present, and future.[102] In the Pseudo-

Clementine *Homilies* 2.6.1, for example, the true prophet (προφήτης . . . ἀληθείας) is defined as "the one who at all times knows everything" (ὁ πάντοτε πάντα εἰδώς). The passage goes on to explain what is meant by πάντα: "things past as they were, things present as they are, things future as they shall be" (τὰ μὲν γεγονότα ὡς ἐγένετο, τὰ δὲ γινόμενα ὡς γίνεται, τὰ δὲ ἐσόμενα ὡς ἔσται).[103] In these texts, then, the one who "knows everything" knows the secrets of human hearts and of the cosmos—past, present, and future.

At the conclusion of the report about Menahem, Josephus claims that many of the Essenes had been granted "the knowledge of divine things" (ἡ τῶν θείων ἐμπειρία, *Ant.* 15.379). This phrase, too, I would suggest, points to esoteric knowledge of an all-encompassing sort.[104]

In his general accounts of the Essenes, Josephus hints at their interest in various esoteric subjects. I have already considered *War* 2.136 and the Qumran evidence for Essene interest in healing. According to *War* 2.142, the Essenes knew the names of the angels and took an oath at the time of their entry into the sect not to reveal them. They also speculated about the nature and ultimate fate of the human soul (*War* 2.154–58; *Ant.* 18.18). The Scrolls reveal that the Essenes at Qumran were interested in the secrets of the heavenly world—in the angels, the divine court, and the movements of sun and stars; in the nature of sin and the secrets of the human heart; in the mysteries of creation and of God's plans for history.[105] The phrases in Josephus' account of Menahem to which I have drawn attention show that there were Essenes outside of Qumran who shared these esoteric interests; they also indicate that, in Josephus' view at least, knowledge of the future was simply one part of the all-encompassing wisdom or knowledge in which the Essenes were proficient.

Simon (War *2.112–13;* Antiquities *17.345–48)*

The last of Josephus' narratives concerning individual Essene prophets is set shortly before the deposition and banishment of Archelaus, son of Herod the Great and ethnarch of Judaea, by the emperor Augustus in 6 C.E. (*War* 2.111; *Ant.* 17.342–44). According to Josephus, Archelaus was warned of his impending fall from power in a dream that was correctly interpreted for him by an Essene named Simon. There are a few discrepancies between the account of the incident in the *War* and the report in the *Antiquities*, but these are minor and can be readily explained; the two accounts agree in substance.

According to the *War*, a few days before he was summoned to trial in Rome, Archelaus had a dream in which he saw nine full-grown ears of corn being eaten by oxen (2.112); according to the *Antiquities*, there were ten ears of corn (17.345). The discrepancy seems to be the result of some confusion on Josephus' part about the length of Archelaus' reign as ethnarch. In *War* 2.111 he says that Archelaus was deposed in the ninth year of his reign, and the details of the dream reflect this chronology. By the time he wrote the *Antiquities*, however, Josephus evidently believed (correctly) that Archelaus had reigned for ten years, and the figures in the account of the dream and its interpretation have been adjusted accordingly. A reign of ten years is also presupposed in *Antiquities* 17.342 and *Life* 5.

Upon awakening from his dreams, Archelaus sent for "the mantics and some of the Chaldaeans" (τοὺς μάντεις καὶ τῶν Χαλδαίων τινάς, *War* 2.112), also described as "those mantics who were concerned with dreams" (τοὺς μάντεις οἷς περὶ ὀνείρατα ἦσαν αἱ ἀναστροφαί, *Ant.* 17.345). Apparently among them was "a certain Simon, an Essene by race" (*War* 2.113; *Ant.* 17.346). Josephus does not describe the interpretations offered by the others, saying only that they conflicted with one another and "did not come to the same result" (*Ant.* 17.346). The two accounts of Simon's interpretation once again disagree in a few details, but agree in substance: the ears of corn signified years and the oxen a revolution or change in Archelaus' situation; the dream as a whole meant that Archelaus' reign would soon come to an end. Just five days later, Josephus reports, Archelaus was summoned to Rome, and the truth and accuracy of Simon's interpretation were thus confirmed (*War* 2.113; *Ant.* 17.348).

The dream described in these accounts is a relatively simple symbolic dream of the sort considered in chapter 2.[106] It is said to have consisted of a series of visual images,[107] each of which signified something in the real world;[108] taken altogether, these images pointed to a particular event expected in the future. In terms of complexity, the dream belongs to the same category as the dreams of the butler and baker and the two dreams of Pharaoh from the Joseph narrative: the images are not fantastic or bizarre, but are drawn from ordinary life; the symbolism is relatively simple, but not so simple that the meaning of the dream is apparent to the dreamer; expert interpretation is required.

Commentators often draw attention to the similarities between Archelaus' dream and the two dreams of Pharaoh recorded in Genesis 41 (= *Ant.* 2.75–86).[109] In both cases, the dreams feature images of corn and oxen, and the ears of corn are understood to signify years. Two quite different conclusions have been drawn from these similarities. First, it is sometimes concluded that the story about Simon and his interpretation of the dream of Archelaus represents a kind of haggadic development of the Joseph narrative.[110] The implications of this proposal, at the historical level, are seldom spelled out. Sometimes it seems to be assumed that the account is pure literary invention; sometimes that a historically reliable kernel has been elaborated with the help of themes and images from the Joseph narrative.

The second conclusion sometimes drawn from the similarities between the two accounts is that Archelaus actually presented Simon with a dream that was reminiscent of Pharaoh's dreams, and that Simon used the scriptural account of these dreams and their interpretation by Joseph to guide him in his interpretation of the dream of Archelaus.[111] Support for this suggestion is thought to be found in the general statement of *War* 2.159, which connects the ability of the Essenes to predict the future with their knowledge of sacred books, and in Josephus' account of his own experience at Jotapata, in which he claims that he was able to understand the meaning of the dreams that God had sent him because of his knowledge of "the prophecies of the sacred books."

It is not impossible that Simon interpreted Archelaus' dream by referring to Genesis 41, but several considerations count against the proposal. First, the similarities between Archelaus' dream and the two dreams of Pharaoh are not actually very extensive. In Pharaoh's case, there are two dreams with the same message; the oxen and corn appear in separate dreams and have precisely the same significance (both represent years); the repetition of the dream serves simply to emphasize that God really does intend to bring about what the two dreams, identically, signify. In the case of Archelaus, on the other hand, oxen and corn appear in one dream and signify different things (oxen portend a change in Archelaus' situation; corn represents years). Moreover, the overall meanings assigned to the dreams are completely different: Pharaoh's dreams mean that seven years of plenty will be followed by seven years of famine; Archelaus' dream that his reign as ethnarch will soon come to an end. I suspect that the similarities between the general frameworks of the two accounts (ruler has symbolic dream and calls upon court wise men to interpret it) and the recurrence of the images of oxen and corn have led commentators to see more correspondences between the dreams of Pharaoh and the dream of Archelaus than actually exist.

These observations also count against the first theory mentioned previously, that the story of Simon's interpretation of the dream of Archelaus should be understood as a haggadic development of the Joseph tradition. Anyone (whether Josephus or his source) who wanted to present Archelaus as a second Pharaoh and Simon as a second Joseph could have done a better job. We have seen evidence that Josephus, in particular, was quite adept at fashioning parallels between ancient and modern figures when he wanted to do so.

To return to the proposal that Simon used Genesis 41 to interpret the dream of Archelaus, it must be emphasized again (the point was made in chapter 2) that *War* 2.159 does not mention dreams. If it could be shown, on other grounds, that Simon's interpretation was based on scripture, then a link might be established between Essene prediction of the future, the interpretation of scripture, and the interpretation of dreams; but this three-way connection is not made in *War* 2.159 itself.

Finally, the significance of the example of Josephus' own practice is difficult to determine. He does claim to have used scripture to interpret the dreams that he remembered at Jotapata, but evidently he did not believe that all symbolic dreams had to be or could be interpreted in this way—none of the others we considered in chapter 2 were. It should be remembered that Josephus distinguished the kind of dreams that he describes in *War* 3.351–54 from relatively simple symbolic dreams of the sort attributed to Archelaus: his own dreams, he implies, were more complex and bizarre; they were the sort of difficult dreams whose interpretation required inspiration. It may be that Josephus thought that scripture, like inspiration, was necessary only for the interpretation of these more complex dreams.

More important than any of these considerations, however, is the fact that Josephus' two accounts of the episode suggest that Simon did not interpret the dream of Archelaus with the aid of scripture, but by another method altogether. According to Josephus, Simon *explained* why he interpreted the dream in the way he did: the ten ears of corn denoted ten years "since there is a harvest in the course of each year" (*Ant.* 17.347); the oxen signified a revolution or a change in Archelaus' situation "since the earth, when ploughed by their labour, cannot remain in the same state as before" (17.347) or "because in ploughing they turn over the soil" (*War* 2.113); the change would be for the worse "since this animal is subject to painful labour" (*Ant.* 17.347).

This account describes the same general type of interpretation that we considered in chapter 2 in connection with the dreams of Pharaoh and his butler and baker. Thus, rather than using Genesis 41 to interpret the dream of Archelaus, Simon appears to have proceeded in exactly the same way that Joseph did. In both cases the method of interpretation employed was basically rational and analogical, taking into account the sequence of events depicted in the dream, the natural properties or cultural associations of the images that were seen, previous interpretations of similar images and dreams, and a whole range of facts about the situation of the dreamer: age, sex, social status, and any recent events affecting him or her significantly.[112] This is a rather analytical description of what was probably, even in Josephus' day, a more or less intuitive process of interpretation. Moreover, it is important to remember that Josephus, along with most Jews, believed such interpretation was not purely a matter of rational calculation but required esoteric wisdom, which came from God.

A few other points require comment. Simon is portrayed by Josephus as a member of a class of professionals who were experts in the interpretation of dreams. These figures are referred to collectively as "mantics" (μάντεις) and "Chaldaeans" (Χαλδαῖοι) and as "those mantics who were concerned with dreams" (οἱ μάντεις οἷς περὶ ὀνείρατα ἦσαν αἱ ἀναστροφαί, *Ant.* 17.345). I shall shortly return to the question of the significance of this terminology; here, I note only that the individuals so designated are members of a class of experts. Moreover, they belong to the royal court. Simon's inclusion in this group once again raises the question of the relationship between the Essenes and the Herods. Here, as in the Menahem narrative, the picture is a mixed one: a large measure of agreement is indicated by Simon's presence in the court; on the other hand, his actual role in events is as a bearer of bad news for Archelaus.

In both the *War* and the *Antiquities* the report concerning Archelaus' dream is followed by an account of a dream experienced by his wife, Glaphyra. At the end of the double account in the *Antiquities*, Josephus inserts an editorial comment (17.354). I have already considered (in chapter 2) the remarks that he makes in this passage about dreams and divine providence. Here I wish to make two comments on the second half of the passage: "Anyone to whom such things seem incredible is welcome to his own opinion but should not interfere with one who adds them to the evidence for virtue." First, Josephus here acknowledges that the account he has given of the dreams of Archelaus and Glaphyra may seem "incredible" (ἀπιστεῖται) to some. We noted the use of similar expressions in the reports concerning Judas and Menahem. Here, as there, the remarks indicate that Josephus realized that the experiences he describes and the gifts that he attributes to the Essenes were extraordinary. Second, he adds a note on virtue. The precise meaning of the text is difficult to determine, but it may support the evidence already considered that suggests that Josephus connected the Essenes' "knowledge of divine things" with their practice of virtue.

Josephus' Essene Prophets and
Pesher Interpretation at Qumran

When discussing the evidence from Josephus for prophetic activity among the Essenes, most scholars combine the accounts of the predictions made by Judas, Menahem, and Simon with the general statement about prediction of the future in *War* 2.159 and conclude that, in all these cases, the predictions that Josephus reports were made on the basis of the interpretation of scripture. A second step is usually taken: *War* 2.159 and, by association, the other three passages are connected with biblical exegesis at Qumran, more specifically, with the composition of pesher commentaries on prophetic books.[113]

I have already expressed doubts about the legitimacy of using the general statement in *War* 2.159 to interpret Josephus' accounts of individual Essene prophets. We saw that the statement is best understood as applying, in the first instance, to the community at Qumran. Those Essenes represented by the Damascus Rule, for example, apparently did not study scripture as intensively as the group at Qumran. The individual Essene prophets mentioned by Josephus may represent a third type, somewhere between the other two, in terms of their devotion to study, but their precise position is unclear; we cannot assume that *War* 2.159 applies to them. Nothing in Josephus' reports concerning Judas and Menahem requires us to conclude that their predictions were based on the interpretation of scripture, and in the case of Simon, I have argued directly against the view.

The second association—between Josephus' reports concerning Essene prediction and pesher exegesis at Qumran—is even more problematic. In the interest of clarity, let me state again what the suggestion is: *War* 2.159 and, by extension, the three accounts concerning individual Essene prophets describe a type of prophetic activity that is essentially the same as that lying behind the Qumran pesharim; the passages from Josephus and the pesharim both illustrate what might be characterized as prediction of the future by means of the (charismatic) interpretation of scripture.

At this level of generalization, that last statement may be true enough. But on closer examination, two problems emerge. First, the Qumran pesharim are not actually very predictive. A large proportion of the interpretations given in the commentaries are explanations of events in the past. Many commentators seem to make a mistake in perspective here. It is perfectly true that the Qumran sectaries who composed the pesharim believed that the prophetic books they were interpreting referred exclusively to the future, that is, to the future *from the point of view of the prophetic author of the texts.* The ancient prophet Habakkuk, they thought, had delivered a number of oracles that he received from God, all of which concerned what was the distant future from his point of view. The true meaning of the oracles was not known even to Habakkuk himself, but was first revealed to the authoritative interpreter, the Teacher of Righteousness. It was he who revealed that all Habakkuk's oracles concerned the last days, that is, the days in which the Qumran community believed it was living, immediately before the End. The pesher commentaries themselves, however, do not refer only, or even primarily, to the future *from the point of view of the Qumran community,* but rather mostly to the past. Indeed, the pesharim, along with the preface to the Damascus Rule, are among the most important sources for the history of the Essenes and the Qumran community. In these texts the Wicked Priest, the Liar, and other past opponents of the party make their appearance; past disputes and divisions are described; and hints are given about the origin of the group. My first point, then, is that the pesharim are not actually very predictive. They are to some extent prediction of the future through the (charismatic) interpretation of scripture, but they are to a much greater extent interpretation of the past through the (charismatic) interpretation of scripture.

Second, most of the predictions that are contained in the pesharim concern the great events predicted for the End: God's judgment of the Wicked Priest, the last judgment, the triumph of the righteous over the wicked, and so on. The following are examples of the type of predictions found in one of the most important of the pesharim, the Commentary on Habakkuk (1QpHab): the nations will not destroy God's people, but rather God's people will judge the nations and the wicked in Israel at the last judgment (5.3–7); the "last time" will be prolonged, but the "men of truth" will not slacken in the service of truth (7.7–14); the wicked will be found guilty at the last judgment (7.15–16); the idols of the nations will not save them on the day of judgment (12.14); the idolatrous and the wicked will be destroyed by God on the day of judgment (13.2–4). There is a vast difference between predictions of this sort and the predictions attributed to Essene prophets by Josephus. "God will destroy the wicked on the day of judgment" is simply not the same kind of statement as "Antigonus will be murdered next Thursday at Strato's Tower." Both are predictions of the future, but the differences between them are enormous.[114] The predictions attributed to Judas, Menaham, and Simon are more precise and restricted, less eschatological in character, than those of the Qumran pesharim. Similarly, it seems to me that Josephus could not possibly be referring to anything like the pesharim in *War* 2.159. What, in that case, could he possibly have meant by saying "seldom, if ever, do they err in their predictions"? Did the sectaries at Qumran actually rise up and judge the nations of the earth? Had God come and judged the wicked and the idolatrous? This second point is thus part of my general campaign to make more precise distinctions between various sorts of predictions. I also believe that we should resist the temptation to use what little we do know about the Essenes to explain everything we do not.

In the passages considered in this chapter, Josephus seems to be describing a type of prophecy that is not precisely the same as that attested by the Qumran pesharim. It is similar in many ways to the sort of prophecy that he himself represents: it is focused on the prediction of events in the public-political sphere; the predictions are relatively narrow and precise; dreams and scripture play a part. This is not to say that this kind of prophecy and pesher interpretation are completely unrelated. Presumably it was thought that anyone who could make the kind of large-scale predictions found in the pesharim would also be able to predict particular events in the way that the Essene prophets are supposed to have done. But the two phenomena should not be identified.

Josephus' Use of Μάντις-Terminology in Connection with the Essenes

I have previously drawn attention to Josephus' use of the word μάντις and related terms in connection with the Essenes. Judas is called a μάντις in *War* 1.80 and *Antiquities* 13.313, and his prediction of the murder of Antigonus is described as a μάντευμα in *War* 1.79 and *Antiquities*

13.312. Simon is not directly labeled a μάντις, but he is portrayed as a member of a group of court professionals who are collectively referred to as μάντεις and Χαλδαῖοι (*War* 2.112; *Ant.* 17.345).

Commentators often attach special significance to the fact that Josephus uses μάντις-terminology rather than προφήτης-terminology to describe the Essenes. Usually it is thought that he intended by this usage to distinguish the sort of predictions the Essenes made from genuine Jewish prophecy. Crone, for example, in his discussion of *War* 2.159, proposes that Josephus did not use προφήτης-terminology in connection with the Essenes because their "ability to foretell the future is not prophecy in the classical O.T. sense"; it is, rather, "presented in Greek fashion as a skill which can be learned."[115] A few pages later, Crone concludes from Josephus' application of μάντις-terminology to the Essenes that "mere prediction was not considered prophecy in the strict sense."[116] Horsley and Hanson do not discuss Josephus' use of μάντις-terminology, but they characterize the kind of prophecy represented by the Essenes as "Hellenistic" in contrast to "classical biblical prophecy."[117] The basic difference between these two types of prophecy is that "the Essene seers' predictions focused narrowly on the fortunes of individual rulers, whereas the classical oracular prophets addressed broad social relationships and placed judgment on royal behavior in an all-inclusive covenantal context."[118] Blenkinsopp acknowledges that the Essenes were essentially predictors of the future, but—in contrast to Crone, Horsley, and Hanson— considers this a fully Jewish and fully prophetic phenomenon. He fails, however, to note the prominence of μάντις-terminology in Josephus' accounts of the Essenes and other Jewish figures and accepts the general view that this terminology serves as a marker for non-Jewish varieties of prophecy.[119]

I argued in chapter 1 (pages 30–34) that Josephus (along with most Jews of his day) did not distinguish prediction of the future from genuine Jewish prophecy in the way that Crone, Horsley, and Hanson propose that he did—here Blenkinsopp is correct. A brief review of Josephus' use of μάντις and related terms will reinforce the point. Josephus uses this terminology in connection with several Jewish figures, and there is a pattern to his usage: μάντις and related terms occur mostly in connection with one general type of prophecy. We shall see that the type was one he regarded very highly.

Josephus uses μάντις-terminology with reference to three Jewish figures in addition to Judas and Simon: Jotham, the son of Gideon; Daniel; and himself. The first of these cases falls outside the general pattern of his usage, and so I mention it only briefly: in *Antiquities* 5.253 the word μαντεία is used to designate Jotham's prediction that the people of Shechem would perish by fire at the hands of Abimelech.[120] The other occurrences of μάντις-terminology with reference to Jews are more significant. Daniel, like Simon the Essene, is never directly called a μάντις, but he is associated with a group of figures in the Babylonian court who are collectively referred to as "the mantics" (οἱ μάντεις, *Ant.* 10.195); other phrases used to designate the same group include "the Chaldaeans" (οἱ Χαλδαῖοι), "the Magi" (οἱ μάγοι), and "the wise" (οἱ σοφοί).[121] There is no doubt that Daniel and his companions are included in this group.[122] These figures, like the μάντεις and Χαλδαῖοι in the court of Archelaus, were specially trained professionals whose duty it was to interpret dreams and omens and to advise on other matters.[123] Finally, Josephus uses μάντις-terminology on two occasions to refer to his own predictions. In *War* 3.405 the verb προμαντεύομαι is used to refer to his prediction of the fall of Jotapata and his own capture, and in *War* 4.625 μαντεία is used of his prediction that Vespasian would become emperor.

Apart from the case of Jotham, Josephus' use of μάντις-terminology links together a group of figures whom I have already associated with one another on other grounds: the Essenes, Daniel, and Josephus himself. There are differences among these figures, and they do not all represent exactly the same prophetic type. For example, whereas Daniel, Simon, and, to some extent, Josephus are court figures, we saw that Judas appears as a political outsider. But they were all practitioners of types of prophecy that had a certain technical dimension—they required special training and skills.

Josephus uses μάντις-terminology with some consistency to refer to prophecy of this more technical sort, whether practiced by Jews or by non-Jews. Apart from Jotham, Daniel, and the other wise men in the Babylonian court, the only biblical figures who are described by Josephus as mantics are Balaam (*Ant.* 4.102–30, 157–58) and the so-called witch of Endor (*Ant.* 6.327–42).[124] The case of the witch of Endor is especially interesting. Josephus describes her as a "ventriloquist" (ἐγγαστρίμυθος) who calls up spirits from the dead (6.329–30); but he also describes practitioners of this "art" (τέχνη, 6.327, 340) as a special "class of mantics" (τοῦτο τὸ γένος τῶν μάντεων, 6.331) and as members of a "profession" (ἐπιστήμη, 6.340).[125]

My own theory about Josephus' use of μάντις-terminology in connection with the Essenes, then, is as follows. Josephus does not call the Essenes προφῆται for the same reason that he does not call himself or others from his own day προφῆται, namely, because he believed that the really great prophets had lived in the past and that he and his contemporaries were, by comparison, unworthy of the title; that is, for reasons of the sort considered in chapter 1. The fact that he calls the Essenes μάντεις does not mean that he thought that they were not prophets. Daniel, after all, was one of a group of μάντεις and, at the same time, "one of the greatest prophets" (*Ant.* 10.266). In his introduction to the story of Saul and the witch of Endor, Josephus reports that Saul had banished from the land "the mantics [οἱ μάντεις], the ventriloquists [οἱ ἐγγαστρίμυθοι], and all practitioners of such arts, *except the prophets* [ἔξω τῶν προφητῶν]" (*Ant.* 6.327, emphasis mine). The mention of the prophets is an addition to scripture (cf. 1 Sam. 28.3) and shows that Josephus considered the kind of skills possessed by the witch to be prophetic. He uses the word μάντις and related terms, then, not to distinguish certain figures from genuine prophets, but rather to point to types of prophecy that required a certain degree of technical expertise. The terminology is not an infallible guide to prophets of this sort: it is sometimes used of individuals who do not fit the type (Jotham), and is not always used of those who do fit the type (e.g., Solomon); but it is used with some consistency by Josephus to refer to more technical varieties of prophecy.

Some of these types of prophecy were international phenomena and not distinctively Jewish; hence the instinctive feeling on the part of many scholars that they were somehow "un-Jewish" or "Hellenistic." On the other hand, they also had a long history within Israelite and Jewish religion by Josephus' day. Josephus does not seem to have been very anxious to distinguish between Jewish and non-Jewish expressions of this general sort of prophecy. Perhaps this is another instance in which the modern scholar has something to learn from him.

Conclusion

I began this chapter by considering Josephus' general comment about the Essenes in *War* 2.159. This passage relates the ability of some of the Essenes to predict the future to their training in "sacred books," "sayings of prophets," and "various purifications." Josephus does not explain precisely how the Essenes used sacred books and sayings of prophets to predict the future—I considered, but rejected, the proposal that he had something like pesher interpretation in mind. Nor does he say just how the Essenes' ability to predict the future was related to their practice of special purity rites.

Though the details of these matters remain unclear, a reasonable guess can be made about how prediction, scripture, and purity were related at a general level. Josephus, like other Jews of his day, believed that God controlled history in a direct and comprehensive way and that events on earth unfolded in accordance with the divine plan. Predicting the future, then, depended on gaining insight into God's character, purposes, and intentions. Scripture, it was believed, had been written by God or (recalling *Against Apion* 1.37) by prophets inspired by God and contained a record of God's actions in the past and his plans for the future. The practice of purifications brought one closer to God by eliminating the impurities that made contact between the human and the divine impossible. Those who studied scripture and practiced special purity rites, then, were in a better position than the ordinary person to perceive and understand God's plans for the future.

Comparison of the general statement in *War* 2.159 with the Community Rule and the Damascus Rule established that the passage probably refers, in the first instance, to the celibate community at Qumran.

For that reason, I cautioned against using *War* 2.159 in a direct way to interpret Josephus' accounts concerning Judas, Menahem, and Simon, all of whom appear to have been from Essene communities outside of Qumran. I suggested that these figures might represent a branch of the Essene movement that falls somewhere between the Qumran sectarians and the group represented by the Damascus Rule in terms of their devotion to study and their practice of purity.

All three of the individual Essene prophets mentioned by Josephus made predictions about events in the public-political realm. In the case of Menahem, prediction of the future was combined with a certain element of moral exhortation, with special emphasis on "justice" and "piety," two terms used by Josephus to summarize the obligations enjoined by the Jewish law. Josephus also believed that the Essenes' ability to predict the future derived, in part, from their character as especially virtuous individuals, where "virtue" is defined as the practice of justice and piety, that is, as obedience to the law. The precise relationship between strict observance of the law and the ability to predict the future is unclear.

We have seen that foreknowledge of the future was only one part of a more comprehensive esoteric knowledge possessed by the Essenes. This wider esoteric knowledge included, among other things, understanding of the art of dream interpretation, and was believed by Josephus and other Jews to be partly a gift from God and partly the result of special technical training. Josephus' use of μάντις-terminology in connection with the Essene prophets emphasizes the element of technical expertise in their activity.

In terms of their social location and role, there is some variation among the individual Essene prophets. All of them make predictions concerning prominent public figures, but they occupy different positions in relation to these figures. Judas appears as a political outsider: he makes a prediction about a member of the ruling Hasmonean family, but has no real connection with this figure or with the court. Menahem is more of a borderline figure: he acclaims Herod king, and thus is more directly involved in political affairs than was Judas; but he probably was not an official adviser or court figure. Finally, Simon is portrayed as an official member of the court, one of a group of professional dream interpreters and advisers, like Daniel before him.

These variations probably reflect the actual political interests and fortunes of the Essenes: as a group, they opposed the Hasmoneans and, at least initially, supported Herod the Great. In relation to the Herodian family, however, the position of these prophets was mixed: Menahem predicted that Herod would be king, but also lectured him on justice and piety and predicted his fall; Simon was a trusted adviser in the court of Archelaus, but announced the end of the Herodian dynasty. After the reign of Archelaus, these figures disappear from public life and from our view.

4

The Sign Prophets

Josephus' account of the revolt against Rome and the events leading up to it includes reports of the activities of several figures who are usually described as sign prophets by scholars.[1] There is some dispute about precisely which figures should be included in this category. My own list of Jewish sign prophets includes the following six individuals or groups:

1. Theudas (*Ant.* 20.97–99)
2. a group of unnamed figures active during the procuratorship of Felix (*War* 2.258–60; *Ant.* 20.167–68)
3. the Egyptian (*War* 2.261–63; *Ant.* 20.169–72)
4. an unnamed figure under Festus (*Ant.* 20.188)
5. another unnamed figure who led his followers to the temple just before it was destroyed in 70 C.E. (*War* 6.283–87)
6. Jonathan, a Sicarius refugee from Palestine who was active in Cyrene after the war (*War* 7.437–50; *Life* 424–25).

In this chapter, I shall review Josephus' accounts concerning these figures and sketch the most important features of the prophetic type they represent. I shall concentrate, in the first instance, on simply describing their actions and behavior, as reported by Josephus, but I shall also attempt to give an account of the intentions and expectations of the sign prophets, insofar as this is possible. That last qualification is a significant one. In order to understand fully what the sign prophets intended by their actions and what they expected to happen, we would need to know a great deal more than we do about what they said and did, about the precise historical circumstances that gave rise to the movements they led, and about the religious beliefs and expectations current among Jews of their day. In what follows, I shall indicate the points at which my own views about the intentions and expectations of the sign prophets differ significantly from the current scholarly consensus and I shall state as clearly as possible what I think we can and cannot say with confidence.

There is some variety among the sign prophets, both in their reported activities and also in their apparent intentions and expectations, but nevertheless enough in the way of common features to justify categorizing them together as representatives of a single prophetic type. Although a full description of these common features will be provided later in this chapter (see pp. 133–43), the following summary may be offered in anticipation:

1. The sign prophets were all leaders of sizable movements.
2. The movements they led were popular movements; that is, their followers were drawn mostly from the common people.
3. These figures presented themselves as prophets. In some cases at least, they appear to have modeled their behavior on certain prophetic figures from the ancient past.
4. These prophets are all reported to have led their followers from one place to another. In several accounts, their destination is described simply as the wilderness or desert; in some cases, specific sites are mentioned, including the Jordan River, the Mount of Olives, and the Temple Mount in Jerusalem.
5. The sign prophets announced to their followers that God himself was about to act in a dramatic way to deliver them. We shall see that it is in most cases extremely difficult to determine precisely how they envisaged this deliverance or what they thought its consequences would be.
6. Finally, in connection with their announcement of imminent divine deliverance, these prophets reportedly promised their followers that God, or they themselves, would perform some sort of miracle. It is from this aspect of their activity, and from the particular terminology that Josephus uses to describe it, that these figures have acquired the name "sign prophets."[2] The nature and purpose of the miracles they promised must be clarified.

Josephus denounces Theudas and the others as "false prophets," "impostors," "deceivers," and "those who misrepresented God." He accuses them of leading the people astray and of contributing to the downfall of Jerusalem and the Jewish nation. In addition to reviewing Josephus' reports about the sign prophets and describing their prophetic type in general terms, I shall also consider the question of why he characterizes them in this way.

One methodological problem will be immediately apparent. I have been writing as if there were some independent source of information about the sign prophets with which we could compare Josephus' accounts, but that is not the case. Theudas and the Egyptian are both mentioned in the book of Acts, but we shall see that these references are confused and of limited historical value. The few other texts sometimes cited by scholars in connection with the sign prophets are difficult to interpret and of doubtful significance.[3]

Thus we are, for all practical purposes, dependent on Josephus alone for information about these prophets. We must assume that there is some correlation between the way he describes them and what they actually said and did. But, as I have noted, Josephus is a hostile witness; his assessment of these figures and even his description of their activities cannot be accepted at face value. Also, he does not tell us all that we should like to know: most of his reports are brief and some of them appear to be rather stylized in form. We must therefore proceed cautiously, paying careful attention to the terminology that Josephus uses to describe these figures and taking into account the ways in which his own convictions may have affected his presentation of them. Finally, we must interpret the scant evidence provided by Josephus against the background of all that is known about circumstances in Palestine in this period and about the beliefs and hopes of those Jews to whom the sign prophets made their appeal.

Josephus' Reports Concerning the Sign Prophets

I shall review Josephus' accounts of the activities of the sign prophets in an order slightly different from their chronological order, beginning with the reports concerning Theudas and the Egyptian. I treat these two accounts together because in both cases the miracle that was promised by the prophet is described by Josephus. In three of the remaining accounts, Josephus uses what appear to be formulaic phrases to refer to the miracles promised by prophets: he speaks of "signs of freedom" (σημεῖα ἐλευθερίας, *War* 2.259) and "the signs of deliverance" (τὰ σημεῖα τῆς σωτηρίας, *War* 6.285); he also uses the compound expressions "signs and apparitions" (σημεῖα καὶ φάσματα, *War* 7.438) and "marvels and signs" (τέρατα καὶ σημεῖα, *Ant.* 20.168). It must be determined, if possible, what Josephus meant by these phrases. One last account (the unnamed figure under Festus, *Ant.* 20.188) does not explicitly mention miracles or signs, but I shall argue that it should be classified with the other passages on the basis of more general considerations.

Theudas (Antiquities 20.97–99)

When Agrippa I died in 44 c.e., he had ruled for three years over an area nearly equal in extent to the kingdom of Herod the Great. At his death, this entire territory was made a Roman province, and Cuspius Fadus was sent out as procurator. In the *War* Josephus passes over the tenure of Fadus (44–?46 c.e.) and his successor, Tiberius Alexander (?46–48 c.e.), with only a summarizing comment: "by abstaining from all interference with the customs of the country [they] kept the nation at peace" (2.220). When he reports events under Fadus in the *Antiquities*, Josephus once again offers a basically positive assessment, but this time there are some hints of friction between the procurator and his subjects. The dispute about who should have control of the high priest's vestments was renewed under Fadus (*Ant.* 20.6–16), and it was also at this time that Theudas made his appearance.[4]

Josephus calls Theudas an "impostor"—the Greek term is γόης, and we shall return to the question of its precise meaning in Josephus. Theudas himself, however, "stated that he was a prophet" (προφήτης . . . ἔλεγεν εἶναι, *Ant.* 20.97). He persuaded his followers to take up their possessions and go with him to the Jordan River, where he promised a miracle: at his command, the river would part, allowing them to cross. Fadus sent out a squadron of cavalry and they took the group by surprise. Many of Theudas' followers were killed or taken prisoner, and Theudas himself was captured and beheaded on the spot. His severed head was displayed in Jerusalem, presumably to discourage other would-be prophets.

It is impossible to determine from Josephus' brief report precisely what Theudas intended or what he and his followers expected. It would appear that the group modeled their actions either on the crossing of the Red Sea at the time of the exodus from Egypt (Exod. 12.29–14.30), or on the miraculous crossing of the Jordan River at the time of the entry into the promised land under the leadership of Joshua (Josh. 3–4).[5] It is difficult to say which of these two models they had in view. The promise to divide the Jordan most naturally suggests the earlier parting of the same river by Joshua, but it may also have been intended as a dramatic re-enactment of the parting of the sea at the time of the exodus. We do not know in which direction the group were traveling, and the fact that they had their possessions with them fits both models equally well.

It may not, in fact, be necessary to decide between the two proposed models. In the biblical version of these events, the crossing of the Jordan under Joshua is explicitly presented as a repetition of the crossing of the sea under Moses, and it is possible that the two events had become fused in popular memory and expectation by the first century C.E.[6] That is to say, the actions of Theudas and his followers may not have been modeled on the crossing of the Red Sea under Moses or the crossing of the Jordan under Joshua, but on both, or rather on a complex combination of the two.[7]

One further point requires discussion. Martin Hengel has suggested, on the basis of the analogy with the biblical account of the exodus, that Theudas and his followers were armed.[8] In this connection, it is important to note a slight difference between the biblical account of the exodus and Josephus' version of the same events. According to the Bible, the Israelites were armed both at the time of the crossing of the Red Sea and at the time of the crossing of the Jordan under Joshua.[9] According to Josephus, however, they were unarmed at the time of the exodus from Egypt and were providentially provided with arms after the crossing of the sea.[10]

There is some evidence that Josephus is here reflecting a wider interpretive tradition.[11] If that is the case, then it would seem unwise to conclude on the basis of the reminiscences of the exodus in Josephus' account of Theudas that he and his followers were armed.

The passage as a whole suggests the opposite. Josephus does not explicitly state that the group were armed, and they appear to have been overcome with ease by a relatively small military force.[12] It is impossible, however, to decide the issue with certainty.

Theudas is mentioned in Acts 5.36, in a speech attributed to Gamaliel I. According to this passage, Theudas "claimed to be somebody" (λέγων εἶναί τινα ἑαυτόν) and collected around four hundred followers. Nothing is said about the precise nature of his activities, but it is reported that "he was slain and all who followed him were dispersed and came to nothing." This conforms fairly closely to Josephus' description, but adds little that is new. As is well known, the chronology of Luke's account is confused: the speech of Gamaliel is set some ten years before Theudas' appearance (according to Josephus' chronology), and yet speaks of him as a figure from the past; indeed, the speech dates Theudas to the period before Judas the Galilean (6 C.E.).[13]

The Egyptian (*War 2.261–63;* Antiquities *20.169–72*)

Josephus' account of the Egyptian is part of a longer narrative summarizing events in Jewish Palestine under Felix, who was procurator from 52 to about 60 C.E. (*War* 2.252–65; *Ant.* 20.160–72). These events included actions taken against certain "brigands" in the countryside, the rise of the Sicarii in Jerusalem, and the appearance there of a group of figures whom Josephus calls "impostors and deceivers." I shall return to this latter group presently. Josephus introduces the Egyptian without indicating his relationship, if any, to these other figures. In the *Antiquities* he states that the Egyptian, like Theudas, "declared that he was a prophet" (προφήτης εἶναι λέγων, 20.169); in the *War* it is reported that he had "gained for himself the reputation of a prophet" (προφήτου πίστιν ἐπιθεὶς ἑαυτῷ, 2.261). Josephus, however, calls him a "false prophet" (ψευδοπροφήτης) and an "impostor" (ἄνθρωπος γόης, both *War* 2.261).

There are substantial differences between the two accounts of the activities of the Egyptian and his followers. In the *Antiquities* he first comes to Jerusalem and raises a following there; in the *War* he appears in the countryside (εἰς τὴν χώραν, 2.261) and draws his followers from the population there.[14] Correspondingly, the *Antiquities* pictures a march from Jerusalem to the Mount of Olives, outside the city walls, while the *War* states that the group traveled from the desert (ἐκ τῆς ἐρημίας, 2.262) to the Mount of Olives. According to the *Antiquities*, the Egyptian claimed that the walls of Jerusalem would fall down at his command, allowing him and his followers to enter; the account in the *War* mentions no such miracle and reports, instead, preparations for a military assault against the city. There is also disagreement about the number of people involved in the incident. The *War* credits the Egyptian with thirty thousand followers (2.261) and states that most of them were killed or taken prisoner in the military engagement with the Romans (2.263). The *Antiquities* describes the Egyptian's following as "the masses of the common people" (τό δημοτικόν πλῆϑος, 20.169), but estimates at only six hundred the number who were killed or taken prisoner by the Romans (20.171).

It is difficult to account for these discrepancies and to know how significant they are. We shall see that Josephus generally tends to "militarize" the sign prophets in the *War*—that is, to assimilate them to, or associate them with, the armed rebels. This is probably part of his more general tendency, in that work, to shift most of the blame for the revolt onto a few individuals or parties on both sides.[15] Among the Jews, those held to be responsible are the armed revolutionaries, who are portrayed as mad and bloodthirsty fanatics, in no way representative of official Judaism or of the Jewish people as a whole. On the Roman side, it is emphasized that it was largely the actions of a few corrupt and unrepresentative procurators (notably Albinus and Florus) that led to war. Apart from these extremists on both sides, Josephus suggests, the revolt could have been avoided. The portrayal of the sign prophets as armed and dangerous revolutionaries fits into this general picture and serves to justify the Romans' brutal response to them. In the case of the Egyptian, this militarization is probably only slightly misleading, since even the account in the *Antiquities* suggests that he and his followers were armed.[16] In the case of the other prophets who were active around the same time, the militarizing account of the *War* is probably more seriously distorting, as we shall see.

In the *Antiquities* Josephus apportions blame for the revolt somewhat more evenly. He is prepared to acknowledge (at least implicitly) that different groups of Jews opposed the Romans for different reasons and in different ways, and no longer seeks to place all of the blame on the rebels or to assimilate all of the opponents of Rome to them. As a result, I suggest, he presents the sign prophets more accurately in the later work as figures of a distinct type.

This explanation may account for some of the discrepancies between the two versions of the Egyptian's activities, but it does not explain the disagreements about his movements from place to place. On this score, it is possible to reconcile the two accounts at least partially by combining them and supposing that the Egyptian showed up in Jerusalem, gathered a crowd there, led them out into the wilderness, where he gathered still more followers, and proceeded to the Mount of Olives. There he promised that the walls of Jerusalem would fall down at his command and prepared to follow up this miraculous event with an armed invasion of the

city. The combination of the miraculous toppling of city walls followed
by an armed invasion is strongly reminiscent of the story of the conquest
of Jericho under Joshua (Josh. 6; cf. *Ant.* 5.22–32), and was almost certainly modeled on that incident. Before the Egyptian's plan could be executed, the Romans moved against him and his followers. Many in the
group were killed or imprisoned, but the Egyptian himself escaped.

The Egyptian is mentioned in the book of Acts, but, as in the case of
Theudas, Luke's account presents a rather confused picture of events.
According to Acts 21.38, when the apostle Paul was arrested in the temple, a Roman tribune mistook him for the Egyptian: "Are you not the
Egyptian, then, who recently stirred up a revolt and led four thousand
men of the Sicarii out into the wilderness?" The chronology is right this
time and other details of the account agree with Josephus' portrayal of
the Egyptian: he "stirred up a revolt" (ἀναστατώσας) and led his followers into the wilderness. But Luke has misidentified the Egyptian's followers as Sicarii: there is no independent evidence linking the two movements, and we may be sure that Josephus would have made it clear if
there were any connection between them. The statement that the Egyptian had four thousand followers disagrees with the figures given both in
the *War* (thirty thousand) and the *Antiquities* (six hundred).

I now proceed to those accounts in which Josephus uses sign terminology to describe the miracles promised by prophets. I shall review the
accounts first and then return to consider the question of the meaning of
the particular terminology he uses.

Unnamed Figures Under Felix
(War *2.258–60;* Antiquities *20.167–68)*

In his account of events under Felix, Josephus includes a brief notice
about the activities of a group of unnamed figures whom he denounces
as "impostors" and "deceivers."[17] The notice is placed immediately
before the report on the Egyptian prophet and immediately after a
description of the chaos created in Jerusalem by the first round of assas-
sinations by the Sicarii. Josephus introduces the unnamed figures in the
War as "another body of villains, with purer hands but more impious
intentions" than the Sicarii (2.258). It is not clear whether he is summarizing the activities of a series of such figures or relating a single incident;
but the fact that, in the *War* at least, he records a single military response
on the part of the Romans suggests that the latter is the case.

Josephus reports that these unnamed figures appeared in Jerusalem
and led their followers out into the desert. According to the *War*, they
promised that "God would there show them signs of liberation" or "freedom" (ἐκεῖ τοῦ θεοῦ δείξοντος αὐτοῖς σημεῖα ἐλευθερίας, 2.259); the
Antiquities reports that they promised "unmistakable marvels and signs
that would be wrought in accordance with God's plan" or "providence"

(ἐναργῆ τέρατα καὶ σημεῖα κατὰ τὴν τοῦ θεοῦ πρόνοιαν γινόμενα, 20.168). Josephus gives no indication of what these signs and marvels were; I shall return to the question below.

The impression created by the account in the *War* is that the freedom promised by these prophets was primarily political freedom, that is, freedom from Roman rule. Josephus accuses them of promoting νεωτερισμοί and μεταβολαί (2.259). The first of these terms, νεωτερισμός, can mean "change" or "innovation" of almost any sort, but Josephus normally uses the word in a more precise way to describe political revolt or political innovation of a revolutionary kind.[18] Thus, it sometimes appears alongside such terms as στάσις ("civil strife"), πόλεμος ἐμφύλιος ("civil war"), and ἀπόστασις ("insurrection").[19] The second of the two terms from *War* 2.259, μεταβολή, is an even more general word for "change," but it, too, sometimes has specifically political connotations in Josephus. In the report about John the Baptist, for example, μεταβολή occurs together with στάσις and νεώτερον in a context where all three terms have political overtones.[20] In addition to accusing the unnamed figures under Felix of promoting νεωτερισμοί and μεταβολαί, the account in the *War* states that the procurator regarded their activities as the preliminary to "insurrection" (ἀπόστασις, 2.260) and, accordingly, sent out a military force against them. As in the case of the Egyptian, this military force is explicitly said to have been "heavily armed" (ὁπλῖται, 2.260), and this reinforces the impression that the group were armed revolutionaries intent on ousting the Romans by force.

The account in the *Antiquities* does not create the same impression. There is no mention there of ἐλευθερία or of νεωτερισμοί, μεταβολαί, or ἀπόστασις, no suggestion that the group were armed, and no report of the use of heavily armed troops against them. I suspect that Josephus has militarized these figures in the *War* for apologetic reasons of the sort described in the preceding section, and that the account in the *Antiquities* presents a more reliable picture of them on the whole. It should be noted that, even in the *War*, Josephus introduces these figures with the remark that they had "purer hands" than the Sicarii (2.258), a description which suggests that they were unarmed and nonviolent, thereby contradicting the general impression created by the rest of the account.

One other feature of Josephus' report deserves comment. In *War* 2.259 he states that these unnamed figures acted "under the pretense of divine inspiration" (προσχήματι θειασμοῦ). It is Josephus' own opinion, of course, that the claim to divine inspiration made by these individuals was only a "pretense." We may assume that they genuinely believed themselves to be inspired, and that those who followed them accepted the claims they made. In the same passage (*War* 2.259), Josephus writes that these prophets "persuaded the multitude to act as if possessed" or "mad" (δαιμονᾶν τὸ πλῆθος ἔπειθον). The reference to the divine inspiration claimed by these figures and the use of the word δαιμονάω to describe the behavior of their followers are sometimes taken to indicate that the group was characterized by some sort cf ecstatic behavior.[21] As we saw in chapter 1, however, Josephus did not have a clear theory about the mechanics of prophetic inspiration and he does not use technical terms for inspiration or inspired behavior in a precise or consistent way. Also, he frequently uses the language of madness or possession to describe the behavior of Jews who opposed Roman rule in one way or another.[22] In such instances, he uses this terminology in a metaphorical way to explain behavior that he regards as incomprehensible—"mad" in the sense of not conforming to what a sensible person like himself would do in a similar situation. I suggest that he is using δαιμονάω in this metaphorical sense in the present passage. What he regards as evidence of madness or possession in this case is not any prophetic-ecstatic behavior, but rather the willingness on the part of the people involved to follow the unnamed prophets out into the desert in the expectation that they would there witness miracles pointing forward to God's deliverance.[23] The word ἀφροσύνη ("folly") is used in a similar way in connection with these same figures in *Antiquities* 20.168 and in the account concerning Theudas (*Ant.* 20.98).

Unnamed Prophet of 70 C.E. *(*War *6.283–87)*

In the course of his narrative describing the destruction of the temple and adjoining buildings in 70 C.E., Josephus recounts the fate of six thousand Jews, "women and children of the populace and a mixed multitude" (ἀπὸ τοῦ δήμου γύναια καὶ παιδία καὶ σύμμικτος ὄχλος, *War* 6.283), who died when the temple portico on which they had taken refuge was set on fire by Roman soldiers. Josephus blames their death on a "false prophet" (ψευδοπροφήτης, 6.285), who had announced to the people in Jerusalem that God commanded them to go up to the temple to receive there "the signs of deliverance" (τὰ σημεῖα τῆς σωτηρίας, 6.285). Once again, no indication is given of what these signs were.[24]

The story of this one prophet and his fate prompts Josephus to make a general comment about the activity of other prophets like him:

> At that time, many prophets [προφῆται] were planted among the people by the tyrants to announce that they should wait for help from God, in order that desertions might be lessened and hope might encourage those who were beyond fear and precaution. When suffering misfortunes, one is quickly persuaded; but when the deceiver actually pictures release from prevailing horrors, then the sufferer wholly abandons himself to hope. (*War* 6.286–87)[25]

I shall return to the question of whether the picture Josephus paints here of some sort of formal cooperation between sign prophets and those involved in the armed resistance—here branded "tyrants"—is accurate.

The passage gives us some idea of what these prophets said and did, if only a general idea. Josephus says that they encouraged the people to "wait for help from God," and he implies that they described to their followers, in vivid terms, the form that this divine assistance would take; at least I suppose this is what he means when he says that such prophets "actually picture[d] [ὑπογράφῃ] release from prevailing horrors" (6.287). It is difficult to imagine what sort of "deliverance" (σωτηρία) or "release" (ἀπαλλαγή) was expected by the prophet who led six thousand apparently defenseless people into the temple precincts in the middle of a fierce battle. It would seem that he expected an act of divine intervention of a very dramatic sort.[26]

Jonathan the Sicarius
(War 7.437–50; Life 424–25)

The last figure who is said to have promised his followers a display of signs and wonders is a certain Jonathan, a Sicarius refugee from Palestine who was active in Cyrene, in North Africa, sometime in the seventies. The account in the *War* is one of two notices that Josephus provides about the activities of the Sicarii after the end of the revolt in Palestine. The first concerns an uprising in Alexandria that was started by a group of Sicarii refugees and that resulted in the demolition, by the Romans, of the Jewish temple at Leontopolis (*War* 7.409–36). The second recounts the activities of Jonathan and his followers in Cyrene (7.437–50).

Josephus introduces Jonathan as "a most villainous man" (πονηρότατος ἄνθρωπος), whose following consisted of "many of the poor" (οὐκ ὀλίγοι τῶν ἀπόρων, 7.438). He is reported to have led his followers from Cyrene into the desert, promising to show them "signs and apparitions" (σημεῖα καὶ φάσματα, 7.438). No description of these miracles is provided. The group's activities went unnoticed by most, but were reported to the Roman governor, Catullus, by "the men of rank" among the Jews (7.439). Catullus dispatched a force of cavalry and infantry, and most of Jonathan's followers were killed or taken prisoner. Jonathan himself escaped from the battle, but was later captured.

Further intrigues followed Jonathan's arrest. According to Josephus, he tried to escape punishment by claiming that he had acted on the instructions of "the wealthiest of the Jews" (7.442). Catullus apparently had his own reasons for wanting to move against this group, and he prompted Jonathan to further accusations. Together they contrived the execution of "all the well-to-do [Jews]" in Cyrene, three thousand in number (7.445). Jonathan went too far, however, when he charged "the most reputable Jews both in Alexandria and Rome" with "sedition" (νεωτερισμός, 7.447). Among those so accused was Josephus himself. He and the others were acquitted when the case was heard by Vespasian, and Jonathan was tortured and burned alive (7.450).

Josephus mentions Jonathan again near the end of the *Life* (424–25), and the account he gives there in some ways supplements, and in other ways contradicts, the report in the *War*. In *Life* 424 Josephus states that the number of Jonathan's followers who were killed when the Romans attacked the group was two thousand. There is no mention, in the *Life*, of a flight into the desert or the promise of signs and apparitions. Jonathan is introduced, instead, as "a certain Jew . . . who had promoted civil strife [στάσις] in Cyrene" (*Life* 424). In the *War* Jonathan's followers are explicitly said to have been unarmed (ἄνοπλοι, 7.440), but *Life* 424 reports that Jonathan accused Josephus of supplying him with arms (ὅπλα) and money. It is unclear how these discrepancies should be explained or what their significance is.

Unnamed Figure Under Festus
(Antiquities 20.188)

Before discussing the significance of the sign terminology used in the three accounts just reviewed, it is necessary to consider one other passage, which concerns an unnamed figure active during the procuratorship of Festus (?60–62 C.E.). Josephus does not provide much information about events in this period. In *War* 2.271 he reports only that Festus captured many "brigands" and put them to death. In the parallel account in the *Antiquities* (20.185–87), he identifies the "brigands" as Sicarii. He also adds this brief notice:

> Festus also sent a force of cavalry and infantry against the dupes of a certain impostor who had promised them salvation and rest from troubles, if they chose to follow him into the wilderness. The force which Festus dispatched destroyed both the deceiver himself and those who had followed him. (*Ant.* 20.188)

There is no mention of a sign in this account and no description of a miracle, and it is possible that this figure should not be classified as a sign prophet. The language of the passage is in some respects reminiscent of Matthew 11.28–30 and of earlier traditions reflected, for example, in Sirach 6.23–31 and 51.23–30.[27] These passages speak of the "rest" (ἀνάπαυσις) that comes from study, instruction, and wisdom. If the phrase παῦλα κακῶν ("rest from troubles") is used in a similar way in the above passage, then the unnamed figure under Festus might be better described as a teacher than as a sign prophet. It might be difficult to see why the Roman procurator would suppress a religious teacher violently, but the case of John the Baptist is instructive in this respect. Josephus reports that Herod Antipas was afraid that John's teaching would lead to a revolt: "Eloquence that had so great an effect on people might lead to some form of civil strife [στάσις], for it looked as if they would be guided by John in everything that they did" (*Ant.* 18.118). A religious teacher could be viewed as a potential political threat, or at least as a threat to public order.

The response of the Romans to the unnamed figure under Festus was not, however, exactly the same as their response to John. John himself was arrested and killed, but no action was taken against those who listened to him and were persuaded by what he taught. In the case under Festus, a military force was sent out against the unnamed figure and his followers. The same response is recorded in the case of the sign prophets (except the one who perished with his followers in the fire that destroyed the temple). In addition, much of the vocabulary of the above passage links the unnamed figure under Festus with the prophets I have been considering: Josephus calls him an "impostor" (ἄνθρωπος γόης) and a "deceiver" (ἀπατήσας); he is said to have promised "salvation" (σωτηρία), and to have led his followers out into the "wilderness" (ἐρημία). On the basis of these similarities, this figure may also be classified as a sign prophet.

The Meaning of Josephus' Sign Terminology

Let us return to the particular phrases that Josephus uses to describe the miracles promised by the sign prophets and see whether it is possible to determine the meaning of these phrases more precisely. In the *War* Josephus states that the unnamed figures under Felix promised their followers that God would show them "signs of liberation" or "freedom" (σημεῖα ἐλευθερίας, 2.259). These same miracles are described in the *Antiquities* as "unmistakable marvels and signs [τέρατα καὶ σημεῖα] that would be wrought in accordance with God's plan" or "providence" (20.168). The prophet who led six thousand Jews to the Temple Mount in 70 C.E. is said to have promised them that they would see "the signs of salvation" or "deliverance" (τὰ σημεῖα τῆς σωτηρίας, *War* 6.285). Finally, Jonathan reportedly promised his followers "signs and apparitions" (σημεῖα καὶ φάσματα, *War* 7.438). The one term common to all of these reports is σημεῖα. It is necessary first to establish the meaning of this term in the passages under consideration. The question of the meaning of the words τέρατα and φάσματα, which are also used to describe the miracles promised by these prophets, will be taken up later.

Σημεῖα as Omens or Portents

The word σημεῖον has a fairly broad range of meanings, most of them attested in Josephus.[28] For the purposes of this discussion, two uses of the term are of interest. First, Josephus sometimes uses σημεῖα to refer to omens or portents: strange phenomena of various sorts that were believed to foreshadow future events and to reveal the will and intentions of the

Deity. Thus, for example, he refers to the omens that predicted Vespasian's rise to power as σημεῖα.[29] He also uses the term, along with τέρας and φάσμα, to describe the omens and portents that preceded and pointed toward the destruction of Jerusalem in 70 C.E. These omens are listed in *War* 6.288–315; they included a star and a comet, a strange light in the temple, a cow that gave birth to a lamb, and other weird and wonderful things.[30]

There are two other passages, both probably from Nicolaus of Damascus, in which σημεῖον and τέρας are used interchangeably of portents or omens of the sort we are discussing. The first is *War* 1.331–32, which recounts Herod's narrow escape on one occasion when a building in which he and his guests had been dining collapsed immediately after their departure. The incident is described as a "miraculous portent" (δαιμόνιόν τι . . . τέρας, 1.331), and Herod is said to have interpreted it as an "omen" (σημεῖον) both of the dangers awaiting him in the military campaign on which he was about to embark and of the certainty of his preservation through these dangers (1.332). The second passage, *War* 1.370–79, concerns an earthquake that occurred in 31 B.C.E. while Herod was waging war against the Arabs. The disaster and the Arab attack that followed it demoralized Herod's troops. According to Josephus, Herod attempted to raise their spirits with a speech (1.373–79) in which he argued, among other things, that the earthquake should not be interpreted as a "portent" (τέρας) of another disaster (1.377); sometimes, he continued, a "sign" (σημεῖον) precedes a natural disaster of this sort, but the disaster itself should not be regarded as portentous (1.377). Herod then referred by way of contrast to the murder, by the Arabs, of the envoys he had sent to them, and suggested that this evil and unnatural act was a "grave portent" (τέρας . . . μέγιστον) of disaster for the Arabs (1.378).[31]

Finally, there are two passages, certainly composed by Josephus, in which τέρας alone is used to refer to omens. The first is *War* 4.286–87, which describes a violent thunderstorm that occurred while the Idumaeans were camped outside Jerusalem, waiting to be admitted to join the rebel forces. In 4.287 Josephus notes that the storm and its accompanying phenomena (winds like a hurricane, rain in torrents, continuous lightning, fearful thunder, and rumblings of earthquake) were clearly "portents" (τὰ τέρατα) of some great calamity. He goes on to say that both the Idumaeans and their moderate opponents in Jerusalem misinterpreted these omens, thinking that they foreshadowed defeat for the rebel cause, whereas in reality (Josephus implies) they signaled doom for the moderate faction and for Jerusalem itself. The second passage is *War* 5.409–12, which forms part of Josephus' long speech to the rebels late in the revolt (5.362–419). Josephus reminds the rebels that the springs in and around Jerusalem, which had been nearly dry before Titus' arrival, flowed copiously as he and his army approached. Josephus refers to this as a "portent" (τέρας, 5.411) and implies that the proper conclusion to be drawn from it was that God had gone over to the side of the Romans (5.412).[32]

Josephus' understanding of the nature and purpose of the omens he designates as σημεῖα, τέρατα, and, on one occasion (*War* 6.297), φάσματα can now be summarized. First, it is worth noting the wide variety of things that could be considered ominous. The passages discussed above include the collapse of a building, an act that violates widely accepted standards of morality (the murder of Herod's envoys), a sudden and unusually violent thunderstorm, the welling up of springs, strange phenomena in the heavens, voices in the temple, predictive prophecies (including written ones, *War* 6.311–13), and unnatural births, among other things. Most of these are strange occurrences, thought to be inexplicable on the basis of natural causes alone. They occur unexpectedly and without warning. Josephus, like most of his contemporaries, assumed that such omens were sent by God (or the gods) and were intended to communicate his (or their) will and intentions. This assumption is made explicit in the editorial remarks included in his description of the omens that preceded the destruction of Jerusalem. In *War* 6.288 Josephus characterizes these omens as "the proclamations of God" (τὰ τοῦ θεοῦ κηρύγματα). Near the close of the list of omens, he comments: "Reflecting on these things, one will find that God cares for human beings, and in all kinds of ways shows His people the way of salvation, while they owe their destruction to folly and calamities of their own choosing" (6.310).[33] This passage points to another important characteristic of omens and portents, as Josephus understood them: the meaning of such signs was frequently ambiguous. More than once Josephus notes that an omen was misinterpreted or interpreted in different ways by different people. Again, this is most clearly illustrated in *War* 6.288–315, but we also saw that the ominous thunderstorm described in *War* 4.286–87 was misinterpreted by both the Idumaeans and the moderates in Jerusalem. The prophetic miracles designated σημεῖα by Josephus are ambiguous in a similar way.

Σημεῖα *as Authenticating Miracles*

One other use of the term σημεῖον in Josephus needs to be considered and is particularly important for understanding the sign prophets. In the *Antiquities* Josephus uses σημεῖον to refer to a certain type of miracle performed by prophets or performed by God through prophets. The figure of Moses is usually thought to be of special significance in this connection. Commentators often point to the similarities between the language Josephus uses to describe the miracles promised by the sign prophets and the language he uses to describe the miracles performed by Moses at the time of the exodus from Egypt.[34] These similarities extend beyond the use of the term σημεῖον and include the use of the language of freedom or liberation, as well as references to God's providence. In *War* 2.259, for example, Josephus writes that the unnamed figures who were active during the procuratorship of Felix promised their followers that God would show them "signs of liberation" or "freedom" (σημεῖα ἐλευθερίας); similarly, in *Antiquities* 2.327 he says that the Israelites at the Red Sea turned against Moses in their despair, "forgetful of all those signs wrought by God in token of their liberation" (πάντων ἐπιλελησμέ-νοι τῶν ἐκ θεοῦ πρὸς τὴν ἐλευθερίαν αὐτοῖς σημείων γεγονότων). According to *Antiquities* 2.286, Moses claimed that the miracles (σημεῖα) he performed before Pharaoh and the Egyptian magicians proceeded "from God's providence and power" (κατὰ ... θεοῦ πρόνοιαν καὶ δύναμιν); similarly, the miracles promised by the unnamed figures under Felix are described in the *Antiquities* as "marvels and signs that would be wrought in accordance with God's plan" or "providence" (τέρατα καὶ σημεῖα κατὰ τὴν τοῦ θεοῦ πρόνοιαν γινόμενα, 20.168).

The conclusion usually drawn from these terminological parallels is that the sign prophets described by Josephus promised miracles like those performed by Moses at the time of the exodus. But caution is needed here. While it is entirely reasonable to suppose that the term σημεῖα has the same basic meaning in Josephus' reports concerning the sign prophets as it does in his account of the exodus, it is important to note precisely which miracles from the exodus tradition Josephus designates as σημεῖα, for his usage in this respect differs significantly from that of the LXX and much of Jewish and Christian tradition.

This fact has not generally been noticed.[35] When scholars say that the sign prophets promised to perform miracles like the ones that Moses had performed, they usually have in mind the great miracles of the exodus and the period in the wilderness—miracles like the plagues, the parting of the sea, and the provision of food and water in the wilderness.[36] This identification reflects the biblical use of the language of "signs and wonders." In the LXX version of Exodus 3–14 (which, in this respect, closely mirrors the MT), the word σημεῖα is used of the three miracles that were taught to Moses on Mount Sinai and also of the Egyptian plagues;[37] in addition, the compound phrase σημεῖα καὶ τέρατα is sometimes used to refer to the plagues.[38] In the rest of the LXX, σημεῖα and the conjunction σημεῖα καὶ τέρατα are frequently used to describe the plagues or the whole complex of miracles associated with the exodus and the wandering in the desert;[39] once again, this corresponds closely to the usage of the Hebrew Bible.[40]

It may be that some of the sign prophets did promise miracles that recalled the great miracles of the exodus and the wilderness period—Theudas apparently did—but it is important to note that this is not pre-cisely what is suggested by the terminological parallels described above between Josephus' accounts of the sign prophets and his account of the exodus under Moses. Josephus' use of the word σημεῖα in connection with the events of the exodus is much more restricted and precise than the usage of the LXX.[41] In *Antiquities* 2.327, already mentioned, the Israelites at the sea are accused of forgetting "all those signs [σημεῖα] wrought by God in token of their liberation." It is not clear from the context whether the signs referred to in this passage are the three miracles taught to Moses on Mount Sinai or the Egyptian plagues or both. Apart from this passage, however, Josephus never refers to the plagues as "signs" (σημεῖα) or as "signs and wonders" (σημεῖα καὶ τέρατα).[42] Nor does he refer to the great miracle of the parting of the sea as a "sign" (σημεῖον), describing it instead as a "miraculous deliverance" (παράλογος σωτηρία, *Ant.* 2.339; παράδοξος σωτηρία, 2.345; 3.1) and a "divine epiphany" (ἐπιφάνεια τοῦ θεοῦ, 2.339). Moreover, Josephus never uses the word σημεῖα or the compound phrase σημεῖα καὶ τέρατα to refer to the whole complex of miracles associated with the exodus.[43] This last fact is especially significant, since he does occasionally treat these miracles as a single complex.[44] He does not, however, refer to them in a shorthand way as "signs" or "signs and wonders" in the way characteristic of much of the LXX.

Apart from the possible exception of *Antiquities* 2.327, Josephus uses the word σημεῖα in his account of the exodus exclusively in connection with the three miracles taught to Moses at the burning bush on Mount Sinai, when he was first commissioned by God to return to Egypt and deliver the Hebrews from slavery.[45] According to Josephus, when Moses expressed uncertainty about how he could possibly persuade the Hebrews to follow him, or convince Pharaoh to permit them to leave, he was equipped by God with three miracles that were supposed to achieve the desired effects: he was taught how to turn his staff into a serpent, how to cause his hand to turn white and then return to normal,[46] and how to turn water into blood (*Ant.* 2.270–73). It is Josephus' more restricted use of σημεῖα to refer to these three miracles that must be considered as a possible parallel to his use of the term in the reports concerning the sign prophets.

According to Josephus, the three signs performed by Moses served several different but related purposes. They were intended, in part, to encourage and strengthen Moses himself. In *Antiquities* 2.276 Josephus writes:

> Moses found those miracles [τὰ σημεῖα ταῦτα] at his service not on that occasion only but at all times, whenever there was need of them; because of this he came to trust more firmly in the oracle from the fire, to believe that God would be his gracious protector, and to hope to be able to deliver his people and to bring disaster upon the Egyptians.[47]

The miracles were also intended to convince those who witnessed them that Moses was God's chosen agent, and thus that they should believe what he said and do what he commanded; thus in *Antiquities* 2.274 Moses is instructed by God to use the three miracles to convince all people "that you are sent by me and do everything at my command." In practice, this meant that the miracles were also intended to persuade the Hebrews that God was about to act to deliver them, since that was the message that Moses, as God's agent, had been sent to proclaim. When Moses performed the three miracles in the presence of the leaders of the Hebrews, they "took courage and were in hopes that all would go well, since God was caring for their safety" (2.280).

The three miracles were, of course, supposed to convince Pharaoh as well as the Hebrews. In this last connection, an important feature of prophetic signs, as Josephus understood them, becomes apparent: such signs are ambiguous and not self-authenticating; they may be accepted as genuine signs or rejected as deceptive tricks.[48] When Moses performed the three signs in the Egyptian court, Pharaoh dismissed them as "juggleries and magic" (τερατουργίαι καὶ μαγείαι, 2.284). Moses retorted by claiming that the miracles did not proceed "from . . . witchcraft or deception of true judgment" (κατὰ γοητείαν καὶ πλάνην τῆς ἀληθοῦς δόξης), as Pharaoh alleged, but "from God's providence and power" (κατὰ δὲ θεοῦ πρόνοιαν καὶ δύναμιν, 2.286). But this protest, and the further miraculous demonstration that followed it, still did not persuade Pharaoh of the truth of Moses' claims. The meaning of prophetic signs, we might say, is in the eye of the beholder.[49]

Before proceeding any further, let us pause to summarize Josephus' understanding of prophetic signs, as revealed by his account of the miracles performed by Moses in Egypt. I began by observing that Josephus, in contrast to the LXX, restricts the use of the word σημεῖα in his exodus account to the three miracles taught to Moses at the time of his commissioning on Mount Sinai. He does not use the term to describe the plagues, the parting of the sea, or the other great miracles of the exodus and the wilderness period. The three miracles that Moses learned at Sinai were intended partly to encourage him in the performance of the task to which God had called him. Their primary purpose, however, was to convince others that he was God's agent, as he claimed to be, and thus that they should believe what he told them of God's intentions and do what he commanded. The signs, that is, were designed to create faith in the one who performed them and in the message he brought from God. I also observed that prophetic signs of this sort are ambiguous in meaning and open to various interpretations. They may be accepted as genuine signs that verify the claims of the one who performs them or be dismissed as deceptive tricks. Finally, Josephus suggests that genuine prophetic signs proceed from, or are in some way related to, God's "providence" (πρόνοια) and "power" (δύναμις).

There are other passages in the *Antiquities* that reveal the same basic understanding of prophetic signs. One of these is *Antiquities* 10.25–29, which records an encounter between King Hezekiah and the prophet Isaiah.[50] As the story opens, Hezekiah has fallen gravely ill. He prays to God, asking that he might be allowed to live long enough to beget an heir to the throne. In response to this prayer, God sends the prophet Isaiah to inform the king that he would recover from his illness within three days, and would live for another fifteen years, and that sons would be born to him. Josephus records what followed this announcement:

> When the prophet at God's command told him these things, he would not believe him because of the severity of his illness and because the news brought to him surpassed belief, and so he asked Isaiah to perform some miraculous sign [σημεῖόν τι καὶ τεράστιον] in order that he might believe in him when he said these things, as in one who came from God. For, he said, things that are beyond belief and surpass our hopes are made credible by acts of a like nature. (*Ant.* 10.28)[51]

The primary purpose of the prophetic sign here, as in the exodus narrative, is to convince the one who witnesses it that the prophet really is God's agent and, thus, that what he says is true ("in order that he might believe in him when he said these things, as in one who came from God"). The observation that such a sign is especially necessary when the message delivered by a prophet is contrary to what one might expect or beyond what one can believe is an editorial insertion into the scriptural text, and presumably reflects Josephus' own view. When Isaiah asked Hezekiah what sign he wished him to perform, the king challenged him to make the sun go backwards. Josephus reports that "when the prophet exhorted God to show this sign to the king, he saw what he wished and was at once freed from his illness" (10.29).[52]

Another passage illustrates especially well how Josephus understood authenticating prophetic signs: *Antiquities* 8.230–45, his version of the story of the man of God from Judah and the prophet of Bethel in 1 Kings 13. Josephus' narrative is interesting for a variety of reasons, but I shall concentrate here on what it reveals of his understanding of prophetic signs.

The story is familiar from the biblical account. Once when Jeroboam was preparing to offer sacrifices on the altar at Bethel, a prophet from Judah, whom Josephus identified with the prophet Iddo mentioned in 2 Chronicles 9.29,[53] appeared and predicted that the priests who ministered at the altar would themselves one day be sacrificed upon it by the righteous King Josiah. The prophet offered a sign (σημεῖον) to confirm that what he said was true: he predicted that the altar would be broken, and that all that was on it would be spilled on the ground (*Ant.* 8.232). When Jeroboam, angered by this prediction, stretched out his hand to order the arrest of the prophet, it was paralyzed and became "numb and lifeless" (8.233); this, too, is regarded as a sign.[54] When the altar collapsed as the prophet had predicted, a repentant Jeroboam begged him to restore his hand, which he consented to do. Refusing an invitation to stay to dinner, the prophet set out for home. He was detained, however, by a local "false prophet" (as Josephus calls him). The extraordinary account of the encounter between these two men is recorded in *Antiquities* 8.236–45.[55]

Josephus makes several editorial additions to the biblical account of these events that indicate how he understood prophetic signs of the type described in the narrative. In *Antiquities* 8.232 he explains that the prophet gave a sign "so that these people may believe that it will be so." He also notes that when the altar collapsed as the prophet had said it would—that is, when the sign occurred as predicted—Jeroboam concluded that "the man was telling the truth and possessed divine foreknowledge" (8.234). Similarly, in another editorial addition, Josephus writes that what happened to the altar and to his hand convinced Jeroboam that the man from Judah was "a truly divine and excellent prophet" (8.243). Finally, Josephus adds to the biblical narrative a speech delivered to Jeroboam by the false prophet of Bethel (8.243–44). In this speech, the false prophet tries to discredit the miraculous signs performed by the visiting prophet. He argues that they were not genuine prophetic signs, but events which could be fully explained on the basis of natural causes: the numbing of the king's hand had been due to fatigue, and the altar, which was new and untried, had simply collapsed from the weight of the sacrificial offerings heaped upon it. He concludes from these things, concerning the man from Judah, that "there was nothing of a prophet either in his person or in what he had spoken" (8.244).[56]

Finally, it should be noted that Josephus has inserted a demand for an authenticating sign of the sort I have been discussing into his version of 1 Kings 22, a text that is, along with 1 Kings 13, one of the most important biblical passages dealing with the problem of distinguishing between true and false prophets.[57] Indeed, not only does he add a demand for an authenticating miracle where none existed in scripture, he also refers back to the incident just discussed. After Micaiah had predicted that the Israelites would be defeated by the Syrians and that King Ahab himself would fall in battle, his prophetic opponent, Zedekiah, tried to reassure the king. According to Josephus, he issued the following challenge in Ahab's presence:

> You shall know whether he [Micaiah] is really true and has the power of the divine spirit; let him right now, when I strike him, disable my hand as Iddo caused the right hand of King Jeroboam to wither when he wished to arrest him. For I suppose you must have heard that this thing happened. (*Ant.* 8.408)[58]

Evidently Josephus assumed that a true prophet, one who "has the power of the divine spirit," should be able to perform a miracle in support of his prophetic claims.[59]

Σημεῖα *in Josephus' Accounts of the Sign Prophets*

Let us return, finally, to Josephus' accounts of the sign prophets. If hc is using the term σημεῖα in these accounts in a way that is consistent with his usage elsewhere, then the signs promised by the first-century prophets were authenticating miracles of the sort I have been discussing. Their primary purpose was to convince people that those who performed them were God's agents and messengers, and that the messages they proclaimed were true and should be accepted and acted upon.[60] When Josephus writes that some of these prophets promised "signs of freedom" (*War* 2.259) or "signs of deliverance" (*War* 6.285), this suggests that they proclaimed a message of freedom or deliverance and promised to perform miracles that would confirm that this message came from God.

A few points require further discussion.

1. We saw earlier that Josephus makes a terminological and conceptual distinction between authenticating miracles and the great liberating acts of God, such as the parting of the sea and the other miracles of the exodus and conquest periods. The former he calls "signs," the latter he calls (among other things) "epiphanies." The differences between these two types of miracles have been summarized very clearly by Otto Betz:

> The epiphany is a marvelous intervention of God which brings liberation to His people in a desperate situation. The sign identifies the liberator and man of God to whom authority has been given as the chosen instrument of God. It lends credit to his commission and creates faith in God, who has sent and authorized him. . . . The epiphany as an act of liberation done by God is evident in an objective, overwhelming way through its great power and effect. The sign (*sēmeion*) takes place on a more modest level and can be met with unbelief. Its truth can be contested; it is open to criticism. The epiphany should be followed by hymns of praise and thanksgiving, sung by those who were saved by it. . . . The adequate response to a *sēmeion* is faith and hope.[61]

This raises the question of whether there are important differences between Theudas and the Egyptian, whose promised miracles clearly fall into the category of epiphanies, and those prophets who are reported to have promised to perform authenticating signs.

This question has not been answered or even very clearly posed in the secondary literature on the sign prophets. Betz's treatment is an especially good example of the confusion surrounding the issue. He is clearly aware that the distinction he makes between epiphanies and signs raises the question of how Theudas and the Egyptian are related to the others. His response, however, is to interpret the signs promised by the other prophets in such a way that they begin to seem like epiphanies and, similarly, to interpret the epiphany-like miracles promised by Theudas and the

Egyptian in such a way that they begin to seem like signs. Thus, for example, he suggests that the phrase "signs of freedom" in *War* 2.259 means "miracles indicating the liberation *and even bringing it about.*"[62] Again, explaining the expressions "signs of freedom" and "signs of salvation," he writes: "The marvelous deeds point to the salvation of God's people, which is at hand. To the Jewish prophets of the first century A.D., *they were even more than signs.* We have to ask whether they understood them to be *the first step toward a revolutionary event and freedom.*"[63] Similarly, he argues that the miracles promised by Theudas and the Egyptian were both signs pointing forward to liberation and acts of liberation themselves.[64]

Betz is here blurring the distinction between signs and epiphanies to which he himself has drawn attention, but the distinction is a real and important one and should be preserved. It seems that, in Josephus' own terms, there was an important difference between Theudas and the Egyptian, on the one hand, and the others: the prophets who promised signs announced the coming liberation and performed miracles to confirm the truth of their message; Theudas and the Egyptian promised to bring the liberation itself. It is of some interest to note, in this connection, that it is only in the case of Theudas and the Egyptian that Josephus reports a direct claim to be a prophet. In addition, only these two, of all the prophets considered in this chapter, indisputably modeled themselves on heroic figures from the past.

2. In the account in the *War* of the unnamed figures under Felix, it is said that they promised their followers that God would show them signs of deliverance (2.259), while the *Antiquities* reports that they promised that they themselves would perform marvels and signs. It would appear that Josephus considered it one and the same thing for a prophet to perform an authenticating miracle and for God to perform such a miracle through the prophet.[65] A clear illustration of this is to be found in the narrative about Isaiah and King Hezekiah considered above: Hezekiah asks *Isaiah* to perform a miracle to confirm the truth of his message, but the prophet "exhorted *God* to show this sign to the king" (*Ant.* 10.28–29, emphasis mine).

3. A problem may be posed by the use of the compound phrases τέρατα καὶ σημεῖα in the account in the *Antiquities* of the unnamed figures under Felix (20.168), and σημεῖα καὶ φάσματα in the account concerning Jonathan the Sicarius (*War* 7.438). Josephus does not elsewhere use the words τέρας and φάσμα to refer to authenticating signs of the sort I have been discussing. I am not sure how significant this is. He does not use either term very frequently: apart from the above passages, φάσμα occurs just once in the whole of Josephus' writings (*War* 6.297), and τέρας only eleven times.[66] With one exception (τέρας in *Ant.* 4.291), all these occurrences refer to omens or portents of the sort considered on pages 123–25. It may be worth pointing out that omens and authenticat-

ing signs, as Josephus understood them, are in many ways similar to one another, the main difference being that signs are produced or predicted by someone, whereas omens occur spontaneously and without warning. Still, it must be admitted that it is unusual for Josephus to use the terms τέρας and φάσμα to designate authenticating signs, as he apparently does in *War* 7.438 and *Antiquities* 20.168.

4. I noted above that the miracles promised by the unnamed figures under Felix are described by Josephus as marvels and signs that would be wrought in accordance with God's "plan" or "providence" (πρόνοια, *Ant.* 20.168). Authenticating signs are also connected with πρόνοια in *Antiquities* 2.286, in the scene describing Moses' conflict with the Egyptian magicians. Josephus evidently believed that authenticating miracles performed by prophets were expressions of God's providence in much the same way that omens and portents were: through such signs, omens, and portents, God revealed his will and intentions to his faithful people.

Characteristic Features of the Sign Prophet as a Type

Let us return to the list of features common to all the sign prophets (given in an abbreviated form in the introduction to this chapter) and consider each item in greater detail.

1. The sign prophets were all leaders of sizable popular movements. The word "sizable" is deliberately vague. Josephus ordinarily describes these groups using general terms for "crowd" (notably πλῆθος, ὄχλος, and δῆμος) that do not indicate numbers very precisely. Occasionally, he gives figures: in *Life* 424 he says that two thousand of Jonathan's followers were killed by the Romans, and he states that the prophet of 70 C.E. had a following of six thousand (*War* 6.283). It is hard to know how accurate these numbers are. In the case of the Egyptian, Josephus gives contradictory figures: according to the *War*, he had thirty thousand followers (2.261), while the *Antiquities* suggests a figure around six hundred (20.171). No direct indication is given of the size of the other movements. The book of Acts, as noted, states that Theudas had a following of around four hundred (5.36) and that the Egyptian led four thousand people into the desert (21.38).

It might be possible to compare the size of the Roman forces sent out against the various groups and thus arrive at an estimate of their relative size, but there are difficulties here as well. The terminology that Josephus uses to describe Roman military contingents, like his terminology for crowds, is usually quite vague as far as numbers are concerned. He reports, for example, that Jonathan and his followers were suppressed by "cavalry and infantry" (ἱππεῖς τε καὶ πεζοί, *War* 7.440). Similarly, the account of the unnamed figure under Festus records the dispatching of "a force of cavalry and infantry" (δύναμις ἱππική τε καὶ πεζική, *Ant.*

20.188) against the prophet and his followers. In neither case is there any
indication of the actual size of the force involved. Josephus is somewhat
more precise in his account of Theudas. He states that Theudas and his
followers were attacked by "a squadron of cavalry" (ἴλη ἱππέων, *Ant.*
20.98). The Greek word ἴλη, here translated "squadron," was used by
Josephus as an equivalent of the Latin *ala*, which denoted a military division of five hundred men.[67] Finally, according to the *Antiquities*, "a large
force of cavalry and infantry" (πολλοὶ ἱππεῖς τε καὶ πεζοί) was required
to suppress the Egyptian and his followers (20.171).

It is unclear, in this last instance, whether a larger Roman force was
necessary because of the sheer number of the Egyptian's followers or
because of their military strength. The force sent out against them was not
only large in comparison with those dispatched to deal with the other
groups, it was also more heavily armed, at least according to the account
in the *War*. There it is stated that Felix sent out "the Roman heavily
armed infantry" (τῶν Ῥωμαϊκῶν ὁπλιτῶν, *War* 2.263) against the Egyptian.[68] This may be an example of the militarization described earlier in
this chapter, or it may be an accurate report: we recall that the Egyptian
and his followers were armed. The use of heavily armed troops against
sign prophets and their followers is recorded in only one other instance,
in the account in the *War* of the unnamed figures under Felix (2.260).
This is almost certainly a case of militarization: we saw that this group
probably was not armed.

Josephus' descriptions of the military forces sent out against the sign
prophets by the Romans thus permit only a very rough ranking of the
various movements in terms of the threat they posed, or were believed to
pose, to public order and to the ruling authorities. The Egyptian and his
followers, it seems, presented the most serious threat. Compared with this
group, the other movements appear to have been considered less dangerous. Even a more precise ranking of this sort would not entirely settle the
question of numbers, for it is not clear how degree of threat or perceived
degree of threat and size should be correlated. A small but well-armed
group might have been thought more dangerous than a large, unarmed
one.

Even though it is impossible to be certain about the precise size of the
movements they led, it is clear that the sign prophets should be distinguished from solitary prophetic figures like Jesus son of Ananias and from
popular prophets like John the Baptist and Jesus of Nazareth.[69] Large
numbers of people apparently came to hear John preach and to be bap-
tized by him, and Jesus of Nazareth also seems to have attracted large
crowds with his healing and teaching; but both men had a relatively small
band of actual disciples and followers. The sign prophets, in contrast, led
sizable groups of people from one place to another in anticipation of
some dramatic act of deliverance.[70]

2. The followers of the sign prophets seem to have come mostly from

the common people. I mentioned above that Josephus uses the words πλῆθος, ὄχλος, and δῆμος to describe these groups in a general way; δημοτικός also occurs.[71] Josephus regularly uses all these terms to refer to the common people. In the passages under consideration here, they have the pejorative connotation of "crowd" or "mob," but still indicate that the followers of the sign prophets were drawn from the common people.[72]

Some of the movements I have been considering seem to have arisen in Jerusalem (unnamed figures under Felix; the Egyptian, according to the *Antiquities;* the prophet of 70 c.e.) or in other towns (Jonathan); the rest may have formed in the countryside. There is little evidence that animosity between the rural population and town-dwellers played a significant role in the formation of these groups. It is only in the account of the Egyptian in the *War* that there is even a hint of such animosity. It is explicitly stated there that the Egyptian recruited his followers "in the countryside" (εἰς τὴν χώραν, *War* 2.261), and that "the whole population" of Jerusalem (πᾶς ὁ δῆμος) fought alongside the Romans against him (2.263). The *Antiquities*, as we have seen, states that the Egyptian appeared in Jerusalem and gathered his followers there; nothing is said in this account about any opposition to the group on the part of the Jerusalem δῆμος.[73]

The followers of the sign prophets, then, were mostly ordinary people from the towns and countryside of Jewish Palestine. It is impossible to be much more precise about the social and economic location of these groups. It is also difficult to know what role social and economic factors played in their formation. It is reasonable to suppose that any social or economic pressures bearing on the common people in this period would have contributed to the rise of movements, like those led by the sign prophets, which sought liberation or deliverance from the existing structures of society. But scholars have so far been unable to trace any specific connections between the origin of these movements and particular events or forces in the social-economic realm.[74] In any case, the movements described by Josephus do not seem to have been primarily social-revolutionary movements: they do not appear to have directly attacked those more privileged than themselves, or to have had a practical strategy for effecting a social-economic revolution. It may be, of course, that Josephus has suppressed the social-revolutionary character of these movements, but there is little evidence for this.

There are some indications that there was a more significant element of class conflict in the disturbances created by Jonathan the Sicarius and his followers in Cyrene than in the other cases. As I noted earlier, Josephus specifically states that Jonathan's followers were drawn from the poor (*War* 7.438). They were opposed, in the first instance, not by the Roman authorities, but by the "men of rank" among the Jews (7.439). After his arrest, Jonathan conspired with the Roman governor Catullus against "the wealthiest of the Jews" (τοὺς πλουσιωτάτους τῶν Ἰουδαίων, 7.442), also described as "the well-to-do" (τοὺς εὐπορίᾳ χρημάτων διαφέροντας, 7.445). The fact that Jonathan was a weaver (ὑφάντης, 7.438) by trade may indicate that he himself was from the lower ranks of society, though this is unclear.[75] Without discussing the matter in detail here, I would suggest that the pronounced social-revolutionary character of Jonathan's activities should be connected with his identity as a Sicarius.[76] We should not generalize from his case to the rest of the sign prophets.

3. Josephus describes these figures in negative terms as impostors and deceivers and so forth, but it is clear that they presented themselves as *prophets* and were regarded as prophets by their followers. Josephus says explicitly that both Theudas and the Egyptian claimed to be prophets. Even where such a positive claim is not reported, the negative terminology Josephus uses in connection with these figures sometimes suggests, indirectly, that they claimed to be prophets. This is obviously true of the term "false prophet," which Josephus uses to describe the Egyptian (*War* 2.261) and the man who led six thousand people into the temple (6.285). Similarly, the allegation that the anonymous figures under Felix acted "under the pretense of divine inspiration" (*War* 2.259) suggests that they claimed to be inspired by God. On one occasion, Josephus slips and actually refers to figures of this type as προφῆται—this is in *War* 6.286, in the general comment that he appends to his account of the prophet in the temple in 70 C.E.

Movements led by prophetic figures of this sort should be distinguished from other types of popular movements known to us from this period, particularly from those led by figures who claimed to be kings.[77] The distinction between these two quite different types of movements is blurred when the sign prophets are described as "messianic prophets," as they often are.[78] The term "messianic" is better reserved for those individuals who claimed to be kings or were acclaimed as kings by their followers.[79] Josephus mentions three such individuals from the period immediately following the death of Herod the Great in 4 B.C.E. and two more from the period of the revolt.[80] The leaders of these messianic movements appear to have had a better understanding of the concrete military and political situation in Palestine than most of the sign prophets did and, correspondingly, a more realistic strategy for achieving their aims. They and their followers were armed and organized, and in some cases exercised effective political control over parts of the country for a period of time.[81]

Though the sign prophet and the popular king, or messiah, thus represent distinct types, they overlap to some extent in the person of the Egyptian.[82] He claimed to be a prophet and promised a miracle as did the other sign prophets; unlike the others, however, he also commanded an armed band of followers and declared his intention to "set himself up as ruler of the people" (τοῦ δήμου τυραννεῖν, *War* 2.262).[83]

At least some of the sign prophets appear to have modeled themselves on ancient prophetic figures. This is most obviously true in the cases of Theudas and the Egyptian. I shall return to the question of whether the other sign prophets also modeled themselves on figures from the past and to the question of how such imitation of ancient figures should be understood.

4. The sign prophets are all reported to have called upon their followers to go with them to a particular place. The "wilderness" or "desert" (ἐρημία or ἔρημος) is usually thought to have special significance in this connection. In three accounts (unnamed figures under Felix, unnamed figure under Festus, and Jonathan), the destination of sign prophets and their followers is described as the wilderness or desert without qualification. In addition, Theudas led his followers to the Jordan River, which is partly in the desert, and the Egyptian apparently led his followers on a march through the wilderness before assembling them on the Mount of Olives.

Many scholars have argued that the fact that these prophets led their followers into the wilderness suggests that they were expecting a miraculous new exodus or conquest and saw themselves as prophetic figures like Moses or Joshua.[84] I am not sure that this is correct as a generalization. In the case of Theudas and the Egyptian, the influence of the exodus and conquest traditions is clear. But the other cases featuring a flight into the wilderness are more difficult to interpret. As a religious motif, the wilderness had wider associations than the exodus and conquest events alone. Also, there were apparently many different reasons for making an exodus into the real wilderness: it was the home of bandits, some members of the armed resistance, and quietistic religious ascetics, among others.[85] In any case, not all the sign prophets were active in the wilderness: one, we recall, led his followers to the Temple Mount in Jerusalem.

5. It may be said with a fair degree of confidence that the sign prophets announced to their followers that God was about to act to deliver them. It is extremely difficult, however, to fill in this general statement with any particular content. What did the sign prophets actually expect was going to happen? How did they visualize the event or events that would lead to the freedom or deliverance they promised their followers?

Some cases are clearer than others. The Egyptian, it seems, believed that God would cause the walls of Jerusalem to fall down and expected that he and his followers would then storm the city and drive out the occupying forces; a new regime would be installed, and the Egyptian himself would be ruler. I suggested above that the prophet who led six thousand unarmed people into the temple in the midst of a raging battle must have expected some very dramatic sort of divine intervention, but it is impossible now to determine what form this was expected to take.[86] Theudas promised a new exodus, or perhaps a new conquest, but how, precisely, was this envisaged? Where it is recorded only that sign prophets promised freedom or salvation or rest from troubles, it is virtually impossible to know what they actually expected.

One thing, however, is reasonably certain: the sign prophets believed that the deliverance they expected and announced would be wrought miraculously by God; it would not be achieved through their own efforts alone. On this point, as on others, there are differences of emphasis among the various sign prophets, differences in the relative importance attached to divine intervention and human effort. The Egyptian thought that God would cause the walls of Jerusalem to fall down, but expected that he and his army would take over from there; the account in the *War* (which, again, may be militarizing) suggests that he even had a practical plan about how to proceed (he would use those who rushed in with him as his bodyguard, and so on). The prophet who led the six thousand people into the temple, on the other hand, seems to have expected a more wholly miraculous act of deliverance. The rest of the sign prophets probably fall somewhere in between these two. As far as we can tell, none of them, apart from the Egyptian and possibly Jonathan, was equipped with weapons or with a practical strategy for effecting the deliverance he announced.

This last fact is of fundamental importance, for it indicates that the sign prophets were not political revolutionaries or insurrectionists in the ordinary sense. This is not to say that the movements they led were in no sense political. On the contrary, it is likely that these movements arose at least partly in response to the experience of foreign domination and that all of them, in one way or another, expected and looked forward to the end of Roman rule. In this sense, they were most definitely political movements. By saying that the sign prophets were not political revolutionaries in the ordinary sense, I mean that they did not have a practical plan for ousting the Romans by force; they were "apolitical" in the sense in which Sanders has defined that term to mean "not involving a plan to liberate and restore Israel by defeating the Romans and establishing an autonomous government."[87] To the extent that their vision of the future included an end to Roman rule, they expected that God himself would bring this about.

The distinction between sign prophets and political revolutionaries, then, does not concern their attitude to Roman rule, but rather their practical tactics and degree of realism, that is, the extent to which they thought it necessary to take into account the realities of the political and military situation in Palestine in their day. It should be emphasized that the distinction between the two types of figures in this respect is not an absolute one: the armed revolutionaries believed that God would fight on their behalf and that victory was impossible without his assistance.[88] But unlike the sign prophets, they also believed that a full and considered military effort was necessary on their part. By the standards of the modern world, which does not put much stock in miraculous divine intervention, the rebels were more realistic in their strategy of opposition to Roman rule than were the sign prophets.

It is sometimes difficult to know where to draw the line between these two types of figures. The Egyptian clearly represents a borderline case in which sign prophet is beginning to merge into political revolutionary. Jonathan the Sicarius might also be considered a practical strategist, depending on whether we follow the account in the *War* (miracles and no arms) or in the *Life* (arms and no miracles). It should be noted, however, that Jonathan's actions were directed not against the Romans, but rather against members of the Jewish aristocracy. If he was a practical revolutionary at all, he might be better described as a social revolutionary than as a political revolutionary.

Josephus cannot always be trusted to distinguish sign prophets from insurrectionists. I pointed out earlier that he implies, in the *War*, that the unnamed prophets who were active during the procuratorship of Felix were political revolutionaries; yet I noted that it is implied in the introduction to that account and in the *Antiquities* that they and their followers were unarmed; from this I concluded that they could not have had a practical strategy for effecting a political revolution. Josephus more than once suggests that sign prophets cooperated in a formal way with the armed rebels in pursuit of a common goal. In *War* 6.286 he claims that prophets like the one who led six thousand women and children into the temple were planted among the people by members of the armed resistance in order to slow the rate of desertions. In other passages, he suggests that the sign prophets cooperated with "brigands" in their expeditions. In *War* 2.264–65, for example, immediately following his account of the unnamed figures under Felix and the Egyptian, Josephus writes that the "impostors" (γόητες),[89] acting together with the "brigands" (ληστρικοί),

> incited numbers to revolt, exhorting them to assert their independence, and threatening to kill any who submitted to Roman domination and forcibly to suppress those who voluntarily accepted servitude. Distributing themselves in companies throughout the country, they looted the houses of the wealthy, murdered their owners, and set the villages on fire.

At the beginning of his account of events under Felix in the *Antiquities*, Josephus again associates impostors and brigands:

> For the country was again infested with bands of brigands [ληστηρίων] and impostors [γοήτων ἀνθρώπων] who deceived the mob. Not a day passed, however, but that Felix captured and put to death many of these impostors and brigands. (*Ant.* 20.160–61)

I consider it extremely unlikely that there was cooperation of the sort described in these last two passages between sign prophets and "brig-

ands." Both passages are editorial summaries of events during the reign
of Felix; as with all of Josephus' editorial summaries, they need to be
checked for accuracy against his actual description of events.[90] When
Josephus describes the activities of the sign prophets elsewhere in the *War*
and the *Antiquities*, there is not a hint of any cooperation of this sort.
Moreover, there are disagreements between the editorial summaries in
the *War* and the *Antiquities*. The parallel to *War* 2.264–65 in the *Antiquities* eliminates the reference to impostors and speaks only of brigands
(*Ant.* 20.172); similarly, the parallel to *Antiquities* 20.160–61 in the *War*
speaks only of brigands and does not mention impostors (*War* 2.253).
Josephus has evidently confused various sorts of figures—genuine brigands, Sicarii, and sign prophets—who were, in reality, quite distinct. All
three types are discussed in his two accounts of events under Felix, and
he has lumped them together in the editorial passages he uses to introduce
and conclude those accounts.

The claim made in *War* 6.286—that the armed rebels used sign
prophets to boost morale among the populace—is more difficult to assess.
I suspect that no such formal cooperation existed, and that Josephus is
simply trying to discredit these prophets by suggesting that they were the
stooges of the rebels. On the other hand, the message announced by these
prophets—that God was about to come to the aid of his people—might
have encouraged those active in the armed resistance, and it is not impossible that there was some cooperation between the two groups.

One problem remains. If the movements led by the sign prophets
(with the partial exception of the Egyptian) were apolitical in the sense
defined earlier, then how can the Roman response to them be explained?
In most cases the Romans sent out troops against these prophets and their
followers. There is a contrast here between the sign prophets, on the one
hand, and John the Baptist and Jesus of Nazareth on the other. In the
latter cases, it was thought sufficient simply to arrest and execute the
leader of the movement; no large troops were employed and no effort was
made to round up and kill all the followers.

John and Jesus, I hope it will be agreed, were definitely apolitical by
my definition. The Roman response to the sign prophets might be taken
to indicate that these figures, in contrast to Jesus and John, were genuine
revolutionaries or at least were perceived as such by the Romans. But it
is possible that the Romans responded differently to the sign prophets not
because they believed that they were any more political than John or
Jesus, but because their followers were much more numerous than in the
cases of John and Jesus, and were all gathered together in one spot, making them, at one and the same time, a more obvious threat to public order
and an easier target for military action.

6. In connection with their announcement of imminent divine deliverance, the sign prophets promised their followers that God, or they
themselves, would perform some sort of miracle. We saw above that a

distinction should be made between the kind of miracles promised by Theudas and the Egyptian and the authenticating signs promised by the others. I suggested that this distinction might point to a difference in the kind of claims these prophets made for themselves.

7. There is one further issue I wish to consider before concluding. In the scholarly literature devoted to them, the sign prophets are almost universally described as "eschatological" prophets. I am not sure this is very helpful, or even accurate, as a general description. When scholars say that the sign prophets were eschatological prophets, they usually mean one or both of two things. Sometimes they mean that the sign prophets conformed, or aimed to conform, to a well-defined expectation of an eschatological prophet that, on this view, was held by many Jews in the first century; usually the expectation of a "prophet like Moses" is in mind.[91] Sometimes scholars mean, more generally, that the sign prophets expected the End, or the inauguration of the eschatological age, or the coming of God's kingdom, or some such thing—in any case, some dramatic event or series of events that would result in the radical transformation of current conditions. The first of these views implies the second, but the second can be maintained without the first; that is, it is possible to think that the sign prophets were eschatological prophets in the general sense without thinking that they were acting out the role of a particular End-time prophet.

I shall not discuss the question of whether there was, in the first century C.E., a well-defined expectation of an eschatological prophet like Moses; it is a large and complicated question that would require a full-length study of its own.[92] For the present, I would only emphasize that some of the arguments made in the preceding pages raise doubts about whether all the sign prophets should be connected with the figure of Moses. There is good reason to believe that Theudas modeled his actions on those of Moses. The Egyptian almost certainly modeled himself on Joshua, who was himself understood as a Mosaic figure. The grounds on which scholars connect the other sign prophets with Moses are twofold: first, the flight into the wilderness that features in many of Josephus' reports is generally thought to be modeled on the exodus from Egypt and the wandering in the wilderness; and, second, the signs and wonders promised by the sign prophets are usually associated with the miracles attributed to Moses in the Bible.

I warned earlier, however, against associating the wilderness too narrowly with the exodus and conquest events, since the term had wider symbolic and historical associations. I also demonstrated at some length that Josephus' use of the language of signs and wonders differs in significant ways from the usage of the Bible. He does not use this language to refer to the great miracles of the exodus, but rather to refer to the more modest sort of miracles that were used to authenticate prophetic claims. Moses was believed to have performed such miracles, and so might have served as a model for the sign prophets; but other prophets performed such signs as well (I considered several examples above); there is no reason to connect them exclusively with Moses. Finally, it should be pointed out that at least one of these prophets cannot reasonably be understood as a Moses-type figure: there is no evidence that the prophet who led the six thousand women and children into the temple was imitating Moses.

On the question of whether the sign prophets should be considered eschatological prophets in the more general sense defined above, I shall make two comments. First, the view that the sign prophets were eschatological prophets is sometimes linked with the view that prophecy had ceased in Israel. The argument runs as follows: most Jews in Josephus' day believed that prophecy had ceased absolutely at some time in the past and would only reappear at the End; thus, when Theudas, the Egyptian, and the others claimed to be prophets, they must have been claiming to be eschatological prophets; they were claiming, in effect, that the spirit of prophecy had returned in them.[93]

In chapter 1, I argued that the belief that prophecy had ceased should not be understood as an absolute dogma, but rather as an expression of a vague nostalgia. Most Jews in this period did not think that prophecy had ceased absolutely: there might no longer be anyone as holy or as great as the prophets of the past, but there were still individuals who had the same sorts of experiences and who said and did the same sorts of things. The idea that prophecy would return at the End is also, it seems to me, an expression of nostalgia: when the End comes and God truly reigns over his people, then great prophets like the ones who lived in the past will once again appear, or, alternatively, we shall all be like the great prophets of old. This does not imply that it was impossible that any prophets would appear in the meantime.

If all of this is correct, then there is no reason to conclude automatically from the fact that a person in this period claimed to be a prophet that he was claiming to be an, or the, eschatological prophet. We may, of course, conclude on other grounds that the sign prophets should be understood as eschatological figures, but the fact that they claimed to be prophets is not, in itself, sufficient proof of this.

Second, before we can confidently label the sign prophets "eschatological," we need to know much more than we do about how they envisaged the event or events that would lead to the freedom or deliverance they promised their followers, and, most importantly, what they thought things would be like afterward. The term "eschatological" is used by scholars in a very imprecise way to describe a whole range of hopes for the future. It seems to me, however, that it is best reserved for events that were expected to result in the radical transformation of conditions as they existed. I realize that this still leaves the problem of defining what "radical transformation" means; it may be preferable to do away with the term "eschatological" altogether and try to define the whole range of future expectations in all their complexity.

In most cases, we know almost nothing about exactly what the sign prophets thought was going to happen when God acted to deliver them, and even less about what they thought things would be like afterward.[94] In the one case where we can make a good guess—that of the Egyptian— the transformation that was expected as a result of God's intervention does not seem very radical: instead of the Romans ruling in Jerusalem, the Egyptian would rule there; there is no indication that anything else was expected to change. I do not think that it is very helpful to label such an expectation "eschatological."

As we have seen, the Egyptian is in some ways an unrepresentative sign prophet. I am prepared, indeed eager, to believe that the other sign prophets had more radical expectations, but there is no conclusive evidence that they did. For this reason, I am hesitant to describe them as eschatological prophets as others have done in the past.

Conclusion: Josephus and the Sign Prophets

Finally, let us consider the question of why Josephus characterizes the sign prophets in the particular way that he does. In addition to calling them "false prophets," he also describes them as "impostors" and "deceivers."[95] The Greek word I have been translating as "impostor" is γόης; the English word "deceiver" usually corresponds to some form of the Greek verb ἀπατάω.[96] The meaning of ἀπατάω is fairly clear, but ψευδοπροφήτης and γόης require some comment.

As is well known, there is no noun for "false prophet" in the Hebrew Bible. The Greek word ψευδοπροφήτης appears for the first time in the LXX, where it is used almost exclusively to refer to the prophetic opponents of Jeremiah.[97] Josephus uses ψευδοπροφήτης in the *Antiquities* to refer to the prophets of Baal,[98] and similarly to describe a group of figures associated with the illegitimate cult center at Bethel.[99] He also calls the old prophet from Bethel mentioned in 1 Kings 13 a false prophet, as we saw earlier.[100] Two other uses of ψευδοπροφήτης in the *Antiquities* come closer to the meaning of the term in Josephus' reports concerning the sign prophets: Zedekiah and the four hundred other prophets who promised victory to King Ahab (1 Kgs. 22) are called ψευδοπροφῆται (*Ant.* 8.402, 406, 409), as are the opponents of the prophet Jeremiah (10.104, 111). In these passages, the label "false prophet" is applied to those who predicted victory in war when in fact, as events confirmed, God had decided to hand his people over to their enemies.

Γόης can mean "magician" or, more generally, "impostor" or "deceiver."[101] These meanings coalesce when the term is used to describe figures like the sign prophets, who announced what God was intending to do and promised to perform miracles to verify their claim to speak for God. We have seen that it is a characteristic feature of such miracles that they are ambiguous and not self-authenticating. They may be accepted as confirmation that the person who performs them is God's agent or be rejected as the sort of tricks that a magician could perform. In Josephus' version of the confrontation between Moses and the Egyptian magicians, Moses protests that his miracles do not proceed from "witchcraft" (γοητεία) or "deception" (πλάνη), but rather from God's "providence" (πρόνοια) and "power" (δύναμις, *Ant.* 2.286). Prophetic signs could be interpreted in either way.[102]

When Josephus calls the sign prophets γόητες, he is implying that they were not really God's messengers, but impostors in the role: the message they proclaimed was of their own devising and did not come from God; the miracles they performed or promised to perform were not genuine prophetic signs, but magical tricks intended to deceive.[103] The message that these prophets proclaimed, we recall, was that God was about to act to deliver his people in some miraculous way. One aspect, at least, of this deliverance would be liberation from Roman rule.

Josephus' rejection of the sign prophets as false prophets, impostors, and deceivers must be understood in connection with his own theological interpretation of the defeat of the Jews by the Romans and the destruction of Jerusalem and the temple. As we saw in chapter 2, he seeks to explain these events, at the religious level, by asserting that God himself, the God of the Jews, had decreed that the Romans should rule the world; God had gone over to the Roman side and was using the Romans to punish his sinful people. On this view, it was not God's intention to deliver the Jews from Roman rule, as the sign prophets believed, but rather that Roman rule should continue, and that the Jews should submit to it. From Josephus' point of view, the sign prophets had misunderstood and misrepresented the purposes and intentions of God and thus had deceived their followers and hastened the destruction of Jerusalem.

Josephus portrays himself, in contrast to the sign prophets, as a true prophetic messenger and servant of God. He claims that the understanding of God's purposes that has just been described was divulged to him in a moment of inspired insight in the cave at Jotapata, when he was trying to decide whether to commit suicide or surrender to the Romans. Later, while walking around the walls of Jerusalem, attempting to persuade the Jews inside to surrender, he expressly compares himself with the prophet Jeremiah. Like Jeremiah, Josephus is implying, he preached an unpopular message of submission to foreign rule and was abused and maligned by his own people. And like Jeremiah, he too had to contend with deceivers and false prophets who promised the people that God would deliver them.

5

Other Prophetic Figures

This chapter examines the remaining accounts in Josephus' writings concerning prophetic figures from the late Second Temple period. In addition to Jesus son of Ananias, whom I considered briefly in chapter 1, these figures include Onias, who was renowned for the effectiveness of his prayers; the Pharisees Pollion and Samaias; and some unnamed pharisaic prophets from the time of Herod the Great. For the most part, Josephus' reports provide only sparse information about the prophetic activities of these individuals, and they are surveyed here largely for the sake of completeness.

Onias (*Antiquities* 14.22–24)

In *Antiquities* 14.22–24 Josephus describes an incident involving a Jew named Onias, known from rabbinic literature as Honi. The earliest rabbinic traditions about Honi describe how he once ended a serious drought by praying to God in a distinctive and insistent manner.[1] Josephus was evidently familiar with these or similar traditions, for he reports that Onias "had once in a rainless period prayed to God to end the drought, and God had heard his prayer and sent rain" (*Ant.* 14.22). He says no more about this feat, however, and the remainder of his account concerns another incident, which took place in Jerusalem sometime close to Passover in the year 65 B.C.E.[2]

The Hasmonean brothers Hyrcanus II and Aristobulus II were, at that time, at war with one another. Hyrcanus had allied himself (through the agency of Antipater, father of Herod the Great) with the Arab king Aretas; their combined troops, along with the citizens of Jerusalem (ὁ δῆμος, *Ant.* 14.20), were besieging Aristobulus, who had sought refuge with the priests inside the temple. According to Josephus, Onias "hid himself when he saw that the civil war continued to rage" (14.22). But Hyrcanus' men sought him out and brought him to their camp, where he was asked to

145

place a curse on Aristobulus and his supporters. Onias made excuses and refused to grant their request, but was eventually "forced to speak by the mob" (14.23). He stood up and offered the following prayer: "O God, king of the universe, since these men standing beside me are your people, and those who are besieged are your priests, I beseech you not to hearken to them against these men nor to bring to pass what these men ask you to do to those others" (14.24).[3] Outraged, "the villains among the Jews" stoned Onias to death (14.24).[4]

It is not clear that Onias is best described as a prophetic figure, but he is included here because Josephus' description of him is in some respects reminiscent of his reports concerning the ancient prophets Balaam and Elijah.[5] Like the foreign μάντις Balaam, who was hired by the Midianites to curse the Israelites (*Ant.* 4.104–30), Onias was recruited by Hyrcanus' supporters to curse the enemy before an important battle. Balaam, instead of cursing the Israelites, blessed them and, in addition (according to Josephus), made some significant long-range predictions.[6] Onias refused to curse Aristobulus and his supporters and prayed instead that God might not hearken to the prayers of either side in the civil war. The report that Onias had once prayed to end a drought (14.22) is reminiscent of the prophet Elijah, though neither the Bible nor Josephus' account of Elijah's rain-making activities mentions prayer.[7]

Josephus introduces Onias as "a righteous man and loved by God" (δίκαιος ἀνὴρ καὶ θεοφιλής, 14.22). We saw in chapter 3 that Josephus frequently uses δίκαιος and related terms to refer specifically to those provisions of the Jewish law that govern relations between humans, with εὐσεβής and cognates referring to laws governing relations between humans and God. Δίκαιος-terminology is also sometimes used by Josephus in a more general sense to indicate obedience to the Mosaic law in both its aspects.[8] It is uncertain which sense is intended here.

The description of Onias as "loved" or "favored by God" (θεοφιλής) is of somewhat greater interest.[9] This term is used by Josephus in connection with several figures, some of them prophetic, whose status as individuals loved or favored by God was manifested in some objective way, either *actively* by their ability to perform miracles of some sort or *passively* by the fact that they enjoyed God's special protection. A few examples will illustrate the point. For Josephus, the fact that Solomon's incantations for exorcising demons were still so powerfully effective in his own day was evidence of the king's understanding, wisdom, and virtue, and also proof of "how God loved him" (τὸ θεοφιλές, *Ant.* 8.49).[10] Similarly, Elisha's ability to perform miracles is cited by Josephus as the basis of his reputation as one "loved by God." Josephus' eulogy of Elisha reads:

> Not long afterward the prophet died; he was a man renowned for righteousness [δικαιοσύνη] and one manifestly held in honour by God [φανερῶς σπουδασθεὶς ὑπὸ τοῦ θεοῦ]; for through his prophetic power he performed astounding and marvellous deeds [θαυμαστὰ . . . καὶ παράδοξα . . . ἔργα],

which were held as a glorious memory by the Hebrews. He was then given a magnificent burial, such as it was fitting for one so dear to God [θεοφιλῆ] to receive. (*Ant.* 9.182)[11]

On the more passive side, God's miraculous deliverance of Daniel's companions from the fiery furnace is said to have persuaded Nebuchadnezzar that they were "righteous and loved by God" (δικαίους καὶ θεοφιλεῖς, *Ant.* 10.215).[12] Similarly, it was probably Daniel's miraculous deliverance from the lions' den that provided the basis for his reputation as a man "loved by God" (θεοφιλής, *Ant.* 10.264).[13]

In the passages cited here, Elisha and the companions of Daniel, like Onias, are described as both "righteous" and "loved by God." In both cases, the description is Josephus' own, unparalleled in scripture. It is not clear just how Josephus understood the relationship between being righteous—that is, obeying the law—and being loved or specially favored by God. The most natural assumption is that he thought that certain individuals were loved by God *because* they were righteous. This is supported, for example, by *Antiquities* 6.294, which states that the prophet Samuel was "a just man [ἀνὴρ δίκαιος] and of a kindly nature and *for that reason* [διὰ τοῦτο] very dear to God [μάλιστα φίλος τῷ θεῷ]."[14] The relationship between the two attributes is, however, more complicated than this, for not every righteous person in Josephus is also said to be loved by God. It is also clear that being loved or specially favored by God did not ensure that one would behave righteously: Josephus notes that Solomon "abandoned the observance of his fathers' customs" even though he had been "the most illustrious of all kings and most beloved by God [θεοφιλέστατος]" (*Ant.* 8.190).

In the case of Onias, his status as one loved by God was apparently manifested in an active way by the nearly automatic efficacy of his prayers: when he prayed, God listened and responded. This had been true in the case of his prayers for rain, and Hyrcanus' supporters evidently supposed that it would be equally true if he were to curse their enemies: they asked Onias to curse Aristobulus and his supporters "just as he had, by his prayers, put an end to the rainless period" (*Ant.* 14.22). The fact that Hyrcanus' men sought out Onias suggests that he had a well-established reputation as an individual whose prayers were particularly effective. As we have seen, Onias was reportedly unwilling to cooperate in this instance: he hid himself at first and, when he was forcibly brought to Hyrcanus' camp, he refused to curse Aristobulus. He seems to have objected especially to civil war, a sentiment shared by Josephus.

We learn nothing else of importance about Onias from Josephus' brief account. There is no indication of what his social position was or even where he was from. The incident recorded in *Antiquities* 14.22–24 took place in Jerusalem, but Onias may have come to the city from elsewhere as a pilgrim to the Passover festival.[15]

Prophetic Figures Among the Pharisees

These figures include Pollion and Samaias and some unnamed Pharisees active in the court of Herod the Great.

Pollion and Samaias
(Antiquities *14.172–76; 15.3–4, 370*)

The Pharisees Pollion and Samaias are mentioned by Josephus in connection with three events during the final years of Hasmonean rule and the reign of Herod the Great: the so-called trial of Herod before Hyrcanus II in 47 or 46 B.C.E.; the capture of Jerusalem by Herod and Sossius in 37 B.C.E.; and the oath of loyalty administered by Herod around the year 20 B.C.E. There is some confusion in the texts about the identity of the main actor in the first two of these events. It appears that both Pollion and Samaias supported Herod during the final siege of Jerusalem in 37 B.C.E., and that Pollion was the more important of the two figures. *Antiquities* 14.176 mentions only Samaias in connection with the siege, but 15.3 states that both Pollion and Samaias were involved and, furthermore, identifies Samaias as a "disciple" (μαθητής) of Pollion. That Pollion played the leading role during the siege would seem to be confirmed by *Antiquities* 15.370, which explains that Pollion and Samaias and their disciples were excused from taking the oath of loyalty in 20 B.C.E. "on Pollion's account." There is less certainty about which of the two figures was involved in Herod's trial. According to *Antiquities* 14.172–76, it was Samaias; according to 15.4, Pollion.[16] I see no way to decide the question of identity in this case, and so I shall refer to the Pharisee who played a part in the trial of Herod as Pollion/Samaias. The prediction reportedly made by this figure during the trial is the only prophetic element in Josephus' accounts concerning Pollion and Samaias, but it is worth surveying all the narratives briefly.

There are two accounts of the trial of Herod in Josephus, one in *War* 1.208–15 and the other in *Antiquities* 14.163–84. They agree, in general terms, on the events that prompted Hyrcanus to summon Herod to trial. In the summer of 47 B.C.E., Hyrcanus and Antipater, Herod's father, were rewarded by Caesar for their assistance in a military campaign in Egypt earlier that year. Among other benefits, Hyrcanus was confirmed as high priest and ethnarch of the Jews, while Antipater was appointed procurator (ἐπίτροπος) of Judaea.[17] Antipater, in turn, nominated his sons Phasael and Herod as governors (στρατηγοί) of Jerusalem and Galilee, respectively. Soon after taking up office, Herod captured and executed the "brigand-chief" (ἀρχιλῃστής) Ezekias and many of his followers (*War* 1.204; *Ant.* 14.158–59). This greatly increased Herod's popularity among the Syrian inhabitants of the region (*War* 1.205; *Ant.* 14.160). At the same time, Antipater and Phasael were also growing in power and influence (*War* 1.206–7; *Ant.* 14.161–62).

Hyrcanus became alarmed, fearing that Antipater and his sons would make a bid for power.[18] His fears were heightened by a group of advisers[19] who urged him, in particular, to call Herod to account for his actions, arguing that his execution of Ezekias and the other "brigands" had been in violation of Jewish law.[20] Hyrcanus was persuaded and ordered Herod to appear before him. He came, accompanied by a military escort (*War* 1.210; *Ant.* 14.169).

Josephus' two accounts diverge at this point.[21] According to the *War*, Sextus Caesar, the legate of Syria, ordered Hyrcanus to clear Herod of the charges brought against him, and Hyrcanus complied. Josephus explains that Hyrcanus was "inclined to take that course on other grounds, for he loved Herod" (1.211). The *Antiquities* also mentions the order from the Syrian legate and states that Hyrcanus wanted to acquit Herod (14.170). But, according to this account, Herod was required to appear before the Sanhedrin. When he arrived, arrayed like a king and surrounded by his armed men, his would-be accusers were overwhelmed: "When Herod stood in the Sanhedrin with his troops, he overawed them all, and no one of those who had denounced him before his arrival dared to accuse him thereafter; instead there was silence and doubt about what was to be done" (14.171).[22]

At this point Pollion/Samaias stood up and addressed the assembly. He criticized Herod for appearing "clothed in purple, with the hair of his head carefully arranged" rather than "letting his hair grow long and wearing a black garment," as was appropriate to a suppliant for mercy (14.172–73). He accused Herod of "putting his own interests above the law," and of being prepared to "outrage justice" by ordering his troops to kill the members of the Sanhedrin if they condemned him "as the law prescribes" (14.173–74). Pollion/Samaias then turned to upbraid Hyrcanus and the other members of the Sanhedrin for tolerating Herod's behavior. Finally, he predicted that Herod, whom they were prepared to release, would one day punish them all (14.174).

Pollion/Samaias' speech apparently convinced some, for Hyrcanus realized that the other members of the Sanhedrin were "bent on putting Herod to death" and "postponed the trial to another day" (14.177). He then secretly advised Herod to flee the city. Herod escaped to Damascus, apparently before a formal verdict was reached by the Sanhedrin. A later passage, however, states that when Herod was contemplating a war of revenge against Hyrcanus, his father urged him to remember with gratitude his "acquittal" (ἄφεσις, 14.182 = *War* 1.214).

This is all rather confusing, and it is very difficult to know what really happened. The account in the *Antiquities* seems to combine two versions of the story, possibly from different sources.[23] The first agrees with the *War*: the legate of Syria ordered Hyrcanus to acquit Herod; Hyrcanus was inclined to do so on other grounds and complied; later, when Herod was contemplating revenge, his father urged him to remember his acquittal through Hyrcanus' intervention. According to the second version of events, Herod appeared before the Sanhedrin, where Pollion/Samaias spoke against him; when it looked like Herod would be convicted, Hyrcanus postponed the proceedings and advised Herod to flee the city; no formal verdict was reached. Both accounts are plausible, and there is no easy way to decide between them. It must therefore remain uncertain whether Pollion/Samaias ever really made the prediction attributed to him in *Antiquities* 14.174 and 15.4. But even if these passages do not describe a historical event, they may still tell us something about prophecy among the Pharisees, or at the very least about Josephus' (or his source's) views on the subject. I shall return to the topic shortly.

The prediction attributed to Pollion/Samaias was fulfilled after Herod and his Roman ally Sossius captured Jerusalem in 37 B.C.E. At that time, Herod rewarded those who had supported his cause and began to track down and execute all those who had opposed him. Included among the latter group were Hyrcanus II and the other members of the Sanhedrin who had (according to the account in *Ant.* 14) brought him to trial some ten years earlier. According to *Antiquities* 14.175–76, Herod decided to spare Pollion/Samaias for two reasons: first, "because of his righteousness" (διὰ τὴν δικαιοσύνην); and, second, "because when the city was . . . besieged by Herod and Sossius, he advised the people to admit Herod." *Antiquities* 15.3 confirms that Pollion and Samaias had urged the Jerusalemites to open the gates to Herod during the siege. It is in this passage, incidentally, that we first learn that Pollion and Samaias were Pharisees.

As I noted briefly in chapter 3, Pollion and Samaias are mentioned again in connection with the oath of loyalty administered by Herod around the year 20 B.C.E. According to *Antiquities* 15.370, Herod tried to persuade these two Pharisees and their disciples to take the oath, but they refused. They were not punished, however, but were "shown consideration on Pollion's account." This appears to be a reference to the support given to Herod by Pollion at the time of the siege.

It is worth commenting on the shifting relationship between Pollion and Samaias and their followers, on the one hand, and Herod the Great. At the trial in 47/46 B.C.E., Pollion/Samaias opposed Herod: he condemned Herod as a lawbreaker and upbraided the other members of the Sanhedrin for not standing up to him and condemning him "as the law prescribes" (14.173). Rather curiously, however, Pollion/Samaias seems to have been remembered chiefly for having predicted that Herod would exact revenge against Hyrcanus and the others. At the time of the final siege of Jerusalem in 37 B.C.E., Pollion and Samaias were on Herod's side. In *Antiquities* 14.176 Josephus suggests that they supported Herod only because they believed that his rule was to be endured as a punishment for sin. This sounds like grudging support at best until we remember that it was also Josephus' attitude to Roman rule, though he also believed, more positively, that God or τύχη had brought the Romans to power.[24] We may take it that Pollion and Samaias actively supported Herod at the time of the siege: they urged the inhabitants of Jerusalem to admit him to the city and were "especially honoured" by Herod in return (15.3).

This shift in attitude on the part of Pollion and Samaias and their followers, from a position critical of Herod to one supportive of him, may at first seem surprising, but can easily be explained if events on the larger political stage are taken into account. Throughout the long civil war between Hyrcanus II, on the one hand, and Aristobulus II and his sons, the Pharisees appear to have sided with Hyrcanus.[25] Antipater and his sons Phasael and Herod also supported Hyrcanus in the beginning. There was, however, a period of rivalry between Hyrcanus and the Herodian family beginning in the summer of 47 B.C.E., after Antipater's position was strengthened by the honors paid him by Caesar. As we have seen, Herod's trial fits precisely into this period. It is perfectly understandable why a pharisaic supporter of Hyrcanus would have opposed Herod and the rest of his family at this juncture: it looked as though they were about to take power. The situation changed dramatically in 40 B.C.E., when Antigonus, the son of Aristobulus II, allied himself with the Parthians and attacked Jerusalem. Hyrcanus and Herod's brother Phasael were taken prisoner. Hyrcanus was mutilated to disqualify him from the office of high priest, and Phasael committed suicide. Herod, who had fled to Rome to ask for support against Antigonus, was appointed king of Judaea and returned to claim his kingdom. At the time of the siege of Jerusalem in 37 B.C.E., then, Herod was fighting on Hyrcanus' side, against their mutual enemy Antigonus. It is easy to see why Pollion and Samaias and the other Pharisees would have supported Herod in these changed circumstances.

In later years, the relationship between Herod and the Pharisees once again became strained. As the king consolidated his power and gradually eliminated his real and imagined opponents (including, in 30 B.C.E., Hyrcanus II), the Pharisees seem to have become increasingly disenchanted with him. By the time of the oath of loyalty in 20 B.C.E., they were critical enough of Herod to refuse to take the oath, but still highly enough regarded to be excused. We shall see in the next section that at least some Pharisees were more actively opposed to Herod by 7 B.C.E.

The only prophetic element in all of this is the prediction to the Sanhedrin attributed to Pollion/Samaias: "Be assured, however, that God is great, and this man [Herod], whom you now wish to release for Hyrcanus' sake, will one day punish you and the king as well" (*Ant.* 14.174). Josephus remarks that Pollion/Samaias "was not mistaken in anything that he said. For when Herod assumed royal power, he killed Hyrcanus and all the other members of the Sanhedrin with the exception of [Pollion/]Samaias" (14.175). The account in *Antiquities* 15.4 also refers to this prediction and makes it clear that it was, in Josephus' view, more than just a politically astute observation: "This same Pollion[/Samaias] had once, when Herod was on trial for his life, reproachfully foretold to Hyrcanus and the judges that if Herod's life were spared, he would one day persecute them all. And in time this turned out to be so, for God fulfilled his words [τοῦ θεοῦ τοὺς λόγους αὐτοῦ τελειώσαντος]."

Josephus provides no more information about this prophecy. In light of the connection he draws, when writing about the Essenes, between strict observance of the law and the ability to predict the future, it is worth noting the prevalence of δίκαιος-terminology in the accounts concerning Pollion/Samaias. In the trial scene, he is introduced as "an upright man [δίκαιος ἀνήρ] and for that reason superior to fear" (14.172). In his speech to the Sanhedrin, he criticizes Herod for breaking the law and outraging justice. According to *Antiquities* 14.176, Herod refrained from punishing Pollion/Samaias after the siege partly "because of his righteousness" (διὰ τὴν δικαιοσύνην). There is no explicit indication of this, but Josephus may have thought there was some connection between Pollion/Samaias' devotion to the law and his ability to predict the future.

Nothing is said directly about the social position of Pollion and Samaias, but they appear to be residents of Jerusalem and fairly prominent members of the community. Pollion/Samaias is depicted as a member of the Sanhedrin convened by Hyrcanus, and both Pharisees were in a position to influence the Jerusalemites to open the gates to Herod at the time of the siege. Many attempts have been made to identify Pollion and Samaias with figures mentioned in rabbinic literature, but no agreement has been reached on the matter.[26]

Pharisaic Intrigues in the Court of Herod the Great (Antiquities 17.41–45)

War 1.567–70 and the parallel in *Antiquities* 17.32–45 describe a secret plot against Herod the Great from the period near the end of his life, probably 7 or 6 B.C.E.[27] The plot involved Herod's eldest son Antipater, Herod's brother Pheroras, and a group of four women: Pheroras' wife (whose own name is never given), her mother and sister, and Antipater's mother. According to the account in the *Antiquities*, the Pharisees were also involved:[28]

> There was also a certain group of Jews priding itself on its strict observance of ancestral custom and claiming to observe laws in which the Deity takes pleasure; by these men the women of the court were ruled. Called Pharisees, they were capable of helping the king greatly because of their foresight [βασιλεῖ δυνάμενοι μάλιστα πράσσειν προμηθεῖς], and yet they were obviously prepared to combat and injure him. (17.41)[29]

As examples of the Pharisees' tendency to combat and injure Herod, Josephus (or his source) refers to several separate, but apparently related, incidents (17.42–45). The account he provides is slightly confusing, and I shall begin by trying simply to unravel the course of events. I shall then ask what the present account contributes to our knowledge of prophecy among the Pharisees.

According to *Antiquities* 17.42, on one occasion when the Jews were required to swear an oath of loyalty to Caesar and to Herod, the Pharisees refused to do so. Herod punished them with a fine, which was paid on their behalf by his brother Pheroras' wife. It is uncertain whether the oath of loyalty mentioned here should be identified with the one referred to in *Antiquities* 15.368–71, which I considered briefly in the preceding section and in chapter 3. That oath was administered around the year 20 B.C.E. Because the oath referred to in *Antiquities* 17.42 is closely connected by the author of the passage with the court intrigues of 7/6 B.C.E., it is most natural (though not necessary) to suppose that it occurred around the same time. There are further discrepancies between the two accounts: *Antiquities* 15.368 does not mention a pledge of loyalty to Caesar, while 17.42 does; 15.370 refers specifically to "Pollion the Pharisee and Samaias and most of their disciples," while 17.42 refers to the Pharisees as a whole ("over six thousand in number"); and, finally, 15.370–71 suggests that Pollion and Samaias and their disciples were excused from taking the oath, while 17.42 states that the Pharisees refused to swear the oath and were punished with a fine.[30] In spite of these discrepancies, I am inclined to think that *Antiquities* 17.42 is a flashback to the earlier oath referred to in 15.368–71, perhaps from a different source.[31] It is possible, however, that the two accounts refer to two different oaths, one imposed around 20 B.C.E. and the other closer to 7/6 B.C.E.

Fortunately, we do not need to decide the matter one way or the other. Though the account of the Pharisees' refusal to swear the oath of loyalty in *Antiquities* 17.42 provides an example of their tendency to combat and injure Herod, it serves chiefly to introduce the report of a second incident, which is of greater interest to us and which was almost certainly connected with the intrigues of 7/6 B.C.E. According to *Antiquities* 17.43, the Pharisees repaid Pheroras' wife for her (past or recent) support by making a prediction:

> In return for her friendliness they foretold [προΰλεγον]—for they were believed to have foreknowledge of things through God's appearances to them [πρόγνωσιν δὲ ἐπεπίστευντο ἐπιφοιτήσει τοῦ θεοῦ]—that by God's decree Herod's throne would be taken from him, both from himself and his descendants, and the royal power would fall to her and Pheroras and to any children that they might have.

This appears to be a straightforward prediction that political power would be transferred from Herod and his descendants to Pheroras and his descendants, that is, from one branch of the Herodian family to another. The implication of the passage, in its present narrative context, is that it was at least partly because of this prediction that Pheroras and his wife

became involved in the plot against Herod. The remark that the royal
power would be transferred to Pheroras and his descendants "by God's
decree" (ὑπὸ θεοῦ ἐψηφισμένης) recalls the view that it was the God of
the Jews who determined who would rule the world and for how long.[32] I
shall return below to the general statement that the Pharisees possessed
"foreknowledge" through "God's appearances to them."

Herod's sister Salome learned of the Pharisees' prediction to Pheroras' wife and reported it to her brother. She also informed him "that the
Pharisees had corrupted some of the people at court" (17.44). Among
those corrupted by the Pharisees, apparently, were a eunuch named
Bagoas, another individual named Karos, and some unnamed members
of Herod's household. Herod reacted swiftly:

> And the king put to death those of the Pharisees who were most to blame
> and the eunuch Bagoas and a certain Karos, who was outstanding among
> his contemporaries for his surpassing beauty and was loved by the king. He
> also killed all those of his [own] household who approved of what the Phari-
> see [ὁ Φαρισαῖος] said. (17.44)

The reference to "the Pharisee" in the singular in the last line is puzzling:
it appears to be either a collective reference to the whole group of Pharisees involved in the plot or a reference to an otherwise unmentioned
leader.[33] Nothing more is said about Karos and his role in the events of
7/6 B.C.E., but the following information is given about the eunuch
Bagoas:

> Now Bagoas had been carried away by them [the Pharisees], being led to
> believe that he would be named father and benefactor of him who, accord-
> ing to a prediction [προρρήσει], would be appointed king. For all things [τὰ
> πάντα] would be in the hands of that one, and he would grant Bagoas the
> ability to marry and beget children of his own. (17.45)[34]

Wikgren understates the case when he writes, in the note to the LCL
translation, that the meaning of this passage is "uncertain."[35] In contrast
to the prediction to Pheroras' wife, this does not appear to be an ordinary
political prediction. It is not clear just what Bagoas was expecting: he is
said, rather confusingly, to have believed that he would be named the
father of a king who would then (after the fact, as it were) give him the
power to conceive children of his own; perhaps the emphasis should be
placed on "would be *named* father." It is clear, however, that the king
expected by Bagoas was no ordinary king: he would have "all things" in
his power and would be able to restore the procreative power of a eunuch.
This seems to imply a radical transformation of reality, and thus qualifies
as an eschatological prediction on the basis of the criterion proposed in
chapter 4. We know nothing, however, of the details of what was
expected. Some commentators have seen a connection between the pre-

diction to Bagoas and Isaiah 56.3–5, but that passage does not seem particularly relevant: it does not promise that the procreative powers of eunuchs will be restored, but rather that God will provide eunuchs with an "everlasting name" that is "better than sons and daughters" (Isa. 56.5). I shall return below to the question of whether Josephus may have some other scriptural passage in mind.

What, if anything, does this tell us about prophecy among the Pharisees? It should be noted, first, that the extended narrative just surveyed is, on the whole, sympathetic to Herod and hostile to the Pharisees. This is one of several features of the passage that have led most commentators to assign it to Herod's courtier and historian, Nicolaus of Damascus.[36] The Pharisees are introduced in *Antiquities* 17.41 as a group of Jews who prided themselves on their strict observance of ancestral custom and "claimed" to observe laws that please God; but the verb in this last expression, προσποιοῦμαι, is probably intended in the negative sense of "falsely claim" or "pretend".[37] The statement that the Pharisees influenced events by controlling "the women of the court" (17.41) is doubtless also meant as an insult. As we saw earlier, the author complains that the Pharisees could have helped Herod but chose instead to combat and injure him (17.41). While *Antiquities* 17.43 states that the Pharisees were believed to possess foreknowledge of the future, the subsequent narrative shows that their predictions to Pheroras' wife and to Bagoas were not in fact fulfilled, thereby implying that their reputation as predictors of the future was undeserved.[38] At the most obvious level, the two predictions appear to be contradictory, the first promising royal power to Pheroras and his descendants, and the second predicting the advent of an eschatological king. This reinforces the impression that the Pharisees were simply interested in stirring up trouble against Herod and were willing to say anything to anybody to achieve this end.

Whatever their motives, it is clear that the Pharisees referred to in this passage claimed to be able to predict the future. We have seen that one of the predictions attributed to them had to do with ordinary political affairs, while the other concerned eschatological events. Nothing is said directly about how the Pharisees claimed to obtain their information about the future, but two possible clues are provided. First, in connection with their prediction to Pheroras' wife, Josephus (or his source) makes the general remark that the Pharisees were believed to have "foreknowledge of things *through God's appearances to them*" (πρόγνωσιν . . . ἐπιφοιτήσει τοῦ θεοῦ, *Ant.* 17.43, emphasis mine).[39] It is not immediately clear what this means. Josephus speaks most directly of God "appearing" to humans in *dreams*.[40] The closest single parallel to the language used of the Pharisees in the passage just quoted is from Josephus' account concerning John Hyrcanus. In *Antiquities* 13.299, a passage considered in chapter 1, Josephus states that Hyrcanus had been deemed worthy of "three of the greatest privileges, the rule of the nation, the office of high-priest, and the gift of prophecy [προφητεία]."[41] He goes on to explain what he means by "the gift of prophecy":

> [F]or the Deity was with him [συνῆν γὰρ αὐτῷ τὸ θεῖον], and gave him foreknowledge of the future [τὴν τῶν μελλόντων πρόγνωσιν], both the ability to foresee the future and to foretell it; so, for example, he foretold of his two elder sons that they would not remain masters of the state. (13.300)[42]

We later learn that John's prediction about his two elder sons was based on a dream:

> Of all his sons Hyrcanus loved best the two elder ones, Antigonus and Aristobulus; and once *when God appeared to him in his sleep* [φανέντα κατὰ τοὺς ὕπνους αὐτῷ τὸν θεὸν], he asked Him which of his sons was destined to be his successor. And when God showed him the features of Alexander, he was grieved that this one should be the heir of all his possessions. (13.322)[43]

In this case, "foreknowledge [πρόγνωσις] of the future" (13.299) is said to have been communicated through a dream in which God "appeared" (φανέντα, 13.322) to the dreamer. This language is quite close to that used in *Antiquities* 17.43, which states that the Pharisees were believed to have "foreknowledge of things through God's appearances to them" (πρόγνωσιν ... ἐπιφοιτήσει τοῦ θεοῦ). It is possible, then, that the appearances of God through which the Pharisees claimed to obtain information about the future occurred in dreams.

There is one possible objection to this proposal: Josephus does not describe any dreams in which *God* appears to the dreamer from the period after Hyrcanus, and it might be suggested that he believed that dreams of this sort belonged to the golden prophetic age in the past and were no longer experienced by people in his own day.[44] But one passage from the *War* suggests that this was not the case. According to *War* 7.349, when Eleazar, the leader of the Sicarii at Masada, was trying to persuade his followers to commit suicide, he compared death to sleep, "in which the soul, undistracted by the body, while enjoying in perfect independence the most delightful repose, holds converse with God [θεῷ δ' ὁμιλοῦσαι] by right of kinship, ranges the universe and foretells many things that are to come." This passage suggests that at least some Jews in Josephus' day believed that it was still possible to "hold converse with God" and learn of the future through dreams.

The second clue provided about the methods used by the Pharisees comes from the account of the prediction to Bagoas. According to Josephus, the Pharisees encouraged Bagoas to believe that he would be named the father and benefactor of the one who would be appointed king "according to a prediction" (προρρήσει, *Ant.* 17.45).[45] It is unclear whether the Pharisees themselves made the prediction about the king or only persuaded Bagoas that it had some significance for him. The word πρόρρησις used here occurs eighteen times in Josephus, sixteen times with the meaning "prediction."[46] A review of some of these passages serves as a reminder that information about the future could, in Josephus' view, be obtained in a variety of ways.[47] In one instance a πρόρρησις is said to have been communicated through a direct oracle from God. According to *Antiquities* 1.257, when Isaac saw that Rebecca, his wife, was "inordinately big with child," he anxiously "consulted God" (ἀνήρετο τὸν θεόν). In response, God "told him" (φράζει) that Rebecca would deliver twins (1.257). Not long after, the twins were born "in accordance with God's prediction" (κατὰ πρόρρησιν τοῦ θεοῦ, 1.258).[48] King Saul, wishing to learn "how matters might turn out for him" (*Ant.* 6.329), sought a "prediction" (πρόρρησις) through prophets and dreams before resorting to the witch of Endor (6.327–36). In the majority of cases, dreams are the source of the predictions that Josephus calls προρρήσεις: sometimes these predictions come through symbolic dreams, and sometimes through message dreams in which God is the messenger.[49] Finally, in two passages πρόρρησις refers to a written prediction contained in scripture. In *War* 7.432 Josephus claims that the building of the Jewish temple at Leontopolis fulfilled the prediction (πρόρρησις) recorded in Isaiah 19.19–22. According to *Antiquities* 4.303, shortly before his death, Moses deposited in the temple "a poem in hexameter verse . . . containing a prediction [πρόρρησις] of future events, in accordance with which all has come and is coming to pass."[50] It is noteworthy that Josephus believed that events in his own day were still unfolding in accordance with Moses' "prediction of future events."

If we can take Josephus' use of πρόρρησις in these passages as a guide (which is not certain because of the source problem in *Ant.* 17.41–45), then the prediction of an eschatological king referred to in *Antiquities* 17.45 may have been made on the basis of a direct divine oracle, a prophetic oracle, a dream, or a prophecy from scripture. It is impossible, without more information, to decide among these alternatives, though my earlier discussion of the mode of God's "appearances" to the Pharisees might incline the choice toward dreams.

If the prediction mentioned in *Antiquities* 17.45 was based on a dream, then it may be significant that the Pharisees are said by Josephus to have a reputation as expert interpreters of the law—in one case (his own), Josephus connects the ability to interpret dreams with knowledge of scripture. If the prediction was based on a scriptural passage, then the Pharisees' interpretive expertise would obviously be relevant. We have also noted that Josephus sometimes relates the ability to predict the future to careful observance of the law. In this connection, it is worth noting that the Pharisees are said by Josephus to have a reputation as both strict interpreters and strict observers of the law.[51]

It is unclear from Josephus' account whether the Pharisees involved in the intrigues of 7/6 B.C.E. were official court figures or not. Sometimes the entire pharisaic party is referred to (for example, in 17.41–42), but the detailed narrative seems to describe the intrigues of a small group of Pharisees with influence in court circles.

Jesus Son of Ananias
(*War* 6.300–309)

Josephus' report concerning Jesus son of Ananias forms part of a list of omens, portents, and prophecies that were believed to have foreshadowed the defeat of the Jews and the destruction of Jerusalem and the temple by the Romans in 70 c.e. (*War* 6.288–315). I have referred to these omens several times in the preceding pages, and it is worth reviewing them now in full: a star resembling a sword appeared over Jerusalem, and a comet was visible for an entire year (6.289); a bright light shone in the temple for half an hour one night during Passover (6.290–91); at the same festival, a cow brought as a sacrifice gave birth to a lamb in the temple court, and the eastern gate of the temple opened of its own accord (6.292–96); a few days later, chariots and armed battalions were seen in the sky (6.296–99); and, at Pentecost, the priests ministering in the temple at night heard a voice say, "We are departing hence" (6.299–300).[52] The report concerning Jesus follows the description of these omens (6.300–309). His appearance and activity are described by Josephus as a portent "even more alarming" than the others (τὸ δὲ τούτων φοβερώτερον, 6.300). The list of omens concludes with the mention of two prophecies, both from "the sacred books" of the Jews.[53] The first predicted that Jerusalem and the sanctuary would be captured whenever the temple should become "four-square" (τετράγωνον); according to Josephus, the rebels fulfilled this condition when they destroyed the Antonia fortress adjacent to the temple (6.311). The second prophecy referred to here is the "ambiguous oracle" predicting that someone from Judaea was about to become ruler of the world (6.312–13); we saw in chapter 2 that Josephus applied this prediction to Vespasian.

A similar, though not identical, list of omens associated with the fall of Jerusalem appears in Tacitus, *Histories* 5.13.[54] The relationship between the two accounts is unclear.[55] The report concerning Jesus is not, however, included in Tacitus' list, and was almost certainly composed by Josephus. He may well have had firsthand knowledge of Jesus and his activities in Jerusalem.

It is important to note the literary context of Josephus' list of omens and portents. In *War* 6.283–84 Josephus reports the death of six thousand Jews who perished in the fire that destroyed the temple in 70 c.e. As we saw in chapter 4, he blames their death on a "false prophet" (ψευδοπροφήτης) who led them into the temple in the expectation that God would there show them "the signs of deliverance" (6.285). Josephus goes on to speak, in more general terms, of the "many prophets" (πολλοί . . . προφῆται) who misled the people at this time by encouraging them "to wait for help from God" (6.286–87). The willingness on the part of so many Jews to trust in the promises of these prophets is contrasted by Josephus with their failure to understand the significance of the omens recorded in 6.288–315:

> Thus it was that the wretched people were deluded at that time by deceivers and those who misrepresented God, while they neither heeded nor believed in the manifest portents that foretold the coming desolation, but, as if thunderstruck and bereft of eyes and mind, disregarded the proclamations of God. (6.288)

He makes a similar comment in 6.310, immediately after his account of Jesus son of Ananias:

> Reflecting on these things, one will find that God cares for human beings, and in all kinds of ways shows His people the way of salvation, while they owe their destruction to folly and calamities of their own choosing.[56]

God, in his providence, had sent the Jews omens and portents warning them of "the coming desolation" (6.288), but they preferred to follow false prophets and deceivers. The omens and portents sent by God, we have seen, included Jesus son of Ananias, who is thus contrasted with the "false prophet" of *War* 6.285 and others like him who, according to Josephus, misrepresented God and misled the people with their promises of deliverance.

Since I reviewed Josephus' report concerning Jesus in chapter 1, only a brief reminder of the course of his prophetic career is necessary here. According to Josephus, Jesus was "an unskilled" or "unlearned peasant" (τῶν ἰδιωτῶν ἄγροικος, *War* 6.300). He came to Jerusalem for the autumn festival of Tabernacles (Sukkoth), probably in the year 62 C.E.[57] At one point during the festival he stood up in the temple and cried out:

> A voice from the east,
> a voice from the west,
> a voice from the four winds;
>
> a voice against Jerusalem and the sanctuary,
> a voice against the bridegroom and the bride,
> a voice against all the people. (6.301)

He repeated his message throughout the festival, and was eventually arrested and punished by the Jewish magistrates of Jerusalem. When their measures had no effect, the magistrates sent him to the procurator Albinus (6.303). There, Jesus was flogged, but still refused to answer questions; instead, he "unceasingly reiterated his dirge over the city" (6.304–5). Albinus concluded from his behavior that Jesus was suffering from "insanity" (μανία) and released him (6.305). From that time on, for seven years and five months, Jesus repeated his lament, until he was struck and killed by a Roman missile during the siege of Jerusalem (6.308–9).

I drew attention in chapter 1 to the compulsive nature of Jesus' behavior. His initial oracle was delivered "suddenly" (ἐξαπίνης, 6.301), and, from that moment on, his concentration on his message was continuous and absolute: he wandered the streets day and night, crying out his oracle of doom; even when severely punished, he did not weep or speak on his own behalf; when released, he repeated his cries for more than seven years, "his voice never flagging nor his strength exhausted" (6.308). During this entire period, according to Josephus,

> he neither approached nor was seen talking to any of the citizens, but daily, like a prayer that he had conned, repeated his lament, "Woe to Jerusalem!" He neither cursed any of those who beat him from day to day, nor blessed those who offered him food: to all men that melancholy presage was his one reply. (6.306–7)

So he continued until the moment of his death.

In my earlier discussion, I compared Jesus' behavior with that of the prophet Jeremiah, but it is evident that there was a difference of degree between the two. Jeremiah repeated his warnings compulsively and was not deterred by punishment or imprisonment; he, too, was deemed insane because of his behavior. But Jeremiah continued to lead a relatively normal life, even functioning as a kind of court adviser to the king. For Jesus, on the other hand, normal life was completely suspended: he lived in the streets, eating whatever was brought to him by sympathizers; he wandered the city day and night, crying out his message of doom, and spoke of nothing else. His obsession was complete.[58]

Jesus' first reported utterance (*War* 6.301, already quoted) takes the form of a prolonged woe or oracle of doom.[59] It is generally thought that Josephus' report preserves the original form of this oracle. It consists of two strophes, each with three lines. The third line of each strophe summarizes and develops the content of the first two lines—a feature usually described as Semitic parallelism.

In the first strophe of the oracle, the origin of the message is described: the voice to which Jesus draws attention comes from the east, from the west, from all four corners of the world. The voice referred to here is sometimes identified with the Bath Qol mentioned in rabbinic literature.[60] In most cases, this "daughter of a voice" functioned as a kind of substitute for the divine voice in a period in which God no longer communicated directly with his people.[61] But, as Aune has shown, in Jewish works from the late Second Temple period, the term "voice" usually refers to direct divine speech—it means "the voice of God." In the Hebrew Bible, this usage is especially common in oracles that announce divine judgment.[62] Aune concludes: "When [Jesus son of Ananias] repeatedly refers to the "voice" coming from all directions (cf. Ps. 29) with negative implications, he is using a well-known, recognizable idiom which refers to the voice of God pronouncing judgment."[63] The voice that Jesus announced was thus not a Bath Qol, but rather the voice of God himself.

The second strophe of the oracle indicates the direction or target of the message: it was directed against Jerusalem and the temple, against the bridegroom and the bride, against all the people. The mention of bridegroom and bride recalls Jeremiah 7.34; 16.9; 25.10; and 33.11. The bridegroom and bride were apparently singled out, in the case of both Jeremiah and Jesus, as those who had most reason to rejoice and be glad. Even the happiest of people, it is implied, will suffer in the coming catastrophe. At other places in Josephus' narrative, Jesus is credited with an abbreviated version of the oracle recorded in *War* 6.301: "Woe to Jerusalem!" (6.304, 306). His last reported utterance parallels his first oracle more closely in terms of content: "Woe once more to the city and to the people and to the temple" (6.309). Though Jesus' oracles warn of a grave threat to Jerusalem, the temple, and the Jews, they do not specify the nature of this threat.[64] Josephus obviously believed that Jesus' ominous predictions had been fulfilled by the events of 70 C.E.

Josephus records a wide range of responses to Jesus. The Jewish magistrates of Jerusalem (οἱ ἄρχοντες, 6.303), also described as "some of the leading citizens" (τῶν . . . ἐπισήμων τινὲς δημοτῶν, 6.302), arrested and punished Jesus. They did so, according to Josephus, because they were "vexed by" or "angry about" (ἀγανακτήσαντες) his predictions (6.302). A more complex rationale for their actions suggests itself when we consider the circumstances in which Jesus first appeared and the political position and role of the Jewish officials.

Jesus came to Jerusalem during the festival of Tabernacles, and it was apparently also during this festival that he was arrested. Near the end of his report about Jesus, Josephus remarks that, throughout his career, "his cries were loudest at the festivals" (6.308). In the politically tense period leading up to the revolt, the great pilgrim festivals in Jerusalem were especially volatile occasions, as numerous reports in Josephus confirm. Hostilities that were normally suppressed were likely to break out at such times, and the smallest incident could quickly escalate into a major disaster. Under Cumanus (procurator from 48 to 52 C.E.), for example, a riot broke out in the temple during the feast of Passover.[65] The disturbance began when a Roman soldier on duty in the temple made an obscene gesture at the crowd. "The whole multitude" (*War* 2.225) called upon Cumanus to punish the offender, and some of the Jews threw stones at the Roman soldiers. Unable to calm the crowd and fearing the outbreak of a serious revolt, Cumanus ordered in reinforcements. When they stormed the temple, the Jews inside panicked, and thousands were killed in the resulting stampede.[66] "Such," Josephus remarks, "were the calamities produced by the indecent behavior of a single soldier" (*Ant.* 20.112). In connection with this incident, he explains that it was standard procedure for the Romans to lay on extra troops during the festivals to prevent a disturbance: "a body of men in arms invariably mounts guard at the feasts, to prevent disorders arising from such a concourse of people."[67]

Though Josephus states in *War* 6.300 that Jesus son of Ananias appeared at a time "when the city was enjoying profound peace and prosperity," we know from his own reports that the procuratorship of Albinus was a period of near anarchy in Jerusalem, when tensions between Romans and Jews, and between pro- and anti-Roman factions among the Jews, were running extremely high.[68] In such circumstances, no one could predict the effect that a prophet of doom might have on the huge crowds that flooded into the city for the festival of Tabernacles. From the point of view of the Jewish magistrates, who were in the difficult position of having to mediate between the Jews and the Romans, it was better to move quickly to eliminate the source of the problem than to risk the outbreak of a serious disturbance.[69]

The procurator Albinus, after questioning Jesus and observing his behavior, concluded that he was harmlessly insane and released him. The Jewish officials were apparently reassured by this decision; they did not attempt to arrest Jesus again. The contrast between Albinus' verdict on Jesus son of Ananias and the verdict of Pontius Pilate on Jesus of Nazareth is worth noting. Jesus of Nazareth was also arrested during a religious festival, and he too had predicted (among other things) the destruction of the temple.[70] But there are three points of contrast to Jesus son of Ananias; Jesus of Nazareth evidently spoke of his own role in the events that he predicted; he had a group of followers; and he performed an action against the temple, albeit a symbolic one. All of this apparently made him more of a threat in the eyes of the Romans. The response of the Romans to Jesus son of Ananias was also markedly different from their response to the sign prophets, who were thought to constitute a genuine threat to public order. Jesus, by contrast, was deemed harmless; he was a nuisance, but nothing more.

The ordinary citizens of Jerusalem were apparently divided in their response to Jesus. *War* 6.307, quoted above, implies that some of them beat him, while others supplied him with food. Horsley has described Jesus as a kind of champion of the cause of the ordinary people against the interests of the ruling classes; he appears to take Jesus' pronouncement against the temple, in particular, as an indication that he opposed the aristocratic leaders of the Jews.[71] But the temple was not—or at least was not only—the symbol of the power of the ruling classes; it was the very center and symbol of Jewish religious life. The prediction of the destruction of the temple implicit in Jesus' oracle of woe would have been resented not only by the members of the Jerusalem aristocracy, but by most Jews.[72] It is also worth noting that Jesus' initial oracle included a pronouncement of doom against "all the people" (τὸν λαὸν πάντα, 6.301). Nothing in the reported utterances of Jesus marks him out as a spokesman for the ordinary people, and Josephus' report shows that reactions to him did not divide along class lines.

The range of responses described by Josephus illustrates what must have been genuine difficulties in assessing the claims of a figure like Jesus. When describing the verdict of the Jewish magistrates on Jesus, Josephus uses the word δαιμόνιος (6.303). It is a nicely ambiguous term: it could be used in connection with spirits of the dead and evil spirits, or in connection with the spirit of God.[73] When Josephus writes that the magistrates concluded that Jesus was "under some supernatural impulse" (δαιμονιώτερον τὸ κίνημα τἀνδρός), he evidently means that they believed that Jesus was possessed. But when he adds his own opinion that this "was indeed the case" (ὅπερ ἦν), he is affirming that Jesus was inspired by God. Albinus, we recall, thought that Jesus was simply insane.

Difficulties of a similar sort are illustrated by the speech of Gamaliel in Acts 5.33–39, though its account of events is confused, as we have seen. Gamaliel advises the members of the Jerusalem council not to act precipitously against Peter and the other Christian apostles. He points to the cases of Theudas and Judas the Galilean as examples. Theudas "claimed to be somebody" and succeeded in gathering a group of followers; "but he was slain and all who followed him were dispersed and came to nothing" (Acts 5.36). Similarly, Judas "also perished, and all who followed him were scattered" (5.37). Gamaliel advises the councilors to wait and see what happens with the Christians: "if this plan or this undertaking is of men, it will fail; but if it is of God, you will not be able to overthrow them" (5.38–39).

It was impossible to determine whether someone who claimed to speak for God really was God's messenger until it was known how things turned out. When composing his report about Jesus son of Ananias, Josephus had the benefit of hindsight. In the year 62 c.e., when Jesus first appeared, Josephus might well have concurred with the Jewish magistrates who judged that Jesus was possessed and sent him to the procurator as a potential troublemaker. But after the defeat of the Jews and the destruction of Jerusalem and the temple, things looked different. Jesus' message of doom, and his claim to speak for God, had, in Josephus' view, been confirmed by the course of events.

Conclusion

The study of Jewish prophecy in the late Second Temple period has been dominated in the past by a particular model of the prophetic office. This model is based on the great classical prophets of the Hebrew Bible and reflects the modern, critical insight that these figures were not primarily predictors of the future, but rather social, moral, and religious reformers, who addressed the situation in their own day and called for radical change.

Some of the figures considered in this study represent, or at least approximate, this model of prophecy. There is, above all, Josephus' portrayal of himself as a new Jeremiah, a prophet-priest who condemned the sins of the rebels, urged them to repent, preached that submission to foreign rule was God's will, and battled against false prophets whose message opposed his own. Jesus son of Ananias may also be viewed as a Jeremiah-type figure in some respects, though I noted some important differences between him and the ancient prophet. Jesus, unlike Jeremiah, was an unskilled peasant with no official role in the political establishment of his day, and his recorded behavior is considerably more compulsive than that attributed to Jeremiah; but the unrelenting message of doom against Jerusalem unites the two figures. The Essene prophet Menahem is also reminiscent of the classical prophets in certain respects. He was remembered, above all, for his prediction that Herod the Great would become king of the Jews; but, according to Josephus, Menahem transcended the role of mere predictor: he also exhorted Herod to practice justice and piety, code words, as we have seen, for the Jewish law in its two aspects.

Theudas and the Egyptian may also be viewed as prophets of a biblical sort, though in their case the model of the prophetic office was provided not by the great classical prophets, but by Moses and Joshua, the leaders at the time of the exodus from Egypt and the entry into the promised land. From Josephus' spare and hostile accounts, we can determine that Theudas, the Egyptian, and the other sign prophets were leaders of large popular movements; that they claimed to be prophets; that they announced to their followers that God was about to act to deliver them in some dramatic way; and that they promised to perform miracles that would either constitute that deliverance itself (in the case of Theudas and the Egyptian) or confirm that they were God's messengers and that what they said was true.

All these figures—Josephus, Jesus son of Ananias, Menahem, and the sign prophets—are recognizably prophetic from the modern-critical point of view. This study of the evidence from Josephus has shown, however, that his definition of prophecy was considerably broader than the modern one. In closing, I want to reemphasize three important features of Josephus' understanding of prophecy that distinguish it from the modern conception: his emphasis on the predictive aspect of prophecy; his special interest in types of prophecy that required technical expertise of one sort or another; and his interest in the connections between prophecy and priesthood.

There is a tendency on the part of modern scholars to distinguish "mere prediction" from "genuine prophecy," but Josephus did not share this view. For him, prophets were, above all, individuals with special insight into the future. The predictions recorded by Josephus vary quite widely in terms of the time-span involved and the scope of the events predicted. At one end of the spectrum are predictions like those attributed to the prophet Daniel, which (according to Josephus) concerned events on the grandest scale (the rise and fall of empires) and in the distant future—some of them still in the future from Josephus' own point of view. At the opposite end of the spectrum are predictions of relatively small-scale events expected in the very near future, like Judas the Essene's prediction of the murder of Antigonus. Predictors of the future in Josephus thus run the gamut from those we would describe as "apocalyptists" to those we might call "seers" or simple "forecasters," but for Josephus, they were all "prophets." He does, to be sure, make some distinctions among these figures. The most important of these derive from his view that the prophets of the past were more glorious than similar figures in his own day. Josephus did not think, for example, that he or other prophets of his day were capable of the kind of grand, distant, and precise predictions made by Daniel. Their abilities were more modest.

When prophecy is so closely identified with prediction of the future, then the criterion for distinguishing between the true and false prophet is a relatively simple one: the true prophet is the one whose predictions come true. It would seem to be primarily on this basis that Josephus makes distinctions among the various popular prophets whose activities he describes: the sign prophets are judged to be false prophets and deceivers because the deliverance they promised their followers did not materialize; Jesus son of Ananias, on the other hand, is considered a true messenger of God because his prediction of destruction was fulfilled when the Romans destroyed Jerusalem and the temple. Similarly, Josephus' high opinion of the Essene prophets Judas, Menahem, and Simon seems to have been based chiefly on their record as accurate predictors. The criterion employed in these cases—the true prophet is the one whose predictions come true—is, of course, especially easy to apply in retrospect, as it usually was by Josephus.

We have seen at several points that predictive prophecy was closely associated by Josephus with God's providential care for his people. Josephus, along with most Jews of his day, believed that God controlled the events of human history in a direct and immediate way, so that everything on earth unfolded in accordance with the divine plan. By revealing his intentions through the prophets, God sought to lead and warn his people and encourage them to follow the path he had chosen for them. The people were, of course, always free to respond as they pleased to God's promptings, and Josephus more than once laments the fact that the Jews failed to respond appropriately.

Josephus was especially interested in varieties of prophecy that required a certain technical expertise. Dream-interpretation was one such enterprise, and one in which Josephus himself claimed extraordinary gifts. We saw in chapter 2 that the claims he makes for himself as an interpreter of dreams put him in a class with Daniel, who was able, through inspiration, to decipher even the most difficult sort of symbolic dreams. Josephus connects his own ability to interpret dreams, in one instance at least, with his knowledge of the prophecies of the sacred books; this knowledge is, in turn, attributed to the special training he received as a priest. Similarly, he claims that it was partly their study of sacred books and sayings of prophets that made the Essenes such successful predictors of the future. Josephus also attributes their success partly to their practice of special purifications and their virtuous mode of life. "Virtue" is defined in this context as the practice of justice and piety, that is, as careful observance of the Jewish law. Josephus' accounts of prophecy among the Pharisees may also hint at a connection between close observance of the law and the ability to predict the future. Finally, according to Josephus, knowledge of the future was, at least in the case of the Essenes, only one part of a wider esoteric knowledge that encompassed everything past, present, and future.

Prophecy and priesthood are linked at numerous points and in various ways by Josephus. We saw, for example, that he was extraordinarily interested in the kind of divination that was performed with the aid of the high-priestly breastplate and regarded such divination as a superior form of prophecy. As I just noted, he connected his own ability to interpret dreams, in one important instance, with his priestly training in scripture. Similarly, he claims that the Essenes' ability to predict the future derived in part from their practice of special purity rites, some of which were distinctively priestly. In the Jeremiah-like speeches he attributes to himself, Josephus emphasizes the importance of the temple and decries its profanation by the rebels.

In addition to being dominated by a particular model of the prophetic office, the study of Jewish prophecy in the late Second Temple period has also been governed by a particular understanding of the status of prophecy in this period. It has usually been thought that most Jews of this time believed that prophecy had ceased completely at some point in the past. In chapter 1, I argued that the belief that prophecy had ceased should not be understood as a hard-and-fast dogma, but rather as one expression of a wider nostalgia for the distant past. As such, it did not rule out the possibility that individuals might still appear who said and did very much the same kinds of things that the ancient prophets had said and done. The differences between ancient and modern prophetic figures were differences of degree, not of kind.

In the introduction I expressed the hope that the results of this investigation might provide a framework for a more comprehensive study of prophecy in the late Second Temple period. The other literary sources for such a study have already been mentioned: they include apocryphal and pseudepigraphical works, rabbinic literature, the Dead Sea Scrolls, and the New Testament, especially the gospels. These sources must be studied individually and on their own terms before a synthesis can be attempted, but this study of the evidence from Josephus provides several starting points for comparative study.

1. Barton's work on postexilic perceptions of prophecy suggests that most Jews in this period shared Josephus' relatively broad understanding of prophecy and his views about the cessation of prophecy. These points must, however, be confirmed and investigated in greater detail. It must be determined, for example, whether Josephus' emphasis on predictive prophecy and his interest in technical varieties of prophecy are truly representative of Jewish views in his day. Similarly, it must be established whether other Jews shared Josephus' interest in priestly varieties of prophecy. If it should turn out that the definition of prophecy varies widely from group to group or source to source, then that phenomenon will have to be explained.

2. We have seen that Josephus was especially interested in prophetic figures from the more literate strata of Palestinian society. The information he provides about prophecy among the Essenes and Pharisees needs to be confirmed and expanded by independent study of the evidence from the Dead Sea Scrolls and rabbinic literature. Josephus' reports about popular prophets are usually (though not always) both brief and hostile. Other sources may provide more information about prophecy among the ordinary people. The gospels may be especially valuable here.

3. Finally, I noted at several points that Josephus does not provide detailed information about the mechanics of prophecy—how prophets were thought to be inspired, how symbolic dreams were interpreted, how sacred books were used to predict the future, and so on. It is to be hoped that other sources might shed greater light on these matters.

Notes

Introduction

1. Important studies that compare Jesus with other Jewish prophets of the period include: Martin Hengel, *The Charismatic Leader and His Followers*, trans. James C. G. Greig, Studies of the New Testament and Its World, vol. 1 (Edinburgh: T. & T. Clark, 1981); Geza Vermes, *Jesus the Jew: A Historian's Reading of the Gospels* (London: Collins, 1973; Philadelphia: Fortress, 1981); P. W. Barnett, "The Jewish Sign Prophets—A.D. 40–70: Their Intentions and Origin," *NTS* 27 (1980–81): 679–97; and E. P. Sanders, *Jesus and Judaism* (London: SCM; Philadelphia: Fortress, 1985). Richard Horsley has written extensively on popular prophecy as part of the historical context of Jesus' ministry; see his "'Like One of the Prophets of Old': Two Types of Popular Prophets at the Time of Jesus," *CBQ* 47 (1985): 435–63 (cited as "Two Types"); "Popular Prophetic Movements at the Time of Jesus: Their Principal Features and Social Origins," *JSNT* 26 (1986): 3–27; and (with John Hanson) *Bandits, Prophets, and Messiahs: Popular Movements at the Time of Jesus* (Minneapolis: Winston Press, 1985). On the meaning of prophecy during this period, see especially John Barton, *Oracles of God: Perceptions of Ancient Prophecy in Israel After the Exile* (London: Darton, Longman and Todd, 1986).

2. On the family tree, see Tessa Rajak, *Josephus: The Historian and His Society* (London: Duckworth, 1983), pp. 15–18.

3. *Life* 12. On the translation of the phrase ἠρξάμην τε πολιτεύεσθαι τῇ Φαρισαίων αἱρέσει κατακολουθῶν, see Steve Mason, *Flavius Josephus on the Pharisees: A Composition-Critical Study*, Studia Post-Biblica, vol. 39 (Leiden: E. J. Brill, 1991), pp. 342–53.

4. On the date of Josephus' works, see Emil Schürer, *The History of the Jewish People in the Age of Jesus Christ (175 B.C.–A.D. 135)*, new English version rev. and ed. Geza Vermes, Fergus Millar, and Martin Goodman (vol. 3 only) (Edinburgh: T. & T. Clark, 1973–87), vol. 1, pp. 46–55 (cited as Schürer-Vermes-Millar, *History*); and Seth Schwartz, *Josephus and Judaean Politics*, Columbia Studies in the Classical Tradition, vol. 18 (Leiden: E. J. Brill, 1990), pp. 9–21. According to *War* 1.3, Josephus first composed an account of the revolt in Aramaic, but that work has not survived. It is possible that there were two editions of the *Antiquities*, and also that book 7 of the *War* is later than books 1–6.

5. Louis Feldman's important article on "Prophets and Prophecy in Jose-

phus" (*JTS* 41 [1990]: 386–422) differs from this work in emphasis. Feldman's study focuses on Josephus' understanding of prophecy and does not extensively analyze the evidence for prophetic figures in this period.

6. On the division of Palestinian society into a ruling class, lower class (also described as the common, or ordinary, people), and an intermediate stratum of literate groups, see Horsley, "Two Types," pp. 444–45. It should be noted (Horsley does not make the point) that most members of the Jewish ruling class would also have been literate.

7. This tendency is clearly exemplified in the chapter on "Prophets and Prophetic Movements" in Horsley and Hanson, *Bandits, Prophets, and Messiahs*, pp. 135–89. The authors adopt a narrow definition of biblical prophecy, portray the popular prophets of Jesus' day as prophets in the biblical mold, and speak of the absence of biblical types of prophecy among the literate groups.

8. See Feldman's note to the LCL translation, vol. 9, pp. 48–49. The only other reference to Jesus in Josephus is in *Ant.* 20.200, where James is identified as "the brother of Jesus who was called the Christ." On the two passages, see Schürer-Vermes-Millar, *History*, vol. 1, pp. 428–41; and John P. Meier, "Jesus in Josephus: A Modest Proposal," *CBQ* 52 (1990): 76–103.

Chapter 1

1. The translation given here is that of W. D. Davies, *Paul and Rabbinic Judaism: Some Rabbinic Elements in Pauline Theology*, 2d ed. (London: SPCK, 1955), p. 331; the Hebrew text is given on p. 330.

2. These texts include: Ps. 74.9; Zech. 13.2–6; 1 Macc. 4.46; 9.27; 14.41; 2 Baruch 85.3; Prayer of Azariah 15; *Against Apion* 1.41 (discussed later); Seder Olam Rabbah 30; bSanhedrin 11a; bYoma 9b, 21b; bSotah 48b (also considered later).

3. The most important discussions of the relevant material are: Ragnar Leivestad, "Das Dogma von der prophetenlosen Zeit," *NTS* 19 (1972–73): 288–99; Barton, *Oracles of God*, pp. 105–16; Roger Beckwith, *The Old Testament Canon of the New Testament Church and Its Background in Early Judaism* (London: SPCK, 1985), pp. 369–76; Frederick E. Greenspahn, "Why Prophecy Ceased," *JBL* 108 (1989): 37–49; Werner Foerster, "Der Heilige Geist im Spätjudentum," *NTS* 8 (1961–62): 117–22; W. D. Davies, *Paul and Rabbinic Judaism*, pp. 208–16; Theodore M. Crone, *Early Christian Prophecy: A Study of Its Origin and Function* (Baltimore: St. Mary's University Press, 1973), pp. 62–68; David E. Aune, *Prophecy in Early Christianity and the Ancient Mediterranean World* (Grand Rapids, Mich.: Eerdmans, 1983), pp. 103–6; and Rudolf Meyer, "Prophecy and Prophets in the Judaism of the Hellenistic-Roman Period," in "προφήτης κτλ.," *TDNT*, vol. 6, pp. 812–19 (cited as "προφήτης").

4. I have altered the LCL translation slightly.

5. See, e.g., Horsley, "Two Types," p. 437; Horsley and Hanson, *Bandits, Prophets, and Messiahs*, p. 146; Joseph Blenkinsopp, "Prophecy and Priesthood in Josephus," *JJS* 25 (1974): 240; Crone, *Early Christian Prophecy*, pp. 63, 143; and Beckwith, *Old Testament Canon*, pp. 371–72.

6. See *Against Apion* 1.1, 54, 217; *Ant.* 1.13; 20.261. *Ant.* 1.5 speaks of "the Hebrew records."

7. Because his argument concerns historical sources only, Josephus says

nothing in the present passage about the authorship of the four books containing "hymns to God and precepts for the conduct of human life," but we may safely assume that he believed that these, too, were written by prophets. The passage can at least be read in this way; see John Barton, "'The Law and the Prophets.' Who Are the Prophets?," *OS* 23 (1984): 5–6; Barton, *Oracles of God*, pp. 48–49; and James Barr, *Holy Scripture: Canon, Authority, Criticism* (Philadelphia: Westminster Press, 1983), p. 55. Moreover, there is some indication that it *should* be read in this way: the four books almost certainly included the book of Psalms, which Josephus believed had been written by the prophet David; see Barton, *Oracles of God*, p. 40.

8. See, e.g., Thackeray's note to the LCL translation of 1.29, vol. 1, pp. 174–75, n. a; also Beckwith, *Old Testament Canon*, p. 82.

9. Modern commentators often regard Josephus' views on the role of priests in relation to scripture as idiosyncratic and unreliable, but I believe both that his views were widely shared and that they reflect the actual historical situation in the Jewish community of his day. More on these topics in chapter 2.

10. Note the μέν . . . δέ construction in 1.37.

11. See Barton, *Oracles of God*, pp. 103–4.

12. See also *Ant.* 4.329, where Josephus says that Moses had no equal as a prophet. The distinction between Moses and the rest of the prophets was a standard one in the Judaism of Josephus' day; see Barton, *Oracles of God*, pp. 63, 94, 117; and Beckwith, *Old Testament Canon*, p. 149.

13. On Joshua as successor to Moses, see *Ant.* 4.165 = Num. 27.15–23; on Elijah and Elisha, see *War* 4.460; *Ant.* 8.352–54; 9.28; and 1 Kgs. 19.15–21; 2 Kgs. 2.9–15.

14. In the Hebrew Bible, Esther's husband is Ahasuerus, who is usually identified with the Persian ruler Xerxes. According to Josephus, however, Esther was not married to Xerxes, but rather to Xerxes' son, Artaxerxes I (*Ant.* 11.184–85). The LXX makes the same mistake; see LCL, vol. 6, p. 403, n. c. Josephus dates the work of Ezra and Nehemiah to the reign of Xerxes, before the time of Esther (*Ant.* 11.120–21, 159).

15. On Josephus' sources for the postbiblical period, see Schürer-Vermes-Millar, *History*, vol. 1, pp. 49–52.

16. The question is whether ἕκαστα, which usually means "all and each severally," here refers to events or to periods of history.

17. I say this without meaning to imply anything at all about the official canonical status of these books. More on this later.

18. Barton, *Oracles of God*, pp. 37–38.

19. See Barton, *Oracles of God*, pp. 59–62, 81–82.

20. Beckwith argues for the former view in *Old Testament Canon*, pp. 371–72. Aune, following van Unnik, argues for the latter in *Prophecy in Early Christianity*, p. 106; cf. W. C. van Unnik, "Die Prophetie bei Josephus," in his *Flavius Josephus als historischer Schriftsteller* (Heidelberg: Lambert Schneider, 1978), p. 48.

21. The passage from Alexander Polyhistor referred to in *Ant.* 1.240–41 contains the only extant fragment of Cleodemus' work, and it has prompted a good deal of speculation concerning the author and his history of the Jews. For a survey of opinions, see David E. Aune, "The Use of ΠΡΟΦΗΤΗΣ in Josephus," *JBL* 101 (1982): 420. See also the translation and introduction by R. Doran in James

H. Charlesworth, ed., *The Old Testament Pseudepigrapha* (London: Darton, Longman and Todd, 1983–85), vol. 2, pp. 883–87.

22. The expression "it is said" (λέγεται, *Ant.* 1.239) was conventionally used to introduce an anonymous tradition; see Aune, "Use of ΠΡΟΦΗΤΗΣ," p. 420.

23. This is almost certainly the sense of the passage; see the next note.

24. Barton, *Oracles of God*, p. 59, assumes that the terms "historians" (συγγραφεῖς) and "prophets" (προφῆται) in *War* 1.18 both refer to the authors of scripture, but it is more likely that they refer to the two groups mentioned in 1.17: the prophets are the Jews before Josephus who accurately recorded the events of Jewish history from "the origin of the nation" to the exile; that is, they are (as in *Against Apion* 1.37–41) the authors of scripture; the historians are the Greeks who translated these works. The entire passage (*War* 1.17–18) has a chiastic structure: authors of scripture / translators of scripture / translators of scripture / authors of scripture. As the note to the LCL translation of *War* 1.17 indicates, the translator-historians Josephus has in mind here probably include those referred to by name in *Against Apion* 1.218.

25. Ἐσσήν, the word used by Josephus, is the transliteration of the Hebrew חשן, which is used in the Hebrew Bible to designate the breastplate of the high priest. According to Josephus, the Greek equivalent is λόγιον (*Ant.* 3.163, 217; 8.93). The LXX normally uses λόγιον to translate חשן.

26. LCL translation, substituting "breastplate" for "*essên.*"

27. See Exod. 28.5–30; Lev. 8.7–8. Josephus describes the ephod and breastplate in *Ant.* 3.162–71 and *War* 5.233–34.

28. Much about the history and practice of priestly divination in ancient Israel remains unclear, and the preceding paragraph represents a summary and simplification of the evidence. For more detailed discussion of the topic, see Roland de Vaux, *Ancient Israel: Its Life and Institutions*, trans. John McHugh, 2d ed. (London: Darton, Longman and Todd, 1965), pp. 349–53; J. Lindblom, "Lot-Casting in the Old Testament," *VT* 12 (1962): 164–78; J. R. Porter, "Ancient Israel," in *Divination and Oracles*, ed. Michael Loewe and Carmen Blacker (London: George Allen and Unwin, 1981), pp. 205–8; Burke O. Long, "The Effect of Divination upon Israelite Literature," *JBL* 92 (1973): 489–97; Aune, *Prophecy in Early Christianity*, pp. 82–83, 138; Blenkinsopp, "Prophecy and Priesthood," pp. 252–54; Edward Robertson, "The 'Ūrīm and Tummīm; What Were They?," *VT* 14 (1964): 67–74; T. C. Foote, "The Ephod," *JBL* 21 (1902): 1–47; W. Muss-Arnolt and Ludwig Blau, "Urim and Thummim," *JE*, vol. 12, pp. 384–86; and the following articles from the *Encyclopaedia Judaica*: "Divination," by Shmuel Ahituv and Louis Isaac Rabinowitz, vol. 6, cols. 111–20; "Ephod," by Yehoshua M. Grintz, vol. 6, cols. 804–6; "Priestly Vestments," by Menahem Haran, vol. 13, cols. 1063–69; and "Urim and Thummim," by Moshe Greenberg, vol. 16, cols. 8–9.

29. The traditional etymology referred to here is reflected in the LXX version of Ezra 2.63 and Neh. 7.65, and in bYoma 73b. The "Urim and Thummim" (אורים ותמים) of Ezra 2.63 is translated in the LXX as [ἕως ἀναστῇ ἱερεὺς] τοῖς φωτίζουσιν καὶ τοῖς τελείοις; the same phrase from Neh. 7.65 becomes [ἕως ἀναστῇ ὁ ἱερεὺς] φωτίσων. The relevant passage in bYoma 73b reads as follows: "Why were they called 'Urim and Thummim'? 'Urim' because they made their words enlightening. 'Thummim' because they fulfil their words." Another group of LXX passages reflects a different etymology that connected "Urim" with "rev-

elation" or "explanation," and "Thummim" with "truth" or "holiness"; see
Exod. 28.30 and Lev. 8.8: δήλωσις, ἀλήθεια; Num. 27.21 and 1 Sam. 28.6: δῆλοι
(for אורים alone); Deut. 33.8: δῆλοι, ἀλήθεια; and 1 Sam. 14.41: δῆλοι, ὁσιότης.
In Sir. 45.10 the Urim and Thummim are apparently referred to as "revealers of
truth," δῆλοι ἀληθείας.

The texts from the Hebrew Bible cited here comprise all the passages in which
the terms אורים and תמים appear. The use of abstract terms for the translation of
these words in the LXX suggests that the identity of the Urim and Thummim had
already been forgotten at the time the LXX translation was made. On the LXX
translations and the etymologies they reflect, see Robertson, "'Ūrīm and Tummīm," pp. 68–69; and Greenberg, "Urim and Thummim," cols. 8–9.

30. *Ant.* 5.120 = Jgs. 1.1–2; *Ant.* 5.159 = Jgs. 20.26–28; *Ant.* 6.115 = 1 Sam.
14.16–20; *Ant.* 6.122–23 = 1 Sam. 14.36–37; *Ant.* 6.254–58 = 1 Sam. 22.9–15;
Ant. 6.271–74 = 1 Sam. 23.1–13; *Ant.* 6.359–60 = 1 Sam. 30.7–8; *Ant.* 7.72–76
= 2 Sam. 5.19–24.

31. *Ant.* 5.120, 159; 6.115, 254, 257, 359; 7.73, 76.

32. *Ant.* 6.271–74 is Josephus' version of 1 Sam. 23.1–13. Three different
oracular inquiries are described in the biblical passage, in vv. 2, 4, and 9–12. The
third of these is explicitly said to have been made through Abiathar the high priest
with the aid of the ephod (vv. 6, 9). The two inquiries described in vv. 2 and 4
were probably also made through Abiathar, though this is not explicitly stated:
the account of these inquiries is immediately preceded by a report of Abiathar's
appearance in David's camp (1 Sam. 22.20–23), and both reports use the word
שאל, which is usually taken to indicate oracular consultation with a priest. Josephus abbreviates the biblical narrative considerably. He eliminates the description of the third inquiry altogether and says simply that David "learned from
God" what was to happen (*Ant.* 6.274). In place of the two consultations described
in 1 Sam. 23.2, 4, Josephus reports a single inquiry, and he says that this was made
"through the prophet" (διὰ τοῦ προφήτου, *Ant.* 6.271). It is possible that Josephus
is here substituting an anonymous prophet for the high priest Abiathar, but more
likely that he is referring to the high priest as "the prophet." It should be noted
that, in the *Antiquities*, as in 1 Samuel, the report of the inquiries made by David
is immediately preceded by an account of Abiathar's arrival in David's camp (*Ant.*
6.269–70).

33. See, e.g., Feldman, "Prophets and Prophecy in Josephus," p. 403.

34. The best examples of this substitution of prophets for the high priest in
the period after David are 1 Kgs. 22.5–28 and 2 Kgs. 3.11–20. There is evidence
that prophets occasionally played a similar role already in the earlier period. The
prophetess Deborah was consulted during the war against the Canaanites (Jgs. 4),
and when Saul was faced with the threat of war against the Philistines, he reportedly sought advice unsuccessfully from dreams, Urim and Thummim, and
prophets before resorting to the "witch" of Endor (1 Sam. 28.6, cf. v. 15).

35. In Sotah 9.12 it is stated that, "when the former prophets died, Urim and
Thummim ceased." The discussion in bSotah 48b concerns the question of the
precise identity of "the former prophets."

36. Attributed to R. Huna. R. Nahman points out that the Urim and Thummim were sometimes ineffectual during the time of David.

37. Attributed to Rabbah b. Samuel.

38. Translation by D. R. A. Hare, from Charlesworth, *Pseudepigrapha*, vol.

2, p. 398, substituting "Holy of Holies" for *Dabeir*. The date of the Lives of the Prophets is uncertain; Hare, along with many others, assigns it to the first century C.E. (pp. 380–81). The passage quoted here associates several different prophetic phenomena with the high priest. Josephus describes the murder of this Zechariah in *Ant.* 9.168–69; note the use of prophetic language in his account.

39. Unattributed.

40. See Ezra 2.63; Neh. 7.65.

41. See, e.g., *Ant.* 8.400–410; 9.33–36.

42. See Blenkinsopp, "Prophecy and Priesthood," pp. 252–53, in agreement.

43. John Strugnell has recently published the text of two fragments from Qumran (4Q375 and 4Q376) that, together with a previously published fragment (1Q29), appear to describe a rite or ordeal for distinguishing between the true and the false prophet. The rite was conducted by the high priest and relied in some way on the flashing of the two sardonyxes on the right and left side of the high-priestly ephod. The original text may also have referred to the oracular use of the breastplate in time of war, though this is less certain. On the fragments and their relation to *Ant.* 3.214–18, see John Strugnell, "Moses-Pseudepigrapha at Qumran: 4Q375, 4Q376, and Similar Works," in *Archaeology and History in the Dead Sea Scrolls: The New York University Conference in Memory of Yigael Yadin*, ed. Lawrence H. Schiffman, JSPS 8 (Sheffield: JSOT Press, 1990), pp. 221–56.

44. There is a variant to the text of *Ant.* 3.214 that reads "sycophants" (συκοφαντῶν) instead of "prophets" (προφητῶν). Feldman has suggested that συκοφαντῶν, as the more difficult reading, should be accepted; see his "Prophets and Prophecy in Josephus," p. 403. Συκοφαντῶν occurs in three manuscripts, S, P, and L. Opinions vary as to the general reliability of these manuscripts. In the introduction to the LCL translation of the *Antiquities*, Thackeray states that the manuscript group R, O, and M, preferred by Niese, is generally superior; he contrasts this group, in particular, with the manuscript pair consisting of S and P, which he considers "seldom trustworthy" when not supported by other witnesses (vol. 4, p. xvii). On this view, προφητῶν would clearly be the preferable reading, and it is the reading adopted by Niese and by Thackeray. Feldman, on the other hand, in *Josephus and Modern Scholarship (1937–1980)* (Berlin: Walter de Gruyter, 1984), praises Niese's text generally, but complains that he "overestimated the value of one group of manuscripts, for example RO in *Antiquities* 1–10, and frequently failed to consider the quality of individual readings case by case" (p. 20). Presumably this is one case where Feldman believes that the reading in S, P, and L is to be preferred.

I find it difficult to know how to assess the manuscript evidence. On more general grounds, the reading προφητῶν is preferable. Priests and prophets were competitors in the sense that both could be consulted for information about God's will and intentions; thus it would be reasonable to compare and contrast them with one another. The tradition in bYoma 73b, quoted previously, and the Qumran fragments referred to in the preceding note both contrast priestly and prophetic oracles, and thereby lend further support to the reading προφητῶν. One may doubt that the principle *lectio difficilior* should always be preferred to intrinsic plausibility.

45. In the thirteenth year of Domitian, and the fifty-sixth year of Josephus' life, *Ant.* 20.267.

46. This is the case whether we use Josephus' chronology or our modern chro-

nology as the basis of our calculations. Josephus knew that John had reigned for thirty-one years (*War* 1.68; *Ant.* 13.299; 20.240). In *War* 6.270 he reckons 639 years (plus a few days) for the period from the second year of Cyrus until the fall of Jerusalem in 70 C.E., and in *Ant.* 13.301, 481 years (plus a few months) from the first year of Cyrus until the accession of Aristobulus I, successor to Hyrcanus. A little simple arithmetic yields the figure of 159 years for the period from the end of John's reign to the destruction of Jerusalem, and 182/3 from the end of John's reign to the completion of the *Antiquities* in 93/4 C.E. Thus, on Josephus' chronology, the two-hundred-year interval mentioned in *Ant.* 3.218, if interpreted precisely, would put the end of priestly divination sometime near the end of the first half of Hyrcanus' reign. On the modern chronology, a precise interval of two hundred years yields the date 107/6 B.C.E. for the end of priestly divination, that is, sometime toward the end of John's reign.

47. See de Vaux, *Ancient Israel*, pp. 258–59.

48. See Jgs. 1.1–2; 18.5–6; 20.18, 23, 26–28; 1 Sam. 14.18–19, 36–37; 22.9–15; 23.2, 4, 9–12; 30.7–8; 2 Sam. 5.19, 23–24.

49. This statement is an addition to scripture.

50. See the passages listed in n. 30. Feldman points out that Greek and Roman histories portray military leaders consulting oracles before engaging in battle; see his "Prophets and Prophecy in Josephus," p. 392. Josephus seems to have this pagan tradition in mind in *Ant.* 3.217: having described the use of the breastplate before a battle, he writes, "Hence [ὅθεν] it is that those Greeks who revere our practices . . . call the breastplate *logion*," i.e., "oracle."

51. The traditional association of the high-priestly vestments with the conduct of war may partly explain the intensity of the debate, which ran throughout the Roman period, about who should have possession of the vestments, the Romans or the Jews. On this debate, see *Ant.* 15.403–408; 18.90–95; 20.6–14. See also Paul Winter, *On the Trial of Jesus*, 2d ed., rev. and ed. T. A. Burkill and Geza Vermes, Studia Judaica, vol. 1 (Berlin: Walter de Gruyter, 1974), pp. 21–26. It is worth noting that the Temple Scroll from Qumran requires the king, before battle, to present himself to the high priest, who would consult God through the Urim and Thummim on the king's behalf; see 11QTemple 58.18–21.

52. Compare Josephus' version of the "law of the king" in *Ant.* 4.223–24 with the original in Deut. 17.14–20. See also *Ant.* 6.36; 8.131; 14.41.

53. There is some evidence that it was not Aristobulus, but his successor, Alexander Jannaeus, who was the first of the Hasmoneans to adopt the title of king. Strabo, 16.2.40 (762), identifies Alexander as the first. Furthermore, on coins which may date from his reign, Aristobulus is designated high priest, but not king, while Alexander Jannaeus is specifically called king. On both points, see Schürer-Vermes-Millar, *History*, vol. 1, pp. 216–17, 227. Josephus, however, believed that Aristobulus had been the first Hasmonean king; see *War* 1.70; *Ant.* 13.301; 20.241.

54. It is generally agreed that Josephus had no written Jewish sources for the period 134–37 B.C.E. For external political affairs, he relied upon Greek sources, including Strabo and Nicolaus of Damascus; for internal affairs, he appears to have depended mostly on Jewish oral tradition, though he may have taken some material from Nicolaus; see Schürer-Vermes-Millar, *History*, vol. 1, pp. 50–51; vol. 3, p. 185.

55. Tosefta Sotah 13.5; bSotah 33a; and ySotah 24b; see Schürer-Vermes-Millar, *History*, vol. 1, p. 210, n. 23.

56. See n. 22. Josephus also introduces the story of Hyrcanus and the voice in the temple with λέγεται (*Ant.* 13.282).

57. Meyer, following Charles, has argued that the descriptions of a future ruler who would combine the three roles of prophet, priest, and king in Test. Levi 8.11–17 and 17.11–18.14 are based on the figure of John Hyrcanus; see Rudolf Meyer, *Der Prophet aus Galiäa: Studie zum Jesusbild der drei ersten Evangelien*, 2d ed. (Darmstadt: Wissenschaftliche Buchgesellschaft, 1970), pp. 60–70; and Meyer, "προφήτης," pp. 825–26; cf. R. H. Charles, *The Testaments of the Twelve Patriarchs* (London: Adam and Charles Black, 1908), pp. lii, 44–46, 62–67. The interpretation of these passages is extremely difficult, however, and the arguments of Charles and Meyer have not won general acceptance.

58. Josephus was proud of his own Hasmonean ancestry; see *Life* 1–6 and *Ant.* 16.187. He also named his first son Hyrcanus (*Life* 5, 426). On Josephus' view of John Hyrcanus, see now also Mason, *Flavius Josephus on the Pharisees*, p. 225.

59. I have altered the LCL translation slightly.

60. My translation.

61. Aune also cites this passage as evidence that Josephus did not restrict the use of the word προφήτης exclusively to figures from the past; see "Use of ΠΡΟΦΗΤΗΣ," p. 419.

62. Several examples of the use of canon-related terminology in this connection are provided in the introductory paragraph of Aune, "Use of ΠΡΟΦΗΤΗΣ," p. 419. Many more examples could be given. Aune himself is not sensitive to the particular points that I make here about the use of canon-related terms and continues to use them in his own work to delimit the period in which prophets were thought to be active. To consider one example, in a discussion of the cessation of prophecy and the use of the word προφήτης in his *Prophecy in Early Christianity*, he refers to the "hiatus between canonical and eschatological prophecy" (p. 81).

63. See the discussion of the canon in Barton, *Oracles of God*, pp. 13–95; the passage from *Against Apion* is discussed on pp. 25–27, 33–34, 37–39, 48–49, 58–60. See also Barton, "'The Law and the Prophets,'" pp. 4–7. In the remainder of this work, I shall use the word "scripture" and its cognates to refer to "those books regarded as authoritative by the person or persons in question" without meaning to imply anything at all about the official canonical status of such books.

64. This is suggested by the fact that he includes the four books of "hymns to God and precepts for the conduct of human life" in the list, even though the discussion concerns historical sources, and also by the comments he makes in 1.42–43, which indicate that the twenty-two books were regarded as authoritative *legal* documents.

65. See Barton, *Oracles of God*, p. 140, and p. 115, which forms the conclusion of a discussion of whether the increasing authority of the law caused the cessation of prophecy. In "'The Law and the Prophets,'" Barton argues that the idea that prophecy belonged to a golden age in the past was an early one that itself played a role in the process leading to the formation of a canon of scripture (see especially pp. 6–7, 15); on this, see also *Oracles of God*, pp. 59–63.

66. In some ways, the whole of the last six chapters of Barton, *Oracles of God*,

is a discussion of the differences between modern-critical and early Jewish perceptions of prophecy, but see especially pp. 131–32.

67. The precise relationship between the interpretation of dreams and the interpretation of scripture is unclear from this passage and will be investigated in chapter 2.

68. See, e.g., Aune, *Prophecy in Early Christianity*, pp. 143–44; and Crone, *Early Christian Prophecy*, p. 92.

69. Barton, *Oracles of God*, pp. 117–18; and Feldman, "Prophets and Prophecy in Josephus," pp. 407–8. Examples of places where Josephus adds references to dreams in narratives concerning prophets include the following: *Ant.* 6.37–40 = 1 Sam. 8.6–10; *Ant.* 7.147 = 2 Sam. 12.1; *Ant.* 8.125 = 1 Kgs. 9.2.

70. On this critical tradition, see J. Lindblom, *Prophecy in Ancient Israel* (Oxford: Basil Blackwell, 1962), p. 201; Barton, *Oracles of God*, p. 127; and Ernst Ludwig Ehrlich, *Der Traum im Alten Testament*, BZAW 73 (Berlin: Alfred Töpelmann, 1953), pp. 155–70.

71. See Barton, *Oracles of God*, pp. 125–28. D. S. Russell, *The Method and Message of Jewish Apocalyptic: 200 BC–AD 100* (London: SCM, 1964), has proposed a similar explanation for the frequent mention of dreams in apocalypses attributed to ancient heroes: "He [the author of the apocalypse] ascribes to the one in whose name he writes such experiences as he would expect to have in a message to himself, and some of these may well have been genuine experiences in which he believed himself to be divinely inspired. . . . His frequent use of dreams, for example, suggests that a good deal of his own message came through dreams" (pp. 158–59).

72. Barton, *Oracles of God*, p. 122.

73. This fact is often cited as evidence that Josephus believed that prophecy had ceased; see, e.g., Blenkinsopp, "Prophecy and Priesthood," pp. 261–62; Crone, *Early Christian Prophecy*, p. 143; and Ernest Best, "The Use and Non-Use of Pneuma by Josephus," *NovT* 3 (1959): 224.

74. The only exceptions are *Ant.* 1.27 (= Gen. 1.1) and *Ant.* 8.114. Out of deference to his non-Jewish readers, Josephus ordinarily uses the phrase θεῖον πνεῦμα rather than πνεῦμα θεοῦ; see Best, "Use and Non-Use," p. 222; and Crone, *Early Christian Prophecy*, p. 142. Both phrases are here translated "spirit of God."

75. The only occurrences of the phrase "spirit of God" in Josephus with reference to prophecy are the following: *Ant.* 4.108, 118, 119 (Balaam); 6.166 (David); 6.222–23 (Saul and his messengers); 8.408 (Micaiah); 10.239 (Daniel). Josephus has added references to the spirit in his account of Balaam. The spirit is mentioned in the Bible only in Num. 23.7 (LXX only) and 24.2 (MT and LXX). *Ant.* 4.118 may correspond to the LXX of Num. 23.7, but the references to the spirit in *Ant.* 4.108, 119 have no parallel in scripture. The Balaam account is the only place in Josephus' entire works where he expresses a view about the nature of prophetic inspiration: in *Ant.* 4.119–22 he gives a description of possession by the spirit of God. The passage is an elaboration of Num. 23.12, which does not mention the spirit. It should also be noted that *Ant.* 4.119 is the only place where Josephus uses τὸ τοῦ θεοῦ πνεῦμα rather than τὸ θεῖον πνεῦμα; see Best, "Use and Non-Use," p. 222. Commentators often take this passage (*Ant.* 4.119–22) to be representative of Josephus' views on prophetic inspiration; see, e.g., Crone, *Early Christian Prophecy*, pp. 142–43; and Gerhard Delling, "Die biblische Pro-

phetie bei Josephus," in *Josephus-Studien: Untersuchungen zu Josephus, dem antiken Judentum und dem Neuen Testament*, ed. Otto Betz, Klaus Haacker, and Martin Hengel (Göttingen: Vandenhoeck und Ruprecht, 1974), pp. 118–19. It is doubtful, however, that the passage should be understood in this way. A large body of extrascriptural traditions grew up around the figure of Balaam, and it is possible that Josephus was influenced by such traditions at this point. He does not assume or elaborate on the theory of prophetic inspiration expressed in *Ant.* 4.119–22 elsewhere in his works.

Apart from the Balaam passages, all Josephus' references to the spirit of God in connection with prophecy are taken over from scripture. There is no real pattern to his retention or elimination of such language as far as I can discern. It is sometimes suggested that he retained πνεῦμα-language only where oracular speech was involved; Best, "Use and Non-Use," p. 223, points out that such a usage would have been familiar to non-Jewish readers. But not all of the passages that mention the spirit of God involve oracular speech: see, e.g., *Ant.* 6.222–23 = 1 Sam. 19.18–24; *Ant.* 10.239 = Dan. 5.14; *Ant.* 6.166 = 1 Sam. 16.13. Moreover, Josephus sometimes eliminates references to the spirit of God from passages that do involve oracular speech; see, e.g., *Ant.* 8.295 = 2 Chron. 15.1; *Ant.* 9.10 = 2 Chron. 20.14; *Ant.* 9.169 = 2 Chron. 24.20. It may be of some interest to note that Josephus consistently eliminates references to the spirit in connection with the performance of superhuman deeds; see, e.g., *Ant.* 6.76 = 1 Sam. 11.6; *Ant.* 5.287 = Jgs. 14.6; *Ant.* 8.333 = 1 Kgs. 18.12; on these passages, see Best, "Use and Non-Use," pp. 224–25.

76. I have altered the LCL translation slightly. For the whole account, see *Ant.* 6.54–57. The biblical parallel is 1 Sam. 10.1–13. Both the MT and the LXX speak of the "spirit of God" in this passage (רוח יהוה, πνεῦμα κυρίου, 1 Sam. 10.6; רוח אלהים, πνεῦμα θεοῦ, 10.10).

77. The biblical parallel is 1 Sam. 19.18–24. Again, the biblical accounts speak of the "spirit of God" (רוח אלהים, πνεῦμα θεοῦ, 1 Sam. 19.20, 23).

78. *Ant.* 6.73–80 = 1 Sam. 11.1–11. The MT and LXX both have "spirit of God" (רוח אלהים, πνεῦμα κυρίου, 1 Sam. 11.6). Josephus has confused the order of the narrative with the result that the connection between the inspiration and the dismembering of the oxen is not as clear as in the biblical account.

79. *Ant.* 8.346 = 1 Kgs. 18.46. The biblical texts speak of the "hand of the Lord" (יד יהוה, χεὶρ κυρίου, 1 Kgs. 18.46).

80. *Ant.* 9.31–37 = 2 Kgs. 3.9–20. Once again, the MT and LXX have "hand of the Lord" (יד יהוה, χεὶρ κυρίου, 2 Kgs. 3.15).

81. See especially *Ant.* 10.112–19; see also 10.89, which reports that Jeremiah repeated his predictions "day after day" (κατὰ πᾶσαν ἡμέραν).

82. As we shall see in chapter 2, Josephus has added explicit references to the destruction of the temple to the biblical account concerning Jeremiah.

83. The adjective δαιμόνιος, which is used to describe Jesus in *War* 6.303, could be used in connection with evil spirits as well as the spirit of God. The general context of Josephus' report about Jesus—a list of omens and portents which were sent by God to warn the Jews of the impending destruction of Jerusalem—suggests that Josephus believed that Jesus was inspired by God, and not by an evil spirit. More on this in chapter 5.

84. I have altered the LCL translation.

85. Crone, *Early Christian Prophecy*, p. 146.

86. See Blenkinsopp, "Prophecy and Priesthood," pp. 242–45; and Christopher T. Begg, "The 'Classical Prophets' in Josephus' *Antiquities*," *Louvain Studies* 13 (1988): 341–57.

87. The text of *Ant.* 10.266 is slightly uncertain, and the word προφητῶν is omitted by the manuscripts R and O. It occurs, however, in the majority of manuscripts, and is also attested by the Latin translation. We know, in any case, that Josephus considered Daniel a prophet, and that he had a high opinion of his gifts.

88. I have altered the LCL translation.

89. See Barton, *Oracles of God*, pp. 5–6, 115–16, 125.

Chapter 2

1. There is uncertainty about the text here. The translation "punish," adopted here, is based on the reading κολάσαι (MSS. P, A, M, and L), from the verb κολάζω, meaning "to punish" or "chastise." Also attested (in a Leyden MS. quoted by Naber) is the reading κλάσαι, from the verb κλάω, meaning "to break" or "break off." This is the reading adopted in the LCL text. A third reading, adopted by Niese and by Naber, is ὀκλάσαι (MSS. V, R, and C), from ὀκλάζω, meaning "to crouch down," "sink," "slacken," "abate." The meaning of the passage is essentially the same, whichever reading is adopted.

2. On the importance of these two ideas in the *War*, see Helgo Lindner, *Die Geschichtsauffassung des Flavius Josephus im Bellum Judaicum: Gleichzeitig ein Beitrag zur Quellenfrage*, Arbeiten zur Geschichte des antiken Judentums und des Urchristentums, vol. 12 (Leiden: E. J. Brill, 1972); Shaye J. D. Cohen, "Josephus, Jeremiah, and Polybius," *History and Theory* 21 (1982): 366–81; and chapter 4 of Rajak, *Josephus*, especially pp. 78–79 and 94–103. In the *War* itself, special attention should be given to the major speeches, in which these two themes recur and are developed.

3. See Rajak, *Josephus*, p. 81, where Josephus' accusations against the rebels are described as "wide-ranging and unspecific." Cohen, "Josephus, Jeremiah, and Polybius," p. 371, has suggested that the sins of which Josephus accuses the rebels correspond closely to those cataloged in Jer. 7, but in both cases the accusations are so general that it is difficult to know how significant the similarities are.

4. For general accusations against the rebels, see especially *War* 4.386–88; 5.401–2; and 7.259–74. On the pollution of the temple by the rebels, see *War* 2.409–17; 4.147–57, 163, 171–72, 201, 242, 261–62, 313; 5.7–10, 15–20, 36–38, 98–104, 562–66; 6.93–102, 118–30, 259. The speech of Josephus in 5.362–419 also emphasizes sins against the temple. Cohen, "Josephus, Jeremiah, and Polybius," pp. 377–78, suggests that Josephus' "obsession with the temple and the temple cult" in this context may be due to the influence of Polybius, but it may simply reflect Josephus' own sensibilities as a priest.

5. Jewish moderates: *War* 2.400; 4.205, 215. Passages where the Romans are said to be more concerned about the temple and its sanctity than the rebels: 4.181–84; 5.19, 362–63, 397, 402, 563–65; 6.101–2, 118–30. As is well known, Josephus maintains that Titus was reluctant to destroy the temple and gave the rebels every opportunity to repent; see, e.g., his remarks in the preface to the *War* (1.10, 27–28).

6. See *War* 5.412. God has abandoned the temple: 2.539; 5.19; 6.127, 299–300. He is fighting on the side of the Romans: 3.293, 484, 494; 4.368; 6.38–41,

411. God is using the Romans to purge the temple of its pollutions: 4.323; 6.110.

7. See *War* 5.19, 415–19; 6.103–7.

8. See Rajak, *Josephus*, pp. 94–98. She cites Jer. 4–6; 21.11ff.; 26; Ezek. 12–18; Hos. 4–13; and Mic. 3 as examples of this sort of sin-and-punishment scheme (p. 95, n. 26). Cohen, "Josephus, Jeremiah, and Polybius," pp. 370–71, refers to Ezek. 33 and the book of Jeremiah.

9. Rajak, *Josephus*, pp. 96–97, discusses 2 Baruch and 4 Ezra.

10. Cohen, "Josephus, Jeremiah, and Polybius," pp. 371–72, ascribes this modification of the traditional scheme to the influence of Polybius.

11. The most important discussion of τύχη in Josephus is Lindner, *Geschichtsauffassung*, pp. 42–48, 85–94, 143–44, 148–49. Lindner's work is distinguished from other treatments of the question by the fact that he connects his discussion of the use of τύχη in Josephus with an analysis of the sources of the *War*.

12. In addition to 3.354, the most important passages are: *War* 2.360, 373, 387; 4.178–79; 5.366–67; 7.203. In *War* 4.622 the rise of Vespasian is attributed to τύχη, πρόνοια, and εἱμαρμένη.

13. Lindner, *Geschichtsauffassung*, pp. 47–48, 143–44; Rajak, *Josephus*, p. 101. On τύχη in Polybius, see F. W. Walbank, *A Historical Commentary on Polybius* (Oxford: Oxford University Press, 1957–79), vol. 1, pp. 16–26; Kurt von Fritz, *The Theory of the Mixed Constitution in Antiquity: A Critical Analysis of Polybius' Political Ideas* (New York: Columbia University Press, 1954), pp. 388–97; W. Warde Fowler, "Polybius' Conception of Τύχη," *Classical Review* 17 (1903): 445–49.

14. Rajak, *Josephus*, p. 99, cites Dan. 7–11 and 4 Ezra 10–13; Cohen, "Josephus, Jeremiah, and Polybius," pp. 372–73, refers to Jer. 27, Job 12.23, Dan. 2.21, and "contemporary apocalyptic literature."

15. On Josephus' interpretation of Dan. 2.31–45, see Lindner, *Geschichtsauffassung*, pp. 43–44; F. F. Bruce, "Josephus and Daniel," *ASTI* 4 (1965): 148–49; and Ulrich Fischer, *Eschatologie und Jenseitserwartung im hellenistischen Diasporajudentum*, BZNW 44 (Berlin: Walter de Gruyter, 1978), pp. 177–80.

16. See *Ant.* 11.336–37, where Josephus reports that Alexander, when paying a visit to Jerusalem, was taken to the temple and shown a copy of the book of Daniel, which stated that "one of the Greeks would destroy the empire of the Persians." According to Josephus, Alexander "believed himself to be the one indicated."

17. Compare *Ant.* 10.206–7 with Dan. 2.33–35 and *Ant.* 10.209 with Dan. 2.40–43.

18. Josephus was not the only Jew of his day to identify the fourth kingdom mentioned in Daniel with Rome. Fischer, *Eschatologie*, p. 179, n. 66, cites 4 Ezra 12.10ff. and 2 Baruch 39.5ff. as examples of the same interpretation. From a later period, see the rabbinic material surveyed in Hermann L. Strack and Paul Billerbeck, *Kommentar zum Neuen Testament aus Talmud und Midrasch* (Munich: Oskar Beck, 1922–28), vol. 4, pp. 1004–6.

19. Lindner, *Geschichtsauffassung*, p. 45. Lindner discusses the differences between Josephus' conception of τύχη and that of Polybius on p. 144. On the latter topic, see also Rajak, *Josephus*, p. 101; and Cohen, "Josephus, Jeremiah, and Polybius," pp. 374, 377, 380–81.

20. Related to the idea that τύχη was temporarily on the side of the Romans,

and that God had decreed that they should rule the world for the present time, is the idea, expressed several times in the speeches in the *War*, that the revolt was "untimely"; see, e.g., *War* 2.355–61; 5.365.

21. See, e.g., Rajak, *Josephus*, pp. 99–100, 102.

22. See especially *War* 6.399, where he states that a particular event demonstrated both "the power of God over unholy men and the fortune of the Romans."

23. See, e.g., *War* 5.39, 412.

24. Cohen, "Josephus, Jeremiah, and Polybius," p. 374.

25. See Rajak, *Josephus*, p. 171. She notes the dual accusation of cowardice and treachery in *War* 3.432–42 and remarks, "The *War* apologia is designed to counter these two charges."

26. I have altered the LCL translation slightly.

27. For glimpses of Josephus' activities in the Roman camp, see *War* 5.114, 261, 325, 360–419, 541–47; 6.93–129, 365; *Against Apion* 1.49; on his situation in Rome, see *Life* 422–23.

28. My claim that the Jotapata narrative is especially important for understanding Josephus' self-presentation in the *War* is a variation on Cohen's argument that it represents the turning point in his assessment of the rebels' guilt; see his "Josephus, Jeremiah, and Polybius," pp. 374–77; and his *Josephus in Galilee and Rome: His Vita and Development as a Historian*, Columbia Studies in the Classical Tradition, vol. 8 (Leiden: E. J. Brill, 1979), pp. 98–100. It is sometimes objected that Josephus, by his own account, already knew most of the things he claims to have learned in the moment of revelation at Jotapata, and thus that the incident should not be understood as a dramatic turning point; so, e.g., Lindner, *Geschichtsauffassung*, pp. 57–59; Per Bilde, *Flavius Josephus Between Jerusalem and Rome: His Life, His Works, and Their Importance*, JSPS 2 (Sheffield: JSOT Press, 1988), p. 51; and Reinhold Mayer and Christa Möller, "Josephus—Politiker und Prophet," in *Josephus-Studien*, ed. O. Betz et al., pp. 283–84. Josephus does say, in *War* 3.136, that he foresaw that the Jews would be defeated even before Jotapata, but this was purely a judgment about military resources and practicalities, and not a perception about the will and purposes of God. Other characters (chiefly those for whom he composed speeches) are credited at an earlier point in the revolt with the insights that Josephus claims to have achieved at Jotapata, namely that God was punishing the rebels for their sins, and that he had decreed that the Romans should rule the world; but Josephus the author of the *War* never attributes these views to Josephus the historical actor before the scene in the cave at Jotapata. Even *Life* 17–19, frequently cited in this connection, concerns practical matters primarily, though it does mention the "good fortune" (εὐτυχία) of Rome. In any case, this passage should be considered in the context of the *Life* as a whole, and should not be conflated with the *War*; so also Cohen, "Josephus, Jeremiah, and Polybius," p. 376, n. 31.

29. Otto Betz has also connected the speech in *War* 5 with the revelation at Jotapata; see his *Offenbarung und Schriftforschung in der Qumransekte*, WUNT 6 (Tübingen: J. C. B. Mohr [Paul Siebeck], 1960), pp. 107–8. Lindner denies that any such connection exists. He argues that the speech cannot be understood as the communication of a message received through revelation; it is, rather, "Mahn- und Anklagerede, durchaus lehrhaft und keineswegs das Wort eines charismatischen Künders" (*Geschichtsauffassung*, p. 57). Van Unnik similarly describes the speech as unprophetic; see his "Die Prophetie bei Josephus," p. 46.

I find these remarks extremely puzzling. The speech in *War* 5 is in fact very similar to many of the oracles of the classical prophets—Lindner himself acknowledges the parallels between Josephus' speech and the book of Jeremiah (p. 33). In any case, the fact that Josephus compares himself with Jeremiah shows that *he* thought that the speech was a prophetic one; moreover, the parallels in content between the speech and the revelation at Jotapata suggest a connection between the two.

30. On what follows, see Rajak, *Josephus*, pp. 185–91. See also Kenneth Scott, *The Imperial Cult Under the Flavians* (Stuttgart: W. Kohlhammer, 1936), pp. 1–19; and Richmond Lattimore, "Portents and Prophecies in Connection with the Emperor Vespasian," *Classical Journal* 29 (1933–34): 441–49.

31. Tacitus, *Hist.* 1.10; 2.4, 78; 4.81–82; 5.13; Suetonius, *Vesp.* 4; 5; 7; *Titus* 5; Dio, *Epit.* 66.1. These omens and prophecies are the *omina imperii* referred to above. Josephus' prediction is mentioned by Suetonius (*Vesp.* 5) and by Dio (*Epit.* 66.1).

32. Rajak, *Josephus*, p. 187.

33. Rajak, *Josephus*, pp. 189–90; Scott, *Imperial Cult*, pp. 1–2, 8–9, 19; and Lattimore, "Portents and Prophecies," pp. 446–47.

34. See Rajak, *Josephus,* pp. 190–91; and Scott, *Imperial Cult*, p. 17.

35. Rajak, *Josephus*, p. 191.

36. Rajak, *Josephus*, p. 188.

37. See, e.g., Lindner, *Geschichtsaffassung*, pp. 63–65; and Fischer, *Eschatologie*, p. 171.

38. In *War* 3.392 Josephus refers to the entire episode as "the war . . . with his own friends."

39. Thackeray's comment on the speech is revealing. In a note to the LCL translation of the lot-drawing episode (vol. 2, p. 687, n. a), he cautions the reader against accepting Josephus' autobiographical notices uncritically as accurate reminiscences. He refers back to the speech as an example of Josephus' unreliability: "That his companions would have tolerated the rhetorical speech on suicide is incredible."

40. On what follows, see Rajak, *Josephus*, pp. 168–73.

41. Rajak, *Josephus*, p. 168.

42. Rajak, *Josephus*, p. 169.

43. Rajak, *Josephus*, p. 172.

44. Rajak, *Josephus*, pp. 170–71.

45. In addition to the collective suicide at Masada, discussed later, see, e.g., the case of the cave-dwelling "bandits" who refused to surrender to Herod (*War* 1.311–13; cf. *Ant.* 14.429–30); the suicide of Simon, a Jew who fought on the side of the Scythopolitans in their conflict against the Jews (*War* 2.469–76); the suicide of some of Josephus' own picked men at Jotapata (*War* 3.331); the collective suicide of five thousand Jews at Gamala (*War* 4.79–81); and the case of two distinguished Jews (priests?), Meirus son of Belgas and Josephus son of Dalaeus, who threw themselves into the flames when the temple was set on fire (*War* 6.280). On these passages, see Louis H. Feldman, "Masada: A Critique of Recent Scholarship," in *Christianity, Judaism and Other Greco-Roman Cults*, ed. Jacob Neusner, SJLA 12.3 (Leiden: E. J. Brill, 1975), pp. 241–42; Martin Hengel, *The Zealots: Investigations into the Jewish Freedom Movement in the Period from Herod I Until 70 A.D.*, trans. David Smith (Edinburgh: T. & T. Clark, 1989), pp.

262–65; and Arthur J. Droge and James D. Tabor, *A Noble Death: Suicide and Martyrdom Among Christians and Jews in Antiquity* (San Francisco: Harper, 1992), pp. 89–92.

46. The use of the word ἀπόνοια in *War* 4.80 may imply disapproval, but the rest of the accounts seem generally admiring.

47. The following works are in general agreement with the interpretation of the Masada narrative given here: Shaye J. D. Cohen, "Masada: Literary Tradition, Archaeological Remains, and the Credibility of Josephus," *JJS* 33 (1982): 385–405; Feldman, "Masada"; Rajak, *Josephus*, pp. 219–22; and Droge and Tabor, *Noble Death*, pp. 92–96. A different interpretation is proposed by David J. Ladouceur in two (closely similar) articles: "Masada: A Consideration of the Literary Evidence," *Greek, Roman, and Byzantine Studies* 21 (1980): 245–60; and "Josephus and Masada," in *Josephus, Judaism, and Christianity*, ed. Louis H. Feldman and Gohei Hata (Detroit: Wayne State University Press, 1987), pp. 95–113.

48. See *War* 7.315–19. In 7.318 Josephus says that the wind changed direction "as if by divine providence" (καθάπερ ἐκ δαιμονίου προνοίας), and in 7.319 that the Romans were thus blessed "by God's aid" (τῇ παρὰ τοῦ θεοῦ συμμαχίᾳ). In the first speech of Eleazar, this incident is referred to as evidence of divine disfavor (7.331–32).

49. Cohen has shown that similar terminology occurs in accounts of collective suicides in other ancient historians, where a generally positive view of the phenomenon is taken; see his "Masada," pp. 391–92.

50. The account of the suicide of Simon the Jew in *War* 2.469–76 presents a similarly mixed view; see especially the concluding remark in 2.476: "So perished a youth who, in virtue of his strength of body and fortitude of soul, deserves commiseration, but who by reason of his trust in aliens met the consequent fate."

51. *War* 3.383, emphasis mine.

52. Rajak mistakenly supposes that the message that Josephus felt he had to survive to deliver concerned the "correct view of the ethics of suicide" (*Josephus*, p. 169). David Daube suggests that Josephus believed he had to instruct the world about "the meaning of Judaism"; see his "Typology in Josephus," *JJS* 31 (1980): 19. It is, however, the prediction to Vespasian that is intended.

53. Daube, "Typology," p. 19, also draws attention to this passage.

54. On the expansion of the text, see Daube, "Typology," pp. 30–31. As is well known, the Slavonic version of the *War* suggests that Josephus manipulated the lots in such a way as to ensure a favorable result for himself.

55. Daube, "Typology," p. 19.

56. On the text here, see n. 1.

57. See, in agreement, Cohen, "Josephus, Jeremiah, and Polybius," pp. 369–70; Fischer, *Eschatologie*, p. 169; Lindner, *Geschichtsauffassung*, pp. 53–54; and O. Betz, *Offenbarung*, pp. 105–7. For the view that the passage concerns the inspired interpretation of scripture, see, e.g., Blenkinsopp, "Prophecy and Priesthood," p. 247; and Aune, *Prophecy in Early Christianity*, p. 139.

58. The Greek is ὧν . . . ἔνθους γενόμενος. There is general agreement that the antecedent of ὧν is τῶν . . . ἱερῶν βίβλων . . . τὰς προφητείας, "the prophecies of the sacred books." Note the chiastic structure of 3.352–53: dreams / prophecies / prophecies / dreams.

59. The construction ἔνθεος plus the genitive does not occur elsewhere in

Josephus. In *Ant.* 9.35 it is said that Elisha "became divinely inspired at the playing of the harp" (πρὸς τὸν ψαλμὸν ἔνθεος γενόμενος). Apart from this passage, Josephus always uses ἔνθεος in an absolute sense; see *War* 4.33, 388; *Ant.* 6.56, 76; 8.346. Liddell and Scott, p. 566, do not give an English equivalent for ἔνθεος plus the genitive, but cite Aeschylus, *Eumenides* 17, where the phrase means "inspired by" or "with." David Levene of Brasenose College, Oxford, has confirmed for me that ἔνθεος plus the genitive normally means "inspired by" or "with" or "from," and that the LCL translation ("inspired to read their meaning") is inaccurate.

60. 'Ανάμνησις αὐτὸν τῶν διὰ νυκτὸς ὀνείρων εἰσέρχεται, 3.351. So also O. Betz, *Offenbarung*, p. 106.

61. See de Vaux, *Ancient Israel*, pp. 353–55; and Steve Mason, "Priesthood in Josephus and the 'Pharisaic Revolution,'" *JBL* 107 (1988): 657. Mason cites Lev. 10.8–11; Deut. 31.9–13; 2 Chron. 15.3; 19.8–11; Ezra 7.1–6, 21; Ezek. 7.26; and Hag. 2.11 (n. 3).

62. See, e.g., de Vaux, *Ancient Israel*, p. 355; and Rajak, *Josephus*, p. 19. Mason, "'Pharisaic Revolution,'" p. 657, attributes this view to Lauterbach, Oesterley, Zeitlin, and Rivkin. Mason himself thinks that such a pharisaic revolution occurred and, in fact, proposes an earlier date for it than is usually accepted.

63. For Pharisees as expert interpreters of the law, see *War* 1.110; 2.162; *Life* 191. It is likely that Judas and Matthias, the two σοφισταί who were involved in the golden eagle incident (*War* 1.648–55; *Ant.* 17.149–67), were also Pharisees; they are described as experts in the interpretation of the law in *War* 1.648 and *Ant.* 17.149. For the claim that the pharisaic interpretation of the law actually constituted the law of the land in Josephus' day, see especially *Ant.* 18.15–17. In this passage, Josephus suggests that, at the time of the revolt of Judas the Galilean (6 C.E.), all public worship was conducted according to the pharisaic interpretation of the law. Even the Sadducees, he says, were obliged to submit to the rulings of the Pharisees, "since otherwise the masses would not tolerate them" (18.17).

64. For a full discussion of the role and influence of the Pharisees in this period, see E. P. Sanders, *Judaism: Practice and Belief 63 BCE–CE 66* (London: SCM; Philadelphia: Trinity Press International, 1992), especially chaps. 18 and 21. For a brief summary of the arguments against the view that the Pharisees governed Palestine at this time, see Sanders, *Jewish Law from Jesus to the Mishnah: Five Studies* (London: SCM; Philadelphia: Trinity Press International, 1990), pp. 101–2.

65. See *War* 7.150; *Ant.* 3.38; 4.302–4; 5.61; 11.336–37. On the practice of storing sacred books in the temple, see Beckwith, *Old Testament Canon*, pp. 80–86.

66. So also Mason, *Flavius Josephus on the Pharisees*, pp. 337–38.

67. I have altered the LCL translation.

68. On the *Antiquities* as a "translation" of the sacred books, see also *Ant.* 1.5.

69. I have altered the LCL translation slightly.

70. I have altered the LCL translation slightly.

71. Rajak describes Josephus' education as pharisaic and suggests that it proceeded along the lines later outlined in the Mishnah and the Talmud; see the discussion in her *Josephus*, pp. 26–34. But quite apart from the very substantial question of whether the pattern of education outlined in these later rabbinic works reflects conditions in Palestine in the period before 70 C.E., Josephus' own

account in the *Life* suggests that his education was priestly and aristocratic, and not pharisaic. He begins the *Life* with a discussion of his priestly and royal pedigree (1–6) and points out that his father was "distinguished . . . by his noble birth" and was "among the most notable men in Jerusalem" (7). He next describes his education (8–9) and goes on to explain that he explored the teachings of the principal Jewish "sects"—including the "sect" of the Pharisees—between the ages of sixteen and nineteen, i.e., after his primary education was completed. So also Mason, *Flavius Josephus on the Pharisees*, pp. 336–38.

72. *Ant.* 4.312–14 (Moses); 10.79 (Jeremiah and Ezekiel); 10.276 (Daniel). See also *Ant.* 4.125, where Josephus says that Balaam predicted events "down to times within my memory."

73. *Ant.* 4.303; 10.35.

74. *War* 4.386–88; 6.108–10, 311–13.

75. *War* 2.112; 3.351, 352, 353; *Ant.* 2.10, 11, 12, 15, 17, 63 (twice), 69, 70, 72 (twice), 75 (twice), 76, 77, 78, 80, 82, 84, 89, 93; 10.194, 195 (three times), 196, 200, 203 (twice), 205, 208, 211, 216, 234; 17.345 (twice), 348; *Life* 208, 210.

76. *Ant.* 2.10, 11, 12, 13, 14, 17, 65, 67, 70, 75, 77, 80, 82; 10.196, 199, 216, 234, 272; 17.345, 346, 348.

77. Ἐνύπνιον: *Ant.* 2.75; 10.196, 198 (twice), 202, 217; φάντασμα: *Ant.* 2.82; 10.272; *War* 3.353.

78. See, e.g., *Ant.* 2.10–11, 63–69; 10.216–17; 17.345–46.

79. In *Ant.* 2.82, e.g., he equates ὄψις and φάντασμα, and in 10.216–17 he uses ἐνύπνιον as a synonym for ὄναρ and ὄψις.

80. Sometimes it is said only that the vision occurred at night, in which case it is only implied (but surely strongly implied) that the visionary was sleeping; sometimes it is said explicitly that a vision was seen in sleep or recalled after waking. A few examples from the main narratives: *Ant.* 2.10, 11, 64, 70, 80, 82; 10.195, 199, 216; 17.345; *War* 3.351; *Life* 208.

81. In the texts cited here, as in his works as a whole, Josephus alternates between τὸ θεῖον and ὁ θεός as designations for God. I can detect no significant pattern to these variations.

82. For a discussion of these two types of dreams, see A. Leo Oppenheim, *The Interpretation of Dreams in the Ancient Near East*, Transactions of the American Philosophical Society, new ser., vol. 46 (Philadelphia: American Philosophical Society, 1956), pp. 186–217.

83. A few examples from the main passages considered here: *Ant.* 2.10, 64; 10.206; 17.345; *War* 2.112.

84. See, e.g., *Ant.* 2.65, 70.

85. On this dream, see Aune, *Prophecy in Early Christianity*, pp. 143–44. Aune classifies the dream oracle, formally, as an "oracle of assurance." The phrase used to describe the appearance of the figure in the dream is ἐπιστάντα μοι (*Life* 208), which Aune identifies as a technical phrase (p. 386, n. 274). The expression (or some variant of it) occurs in some of Josephus' other accounts of message dreams; see, e.g., *Ant.* 1.313; 2.170–75, 210–16; 5.215–16; *War* 2.114–16 = *Ant.* 17.349–53.

86. For examples of message dreams, see the passages cited in the preceding note and also *War* 5.381; *Ant.* 1.208; 8.125–29; 11.327–28, 333–35; 12.112. For an example of a dream of mixed form, see *Ant.* 1.278–83.

87. See *Ant.* 2.82–83 for further expressions of Pharaoh's anxiety.

88. See also *Ant.* 10.235, where it is said that the vision caused him to feel "anxiety" (ἀγωνία) and "distress" (λύπη).

89. See the description of Daniel's reaction in the biblical account: "And I, Daniel, was overcome and lay sick for some days; then I rose and went about the king's business; but I was appalled by the vision and did not understand it" (Dan. 8.27).

90. Consider, e.g., the first two dreams of Joseph, *Ant.* 2.11–16.

91. I have altered the LCL translation slightly.

92. So also S. Zeitlin, "Dreams and Their Interpretation from the Biblical Period to the Tannaitic Time: An Historical Study," *JQR* 66 (1975–76): 12.

93. In addition to the examples discussed here, see, from the main passages, *Ant.* 2.14, 63; 10.216, 239, 241, 243–45, 272–74; *War* 2.112.

94. I have altered the LCL translation slightly.

95. Using the passive forms of σημαίνω and δηλόω; see, e.g., *Ant.* 2.11, 15, 17, 69, 78; 10.200, 238, 245.

96. Verbs commonly used by Josephus to describe the interpretation of dreams include κρίνω (*Ant.* 2.11; 10.217, 234, 272), φράζω (*Ant.* 2.14, 65, 70, 77, 80; 10.196, 239, 245), and ἐξηγέομαι (*War* 2.113 = *Ant.* 17.347).

97. The one symbolic dream not included in my selection of passages is also of this type; see *Ant.* 5.218–22 = Jgs. 7.9–15.

98. I have altered the LCL translation slightly.

99. According to Gen. 37.3, Jacob loved Joseph more than the others "because he was the son of his old age."

100. See *Ant.* 2.63, 65, 76, 80, 87, 91.

101. See *Ant.* 10.194, 237, 239, 240, 241. The court professionals who are called upon to interpret dreams are called "wise men" (τοφοί) in 10.197–98.

102. On esoteric wisdom, see Hans-Peter Müller, "Mantische Weisheit und Apokalyptik," VTS 22 (1972): 268–93; Martin Hengel, *Judaism and Hellenism: Studies in Their Encounter in Palestine During the Early Hellenistic Period*, trans. John Bowden (London: SCM, 1974), vol. 1, pp. 202–18; and Barton, *Oracles of God*, pp. 128–30. All three authors point to the similarities between prophecy, mantic wisdom, and apocalyptic.

103. Gen. 41.45 simply gives the Egyptian name without explaining its meaning. According to Philo, the name that Pharaoh gave Joseph was "based on his art of dream interpretation" (*On Joseph* 121).

104. For similar expressions, see *Ant.* 10.196, 204, 239. In 10.210 Josephus refers the reader who wants to know more about "the hidden things that are to come" to the book of Daniel.

105. See especially *Ant.* 10.203; also 10.198–202. According to Josephus, Daniel's own vision at Susa was interpreted directly by God; see 10.271–72.

106. On Joseph, see Gen. 40.8; 41.16, 38–39; these passages are discussed immediately below. On Daniel, see the following passages, where it is said that he had "the spirit of the holy god(s)": Dan. 4. 5 (= MT; ET v. 8); 4.6 (ET v. 9); 4.15 (ET v. 18); 5.11, 14; according to Dan. 5.12 and 6.4 (ET v. 3), Daniel possessed "an excellent spirit." That the ability to interpret dreams comes from God is emphasized especially in Dan. 2.27–30; see also 2.17–23 and 2.47, where God is praised as a "revealer of mysteries." Daniel's own visions (chaps. 7–12) are interpreted by angels.

107. On Daniel, see the passages listed in n. 105 and *Ant.* 10.194 (the Deity

manifests himself to Daniel); 10.239 ("the divine spirit" attends him); 10.250 (Daniel is believed to have "the divine" in him); and 10.267 (Daniel "spoke with God").

108. Compare Gen. 40.1–8 and *Ant.* 2.62–63; Gen. 41.14–24 and *Ant.* 2.79–83; Gen. 41.25–44 and *Ant.* 2.84–90.

109. To my knowledge, the only scholar who has noticed Josephus' omission of these passages is Ehrlich; see his *Traum im Alten Testament*, pp. 72, 84. He speculates (p. 72) that Josephus omitted Gen. 40.8 because he realized that his Hellenistic readers would find the notion that dream interpretations came from God laughable, since they were accustomed (according to Ehrlich) to interpret dreams with the aid of dream books. He also suggests that Josephus may have omitted Gen. 40.8 and 41.16 as part of a general tendency to emphasize the abilities of Joseph himself (pp. 72, 84). No explanation is offered for the omission of Gen. 41.38–39, though it is noted on p. 84. Ehrlich remarks that the omission of these passages distinguishes Josephus from "the Midrash" and Philo (p. 84).

110. This might be compared to the distinction that Josephus makes in *Against Apion* 1.37–41 between Moses and the successors to Moses: all were inspired, but Moses was especially inspired.

111. Otto Betz has suggested that the word συμβάλλω points toward a particular type of interpretation-through-comparison; see his *Offenbarung*, pp. 106, 108. This suggestion is not, however, supported by the careful analysis of W. C. van Unnik, "Die rechte Bedeutung des Wortes treffen, Lukas 2, 19," in *Verbum: Essays on Some Aspects of the Religious Function of Words*, ed. H. W. Obbink, A. A. van Ruler, and W. C. van Unnik, Studia Theologica Rheno-Traiectina, vol. 6 (Utrecht: Kemink and Zoon, 1964), pp. 129–47.

112. See p. 52 and n. 59.

113. O. Betz, *Offenbarung*, p. 106.

114. See, e.g., Aune, *Prophecy in Early Christianity*, p. 140; Meyer, *Prophet aus Galiläa*, p. 55; Lindner, *Geschichtsauffassung*, pp. 69–70; and Marianus de Jonge, "Josephus und die Zukunftserwartungen seines Volkes," in *Josephus-Studien*, ed. O. Betz et al., p. 210.

115. See, in agreement, Cohen, "Josephus, Jeremiah, and Polybius," p. 370; Rajak, *Josephus*, p. 191; and Fischer, *Eschatologie*, pp. 168–74.

116. "Typology in Josephus," *JJS* 31 (1980): 18–36. For the general description of typological thinking that follows here, see pp. 21–25.

117. Daube, "Typology," p. 25.

118. Daube, "Typology," p. 26.

119. Daube, "Typology," pp. 26–36; see also his "'I Believe' in *Jewish Antiquities* xi.237," *JJS* 27 (1976): 142–46.

120. *War* 5.376–400.

121. On these parallels, see Cohen, "Josephus, Jeremiah, and Polybius"; Daube, "Typology," pp. 26–27, 33; and de Jonge, "Zunkunftserwartungen," p. 207.

122. On Jeremiah as a priest, see Jer. 1.1 and *Ant.* 10.80. Josephus states only that Jeremiah was a priest "by descent" (τῷ γένει), but probably also implies that he actually served as a priest; see Daniel R. Schwartz, "Priesthood and Priestly Descent: Josephus, *Antiquities* 10.80," *JTS* 32 (1981): 129–35.

123. On Jeremiah, see *War* 5.392; *Ant.* 10.89, 104, 112, 117–18, 125–28. Jeremiah also predicted that Israel would be restored after an exile of seventy years;

see *Ant*. 10.113; 11.1–2. These passages provide a fair summary of the preaching of Jeremiah as it is recorded in scripture. For general discussions of the relationship between the book of Jeremiah and Josephus' account in the *Antiquities*, see Christian Wolff, *Jeremia im Frühjudentum und Urchristentum*, TU 118 (Berlin: Akademie, 1976), pp. 10–15; Delling, "Biblische Prophetie," pp. 116–17; and Begg, "The 'Classical Prophets' in Josephus' *Antiquities*," pp. 351–55. For Josephus' message, see *War* 5.114, 261, 362–419; 6.93–110, 365.

124. See Jer. 37.11–15 and *Ant*. 10.114–15 on the accusations against Jeremiah.

125. See *War* 5.375, 541–47; 6.98, 108, 365.

126. See Jer. 38.1–4 and *Ant*. 10.119.

127. See Jer. 26; 37.11–21; 38.1–13 and *Ant*. 10.90–93, 114–15, 117–23. Though he was technically a prisoner in the Roman camp, Josephus acknowledges that he was "treated . . . with a respect beyond the common lot of a prisoner" (*War* 3.438). He was never imprisoned by the Jews, though his parents were (*War* 5.533, 544–47), a point noted by Daube, "Typology," p. 26.

128. Daube suggests that it was because Josephus saw himself as a new Jeremiah that he believed that the old Jeremiah had predicted the destruction of Jerusalem by the Romans; see his "Typology," p. 27. This is, however, unlikely. After the destruction of the temple in 70 c.e., many Jews identified the Babylonians of the book of Jeremiah with the Romans and believed that the second destruction, as well as the first, had been predicted by Jeremiah; see Cohen, "Josephus, Jeremiah, and Polybius," p. 371; and Wolff, *Jeremia im Frühjudentum und Urchristentum*, pp. 11–12.

129. There are references to the temple or the temple service or the holy things or the holy precincts in the following passages in the speech: 5.362–63, 377, 380–81, 383, 384 (ark), 389, 391, 394, 397, 400, 402, 405, 406, 411, 412, 416. Daube also notes the prominence of the temple in this speech; see his "Typology," pp. 26–27.

130. See Cohen, "Josephus, Jeremiah, and Polybius," p. 378, in agreement. The temple is mentioned in Jer. 7, as Cohen notes; see also Jer. 26. Cohen attributes the prominence of the temple in Josephus' works to the influence of Polybius (pp. 377–78).

131. Emphasis mine. Daube notes the addition of references to the temple in *Ant*. 10.126, 128; see his "Typology," p. 26. Ralph Marcus also observes that the temple is not mentioned in Jer. 38; see his note to the LCL translation, vol. 6, p. 228, n. a.

132. Emphasis mine. The reference to the Persians and Medes is also unscriptural, and reflects Josephus' interpretation of Dan. 2, which I considered above.

133. See, e.g., *Ant*. 10.112 = Jer. 37.8; and *War* 5.391, quoted earlier. See also *War* 5.411 and 6.103–4, which do not refer to Jeremiah, but which concern events in his day.

134. On Josephus' handling of the book of Daniel in general, see Bruce, "Josephus and Daniel," pp. 148–51; and Geza Vermes, "Josephus' Treatment of the Book of Daniel," *JJS* 42 (1991): 149–66.

135. On Josephus' royal pedigree, see *Life* 2. According to Dan. 1.3, the exiles brought to Nebuchadnezzar's court were "of the royal family and of the nobility"; Dan. 1.6 states that Daniel and his companions were "of the tribe of Judah." Josephus describes them as relatives of king Zedekiah, see *Ant*. 10.186, 188.

136. On Daniel, see Dan. 1.3–4, 17–20; *Ant.* 10.187, 189, 194; on Josephus, see *Life* 8–9.

137. On Daniel, see *Ant.* 10.276. See the note on the text in the LCL edition. Even if the longer text is rejected, it is clear (e.g., from his interpretation of the statue made of four metals) that Josephus believed that Daniel had predicted the destruction of Jerusalem by the Romans.

138. I have altered the LCL translation slightly.

139. There is a lacuna in the text of 10.256, so it is unclear precisely what Josephus said about Daniel's enemies there, but the word φθόνος does appear.

140. This is a possibility also noted by Daube in connection with the Joseph narrative; see his "Typology," p. 27; and his "'I Believe,'" p. 145. On the theme of envy in Josephus, see Mason, *Flavius Josephus on the Pharisees*, pp. 225–27.

141. On the entire incident, see *Life* 84–103 and the parallel in *War* 2.614–25.

142. It should be remembered that the passage I am considering immediately precedes the account of the particular plot mentioned earlier (*Life* 84–85).

143. See also 10.258, 262. Daniel's escape from the lions' den is also viewed as providential in scripture; see Dan. 6.16, 20, 22, 27.

144. More on this episode in chapter 4.

145. See de Jonge, "Zunkunftserwartungen," pp. 206–7, in agreement.

146. Gen. 39.1–6 = *Ant.* 2.39–40.

147. See *Ant.* 2.10, 13, 27.

148. Daube, "Typology," pp. 20–21. As Daube notes, the reliability of Josephus' account has been questioned both on general grounds and because of the existence of other Jewish traditions attributing a similar prediction to Johanan ben Zakkai. On these traditions, see Rajak, *Josephus*, pp. 188–89; Abraham Schalit, "Die Erhebung Vespasians nach Flavius Josephus, Talmud und Midrasch: Zur Geschichte einer messianischen Prophetie," *ANRW* II.2 (1975): 208–327; and Horst R. Moehring, "Joseph ben Matthia and Flavius Josephus: The Jewish Prophet and Roman Historian," *ANRW* II.21.2 (1984): 864–944.

149. Daube, "Typology," p. 32.

Chapter 3

1. For a summary of the evidence, see Geza Vermes, *The Dead Sea Scrolls: Qumran in Perspective*, 2d ed. (London: SCM, 1982), pp. 126–30 (cited as *Perspective*); and Schürer-Vermes-Millar, *History*, vol. 2, pp. 583–85. On the parallels between Josephus and the Scrolls, see Todd S. Beall, *Josephus' Description of the Essenes Illustrated by the Dead Sea Scrolls*, SNTSMS 58 (Cambridge: Cambridge University Press, 1988) (cited as *Description*); but note the critical comments made by Philip Davies in his review of Beall's work in *JTS* 41 (1990): 164–69. There is still a great deal of debate about the origins and early development of the Essene movement, including the question of the historical relationship between the Qumran sect and other Essene groups, but these topics do not directly concern us here. I summarize the dominant hypothesis about Qumran origins on p. 97; I provide references there to recent scholarly works that are critical of this hypothesis.

2. The discovery of the bones of a few women and children in the graves near

Qumran has led some scholars to question whether the sectaries who lived there were in fact celibate. On the debate, see Sanders, *Practice and Belief*, p. 344 and p. 529, n. 6, and the works referred to there. I remain convinced (and this is still the scholarly consensus) that the group represented by the Community Rule (1QS) was celibate, since the work contains many special purity laws, but none relating to women.

3. Vermes, following de Vaux, estimates the population of Qumran at 150 to 200 people at a time; see his *Perspective*, p. 88. E. M. Laperrousaz has proposed a figure of 300 to 400; see the detailed discussion in his *Qoumrân, l'établissement essénien des bords de la Mer Morte* (Paris: A. & J. Picard, 1976), pp. 99–109.

4. Josephus, *Ant.* 18.20; Philo, *Every Good Man Is Free* 75.

5. For a good discussion of the two basic types of Essenes, including a summary of the differences between them, see Vermes, *Perspective*, pp. 87–109.

6. The Damascus Rule is traditionally divided into the statutes (pages 9–16) and the exhortation (pages 1–8, 19–20). The statutes legislate for married Essenes who lived away from Qumran; the exhortation includes material that refers to both celibate and noncelibate members; see Vermes, *Perspective*, pp. 87, 107–8; and Michael A. Knibb, *The Qumran Community*, Cambridge Commentaries on Writings of the Jewish and Christian World, 200 BC to AD 200, vol. 2 (Cambridge: Cambridge University Press, 1987), pp. 14–15, 17.

7. The general point and the specific example considered here are discussed in Sanders, *Practice and Belief*, p. 348.

8. For community of goods at Qumran, see 1QS 1.11–13; 5.1–3; 6.17–22, 24–25. Vermes also remarks on the different practices of the two communities; see his *Perspective*, p. 105. Beall proposes that 1QS and CD, on this point as on others, represent different stages in the development of the Essene movement; see his *Description*, pp. 44–45.

9. On these accounts, see Geza Vermes and Martin D. Goodman, eds., *The Essenes According to the Classical Sources*, Oxford Centre Textbooks, vol. 1 (Sheffield: JSOT Press, 1989).

10. See Sanders, *Practice and Belief*, p. 345.

11. The passage is difficult to interpret for a number of reasons, but this seems to be its meaning. On the textual problems and the translation of the passage, see Feldman's note to the LCL translation, vol. 9, pp. 16–17, n. a.

12. On the sources for Josephus' general accounts of the Essenes, see Morton Smith, "The Description of the Essenes in Josephus and the Philosophumena," *HUCA* 29 (1958): 273–313, and the works referred to there. A different case is argued by S. Zeitlin in "The Account of the Essenes in Josephus and the Philosophumena," *JQR* 49 (1958–59): 292–300.

13. There is disagreement about precisely where Nicolaus' narrative broke off. Most commentators think that it ended at *War* 2.111, i.e., before the account of Simon's interpretation of Archelaus' dream; see, e.g., Thackeray's note to the LCL translation, vol. 2, p. 364, n. a; and Vermes and Goodman, *The Essenes According to the Classical Sources*, p. 37. Gustav Hölscher argued that Nicolaus' narrative extended through *War* 2.116 and included the report concerning Simon; see his article on "Josephus," *RE*, vol. 9 (1916), col. 1944.

14. See chapter 1, n. 22.

15. I have altered the LCL translation. The Greek is: Εἰσὶν δ' ἐν αὐτοῖς οἳ

καὶ τὰ μέλλοντα προγινώσκειν ὑπισχνοῦνται, βίβλοις ἱεραῖς καὶ διαφόροις ἁγνείαις καὶ προφητῶν ἀποφθέγμασιν ἐμπαιδοτριβούμενοι · σπάνιον δ' εἴ ποτε ἐν ταῖς προαγορεύσεσιν ἀστοχοῦσιν.

16. The Greek is: συντηρήσειν . . . τά . . . τῆς αἱρέσεως αὐτῶν βιβλία. "Preserve," in this context, may mean "preserve as a secret."

17. See the works discussed in section C ("Bible Interpretation") of Geza Vermes, *The Dead Sea Scrolls in English*, 3d ed. (Harmondsworth: Penguin, 1987), pp. 249–302.

18. See Roland de Vaux, *Archaeology and the Dead Sea Scrolls*, The Schweich Lectures of the British Academy, 1959, rev. English ed. (London: Oxford University Press, 1973), pp. 29–33.

19. I have altered the LCL translation.

20. The passage from *Ant.* 8 is mentioned in this connection by Thackeray in the note to the LCL translation, vol. 2, pp. 374–75, n. c; see also Beall, *Description*, pp. 153–54, n. 175; Vermes, *Jesus the Jew*, pp. 62–63; Hengel, *Judaism and Hellenism*, pp. 240–41; and O. Betz, *Offenbarung*, p. 69.

21. This is suggested by the use of συντάσσομαι in *Ant.* 8.45 and συντίθημι in 8.47, and by the fact that the passage as a whole is appended to a summary description of Solomon's (other) writings.

22. Vermes, *Jesus the Jew*, p. 239, n. 23; and Morton Smith, "The Occult in Josephus," in *Josephus, Judaism, and Christianity*, ed. Feldman and Hata, p. 241, have both suggested that the root used on this occasion was that of the *baaras* plant; see *War* 7.180–85, where Josephus says that this root was used to expel demons. The parallels between *War* 2.136 and *Ant.* 8.42–49 have led many commentators to speculate that Eleazar, the exorcist named in the passage from the *Antiquities*, was an Essene, but this is not certain. The interest in magic and medicine that the two passages attest was not restricted to Essene circles. For a general discussion of the passage from *Ant.* 8 and related traditions about Solomon, see Dennis C. Duling, "The Eleazar Miracle and Solomon's Magical Wisdom in Flavius Josephus's *Antiquitates Judaicae* 8.42–49," *HTR* 78 (1985): 1–25.

23. See, e.g., Tobit 6.13–17; 8.1–3; 1 Enoch 7.1; 8.3; 10.4–8; Jubilees 10.10–14; Genesis Apocryphon (1QapGen) 20.16–29; and the Prayer of Nabonidus (4QprNab). For a discussion of these passages and others like them, see Vermes, *Jesus the Jew*, pp. 61–62, 65–68; and Beall, *Description*, pp. 72–73.

24. This proposal was originally made by Vermes; see "The Etymology of 'Essenes,'" in his *Post-Biblical Jewish Studies*, SJLA 8 (Leiden: E. J. Brill, 1975), pp. 8–29 (= *RQ* 2 [1960]: 427–43). See also Schürer-Vermes-Millar, *History*, vol. 2, pp. 559–60; and John Kampen, "A Reconsideration of the Name 'Essene' in Greco-Jewish Literature in Light of Recent Perceptions of the Qumran Sect," *HUCA* 57 (1986): 63–64.

25. Identity with the canon is argued or assumed, e.g., by Crone, *Early Christian Prophecy*, p. 120; Beall, *Description*, p. 153, n. 165; and A. Dupont-Sommer, *The Essene Writings from Qumran*, trans. Geza Vermes (Oxford: Basil Blackwell, 1961), pp. 34–35, n. 3. In agreement with the position taken here, see Hengel, *Judaism and Hellenism*, p. 240: "the 'holy books' cannot have been limited to the Torah and the prophets, but must also have included apocalyptic and astrological-mantic writings."

26. This seems to be the meaning of the passage; see Vermes, *Perspective*, p. 104.

27. The same conclusion is reached in Schürer-Vermes-Millar, *History*, vol. 3, pp. 411–12. There is some disagreement about whether the Temple Scroll should be classified as a sectarian document; various opinions are expressed in the essays published in George J. Brooke, ed., *Temple Scroll Studies: Papers Presented at the International Symposium on the Temple Scroll, Manchester, December 1987*, JSPS 7 (Sheffield: JSOT Press, 1989). For an argument in favor of the sectarian classification, see Schürer-Vermes-Millar, *History*, vol. 3, pp. 412–14.

28. See Dupont-Sommer, *Essene Writings*, pp. 34–35, n. 3; Blenkinsopp, "Prophecy and Priesthood," p. 247 and n. 30; and Horsley, "Two Types," p. 447 and n. 25 (following Blenkinsopp).

29. On what follows, see Beall, *Description*, pp. 109–10. Crone has also argued against the emendation in *Early Christian Prophecy*, p. 120.

30. Blenkinsopp's note ("Prophecy and Priesthood," p. 247, n. 30), which suggests that he is simply adopting one reading as opposed to another, is misleading.

31. It is certainly to these purity practices that Josephus refers in *War* 2.159 and not to the practice of ascetical exercises of a more general sort (especially fasting), which were thought by some Jews to prepare one for receiving divine revelations. The latter suggestion is made by Crone, *Early Christian Prophecy*, p. 120; and Meyer, *Prophet aus Galiläa*, pp. 43–45.

32. It is virtually certain that the Essenes' avoidance of oil was based on purity concerns, as Josephus implies, and was not simply part of their more general asceticism and rejection of luxury, as has sometimes been thought. The most likely explanation of the practice is the one proposed by Joseph Baumgarten in "The Essene Avoidance of Oil and the Laws of Purity," in his *Studies in Qumran Law*, SJLA 24 (Leiden: E. J. Brill, 1977), pp. 88–97 (= *RQ* 6 [1967]: 183–93): oil, as a liquid, was an especially powerful conveyor of impurity; those who wished to avoid contracting impurity through contact with unclean persons or things would thus avoid using oil on the skin. For similar reasons (because liquids convey uncleanness more easily than solid food) initiates at Qumran were allowed to share in the community's Pure Meal one year before they were allowed to share in its Pure Drink (1QS 6.16–21; cf. 7.18–20). Yigael Yadin has suggested another possible explanation of the avoidance of oil that also has to do with purity: the Essenes at Qumran may have avoided oil because, in their view, it was supposed to be purified in an annual first-fruits festival, part of which was to take place in the temple; as long as the sectaries boycotted the temple (more on this below), the oil could not be purified; see Yadin, *The Temple Scroll* (Jerusalem: Israel Exploration Society, 1977–83), vol. 1, pp. 111–14.

33. *War* 2.123, 129, 131, 137, 161. In *War* 2.123 Josephus says that the Essenes "always" (διαπαντός) dressed in white, but probably only the ceremonial robes—and not the loincloths—were white; see *War* 2.137, where he distinguishes between the loincloth and the white garment. On this point, see Schürer-Vermes-Millar, *History*, vol. 2, p. 564, n. 10, in agreement.

34. It is clear that these were purificatory baths that involved immersion. In all three cases, the verb used by Josephus is ἀπολούομαι, which means "bathe." In first-century Palestine, "bathing" was generally taken to mean immersion; see Sanders, *Jewish Law*, pp. 214–15. In *War* 2.129 the premeal bath is described as a "purification" (ἁγνεία) that makes one "clean" or "pure" (καθαρός). Similarly, Josephus says that the Essenes bathed after defecation "as if defiled" (καθάπερ

μεμιασμένοις, 2.149). Contact with a junior member of the community is compared to "contact with an alien" (2.150).

35. This is true in spite of the fact that Josephus provides other explanations for these practices: see *War* 2.120–21 on celibacy; *Ant.* 18.21 on celibacy and opposition to slavery. For the argument that these practices were related to purity concerns, see George Wesley Buchanan, "The Role of Purity in the Structure of the Essene Sect," *RQ* 4 (1963): 399–406. On celibacy, see also Vermes, *Perspective*, pp. 181–82; and *Jesus the Jew*, pp. 99–102. Vermes notes the existence of scattered traditions that connect celibacy (but not purity more generally) with prophecy. Beall, *Description*, pp. 41–42, mentions other factors in addition to purity that might have played a role as far as celibacy was concerned.

36. I here use "Pure Meal" for the terms that are usually translated literally as "the Purity" (various forms of טהרה), since it is generally agreed that they refer primarily to the food of the community; see Vermes, *Perspective*, pp. 95–96. "Pure Drink" is משקה הרבים (1QS 6.20; 7.20).

37. See Beall, *Description*, pp. 56–57, and the works referred to there.

38. The meal referred to in 1QS 6.4–5 should probably be considered a Pure Meal, even though it is not explicitly designated as such. I leave out of consideration a passage from the Messianic Rule (1QSa 2.17–21) that describes a similar meal to be held in the presence of the Messiah of Israel. It is unclear precisely how this meal was related to the everyday meals of the community represented by 1QSa.

39. *War* 2.129, 139. According to 1QS 5.13, those who were not members of the covenant could not share in the Pure Meal or the bath that preceded it. New members were barred from the Pure Meal for a full year after their admission to the sect (1QS 6.16–17), and were prevented from sharing the Pure Drink for another year beyond that (6.20–21). A number of offenses were punished by temporary exclusion from the Pure Meal; see 1QS 6.24–25; 7.2–3, 15–16, 18–20; 8.16–18, 24.

40. It is unclear whether these procedures were followed at every meal, which is what Josephus implies, or only on special occasions. Sanders has recently argued that the meal described by Josephus and referred to as the Pure Meal in 1QS was not the twice-daily common meal of the community, but rather a special type of meal held to celebrate the annual first-fruit festival(s) and perhaps other religious festivals and solemn gatherings of the community. Such meals might have occurred reasonably frequently, but not daily; Josephus is exaggerating when he suggests that the Essenes ate all their meals in this fashion. For a detailed discussion of the problem, see Sanders, *Practice and Belief*, pp. 353–56.

41. See *Ant.* 3.102–87 and *War* 5.229–36 for Josephus' description of the priestly vestments. The everyday vestments of the priests and the high priest were made of fine linen, which was apparently unbleached and not considered perfectly white. According to the rabbis, white priestly vestments were reserved for very special occasions: they were worn by the high priest during part of the service on the Day of Atonement (Yoma 3.6; 7.1, 4) and by an ordinary priest when preparing the ashes of the red heifer, which removed corpse-impurity (Parah 4.1). According to the War Rule (1QM), the seven priests who were to lead the final eschatological battle would be clothed in "garments of fine white linen" (7.10). For a detailed discussion of these matters, see "The Priestly Vestments" in Sanders, *Practice and Belief*, pp. 92–102.

42. Sanders suggests that the wearing of linen loincloths by the Essenes may have been "a priestly gesture" (*Practice and Belief,* p. 98).

43. According to Josephus, when King David learned that Bathsheba's child had died, he changed into "a white garment" (ἐσθῆτα λευκήν) and went up to the tabernacle (*Ant.* 7.156); scripture says merely that he "changed his clothes" (2 Sam. 12.20). Similarly, Archelaus, after mourning his father for seven days, put on "a white garment" (ἐσθῆτα λευκήν) before going up to the temple to address the people (*War* 2.1). Anticipating the arrival of Alexander the Great, the high priest Jadduas instructed the Jews of Jerusalem to put on their "white garments" (λευκαῖς ἐσθῆσιν) to go out to meet him (*Ant.* 11.327, 331). Finally, according to Ta'anith 4.8, on 15 Ab and the Day of Atonement, the daughters of Jerusalem "used to go forth in white raiments." These passages are discussed in Sanders, *Practice and Belief,* pp. 96–98.

44. On what follows, see Sanders, *Jewish Law,* pp. 134–35.

45. A portion of the peace offering was returned to the person who had brought it and was taken away and shared among his family and friends, all of whom were required to be pure when they ate it. The deuteronomic or second tithe was also consumed by laypeople in a state of purity. When eating Passover, Jews were required to be free of corpse-impurity, which in practice meant the removal of other types of impurity as well. On these topics, see Sanders, *Jewish Law,* pp. 135, 148, 193.

46. Schürer-Vermes-Millar, *History,* vol. 2, p. 295, n. 10, cites Yoma 3.2 in connection with defecation. Danby's translation of the passage reads as follows: "This was the rule in the Temple: whosoever covered his feet must immerse himself, and whosoever made water must sanctify his hands and his feet." That is, immersion was required after defecation, and the washing of hands and feet after urination. Tamid 1.1 mentions toilets in the temple that were used by the priests. The same passage presupposes the existence of an immersion pool in the temple and requires any priest who had an involuntary emission of semen while sleeping over in the temple to immerse himself, wait until the gates were opened in the morning, and then leave the temple. If priests on duty in the temple immersed after defecation and emission of semen, it is likely that they did so also in the case of other minor impurities.

47. This is implied by Hagigah 2.7, which concerns midras-impurity; see the discussion in Sanders, *Jewish Law,* pp. 205–7.

48. On the general point that priests outside the temple did not maintain the same degree of purity as when they were serving in the temple, see Sanders, *Jewish Law,* p. 206, again commenting on Hagigah 2.7. On reliance on a once-a-day pre-meal immersion, see Sanders, *Practice and Belief,* pp. 228, 358.

49. Lev. 15.18.

50. See Vermes, *Perspective,* p. 181.

51. On the proposed etymology and the problems with it, see Vermes, "Etymology of 'Essenes,'" pp. 11–12; and Kampen, "Reconsideration of the Name 'Essene,'" pp. 67–68.

52. This is the view taken by O. Betz, *Offenbarung,* pp. 69–70, 136, and by most commentators.

53. See CD 12.11–15. The command to "be separated from uncleanness" in CD 7.3 is usually taken as a reference to these laws. In CD 9.20–23, reference is made to the Pure Meal.

54. See CD 10.10–13. According to 11.21–22, anyone entering the temple (?) had to wash himself first. Josephus also mentions that the "other order of Essenes" bathed, *War* 2.161.

55. See, e.g., CD 11.18–21; 12.15–18. Rules governing sex and contact with outsiders will be considered shortly.

56. See 1QS 1.10; 5.1–2; 8.12–14; 9.8–9, 16–17. See also *War* 2.139, where Josephus indicates that the oath of entry into the Essene community included the promise "to hate the unjust forever."

57. The "Book of Meditation" was probably the five books of Moses; see Vermes, *Perspective*, p. 113. For a survey of some other possibilities, see Beall, *Description*, pp. 71–72.

58. The Messianic Rule seems to refer to the same type of community as the Damascus Rule and provides a more detailed description of the kind of instruction given to members of this community. According to 1QSa 1.4–5, all the members, including women and children, were to be instructed in "the precepts of the Covenant" and "all their statutes." Male children were to be instructed for ten years in the Book of Meditation, the precepts of the Covenant, and "their statutes" (1.6–8). The significance of these passages is unclear, however, because of the fact that the document as a whole concerns events in the messianic age; see Vermes, *Dead Sea Scrolls in English*, p. 100; and Knibb, *Qumran Community*, p. 145. It is difficult to know to what extent the work reflects contemporary practice within the community, if at all.

59. See Vermes, *Perspective*, p. 97, in agreement.

60. Strato's Tower was rebuilt by Herod the Great and renamed Caesarea; see *War* 1.408–15; *Ant.* 14.76; 15.331–41; and Schürer-Vermes-Millar, *History*, vol. 2, pp. 115–18.

61. Six hundred στάδιοι, *War* 1.79 and *Ant.* 13.312.

62. Aune classifies this report as an oracle story, "a particular type of Greco-Roman anecdote in which an oracular utterance which appears in danger of proving untrue is fulfilled in an unexpected way through the recognition that the oracle had a double meaning" (*Prophecy in Early Christianity*, p. 145).

63. See Philip R. Davies, *The Damascus Covenant: An Interpretation of the "Damascus Document,"* JSOTS 25 (Sheffield: JSOT Press, 1983), pp. 135–36. Sanders, while agreeing with the position accepted here, points out that it is at least conceivable that the rule in CD 12.1–2 was observed by a Jerusalem group: "If married Essenes had sex only for the sake of procreation, they could have lived in Jerusalem and spent only enough time outside it for the woman to conceive each year" (*Practice and Belief*, p. 347).

64. Schürer-Vermes-Millar, *History*, vol. 2, p. 563, n. 5.

65. Yadin identifies "the place called Bethso" (*War* 5.145) as a latrine, taking the name "Bethso" (βηθσώ) to be a transliteration of the two Hebrew words בית, "house," and צואה, "excrement"; see his *Temple Scroll*, vol. 1, pp. 302–3.

66. Yadin, *Temple Scroll*, vol. 1, pp. 303–4. See the discussion of the related material from the Scrolls in vol. 1, pp. 294–301.

67. According to the *War*, from where Judas was sitting he could see Antigonus "passing through the temple" (παριόντα διὰ τοῦ ἱεροῦ, 1.78); the *Antiquities* has "passing by" or "entering the temple" (παριόντα τὸ ἱερόν, 13.311).

68. For a dissenting view, see Beall, *Description*, pp. 115–19. Beall's argument (that the Qumran community did participate to some extent in the temple

cult) is weakened by his indiscriminate use of material from 1QS, CD (exhortation and statutes), 1QM, Josephus, and Philo as evidence for the views of the Qumran community.

69. See Schürer-Vermes-Millar, *History*, vol. 2, p. 582, and the works referred to there.

70. *Ant.* 18.19, which I considered briefly above, is sometimes thought to describe the practice of the Qumran community: they did not sacrifice in the temple because of a disagreement about the purification rites required for admission, but they continued to send votive offerings to the temple. In view of the sect's extreme antipathy toward the priestly leaders of the temple, however, even this seems unlikely.

71. On the evidence from CD for the practice of non-Qumran Essenes, see Philip R. Davies, "The Ideology of the Temple in the Damascus Document," *JJS* 33 (1982): 287–301; and his *Damascus Covenant*, pp. 134–40.

72. Recall Josephus' comments about the accuracy of Essene predictions in *War* 2.159: "seldom, if ever, do they err in their predictions."

73. Γνώριμοι: *War* 1.78; *Ant.* 13.311; ἑταῖροι: *Ant.* 13.311; μανθάνοντες: *War* 1.78.

74. Liddell and Scott, pp. 355, 700.

75. See, e.g., Blenkinsopp, "Prophecy and Priesthood," p. 258; Crone, *Early Christian Prophecy*, p. 121; Meyer, *Prophet aus Galiläa*, p. 42; Meyer, "προφήτης," p. 823; and Otto Michel, "Spätjüdisches Prophetentum," in *Neutestamentliche Studien für Rudolf Bultmann*, ed. W. Eltester, BZNW 21 (Berlin: Alfred Töpelmann, 1954), p. 60.

76. Τὸ μάντευμα: *War* 1.79 = *Ant.* 13.312; ὁ μάντις: *War* 1.80 = *Ant.* 13.313.

77. There is no parallel to this material in the *War*.

78. On Herod's "trial" before the Sanhedrin, which took place in 47 or 46 B.C.E., see *War* 1.208–15; *Ant.* 14.163–84; 15.4; and pp. 148–50. On the later episode, see *Ant.* 14.176; 15.3; and p. 150. In both cases, there is evident confusion about whether Pollion or Samaias was the principal actor, as we shall see in chapter 5.

79. There has been speculation about the identity of this Menahem; see the note to the LCL translation, vol. 8, pp. 180–81, n. d; and Meyer, *Prophet aus Galiläa*, pp. 44 and n. 14. Meyer identifies Menahem with a one-time colleague of Hillel.

80. Aune classifies this prediction, formally, as a recognition oracle and connects it with Josephus' and Johanan ben Zakkai's predictions to Vespasian, Akiba's acclamation of Bar Kochba as Messiah, and Samuel's prediction of David's kingship; see his *Prophecy in Early Christianity*, p. 146.

81. This pat on the backside is sometimes described as a prophetic symbolic action; see, e.g., Meyer, *Prophet aus Galiäa*, p. 143, n. 16; Meyer, "προφήτης," p. 823; and O. Betz, *Offenbarung*, p. 104. This seems a little extreme to me.

82. Philo also states that the Essenes rejected oaths; see *Every Good Man Is Free* 84.

83. The entry oath is mentioned in CD 15.5–10, other oaths in 9.8–12; 15.1–5; 16.6–8, 10–12. On these passages, see Beall, *Description*, pp. 68–70.

84. See A. I. Baumgarten, "*Korban* and the Pharisaic *Paradosis*," *Journal of the Ancient Near Eastern Society* 16–17 (1984–85): 9.

85. For the summary of Essene history that follows, see Knibb, *Qumran Community*, pp. 6–10; and Vermes, *Perspective*, pp. 137–62. The prevailing consensus about the origins of the Qumran community has recently been challenged by, e.g., P. R. Davies, *Damascus Covenant*; and Phillip R. Callaway, *The History of the Qumran Community: An Investigation*, JSPS 3 (Sheffield: JSOT Press, 1988).

86. On these events, see the section on Herod the Great in Schürer-Vermes-Millar, *History*, vol. 1, pp. 287–329.

87. The site at Qumran was extensively damaged by an earthquake that is usually dated to the year 31 B.C.E., six years into the reign of Herod; it was not rebuilt until shortly after Herod's death, sometime between 4 B.C.E. and 1 C.E. There is some disagreement about whether the site was totally abandoned during this period (for contrasting views, see de Vaux, *Archaeology*, pp. 20–24; and Vermes, *Perspective*, pp. 33–34), but general agreement that community life was not revived until the period of rebuilding after Herod's death. We do not know where the members of the Qumran community went during this period, but the fact that they did not immediately rebuild their isolated desert settlement may be a further indication of good relations between Herod and the Essenes: even the strictest members of the party, it seems, felt comfortable living in Herod's territory.

88. According to Josephus, Herod was nearly seventy years old when he died in 4 B.C.E. (*War* 1.647; *Ant.* 17.148), and so was born in 74/73 B.C.E. I am not certain at what age children would have attended school, though the upper age limits are suggested by Josephus: he says that he himself was already an expert at fourteen, and that he sought some practical experience (outside school) of the various Jewish sects at age sixteen (*Life* 9–10).

89. Antipater's father was appointed governor (στρατηγός) of Idumaea by Alexander Jannaeus; see *Ant.* 14.10. It is usually assumed that Antipater inherited this office; see, e.g., Schürer-Vermes-Millar, *History*, vol. 1, p. 234. On Antipater's initial intervention in Judaean affairs, see *War* 1.123ff.; *Ant.* 14.8ff.

90. Since the oath of loyalty was introduced around 20 B.C.E., Josephus must be thinking of a time before this date. The period from 23–20 B.C.E. was an especially successful one for Herod. For one thing, he acquired a great deal of territory in these years; see Schürer-Vermes-Millar, *History*, vol. 1, p. 319.

91. The palace in Jerusalem and the royal apartments at Herodium, Machaerus, and Masada all seem to have been built around this time; see Schürer-Vermes-Millar, *History*, vol. 1, pp. 304–8.

92. So also O. Betz, *Offenbarung*, p. 103.

93. "Justice": δικαιοσύνη, *Ant.* 15.375; δίκαιον, 15.376; "piety": εὐσέβεια, 15.375, 376. Horsley has also drawn attention to the combination of prediction and moral exhortation in Menahem's speech; see his "Two Types," p. 448.

94. See, e.g., *Ant.* 8.121, 280; 18.117. The connection with the law is especially clear in *Ant.* 7.374, 384; 10.49ff. Similarly, the pair "injustice" and "impiety" could be used to summarize wholesale offenses against the law; see, e.g., *War* 7.260. On the combination of justice and piety in Josephus, see Adolph Büchler, *Types of Jewish-Palestinian Piety from 70 B.C.E to 70 C.E.: The Ancient Pious Men*, Jews' College Publications, no. 8 (London: Jews' College, 1922), pp. 161–64; and Mason, *Flavius Josephus on the Pharisees*, pp. 86–87.

95. See, e.g., *Ant.* 6.265 (Saul); 7.356, 374, 384 (Solomon); 8.314 (Asa); 8.394 and 9.16 (Jehoshaphat); 9.236 (Jotham); 10.49ff. (Josiah).

96. I have altered the LCL translation slightly.

97. See vol. 5, p. 733, n. c.

98. See especially *War* 2.120 and *Ant.* 18.20.

99. In both cases, the word for "virtue" is καλοκαγαθία. It is an unusual word in Josephus: apart from the present passage it occurs only in *Ant.* 16.178, in what is clearly an editorial passage (16.174–78). There καλοκαγαθία is connected with "justice" (τὸ δίκαιον), which, in turn, is said to be the special concern of the Jewish law (16.177).

100. See W. C. van Unnik, "A Greek Characteristic of Prophecy in the Fourth Gospel," in *Text and Interpretation: Studies in the New Testament Presented to Matthew Black*, ed. E. Best and R. McL. Wilson (Cambridge: Cambridge University Press, 1979), pp. 211–29. The most common form of the expression is πάντα or ἅπαντα plus a verb for "knowing," usually some form of οἶδα or ἐπίσταμαι. Van Unnik cites examples of the use of the expression from the following widely diverse sources: the gospel of John, Dio Chrysostom, Hippolytus, Proclus, Aristocles, Origen, Philostratus, 3 Baruch, 2 Enoch, Josephus, the Pseudo-Clementine *Homilies*, Sophocles, Euripides, Quintus Smyrnaeus, Hesychius, the Berlin Magical Papyrus, and the London Magical Papyrus. He discusses *Ant.* 15.375 on pp. 222–23.

101. *Orationes* 33.4, cited by van Unnik, "Greek Characteristic," p. 219.

102. See, e.g., 2 Enoch 39.2 (A); Pseudo-Clementine *Homilies* 2.10.1; and Virgil, *Georgica* 4.392–93, all cited by van Unnik in "Greek Characteristic," pp. 221; 223, n. 2; and 225–26, respectively. On the threefold formula referring to past, present, and future, see van Unnik, "A Formula Describing Prophecy," *NTS* 9 (1962–63): 86–94.

103. Van Unnik, "Greek Characteristic," p. 223.

104. O. Betz refers it, more narrowly, to the knowledge of scripture mentioned in *War* 2.159; see his *Offenbarung*, p. 103.

105. On the scope and character of Essene knowledge, see Hengel, *Judaism and Hellenism*, pp. 242–43, 251–52. Since Hengel wrote, the Qumran Songs of the Sabbath Sacrifice (4Q400–407, 11Q5–6, and a fragment found at Masada) have been published. These poems, describing the angelic liturgy in the heavenly sanctuary, add to our knowledge of Essene interest in esoteric matters. See Carol Newsom, *Songs of the Sabbath Sacrifice: A Critical Edition*, Harvard Semitic Studies, no. 27 (Atlanta: Scholars Press, 1985).

106. There is nothing remarkable about the terminology used to describe the dream; it is called an ὄναρ/ὄνειρον in *War* 2.112 and *Ant.* 17.345, 347, and an ὄψις in *Ant.* 17.345, 346, 348.

107. Note the visual language in *War* 2.112 (ἰδεῖν, ὁρᾶν) and *Ant.* 17.345 (θεασάμενος, θεωρεῖν).

108. See σημαίνειν (of dream as a whole) in *War* 2.112. In 2.113 a correspondence is made between ears of corn and years, and oxen and revolution, but no technical terminology is used. In *Ant.* 17.346 the dream as a whole is said to "point to" or "refer to" (φέρειν) a change in Archelaus' situation. In 17.347 the oxen "indicate" (ἀποσσαφεῖν) suffering and a change in Archelaus' situation, while the ears of corn "denote" (ὁρίζειν) years.

109. See, e.g., Thackeray's note to the LCL translation, vol. 2, p. 365, n. e; Crone, *Early Christian Prophecy*, p. 122; O. Betz, *Offenbarung*, p. 104; Beall, *Description*, p. 109; Ehrlich, *Traum im Alten Testament*, p. 85; and R. Beckwith,

"The Significance of the Calendar for Interpreting Essene Chronology and Eschatology," *RQ* 10 (1980): 201.

110. This is the view of Thackeray and Ehrlich; see the works cited in the preceding note.

111. So, e.g., Beckwith, "Significance of the Calendar," p. 201. O. Betz seems to hover undecided between the two views; see his *Offenbarung*, p. 109.

112. The method described here is similar in many ways to that developed later by Artemidorus for the interpretation of "allegorical" dreams. For an excellent account of the basic principles of Artemidorus' theory of the interpretation of dreams, see S. R. F. Price, "The Future of Dreams: From Freud to Artemidorus," *Past and Present* 113 (1986): 3–37, especially pp. 9–16, 22–31. See also C. A. Behr, *Aelius Aristides and the Sacred Tales* (Amsterdam: Adolf M. Hakkert, 1968), pp. 171–95.

113. See, e.g., Blenkinsopp, "Prophecy and Priesthood," p. 247; Aune, *Prophecy in Early Christianity*, pp. 133–34; Crone, *Early Christian Prophecy*, p. 120; Horsley and Hanson, *Bandits, Prophets, and Messiahs*, pp. 155–57; Horsley, "Two Types," pp. 447–48; and Beall, *Description*, pp. 109–11.

114. Foerster also remarks on the differences between the kind of predictions made in the pesharim and those attributed to the Essene prophets by Josephus; see his "Der Heilige Geist im Spätjudentum," p. 134.

115. Crone, *Early Christian Prophecy*, pp. 119–20.

116. Crone, *Early Christian Prophecy*, p. 123.

117. Horsley and Hanson, *Bandits, Prophets, and Messiahs*, p. 155.

118. Horsley and Hanson, *Bandits, Prophets, and Messiahs*, p. 156.

119. Blenkinsopp, "Prophecy and Priesthood," pp. 246–47.

120. See *Ant.* 5.239 for the original prediction. In the Bible, Jotham utters a curse, not a prediction; see Jgs. 9.16–20, 57.

121. "Chaldaeans": *Ant.* 10.195, 198, 199, 203, 234; "Magi": *Ant.* 10.195, 198, 199, 203, 216, 234, 235, 236; "the wise": *Ant.* 10.197, 198. These terms are used more or less interchangeably.

122. See especially *Ant.* 10.199.

123. See *Ant.* 10.187–89, 194 on the education received by Daniel and his companions. On the status of these figures as a professional class, see *Ant.* 10.234, where they are described as a "class" (γένος), who "could interpret signs and dreams."

124. For the use of μάντις-terminology in connection with Balaam, see *Ant.* 4.104, 112, 157.

125. In addition to the instance cited here, μάντις-terminology is used of the "witch" in *Ant.* 6.327, 330, 331, 338. In the LXX account, such terminology occurs only in 1 Sam. 28.8.

Chapter 4

1. This label was first attached to these figures by Barnett in his "Jewish Sign Prophets," p. 679. Certain objections have been raised against the use of this title; see the next note.

2. Horsley has objected to the use of this label to describe the figures considered in this chapter on the grounds that the promise of signs was not a distinctive feature of their activity; see his "Popular Prophetic Movements," pp. 8–9. By

Horsley's count, signs are mentioned in only one of the relevant accounts, the one concerning the unnamed figures under Felix; in the remaining accounts, no sign terminology is used, nor, he argues, can the actions recorded in those accounts be construed as signs. He prefers to describe these figures as "action prophets" or "prophets who led movements," and states that "the distinctive thing which all of these prophets had in common is that they all led their followers into (antici- pated) participation in some great liberating action by God" (p. 8).

It can be agreed that the announcement of imminent divine deliverance and the call to join in some action that anticipated this deliverance were central fea- tures of these prophetic movements. Also, as we shall see, it is possible that a dis- tinction should be made between the kinds of miracles promised by Theudas and the Egyptian, on the one hand, and the signs promised by the rest of the prophets; if so, then "sign prophet" might not be an appropriate designation for Theudas and the Egyptian. But Horsley has played down the significance of the miracles and signs promised by these prophets to an unacceptable degree. He does not include in his list of action prophets either the prophet who led his followers to the Temple Mount in 70 C.E. or Jonathan, both of whom are said to have prom- ised signs. By my reckoning, then, there is only one account (concerning the unnamed figure under Festus) that mentions neither sign nor miracle. Thus, the promise to perform miracles of some sort does appear to have been a distinctive feature of the activity of these figures, and "sign prophets" may be retained as a convenient designation for them.

3. It is often suggested that Matt. 24.11, 24–26 / Mark 13.22 refer to the sign prophets mentioned by Josephus. Barnett includes bSanhedrin 67a in a list of pas- sages that may refer to the Egyptian ("Jewish Sign Prophets," p. 694, n. 2), and Crone notes the suggestion that the Egyptian should be identified with the Ben Stada mentioned in bShabbath 104b (*Early Christian Prophecy*, p. 332, n. 20).

4. On the dispute over the high-priestly vestments, see chapter 1, n. 51. On the name Θευδᾶς, see Schürer-Vermes-Millar, *History*, vol. 1, p. 456, n. 6, and the works referred to there.

5. According to 2 Kgs. 2, both Elijah (v. 8) and Elisha (v. 14) parted the Jor- dan while fifty of the sons of the prophets looked on from a distance. Horsley and Hanson have described these two miraculous partings of the river as "prophetic signs of imminent deliverance reminiscent of Moses and the crossing of the sea and of Joshua and the crossing of the Jordan" (*Bandits, Prophets, and Messiahs*, p. 141) and have suggested that they may have provided the model for Theudas (p. 167). But the connection between the Elijah-Elisha story and the exodus-con- quest events is unclear, to say the least. In 2 Kgs. 2, the parting of the Jordan is not part of a miraculous deliverance of any sort, but serves rather to demonstrate that the power of the spirit had been transferred from Elijah to Elisha. I therefore consider it unlikely that the Elijah-Elisha story served as a model for Theudas and his followers.

6. The parallel between the two events is made explicit in Joshua 3.7; 4.14, 23. In Josephus' version (*Ant.* 5.16–19), no direct comparison is made between them. Also, the crossing of the Jordan is not as dramatically miraculous in Jose- phus as it is in the Bible. In Josh. 3–4, the waters of the Jordan are stopped com- pletely when the feet of the priests carrying the ark first touch them; according to Josephus, God merely reduced the volume of the river so that it was fordable.

7. According to 4 Ezra 13.46–47, in "the last times," God will stop the chan-

nels of the Euphrates River so that the ten tribes in exile can return to Mount Zion, the place of eschatological judgment. This passage appears to be based on Isa. 11.15–16, which also speaks of a miraculous parting of the Euphrates and expressly compares it to the parting of the sea at the time of the exodus from Egypt.

8. Hengel, *Zealots*, p. 230, n. 5.

9. Exod. 13.18; Josh. 1.14; 4.12–13.

10. Israelites unarmed: *Ant.* 2.321, 326; provided with arms after crossing the sea: 2.349. The description that Josephus gives of the exodus in one of his speeches to the rebels in Jerusalem also implies that the Israelites were unarmed when they left Egypt (*War* 5.382–83). Moreover, Josephus includes the miraculous provision of arms after the crossing of the sea in some of his summarizing recitals of the miracles of the exodus and conquest; see, e.g., *Ant.* 3.18; 4.44.

11. Thackeray suggests that Josephus may be borrowing from Demetrius; see his note to the LCL translation, vol. 4, p. 305, n. d. Others have suggested the influence of the works of Ezekiel the tragedian; see, e.g., Louis H. Feldman, "Use, Authority and Exegesis of Mikra in the Writings of Josephus," in *Mikra: Text, Translation, Reading and Interpretation of the Hebrew Bible in Ancient Judaism and Early Christianity*, ed. Martin Jan Mulder, CRINT, sec. 2, vol. 1 (Assen: Van Gorcum; Philadelphia: Fortress, 1988), p. 474.

12. A "squadron of cavalry" (ἴλη ἱππέων, *Ant.* 20.98). The notes to the LCL translation of *Ant.* 19.365 and 20.98 connect Josephus' use of ἴλη with the Latin *ala* and suggest that an *ala* consisted of five hundred or one thousand men. According to Lewis and Short, *ala*, as a military division, "usually consisted of about 500 men" (p. 79).

13. On Acts 5.36 and its relationship to Josephus' account concerning Theudas, see Schürer-Vermes-Millar, *History*, vol. 1, pp. 456–57, n. 6, and the works referred to there. It is sometimes proposed that Acts is referring to a different Theudas, but this is extremely unlikely.

14. Χώρα can mean "country" both in the sense of "country" as opposed to "city" (in which case its meaning comes close to ἐρημία), and in the sense of "land" or "territory" (Liddell and Scott, p. 2015). So, when Josephus says that the Egyptian came εἰς τὴν χώραν, he might mean simply that he came from Egypt to Judaea or, more specifically, that he came to the countryside as opposed to the city. The second of these alternatives seems more likely, since Josephus, after saying in *War* 2.261 that the Egyptian appeared εἰς τὴν χώραν, states that he then led his followers ἐκ τῆς ἐρημίας (2.262), without suggesting that he had previously led them into the wilderness from somewhere else.

15. For the following explanation, which seeks to account for the discrepancies between the reports in the *War* and the *Antiquities* by pointing to the different apologetic emphases of the two works, see Cohen, *Josephus in Galilee and Rome*, pp. 154–60, 234–42; he comments on Josephus' portrayal of the sign prophets who appeared during the procuratorship of Felix on p. 157 and in n. 185. I deliberately speak of the different apologetic *emphases* of the two works; the continuities between them are not to be denied.

16. Noting (correctly) that the account in the *Antiquities* suggests that the Egyptian modeled his actions on those of Joshua, Horsley concludes that he and his followers were unarmed and nonviolent; see his "Two Types," p. 460; and (with Hanson) *Bandits, Prophets, and Messiahs*, p. 170. Horsley emphasizes that

"the battle-of-Jericho prototype was clearly *ritual* warfare" ("Two Types," p. 460, emphasis in original). Ritual warfare it may have been, but it was not nonviolent. According to the biblical account (Josh. 6), the miraculous collapse of the walls of Jericho was followed by an armed invasion and the slaughter, "with the edge of the sword," of most of the inhabitants of the city (6.21). Josephus' account of the incident (*Ant.* 5.22–32) is, in this respect, closely similar. Horsley's romanticism has even led him to deny a military element in the account in the *War.* He states that the "tone of military encounter" in Thackeray's translation is "merely ambiguous" in the Greek ("Two Types," p. 460). On the contrary, much of the language of the account suggests unambiguously that the Egyptian and his followers were planning an armed attack against Jerusalem. According to Josephus, the Egyptian "was prepared to use force to enter Jerusalem" (οἷός τε ἦν εἰς Ἱεροσόλυμα παρελθεῖν βιάζεσθαι, *War* 2.262), intended "to overpower" (κρατεῖν, 2.262) the Roman garrison in the city, and planned to use those who rushed in with him as his "bodyguard" (δορυφόροι, 2.262). In addition, it is said that Felix anticipated the Egyptian's "attack" (ὁρμή, 2.263), another term that suggests a military assault. On the violent and military connotations of this type of language, see Ernest Moore, "ΒΙΑΖΩ, ΑΡΠΑΖΩ and Cognates in Josephus," *NTS* 21 (1974–75): 519–43.

17. Πλάνοι ... ἄνθρωποι καὶ ἀπατεῶνες, *War* 2.259; οἱ ... γόητες καὶ ἀπατεῶνες ἄνθρωποι, *Ant.* 20.167.

18. Νεωτερισμός refers to innovation in the cultic-religious sphere in *Ant.* 5.101, 111; 9.204. In every other instance, it refers to politically revolutionary change or to outright revolt: *War* 5.152; 6.343; 7.447; *Ant.* 8.203; 13.425; 15.30 (with μεταβολή), 353, 424; 17.289, 314; 19.327; 20.106, 113, 133; *Life* 17, 23, 56, 184.

19. With στάσις: *War* 5.152; 6.343; with πόλεμος ἐμφύλιος: *War* 6.343; with ἀπόστασις: *Life* 17.

20. *Ant.* 18.118. Other passages in which μεταβολή is used to refer to political change or agitation include the following: *War* 1.23, 171; 4.231, 592; *Ant.* 1.13; 15.30 (with νεωτερισμός), 264; *Life* 36 (with πόλεμος and νεώτερον), 87 (with νεώτερον and στάσις).

21. See, e.g., Crone, *Early Christian Prophecy*, p. 131: "The use of the term δαιμονᾶν suggests that these groups appeared as enthusiastic or even frenzied pneumatics."

22. Hengel, *Zealots*, p. 16. Hengel refers to the use of ἀπόνοια, ἄνοια, and μανία in this context and cites the following examples (n. 67): *War* 2.265; 3.454, 479; 4.362; 5.34, 121, 424, 436; 6.20; 7.213, 267, 412; *Ant.* 17.263, 271; 18.25; *Life* 18. The only other occurrence of δαιμονάω, the verb used in the current passage, is in *War* 7.389, where it is used to describe the behavior of the Sicarii on Masada, eager, as if possessed, to commit suicide.

23. So also Horsley, "Two Types," p. 456: "To the latter [Josephus] it appeared as sheer madness that large numbers of the peasantry were inspired to abandon their fields and villages and to follow these charismatic leaders out into the desert, in anticipation of divine deliverance." Cf. *Ant.* 2.340, where the Egyptians think the Hebrews "mad" (μαίνεσθαι) for stepping into the Red Sea.

24. Horsley does not classify this figure as a sign prophet (or, in his terminology, an "action prophet"), but rather as an "oracular" prophet who promised deliverance ("Two Types," p. 453), though he acknowledges in another work that this

particular figure is "difficult to categorize by type" ("Popular Prophetic Movements," p. 8). But the fact that this prophet proclaimed a message does not distinguish him from the other sign prophets, and the report that he promised signs of deliverance and had six thousand followers puts him squarely in their camp.

25. My translation.

26. Horsley connects this prophet's promise of divine deliverance with the vision of the heavenly armies recorded in *War* 6.296–99 ("Two Types," p. 453). The argument seems to run as follows: the report in *War* 6 is only one of many passages in Jewish literature of the period concerning the role of the heavenly armies; such traditions attest a widespread expectation that God's heavenly armies would miraculously deliver the Jews at the End. The prophet in our present passage, Horsley suggests, may have expected just such a miraculous deliverance. Hengel connects Josephus' report about this prophet with speculation concerning the seventy weeks of years in Daniel (*Zealots*, pp. 242–43). He argues that the end of this period was believed to be imminent, and in fact was expected precisely on 10 Ab 70 c.e., the date on which Josephus says that the temple was destroyed. Hengel suggests that this prophet deliberately chose that day to lead his followers up to the temple (note the expression "on that day" in *War* 6.285), expecting the appearance of the Son of man as predicted in Daniel. A similar interpretation is given by Meyer, *Prophet aus Galiläa*, pp. 54–55. Both Hengel and Meyer are dependent on the analysis of Strack-Billerbeck, *Kommentar*, vol. 4, pp. 1001–11.

27. On Matt. 11.28–30 and related texts, see H. D. Betz, "The Logion of the Easy Yoke and of Rest (Matt. 11:28–30)," *JBL* 86 (1967): 10–24.

28. I give only a few examples: σημεῖον can mean "signal": *War* 2.172, 579; 3.105; 6.70; *Ant.* 5.46, 161; 12.404; 18.61; *Life* 322; "password": *War* 2.551; 3.88; and frequently in *Ant.* 19.29–256; "proof" or "evidence": *Ant.* 1.125, 127; 16.363. For the whole range of possible meanings of σημεῖον, see the entry in Liddell and Scott, p. 1593; and also K. H. Rengstorf, "σημεῖον," *TDNT*, vol. 7, pp. 200–261.

29. *War* 1.23; 3.404; 4.623. Σημεῖον is the only term for "omen" or "portent" that Josephus uses in connection with the *omina imperii*.

30. I shall return to this list of omens in chapter 5. It is sometimes said that Josephus distinguishes clearly between the terms σημεῖον and τέρας; see especially Rengstorf, "σημεῖον," pp. 224–25. This does not, however, appear to be the case. He certainly does not make a clear distinction in the present passage (*War* 6.288–315). In the introduction to the *War*, Josephus refers to the omens listed in 6.288–315 as σημεῖα καὶ τέρατα (1.28). In the passage itself, he uses the terms σημεῖον (three times), τέρας (twice), and φάσμα (once) to describe the omens. As far as I can tell, he uses these three terms as if they were completely synonymous. In 6.288 he uses τέρατα to summarize the list as a whole; at the conclusion of the passage (6.315), σημεῖα is used in the same way. In 6.295 he uses τέρας to describe the miraculous opening of the temple gate; in 6.296 he uses σημεῖον to describe the same incident. In 6.297 he describes the appearance of armies in heaven as "a miraculous apparition" (φάσμα τι δαιμόνιον); in 6.298 σημεῖον is used to refer to the same incident.

31. There is a parallel to *War* 1.370–79 in *Ant.* 15.121–46. No sign terminology is used in the account in the *Antiquities*, but a similar argument is made against interpreting the earthquake as an indication of God's displeasure; see *Ant.* 15.144–45.

32. In *War* 5.411 Josephus states that the same miracle occurred when the Babylonians, under Nebuchadnezzar, approached Jerusalem before the destruction of the first temple. No such miracle is recorded in scripture; see the note to the LCL translation, vol. 3, p. 329, n. e.

33. I have altered the LCL translation.

34. See, e.g., Barnett, "Jewish Sign Prophets," pp. 682–83; Horsley, "Two Types," p. 455; Horsley, "Popular Prophetic Movements," p. 4; and Hengel, *Zealots*, pp. 114–15.

35. To my knowledge, Otto Betz is the only scholar to have appreciated the difference between Josephus' usage of σημεῖον and that of the LXX; see his "Das Problem des Wunders bei Flavius Josephus im Vergleich zum Wunderproblem bei den Rabbinen und im Johannesevangelium," in *Josephus-Studien*, ed. O. Betz et al., p. 30.

36. See, e.g., Horsley, "Two Types," p. 456: "The 'tokens of deliverance' and the 'signs and wonders' are clearly allusions to the great historical acts of deliverance wrought by God in the exodus from slavery in Egypt, the way through the wilderness, and perhaps the entry into the promised holy land." See also Horsley and Hanson, *Bandits, Prophets, and Messiahs*, p. 162: "Thus their procession into the wilderness and the marvels and signs anticipated there as tokens of their own deliverance were surely conceived in analogy with the great liberating acts of God in the formative history of Israel"; they go on to quote Deut. 26.7–8. Barnett speculates about exactly which σημεῖα the sign prophets expected: "Were they expecting manna and/or quails to drop from the heavens? Would a 'Moses' figure strike a rock for the water to gush forth? Perhaps the Jordan would turn to blood?" ("Jewish Sign Prophets," p. 683).

37. Of the three miracles of Moses: Exod. 4.8, 9, 17, 28, 30; of the plagues: 8.19 (ET 8.23); 10.1, 2. In every instance, σημεῖον translates the Hebrew אות.

38. Exod. 7.3; 11.9, 10. In this case the correspondence with the MT is not so exact. In Exod. 7.3 σημεῖα represents the Hebrew אותת and τέρατα represents מופתים; but in 11.9 and 11.10, the Hebrew מופתים has been translated by the compound phrase σημεῖα καὶ τέρατα.

39. Σημεῖα alone: Num. 14.11, 22; Sir. 45.3; σημεῖα καὶ τέρατα: Deut. 4.34; 6.22; 7.19; 11.3; 26.8; 29.2; 34.11; Neh. 9.10; Pss. 77.43 (ET 78.43); 104.27 (ET 105.27); 134.9 (ET 135.9); Wisd. Sol. 10.16; Jer. 39.20–21 (ET 32.20–21); Baruch 2.11. It is often difficult to know whether the phrase "signs and wonders" in these passages refers specifically to the plagues or more generally to the miracles of the exodus as a whole. As can be seen from the list, the use of the compound phrase σημεῖα καὶ τέρατα is especially characteristic of material from the deuteronomic school, though it is found elsewhere.

40. In all of the passages listed in the preceding note that correspond to passages from the Hebrew Bible, σημεῖα translates the Hebrew אותת; in all but one, τέρατα translates מופתים (Deut. 11.3 has מעשים, "deeds").

41. See O. Betz, "Problem des Wunders," p. 30, in agreement.

42. O. Betz, "Problem des Wunders," p. 30 and n. 36; and O. Betz, "Miracles in the Writings of Flavius Josephus," in *Josephus, Judaism, and Christianity*, ed. Feldman and Hata, p. 235, n. 35. Josephus calls the plagues πάθη ("sufferings," *Ant.* 2.293, 299); πληγαί ("plagues," 2.296, 305); προσβολαὶ κακοῦ ("evil happenings," 2.300, 309); and κακά ("evil," 2.304).

43. See O. Betz, "Problem des Wunders," p. 30, on σημεῖα; he does not comment on the compound phrase.

44. See, e.g., *Ant.* 3.17–18, 86; 4.43–45.

45. *Ant.* 2.274, 276, 280, 283, 284.

46. According to Exod. 4.6, Moses' hand turned "leprous, as white as snow." Josephus avoids the mention of leprosy, apparently because of accusations like those reflected in *Ant.* 3.265–68 and *Against Apion* 1.279–85; see O. Betz, "Miracles," p. 234, n. 31.

47. I have modified the LCL translation slightly.

48. Deut. 13.2–6 (ET 13.1–5), frequently cited in this connection, also assumes that prophetic signs are ambiguous in this sense. A prophet who can perform "a sign or a wonder" (LXX: σημεῖον ἤ τέρας) might nevertheless prove to be a false prophet who attempts to lead the people into idolatry. This is one of the few deuteronomic passages in which σημεῖον and τέρας are used to designate authenticating miracles of the sort we are discussing.

49. On the use of miracles to authenticate a prophetic claim and the inconclusiveness of such a demonstration, see Sanders, *Jesus and Judaism*, pp. 170–72.

50. The biblical parallels are 2 Kgs. 20.1–11 and Isa. 38.1–22.

51. I have altered the LCL translation slightly.

52. A note on the terminology used by Josephus in comparison with that of the biblical account: Josephus uses the word σημεῖον to describe the sign performed by Isaiah in *Ant.* 10.29 (twice); in 10.28, as we have seen, he uses the phrase σημεῖόν τι καὶ τεράστιον. The LXX has σημεῖον in every instance (2 Kgs. 20.8, 9; Isa. 38.7, 22), and, in every case, this term translates the Hebrew אות.

53. According to the note to the LCL translation (vol. 5, p. 697, n. d), the same identification was made in rabbinic tradition.

54. See *Ant.* 8.236–37, 244; in 8.408, which refers back to this incident, it is assumed that the paralyzing of the king's hand was an authenticating miracle of the sort discussed here. I shall return to this last passage.

55. The biblical parallel is 1 Kgs. 13.11–34.

56. In the MT the word מופת is used of the signs offered by the man of God (1 Kgs. 13.3, 5); the LXX translates this term τέρας throughout. Josephus, however, consistently uses the term σημεῖον to refer to the signs (*Ant.* 8.232, 236, 244).

57. See especially 1 Kgs. 22.5–28 = *Ant.* 3.400–410.

58. I have altered the LCL translation slightly.

59. There are other passages in the *Antiquities* that could be discussed. *Ant.* 8.347 speaks of σημεῖα performed by Elijah; it is not clear to what this refers. In *Ant.* 9.23 Elijah prays for fire to come down from heaven and consume the soldiers who had been sent to seize him, in order "to prove whether he was a true prophet." In *Ant.* 6.53–57 the prophet Samuel predicts certain σημεῖα that will confirm his message to Saul that God had appointed him king over Israel. In *Ant.* 6.88–94 Samuel conjures up a thunderstorm as a σημεῖον of God's displeasure at the election of a king.

60. There is no evidence for Barnett's contention that the sign prophets regarded the signs they promised as " 'levers' by which to activate, even force, the hand of God to speedily bring his 'Salvation'" ("Jewish Sign Prophets," p. 688).

61. O. Betz, "Miracles," p. 223; see also pp. 224–25.

62. O. Betz, "Miracles," p. 227, emphasis mine.

63. O. Betz, "Miracles," p. 227, emphasis mine.

64. O. Betz, "Miracles," pp. 228–29.

65. See O. Betz, "Miracles," p. 228, in agreement.

66. *War* 1.28, 331, 377, 378; 4.287; 5.411; 6.288, 295; *Ant.* 2.265; 4.43, 291.

67. See n. 12.

68. Sanders, noting the use of the term ὁπλίτης in this passage, describes the contrast between the Egyptian and the other sign prophets in the following way: "Putting down the Egyptian, it appears, required a pitched battle. . . . Theudas and the others may have been suppressed by something closer to police action" (*Jesus and Judaism*, p. 303).

69. So also Horsley, "Two Types," p. 454.

70. On the contrast between the sign prophets and Jesus of Nazareth in terms of the nature of their call to people to follow them, and the number of their followers, see Hengel, *Charismatic Leader*, p. 59; on the question of numbers, see also Sanders, *Jesus and Judaism*, pp. 302–4.

71. Πλῆθος is used of the followers of the unnamed figures under Felix (*War* 2.259); ὄχλος of the followers of Theudas (*Ant.* 20.97), the unnamed figures under Felix (*Ant.* 20.167), and the prophet of 70 C.E. (*War* 6.283); δῆμος of the followers of the prophet of 70 C.E. (*War* 6.283); and δημοτικός of the followers of the Egyptian (*Ant.* 20.169) and the prophet of 70 C.E. (*War* 6.277).

72. On Josephus' use of δῆμος and πλῆθος, see V. A. Tcherikover, "Was Jerusalem a 'Polis'?," *IEJ* 14 (1964): 66. In the account of the Egyptian in the *War*, δῆμος is used to refer to the citizens or residents of Jerusalem who opposed the prophet (2.262–63).

73. Horsley, generalizing from the account of the Egyptian in the *War*, suggests that the followers of the sign prophets generally came from the countryside rather than the cities; see his "Popular Prophetic Movements," pp. 12–13.

74. Horsley similarly concludes that "we can make only rough connections between the broad general social historical situation and prophetic words and actions." As he points out, Barnett's discussion of the sign prophets ironically illustrates the point: "He [Barnett] sketches the 'context' for each of the 'sign prophets' but then apparently can make no specific connections between a given prophet and his 'context'"; see Horsley, "Popular Prophetic Movements," p. 18.

75. "Weaver" appears in one of the rabbinic lists of despised trades discussed by Joachim Jeremias in *Jerusalem in the Time of Jesus: An Investigation into Economic and Social Conditions During the New Testament Period*, trans. F. H Cave and C. H. Cave (London: SCM, 1969), pp. 303–12.

76. On the social-revolutionary concerns of the Sicarii, see David M. Rhoads, *Israel in Revolution: 6–74 C.E.: A Political History Based on the Writings of Josephus* (Philadelphia: Fortress, 1976), pp. 111–22; and Richard A. Horsley, "Menahem in Jerusalem: A Brief Messianic Episode Among the Sicarii—Not 'Zealot Messianism,'" *NovT* 27 (1985): 334–48.

77. So also Barnett, "Jewish Sign Prophets," pp. 686–87; Horsley, "Popular Prophetic Movements," p. 7; and de Jonge, "Zukunftserwartungen," pp. 218–19.

78. For example, by David Hill, "Jesus and Josephus' 'Messianic Prophets,'" in *Text and Interpretation*, ed. E. Best and R. McL. Wilson, pp. 143–54; by Meyer, "προφήτης," pp. 826–27; Meyer, *Prophet aus Galiläa*, pp. 82–88; and by Hengel, *Zealots*, pp. 229–33.

79. See Richard A. Horsley, "Popular Messianic Movements Around the Time of Jesus," *CBQ* 46 (1984): 473; and Horsley, "Popular Prophetic Movements," p. 7. Even this usage of "messianic" may be misleading if it is taken to imply that all such figures claimed to be *eschatological* kings.

80. At the time of the death of Herod: Judas, Simon, and Anthronges (*War* 2.55–65; *Ant*. 17.269–85); during the revolt: Menahem the Sicarius (*War* 2.433–48) and Simon son of Gioras. On these figures, see Horsley, "Popular Messianic Movements" and "Menahem in Jerusalem."

81. On the question of "realism," see Horsley, "Two Types," p. 462; and Horsley, "Ancient Jewish Banditry and the Revolt Against Rome, A.D. 66–70," *CBQ* 43 (1981): 422–24, which compares and contrasts bandits, prophets, messiahs, and Sicarii in terms of their degree of realism. I shall return to the question when I consider the relationship between sign prophets and armed rebels.

82. Barnett, "Jewish Sign Prophets," pp. 683, 687; and Crone, *Early Christian Prophecy*, pp. 134–35.

83. Horsley rejects this interpretation, according to which the Egyptian combined aspects of the role of sign prophet and popular king; see his "Popular Prophetic Movements," pp. 7–8. He argues that τοῦ δήμου τυραννεῖν does not mean "set oneself up as a tyrant" or "king," but indicates, instead, that the Egyptian presented himself as a popular democratic leader. He also claims that Josephus used the distinctive language of "claiming the kingship" and "donning the diadem" when describing messianic figures; such terminology is missing in the case of the Egyptian.

84. This interpretation is virtually universal; see, e.g., Horsley, "Two Types," p. 456; and Barnett, "Jewish Sign Prophets," pp. 682–83, 685.

85. On the range of religious associations connected with the desert or wilderness, and the various possible reasons for making an exodus there, see Hengel, *Zealots*, pp. 249–53. While recognizing that it had wider associations, Hengel connects the desert motif in Josephus' reports about the sign prophets with the exodus-conquest traditions.

86. See n. 26 for some speculations about what this prophet expected.

87. Sanders, *Jesus and Judaism*, p. 296.

88. See Rhoads, *Israel in Revolution*, p. 168.

89. I assume that γόητες, here and in *Ant*. 20.160–61, refers to sign prophets, since that is how Josephus uses the term in the rest of the account of events under Felix; see *War* 2.261 and *Ant*. 20.167.

90. So also Horsley, "Two Types," p. 444, commenting on *War* 2.264.

91. The classic works on the expectation of a particular eschatological prophet generally distinguish at least two types: the "prophet like Moses" or "new Moses" and "the returning Elijah" or "new Elijah"; see Horsley, "Two Types," pp. 437–43, and the works referred to there.

92. On the expectation of an eschatological prophet like Moses, see Howard M. Teeple, *The Mosaic Eschatological Prophet*, JBL Monograph Series, vol. 10 (Philadelphia: SBL, 1957); Wayne A. Meeks, *The Prophet-King: Moses Traditions and the Johannine Christology*, NovTS 14 (Leiden: E. J. Brill, 1967); and Joachim Jeremias, "Μωυσῆς," *TDNT*, vol. 4, pp. 848–73.

93. See, e.g., Aune, *Prophecy in Early Christianity*, pp. 127–28: "Theudas claimed to be a prophet, and in view of the rarity of that label during the late Second Temple period, he must have regarded himself as an *eschatological* prophet" (emphasis in original); or Hill, "Jesus and Josephus' 'Messianic Prophets,'" p. 148, on Theudas and the Egyptian: "Since their claim of prophecy could be made only within the context of events heralding the messianic times (when the prophetic spirit was expected to be active again), we may justifiably suggest that these

two individuals, at least, believed themselves to be involved in the imminent messianic release of the nation." This kind of reasoning is extremely common in studies of Jesus as prophet.

94. Horsley proposes that the sign prophets expected "the divine transformation of the socio-political order . . . into the society of justice willed and ruled by God" ("Two Types," p. 456; cf. (with Hanson) *Bandits, Prophets, and Messiahs*, p. 161), but this is pure speculation.

95. "False prophet": *War* 2.261 (Egyptian) and *War* 6.285 (prophet of 70 C.E.); "impostor": *War* 2.261 (Egyptian), *War* 2.264 (summary), *Ant.* 20.97 (Theudas), *Ant.* 20.160 (summary), *Ant.* 20.167 (unnamed figures under Felix), and *Ant.* 20.188 (unnamed figure under Festus); "deceiver": *War* 2.259 and *Ant.* 20.167 (unnamed figures under Felix), *War* 6.287 (prophets like the prophet of 70 C.E.), *Ant.* 20.98 (Theudas), and *Ant.* 20.188 (unnamed figure under Festus). The followers of the sign prophets are sometimes referred to as "the deceived": *War* 2.261 (Egyptian) and *Ant.* 20.188 (unnamed figure under Festus).

96. *War* 2.259 has πλάνοι; *War* 6.287, ἐξαπατάω.

97. Jer. 6.13; 33(ET 26).7, 8, 11, 16; 34(ET 27).9; 35(ET 28).1; 36(ET 29).1, 8; the only occurrence of the term outside the book of Jeremiah is Zech. 13.2. On the LXX usage, see J. Reiling, "The Use of ΨΕΥΔΟΠΡΟΦΗΤΗΣ in the Septuagint, Philo and Josephus," *NovT* 13 (1971): 147–56.

98. *Ant.* 8.318; 9.133, 134, 137.

99. *Ant.* 8.242; 10.66. There is no reference to prophets at all, whether true or false, in the biblical texts corresponding to these passages (*Ant.* 8.242 = 1 Kgs. 13.32; *Ant.* 10.66–67 = 2 Kgs. 23.15–16).

100. *Ant.* 8.236, 241. In the Bible, he is simply called a prophet (1 Kgs. 13.11, 18, 20, 25, 26 [MT only], 29).

101. On the meaning of γόης, see Liddell and Scott, p. 356; Gerhard Delling, "γόης," *TDNT*, vol. 1, pp. 737–38; and Smith, "The Occult in Josephus," pp. 250–52.

102. Γόης and related terms are used with reference to Moses in other passages in Josephus. In *Ant.* 2.320 Pharaoh laments the fact that the γοητεία of Moses had caused him to release the Hebrews; it is unclear whether γοητεία here refers to the three miracles of Moses, the plagues, or Moses' speeches on behalf of the Hebrews. In *Against Apion*, Josephus defends Moses against the charge that he was "an impostor and a deceiver" (γόης καὶ ἀπατεών, 2.145, 161), an accusation that, according to Josephus, was made by Apollonius Molon, Lysimachus, and others (2.145). It would appear that, in this instance, the charge of being an impostor and deceiver was not connected with the performance of miracles, for Josephus defends Moses by arguing that he was an excellent legislator and leader of the people, and says nothing at all about miracles. In other passages, too, γόης and related terms are used of individuals who are not depicted as miracle workers: John of Gischala (*War* 4.85), Castor the Jew (*War* 5.317), and Justus of Tiberius (*Life* 40).

103. Philo also contrasts the γόης and the προφήτης: "Further if anyone cloaking himself under the name and guise of a prophet and claiming to be possessed by inspiration lead us on to the worship of the gods recognized in the different cities, we ought not to listen to him and be deceived by the name of prophet. For such a one is no prophet, but an impostor [γόης], since his oracles and pronouncements are falsehoods invented by himself" (*Special Laws* 1.315, cited by

Feldman in the LCL translation of Josephus, vol. 10, p. 52, n. b). The topic here is idolatry, and there is no mention of miracles (though the passage appears to refer to Deut. 13.2–6 [ET 1–5]), but the basic meaning of γόης assumed by Philo is close to the meaning of the word in Josephus' reports concerning the sign prophets: a γόης is someone who claims to speak for God, but who, in reality, speaks "falsehoods invented by himself."

Chapter 5

1. The principal rabbinic texts are Ta'anith 3.8 and bTa'anith 23a. On these and other rabbinic traditions about Honi, see Vermes, *Jesus the Jew*, pp. 69–72, 80–82; Büchler, *Types of Jewish-Palestinian Piety*, pp. 196–264; and William Scott Green, "Palestinian Holy Men: Charismatic Leadership and Rabbinic Tradition," *ANRW* II.19.2 (1979): 619–47.

2. On the date, see Schürer-Vermes-Millar, *History*, vol. 1, p. 236, n. 7. The *War* does not mention Onias. In *Ant.* 14.19–29 Josephus has expanded *War* 1.126–27 by the addition of two apparently traditional stories, the first involving Onias (*Ant.* 14.22–24), and the second describing fraudulent negotiations over the provision of sacrificial animals for the Passover festival (14.25–28). As the double mention of Passover (14.21, 25) and the duplication of explanations for God's punishment of the Jews (14.25, 28) show, Josephus has not combined his sources completely smoothly. For rabbinic parallels to the story about the Passover sacrifices, see bMenahoth 64b, bSotah 49b, and bBaba Kamma 82b.

3. I have altered the LCL translation slightly.

4. bTa'anith 23a provides a different, and highly legendary, account of Onias/Honi's death.

5. At the general level considered here, Josephus' depictions of Balaam and Elijah closely reflect the Bible.

6. See Josephus' editorial remarks on the predictions of Balaam in *Ant.* 4.125.

7. See *Ant.* 8.343–46 = 1 Kgs. 18.41–46. Green has proposed that Honi used magical techniques to bring rain, and that the mention of prayers in the earliest rabbinic accounts of his rain-making activities is a "rabbinizing" feature; see his "Palestinian Holy Men," especially pp. 626–39. By Green's standards, Josephus' account is already rabbinized, for, as we have seen, it clearly states that Onias "had *prayed* to God to end the drought, and God had heard his *prayer*" (*Ant.* 14.22, emphasis mine). Two of Honi's grandsons, Hanan and Abba Hilkiah, were also famous as rain-makers; see Vermes, *Jesus the Jew*, p. 72; and Büchler, *Types of Jewish-Palestinian Piety*, pp. 201–3.

8. See Büchler, *Types of Jewish-Palestinian Piety*, pp. 158–60.

9. The Greek word θεοφιλής sometimes has the meaning "loving God," rather than "loved by God"; see Liddell and Scott, p. 792. The second sense seems, however, to be intended in every instance in Josephus; so also the translators of the LCL text and Rengstorf (vol. 2, p. 340).

10. This is an editorial comment of Josephus, unparalleled in scripture.

11. Most of this passage, including the remarks on Elisha's righteousness and his status as one loved by God, are additions to scripture; compare *Ant.* 9.182–83 with 2 Kgs. 13.20–21.

12. Once again, the remark is an addition to scripture; cf. Dan. 3.26–30.

13. This, too, is unscriptural; cf. Dan. 6.28. In addition to the examples cited here, θεοφιλής occurs in the following passages in Josephus: *War* 1.331 and *Ant.* 14.455 (Herod the Great); *War* 5.381 (the ancient Israelites generally); *Ant.* 1.106 ("the ancients" in general, and especially Noah); 1.346 (Isaac); and 6.280 (David). See also the use of the phrase φίλος τῷ θεῷ or some variant in the following: *War* 7.327 (the Jews as a whole); *Ant.* 4.199 (laws defining behavior that is "pleasing to God"); 5.116 (the practice of piety alone retains "the friendship of the Deity"); and 5.213 (Gideon).

14. Emphasis mine. See also *Ant.* 8.300: the king who rules "justly" (δικαίως) and "piously" (εὐσεβῶς) is "pleasing to God" (τῷ θεῷ φίλα).

15. So also Vermes, *Jesus the Jew*, p. 72. The rain-making incident described in the rabbinic traditions seems also to be set around Passover; see especially the references to Passover ovens in Ta'anith 3.8.

16. The Epitome and the Latin version have "Samaias" in *Ant.* 15.4, and that reading is adopted by Naber. But, as the *lectio difficilior* and the reading attested by all the major manuscripts, "Pollion" is preferable.

17. On these arrangements, see Schürer-Vermes-Millar, *History*, vol. 1, pp. 271–72.

18. According to the *War*, Herod and Phasael's successes "caused Hyrcanus a secret pang" (1.208). In the *Antiquities* Hyrcanus' suspicions are first aroused by his advisers (14.163–67).

19. *War* 1.208: "malicious persons at court"; *Ant.* 14.163: "the leading Jews"; 14.165: "the chief Jews."

20. In the *War* it is implied that Jewish law required that an execution be carried out only after some kind of trial and on the "oral or written instructions" of the head of state (1.209). According to *Ant.* 14.167, Jewish law "forbids us to slay a man, even an evildoer, unless he has first been condemned by the Sanhedrin to suffer this fate." The approval of the ruler was also required (also 14.167).

21. On what follows, see Sanders, *Practice and Belief*, pp. 479–80. For a more detailed discussion of the two accounts of Herod's trial, see James S. McClaren, *Power and Politics in Palestine: The Jews and the Governing of Their Land, 100 BC–AD 70*, JSNTS 63 (Sheffield: JSOT Press, 1991), pp. 67–79.

22. I have altered the LCL translation slightly.

23. See Sanders, *Practice and Belief*, p. 479. A similar, though not identical, trial from the time of Alexander Jannaeus is reported in bSanhedrin 19a-b.

24. On Roman rule as a punishment for sin, see pp. 38, 40–41. Mason also notes the similarity between the view attributed to Pollion/Samaias in *Ant.* 14.176 and Josephus' attitude to Roman rule; see his *Flavius Josephus on the Pharisees*, p. 262, n. 17.

25. That the Pharisees started out on the side of Hyrcanus II may be inferred from Josephus' account of divisions during the reigns of Alexander Jannaeus and Alexandra Salome. On one side were Jannaeus, "the eminent," Aristobulus II, and his son Antigonus; on the other, Salome Alexandra, the Pharisees, Hyrcanus II, and the Herodian family. On these alignments, see Sanders, *Practice and Belief*, pp. 390–91. The Pharisees' later actions are all consistent with continued support of Hyrcanus II.

26. On the proposed identifications, see Blenkinsopp, "Prophecy and Priesthood," p. 257, and the literature cited there.

27. Herod's sons, Alexander and Aristobulus, were executed in 7 B.C.E. The events described in *War* 1.567–70 and *Ant.* 17.32–45 took place sometime shortly afterward.

28. The *War* does not directly mention the Pharisees' involvement in the intrigues of 7/6 B.C.E., but it reports that Pheroras' wife was subsequently accused by Herod of "subsidizing the Pharisees to oppose him" (1.571). This is probably a reference to her payment of a fine on behalf of the Pharisees in connection with an oath of loyalty imposed by Herod, though this is not certain. More on the oath and the fine below.

29. My translation. For a different rendering of the phrase βασιλεῖ δυνάμενοι μάλιστα πράσσειν προμηθεῖς, see Mason, *Flavius Josephus on the Pharisees*, pp. 263, 266–67.

30. The meaning of *Ant.* 15.370 is not entirely clear. It may mean that Pollion and Samaias and their disciples refused to take the oath, but were not punished in the same way as the others who refused, namely, with death. This would not exclude the possibility of a fine; so Mason, *Flavius Josephus on the Pharisees*, p. 276. The continuation of the passage suggests, however, that Pollion and the others were excused from taking the oath, for 15.371 states that the Essenes were "also" (καί) "excused" (ἀφείθησαν) from the necessity of swearing the oath.

31. So also Daniel R. Schwartz, "Josephus and Nicolaus on the Pharisees," *JSJ* 14 (1983): 160. Schwartz attributes 15.370 to Josephus, and 17.41–42 to Nicolaus of Damascus.

32. See pp. 38–40.

33. Mason (*Flavius Josephus on the Pharisees*, p. 279) takes the expression to be a collective singular and draws attention to the use of the same phrase in *Ant.* 18.17; Sanders (*Practice and Belief*, p. 532, n. 4) suggests that the singular "points towards a leader."

34. My translation.

35. Vol. 8, p. 393, n. b.

36. See, e.g., D. R. Schwartz, "Josephus and Nicolaus on the Pharisees," pp. 159–61. For an argument in favor of Josephan authorship, see Mason, *Flavius Josephus on the Pharisees*, pp. 260–80.

37. See Mason, *Flavius Josephus on the Pharisees*, p. 265. Mason attributes the negative characterization of the Pharisees to Josephus.

38. Bagoas was executed immediately (*Ant.* 17.44); Pheroras died later (17.58–59).

39. Following the LCL rendering, I here translate the Greek singular ἐπιφοιτήσις with the English plural "appearances." Both ἐπιφοιτήσις and the cognate verb ἐπιφοιτάω often refer to habitual or frequent appearances; see Liddell and Scott, p. 671. Apart from the present passage, ἐπιφοιτήσις occurs in Josephus only in *Ant.* 19.223, where it is used of a "concourse" of soldiers—a "coming together," "gathering," or "crowd."

40. See, e.g., *Ant.* 1.279–83, 313; 2.172–75, 210–16; 5.215–16; 6.38–39; 11.327–28.

41. See also *War* 1.68.

42. I have altered the LCL translation. See also *War* 1.69.

43. Emphasis mine. There is no parallel in the *War* to this account of John's dream.

44. The message dreams of Josephus (*Life* 208–10) and Glaphyra (*War* 2.114–16 / *Ant*. 17.349–53) do not feature God as the messenger.

45. It is possible that the phrase τοῦ ἐπικαταστασθησομένου προρρήσει βασιλέως in *Ant*. 17.45 means "the one who would be appointed king *by a proclamation*," but this is unlikely: as we shall see immediately below, πρόρρησις is almost always used by Josephus in the sense of "prediction." I see no grounds for the translation given in the LCL: "the one who would some day be set over the people *with the title* of king" (emphasis mine).

46. In *Ant*. 1.225 and *Against Apion* 2.190 πρόρρησις has the meaning "commandment" or "precept."

47. In addition to the occurrences of πρόρρησις surveyed here, see also *Ant*. 4.105 (of Balaam); 9.120 (of Elijah); and *Against Apion* 1.258 (of a prediction written by an Egyptian seer).

48. As the note to the LCL translation (vol. 4, pp. 126–27, n. a) indicates, *Ant*. 1.257–58 condenses the account in Gen. 25.21–28. In the biblical account, Isaac first prays that Rebecca might conceive a child (v. 21); Rebecca then "inquires of God" and receives the oracle about the twins (vv. 22–23).

49. Predictions through symbolic dreams: *Ant*. 2.15, 65, 72; through message dreams, with God as the messenger: *Ant*. 1.284, 314; 2.217, 229; 6.43.

50. This is apparently a reference to Deut. 32.1–43; see the note in the margin of the LCL translation, vol. 4, p. 621.

51. Strict interpreters: *War* 1.110; 2.162; and *Life* 191; strict observers: *Ant*. 17.41.

52. It is difficult to say when Josephus thought these omens had occurred. No date is assigned to the appearance of the star and the comet. The other omens are said to have occurred during Passover (the light in the temple, the cow and the lamb, and the opening of the temple gate), between Passover and Pentecost (armies in the sky), and during Pentecost (the voice in the temple). Presumably a single cycle of festivals is intended, but Josephus does not specify the year. According to *War* 6.290, the last five portents occurred "before the revolt and the commotion that led to war." That suggests a date sometime before the defeat of Cestius in November of 66 C.E. In *War* 2.650, however, Josephus mentions the omens in connection with events which took place after Cestius' defeat but before the beginning of Vespasian's campaign in Galilee in the spring of 67 C.E. As we shall see, Jesus son of Ananias probably began his activity in Jerusalem in the autumn of 62 C.E.

53. The first prophecy is said to be recorded "in their oracles" (ἐν τοῖς λογίοις, 6.311); the second was "likewise in their sacred books" (ὁμοίως ἐν τοῖς ἱεροῖς . . . γράμμασιν, 6.312). The concluding reflection in *War* 6.315 makes it clear that these prophecies are included in the list of omens and portents being considered here; see Fischer, *Eschatologie*, p. 161.

54. Tacitus mentions (in the following order) the vision of armies in the sky, the mysterious light in the temple, the opening of the gate of the temple, the voice announcing "that the gods were leaving it," and the prediction concerning the ruler from Judaea. This last prediction is also mentioned by Suetonius in *Vesp*. 4. Both Tacitus and Suetonius, like Josephus, refer the prediction to Vespasian.

55. On the two accounts and the relationship between them, see Fischer, *Eschatologie*, pp. 161–67; Lindner, *Geschichtsauffassung*, pp. 126–32; and S. V.

McCasland, "Portents in Josephus and in the Gospels," *JBL* 51 (1932): 323–35. On Josephus' list, see also Otto Michel, "Apokalyptische Heilsansagen im Bericht des Josephus (*BJ* 6,290f., 293–95); ihre Umdeutung bei Josephus," in *Neotestamentica et Semitica: Studies in Honour of Matthew Black*, ed. E. Earle Ellis and Max Wilcox (Edinburgh: T. & T. Clark, 1969), pp. 240–44.

56. I have altered the LCL translation of both these passages slightly.

57. According to Josephus, Jesus appeared "four years before the war" (*War* 6.300), during the procuratorship of Albinus (6.305). Albinus was procurator from 62–64 C.E. It appears that the defeat of Cestius (November 66 C.E.) is here being taken as the beginning of the war and that Jesus appeared in the autumn of 62 C.E.

58. Moshe Greenberg has drawn attention to certain parallels in this respect between Jesus and the prophet Ezekiel; see his "On Ezekiel's Dumbness," *JBL* 77 (1958): 101–5.

59. On what follows, see Crone, *Early Christian Prophecy*, p. 136; and Aune, *Prophecy in Early Christianity*, p. 136.

60. See, e.g., Michel, "Spätjüdisches Prophetentum," p. 61.

61. See, e.g., Tosefta Sotah 13.2, quoted on p. 7.

62. On these points, see Aune, *Prophecy in Early Christianity*, pp. 136–37.

63. Aune, *Prophecy in Early Christianity*, p. 137.

64. Aune singles this out as a feature that distinguishes the oracle attributed to Jesus in *War* 6.301 from the woe oracles recorded in the Hebrew Bible; see his *Prophecy in Early Christianity*, p. 136.

65. On what follows, see *War* 2.224–27; *Ant.* 20.105–12.

66. According to *War* 2.227, "upwards of thirty thousand" died (though see the variant); *Ant.* 20.112 has "twenty thousand." Even allowing for some exaggeration, a very large number of people must have been killed.

67. *War* 2.224; cf. *Ant.* 20.106–7.

68. See *War* 2.272–76; *Ant.* 20.200–223.

69. The view attributed to the high priest Caiaphas in John 11.50 very likely reflects the actual stance of the Jewish leadership in a situation like this: it was better for one potential troublemaker to die than for the whole nation to be caught up in a conflagration. The evangelist intends this to be a reference to Jesus' saving death, but it can be understood at this more obvious and pragmatic level; see Sanders, *Jesus and Judaism*, p. 305.

70. See Matt. 24.1–2 // Mark 13.1–2 // Luke 21.5–6; Matt. 26.61 // Mark 14.58.

71. See Horsley, "Two Types," pp. 450–51, 453–54; and Horsley and Hanson, *Bandits, Prophets, and Messiahs*, pp. 143–45 (on the biblical prophets with whom Horsley compares Jesus), 174.

72. See Sanders, *Jesus and Judaism*, pp. 270–71, on the reaction to Jesus of Nazareth's threat against the temple.

73. For the use of δαιμόνιος in connection with an evil spirit, see, e.g., *Ant.* 6.214. The term is more often used in connection with things divine; see, e.g., *War* 1.82; 3.341; 4.622; 6.296; 7.82, 318; *Ant.* 13.314.

Bibliography

Ahituv, Shmuel, and Louis Isaac Rabinowitz. "Divination." *Enc. Jud.*, vol. 6, cols. 111–20.

Attridge, Harold W. *The Interpretation of Biblical History in the Antiquitates Judicae of Flavius Josephus.* Harvard Dissertations in Religion, no. 7. Missoula, Mont.: Scholars Press, 1976.

Aune, David E. *Prophecy in Early Christianity and the Ancient Mediterranean World.* Grand Rapids, Mich.: Eerdmans, 1983.

———. "The Use of ΠΡΟΦΗΤΗΣ in Josephus." *JBL* 101 (1982): 419–21.

Barnett, P. W. "The Jewish Eschatological Prophets A.D. 40–70 in Their Theological and Political Setting." Ph.D. diss., University of London, 1977.

———. "The Jewish Sign Prophets—A.D. 40–70: Their Intentions and Origin." *NTS* 27 (1980–81): 679–97.

Barr, James. *Holy Scripture: Canon, Authority, Criticism.* Philadelphia: Westminster Press, 1983.

Barton, John. "'The Law and the Prophets.' Who Are the Prophets?" *OS* 23 (1984): 1–18.

———. *Oracles of God: Perceptions of Ancient Prophecy in Israel after the Exile.* London: Darton, Longman and Todd, 1986.

Baumgarten, A. I. "*Korban* and the Pharisaic *Paradosis.*" *Journal of the Ancient Near Eastern Society* 16–17 (1984–85): 5–17.

Baumgarten, Joseph M. "The Essene Avoidance of Oil and the Laws of Purity." In his *Studies in Qumran Law.* SJLA 24. Leiden: E. J. Brill, 1977. Pp. 88–97 (= *RQ* 6 [1967]: 183–93).

Beall, Todd S. *Josephus' Description of the Essenes Illustrated by the Dead Sea Scrolls.* SNTSMS 58. Cambridge: Cambridge University Press, 1988.

Beckwith, Roger. *The Old Testament Canon of the New Testament Church and Its Background in Early Judaism.* London: SPCK, 1985.

———. "The Significance of the Calendar for Interpreting Essene Chronology and Eschatology." *RQ* 10 (1980): 167–202.

Begg, Christopher T. "The 'Classical Prophets' in Josephus' *Antiquities.*" *Louvain Studies* 13 (1988): 341–57.

Behr, C. A. *Aelius Aristides and the Sacred Tales.* Amsterdam: Adolf M. Hakkert, 1968.

Best, Ernest. "The Use and Non-Use of Pneuma by Josephus." *NovT* 3 (1959): 218–25.

Betz, H. D. "The Logion of the Easy Yoke and of Rest (Matt. 11:28–30)." *JBL* 86 (1967): 10–24.

Betz, Otto. "Miracles in the Writings of Flavius Josephus." In *Josephus, Judaism, and Christianity*, ed. Louis H. Feldman and Gohei Hata. Detroit: Wayne State University Press, 1987. Pp. 212–35.

———. *Offenbarung und Schriftforschung in der Qumransekte.* WUNT 6. Tübingen: J. C. B. Mohr (Paul Siebeck), 1960.

———. "Das Problem des Wunders bei Flavius Josephus im Vergleich zum Wunderproblem bei den Rabbinen und im Johannesevangelium." In *Josephus-Studien: Untersuchungen zu Josephus, dem antiken Judentum und dem Neuen Testament*, ed. Otto Betz, Klaus Haacker, and Martin Hengel. Göttingen: Vandenhoeck und Ruprecht, 1974. Pp. 23–44.

Bilde, Per. "The Causes of the Jewish War According to Josephus." *JSJ* 10 (1979): 179–202.

———. *Flavius Josephus between Jerusalem and Rome: His Life, His Works, and Their Importance.* JSPS 2. Sheffield: JSOT Press, 1988.

Blenkinsopp, Joseph. "Prophecy and Priesthood in Josephus." *JJS* 25 (1974): 239–62.

Brooke, George J., ed. *Temple Scroll Studies: Papers Presented at the International Symposium on the Temple Scroll, Manchester, December 1987.* JSPS 7. Sheffield: JSOT Press, 1989.

Bruce, F. F. "Josephus and Daniel." *ASTI* 4 (1965): 148–62.

Buchanan, George Wesley. "The Role of Purity in the Structure of the Essene Sect." *RQ* 4 (1963): 397–406.

Büchler, Adolph. *Types of Jewish-Palestinian Piety from 70 B.C.E to 70 C.E.: The Ancient Pious Men.* Jews' College Publications, no. 8. London: Jews' College, 1922.

Callaway, Phillip R. *The History of the Qumran Community: An Investigation.* JSPS 3. Sheffield: JSOT Press, 1988.

Charles, R. H. *The Testaments of the Twelve Patriarchs.* London: Adam and Charles Black, 1908.

Charlesworth, James H., ed. *The Old Testament Pseudepigrapha.* 2 vols. London: Darton, Longman and Todd, 1983–85.

Cohen, Shaye J. D. *Josephus in Galilee and Rome: His Vita and Development as a Historian.* Columbia Studies in the Classical Tradition, vol. 8. Leiden: E. J. Brill, 1979.

———. "Josephus, Jeremiah, and Polybius." *History and Theory* 21 (1982): 366–81.

———. "Masada: Literary Tradition, Archaeological Remains, and the Credibility of Josephus." *JJS* 33 (1982): 385–405.

Crone, Theodore M. *Early Christian Prophecy: A Study of Its Origin and Function.* Baltimore: St. Mary's University Press, 1973.

Cross, Frank Moore, Jr. *The Ancient Library of Qumran and Modern Biblical Studies.* The Haskell Lectures, 1956–57. Rev. ed. Garden City, N.Y.: Doubleday Anchor Books, 1961.

Danby, Herbert, trans. *The Mishnah.* Oxford: Oxford University Press, 1933.

Daube, David. "'I Believe' in *Jewish Antiquities* xi.237." *JJS* 27 (1976): 142–46.

————. "Typology in Josephus." *JJS* 31 (1980): 18–36.

Davies, Philip R. *The Damascus Covenant: An Interpretation of the "Damascus Document."* JSOTS 25. Sheffield: JSOT Press, 1983.

————. "The Ideology of the Temple in the Damascus Document." *JJS* 33 (1982): 287–301.

————. Review of *Josephus' Description of the Essenes Illustrated by the Dead Sea Scrolls*, by Todd S. Beall. In *JTS* 41 (1990): 164–69.

Davies, W. D. *Paul and Rabbinic Judaism: Some Rabbinic Elements in Pauline Theology.* 2d ed. London: SPCK, 1955.

Delling, Gerhard. "Die biblische Prophetie bei Josephus." In *Josephus-Studien: Untersuchungen zu Josephus, dem antiken Judentum und dem Neuen Testament*, ed. Otto Betz, Klaus Haacker, and Martin Hengel. Göttingen: Vandenhoeck und Ruprecht, 1974. Pp. 109–21.

————. "γόης." *TDNT*, vol. 1, pp. 737–38.

————. "Josephus und das Wunderbare." *NovT* 2 (1958): 291–309.

Droge, Arthur J., and James D. Tabor. *A Noble Death: Suicide and Martyrdom Among Christians and Jews in Antiquity.* San Francisco: Harper, 1992.

Duling, Dennis C. "The Eleazar Miracle and Solomon's Magical Wisdom in Flavius Josephus's *Antiquitates Judaicae* 8.42–49." *HTR* 78 (1985): 1–25.

Dupont-Sommer, A. *The Essene Writings from Qumran.* Trans. G. Vermes. Oxford: Basil Blackwell, 1961.

Ehrlich, Ernst Ludwig. *Der Traum im Alten Testament.* BZAW 73. Berlin: Alfred Töpelmann, 1953.

Epstein, I., ed. *The Babylonian Talmud.* 35 vols. London: Soncino Press, 1935–52.

Fascher, Erich. Προφήτης: *Eine sprach- und religionsgeschichtliche Untersuchung.* Giessen: Alfred Töpelmann, 1927.

Feldman, Louis H. "Flavius Josephus Revisited: The Man, His Writings, and His Significance." *ANRW* II.21.2 (1984): 763–862.

————. "The Identity of Pollio, the Pharisee, in Josephus." *JQR* 49 (1958–59): 53–62.

————. *Josephus and Modern Scholarship (1937–1980).* Berlin: Walter de Gruyter, 1984.

————. *Josephus: A Supplementary Bibliography.* With an Introduction by Morton Smith. New York: Garland, 1986.

————. "Masada: A Critique of Recent Scholarship." In *Christianity, Judaism and Other Greco-Roman Cults*, ed. Jacob Neusner. SJLA 12.3. Leiden: E. J. Brill, 1975. Pp. 218–48.

————. "Prophets and Prophecy in Josephus." *JTS* 41 (1990): 386–422.

————. "Use, Authority and Exegesis of Mikra in the Writings of Josephus." In *Mikra: Text, Translation, Reading and Interpretation of the Hebrew Bible in Ancient Judaism and Early Christianity*, ed. Martin Jan Mulder. CRINT, sec. 2, vol. 1. Assen: Van Gorcum; Philadelphia: Fortress, 1988. Pp. 455–518.

Fischer, Ulrich. *Eschatologie und Jenseitserwartung im hellenistischen Diasporajudentum.* BZNW 44. Berlin: Walter de Gruyter, 1978.

Fitzmyer, Joseph A. *The Dead Sea Scrolls: Major Publications and Tools for Study.* 2d ed. SBL Sources for Biblical Study, no. 8. Missoula, Mont.: Scholars Press, 1977.

Foerster, Werner. "Der Heilige Geist im Spätjudentum." *NTS* 8 (1961–62): 117–34.

Foote, T. C. "The Ephod." *JBL* 21 (1902): 1–47.

Fowler, W. Warde. "Polybius' Conception of Τύχη." *Classical Review* 17 (1903): 445–49.

Fritz, Kurt von. *The Theory of the Mixed Constitution in Antiquity: A Critical Analysis of Polybius' Political Ideas.* New York: Columbia University Press, 1954.

Goodman, Martin. *The Ruling Class of Judaea: The Origins of the Jewish Revolt Against Rome A.D. 66–70.* Cambridge: Cambridge University Press, 1987.

Green, William Scott. "Palestinian Holy Men: Charismatic Leadership and Rabbinic Tradition." *ANRW* II.19.2 (1979): 619–47.

Greenberg, Moshe. "On Ezekiel's Dumbness." *JBL* 77 (1958): 101–5.

———. "Urim and Thummim." *Enc. Jud.*, vol. 16, cols. 8–9.

Greenspahn, Frederick E. "Why Prophecy Ceased." *JBL* 108 (1989): 37–49.

Grintz, Yehoshua M. "Ephod." *Enc. Jud.*, vol. 6, cols. 804–6.

Hanson, John S. "Dreams and Visions in the Graeco-Roman World and Early Christianity." *ANRW* II.23.2 (1980): 1395–1427.

Haran, Menahem. "Priestly Vestments." *Enc. Jud.*, vol. 13, cols. 1063–69.

Hengel, Martin. *The Charismatic Leader and His Followers.* Trans. James C. G. Greig. Studies of the New Testament and Its World, vol. 1. Edinburgh: T. & T. Clark, 1981.

———. *Judaism and Hellenism: Studies in Their Encounter in Palestine During the Early Hellenistic Period.* Trans. John Bowden. 2 vols. in 1 part. London: SCM, 1974.

———. *The Zealots: Investigations into the Jewish Freedom Movement in the Period from Herod I Until 70 A.D.* Trans. David Smith. Edinburgh: T. & T. Clark, 1989.

Hill, David. "Jesus and Josephus' 'Messianic Prophets.'" In *Text and Interpretation: Studies in the New Testament Presented to Matthew Black*, ed. E. Best and R. McL. Wilson. Cambridge: Cambridge University Press, 1979. Pp. 143–54.

Hölscher, Gustav. "Josephus." *RE*, vol. 9 (1916), cols. 1934–2000.

Horsley, Richard A. "Ancient Jewish Banditry and the Revolt Against Rome, A.D. 66–70." *CBQ* 43 (1981): 409–32.

———. "'Like One of the Prophets of Old': Two Types of Popular Prophets at the Time of Jesus." *CBQ* 47 (1985): 435–63.

———. "Menahem in Jerusalem: A Brief Messianic Episode among the Sicarii—Not 'Zealot Messianism.'" *NovT* 27 (1985): 334–48.

———. "Popular Messianic Movements Around the Time of Jesus." *CBQ* 46 (1984): 471–95.

———. "Popular Prophetic Movements at the Time of Jesus: Their Principal Features and Social Origins." *JSNT* 26 (1986): 3–27.

Horsley, Richard A., and John S. Hanson. *Bandits, Prophets, and Messiahs: Popular Movements at the Time of Jesus.* Minneapolis: Winston Press, 1985.

Jeremias, Joachim. *Jerusalem in the Time of Jesus: An Investigation into Economic and Social Conditions During the New Testament Period.* Trans. F. H. Cave and C. H. Cave. London: SCM, 1969.

———. "Μωυσῆς." *TDNT*, vol. 4, pp. 848–73.

Jonge, Marianus de. "Josephus und die Zukunftserwartungen seines Volkes." In *Josephus-Studien: Untersuchungen zu Josephus, dem antiken Judentum und dem Neuen Testament*, ed. Otto Betz, Klaus Haacker, and Martin Hengel. Göttingen: Vandenhoeck und Ruprecht, 1974. Pp. 205–19.

Kampen, John. "A Reconsideration of the Name 'Essene' in Greco-Jewish Literature in Light of Recent Perceptions of the Qumran Sect." *HUCA* 57 (1986): 61–81.

Kittel, Gerhard, and Gerhard Friedrich, eds. *Theological Dictionary of the New Testament*. Trans. and ed. G. W. Bromily. 9 vols. Grand Rapids, Mich.: Eerdmans, 1964–76.

Knibb, Michael A. *The Qumran Community*. Cambridge Commentaries on Writings of the Jewish and Christian World, 200 BC to AD 200, vol. 2. Cambridge: Cambridge University Press, 1987.

Ladouceur, David J. "Josephus and Masada." In *Josephus, Judaism, and Christianity*, ed. Louis H. Feldman and Gohei Hata. Detroit: Wayne State University Press, 1987. Pp. 95–113.

———. "Masada: A Consideration of the Literary Evidence." *Greek, Roman, and Byzantine Studies* 21 (1980): 245–60.

Laperrousaz, E. M. *Qoumrân, l'établissement essénien des bords de la Mer Morte*. Paris: A. & J. Picard, 1976.

Lattimore, Richmond. "Portents and Prophecies in Connection with the Emperor Vespasian." *Classical Journal* 29 (1933–34): 441–49.

Leivestad, Ragnar. "Das Dogma von der prophetenlosen Zeit." *NTS* 19 (1972–73): 288–99.

Lewis, Charlton T., and Charles Short. *A Latin Dictionary*. Oxford: Oxford University Press, 1879.

Liddell, Henry George, and Robert Scott. *A Greek-English Lexicon*. 9th ed., rev. and augmented by Henry Stuart Jones. Oxford: Oxford University Press, 1940.

Lindblom, J. *Gesichte und Offenbarungen: Vorstellungen von göttlichen Weisungen und übernatürlichen Erscheinungen im ältesten Christentum*. Skrifter utgivna av. Kungl. Humanistiska Vetenskapssamfundet i Lund 65. Lund: Gleerup, 1968.

———. "Lot-Casting in the Old Testament." *VT* 12 (1962): 164–78.

———. *Prophecy in Ancient Israel*. Oxford: Basil Blackwell, 1962.

———. "Die Vorstellung vom Sprechen Jahwes zu den Menschen im Alten Testament." *ZAW* 75 (1963): 263–88.

Lindner, Helgo. *Die Geschichtsauffassung des Flavius Josephus im Bellum Judaicum: Gleichzeitig ein Beitrag zur Quellenfrage*. Arbeiten zur Geschichte des antiken Judentums und des Urchristentums, vol. 12. Leiden: E. J. Brill, 1972.

Lohse, Eduard, trans. and ed. *Die Texte aus Qumran*. Darmstadt: Wissenschaftliche Buchgesellschaft, 1964.

Long, Burke O. "The Effect of Divination upon Israelite Literature." *JBL* 92 (1973): 489–97.

MacMullen, Ramsay. *Enemies of the Roman Order: Treason, Unrest, and Alienation in the Empire*. Cambridge, Mass.: Harvard University Press, 1966.

Mason, Steve. *Flavius Josephus on the Pharisees: A Composition-Critical Study*. Studia Post-Biblica, vol. 39. Leiden: E. J. Brill, 1991.

———. "Priesthood in Josephus and the 'Pharisaic Revolution.'" *JBL* 107 (1988): 657–61.

Mayer, Reinhold, and Christa Möller. "Josephus—Politiker und Prophet." In *Josephus-Studien: Untersuchungen zu Josephus, dem antiken Judentum und dem Neuen Testament*, ed. Otto Betz, Klaus Haacker, and Martin Hengel. Göttingen: Vandenhoeck und Ruprecht, 1974. Pp. 271–84.

McCasland, S. V. "Portents in Josephus and in the Gospels." *JBL* 51 (1932): 323–35.

———. "Signs and Wonders." *JBL* 76 (1957): 149–52.

McClaren, James S. *Power and Politics in Palestine: The Jews and the Governing of Their Land, 100 BC–AD 70*. JSNTS 63. Sheffield: JSOT Press, 1991.

Meeks, Wayne A. *The Prophet-King: Moses Traditions and the Johannine Christology*. NovTS 14. Leiden: E. J. Brill, 1967.

Meier, John P. "Jesus in Josephus: A Modest Proposal." *CBQ* 52 (1990): 76–103.

Meyer, Rudolf. "Prophecy and Prophets in the Judaism of the Hellenistic-Roman Period." In "προφήτης κτλ." *TDNT*, vol. 6, pp. 812–28.

———. *Der Prophet aus Galiläa: Studie zum Jesusbild der drei ersten Evangelien*. 2d ed. Darmstadt: Wissenschaftliche Buchgesellschaft, 1970.

Michel, Otto. "Apokalyptische Heilsansagen im Bericht des Josephus (*BJ* 6,290f., 293–95); ihre Umdeutung bei Josephus." In *Neotestamentica et Semitica: Studies in Honour of Matthew Black*, ed. E. Earle Ellis and Max Wilcox. Edinburgh: T. & T. Clark, 1969. Pp. 240–44.

———. "Spätjüdisches Prophetentum." In *Neutestamentliche Studien für Rudolf Bultmann*, ed. W. Eltester. BZNW 21. Berlin: Alfred Töpelmann, 1954. Pp. 60–66.

Michel, Otto, and Otto Bauernfeind, trans. and eds. *Flavius Josephus, De bello judaico: Zweisprachige Ausgabe der sieben Bücher*. 3 vols. in 4 parts. Bad Homburg: Hermann Gentner, 1960 (vol. 1); Munich: Kösel, 1963–69 (vols. 2–3).

Moehring, Horst R. "Joseph ben Matthia and Flavius Josephus: The Jewish Prophet and Roman Historian." *ANRW* II.21.2 (1984): 864–944.

Montgomery, James A. "The Religion of Flavius Josephus." *JQR* 11 (1920–21): 277–305.

Moore, Ernest. "ΒΙΑΖΩ, ΑΡΠΑΖΩ and Cognates in Josephus." *NTS* 21 (1974–75): 519–43.

Müller, Hans-Peter. "Mantische Weisheit und Apokalyptik." VTS 22 (1972): 268–93.

Muss-Arnolt, W., and Ludwig Blau. "Urim and Thummim." *JE*, vol. 12, pp. 384–86.

Naber, Samuel A., ed. *Flavii Josephi opera omnia post Immanuelem Bekkerum*. 6 vols. in 3 parts. Leipzig: Teubner, 1888–96.

Newsom, Carol. *Songs of the Sabbath Sacrifice: A Critical Edition*. Harvard Semitic Studies, no. 27. Atlanta: Scholars Press, 1985.

Niese, Benedict, ed. *Flavii Josephi opera*. 7 vols. Berlin: Weidmann, 1885–95 (= *editio maior*).

Oppenheim, A. Leo. *The Interpretation of Dreams in the Ancient Near East*. Transactions of the American Philosophical Society, new ser., vol. 46. Philadelphia: American Philosophical Society, 1956. Pp. 179–373.

Porter, J. R. "Ancient Israel." In *Divination and Oracles*, ed. Michael Loewe and Carmen Blacker. London: George Allen and Unwin, 1981. Pp. 191–214.

Price, S. R. F. "The Future of Dreams: From Freud to Artemidorus." *Past and Present* 113 (1986): 3–37.

Rajak, Tessa. "Josephus and the 'Archaeology' of the Jews." *JJS* 33 (1982): 465–77.

———. *Josephus: The Historian and His Society.* London: Duckworth, 1983.

Reiling, J. "The Use of ΨΕΥΔΟΠΡΟΦΗΤΗΣ in the Septuagint, Philo and Josephus." *NovT* 13 (1971): 147–56.

Rengstorf, K. H. "σημεῖον." *TDNT*, vol. 7, pp. 200–261.

———. "τέρας." *TDNT*, vol. 8, pp. 113–26.

———, ed. *A Complete Concordance to Flavius Josephus.* 4 vols. Leiden: E. J. Brill, 1973–83.

Rhoads, David M. *Israel in Revolution: 6–74 C.E.: A Political History Based on the Writings of Josephus.* Philadelphia: Fortress, 1976.

Robertson, Edward. "The 'Ūrīm and Tummīm; What Were They?" *VT* 14 (1964): 67–74.

Roth, Cecil, ed. *Encyclopaedia Judaica.* 16 vols. Jerusalem: Keter, 1971–72.

Russell, D. S. *The Method and Message of Jewish Apocalyptic: 200 BC–AD 100.* London: SCM, 1964.

Sanders, E. P. *Jesus and Judaism.* London: SCM; Philadelphia: Fortress, 1985.

———. *Jewish Law from Jesus to the Mishnah: Five Studies.* London: SCM; Philadelphia: Trinity Press International, 1990.

———. *Judaism: Practice and Belief 63 BCE–CE 66.* London: SCM; Philadelphia: Trinity Press International, 1992.

Schalit, Abraham. "Die Erhebung Vespasians nach Flavius Josephus, Talmud und Midrasch: Zur Geschichte einer messianischen Prophetie." *ANRW* II.2 (1975): 208–327.

———. "Josephus Flavius." *Enc. Jud.*, vol. 10, cols. 251–65.

Schiffman, Lawrence H. *Sectarian Law in the Dead Sea Scrolls: Courts, Testimony and the Penal Code.* Brown Judaic Studies, no. 33. Chico, Cal.: Scholars Press, 1983.

Schürer, Emil. *The History of the Jewish People in the Age of Jesus Christ (175 B.C.–A.D. 135).* New English version rev. and ed. Geza Vermes, Fergus Millar, and Martin Goodman (vol. 3 only). 3 vols. in 4 parts. Edinburgh: T. & T. Clark, 1973–87.

Schwartz, Daniel R. "Josephus and Nicolaus on the Pharisees." *JSJ* 14 (1983): 157–71.

———. "Priesthood and Priestly Descent: Josephus, *Antiquities* 10.80." *JTS* 32 (1981): 129–35.

Schwartz, Seth. *Josephus and Judaean Politics.* Columbia Studies in the Classical Tradition, vol. 18. Leiden: E. J. Brill, 1990.

Scott, Kenneth. *The Imperial Cult Under the Flavians.* Stuttgart: W. Kohlhammer, 1936.

Singer, Isidore, ed. *The Jewish Encyclopedia.* 12 vols. London: Funk and Wagnalls, 1901–6.

Smallwood, E. Mary. *The Jews Under Roman Rule: From Pompey to Diocletian.* SJLA 20. Leiden: E. J. Brill, 1976.

Smith, Morton. "The Description of the Essenes in Josephus and the Philosophumena." *HUCA* 29 (1958): 273–313.

———. "The Occult in Josephus." In *Josephus, Judaism, and Christianity*, ed. Louis H. Feldman and Gohei Hata. Detroit: Wayne State University Press, 1987. Pp. 236–56.

Sparks, H. F. D. *The Apocryphal Old Testament*. Oxford: Oxford University Press, 1984.

Stern, Menahem. *Greek and Latin Authors on Jews and Judaism*. 3 vols. Jerusalem: Israel Academy of Sciences and Humanities, Jerusalem Academic Press, 1974–84.

———. "Sicarii and Zealots." In *Society and Religion in the Second Temple Period*, ed. M. Avi-Yonah and Zvi Baras. *The World History of the Jewish People*, ed. B. Netanyahu et al., vol. 8. Jerusalem: Massada, 1977. Pp. 263–301.

Strack, Hermann L., and Paul Billerbeck. *Kommentar zum Neuen Testament aus Talmud und Midrasch*. 4 vols. in 5 parts. Munich: Oskar Beck, 1922–28.

Strugnell, John. "Moses-Pseudepigrapha at Qumran: 4Q375, 4Q376, and Similar Works." In *Archaeology and History in the Dead Sea Scrolls: The New York University Conference in Memory of Yigael Yadin*, ed. Lawrence H. Schiffman. JSPS 8. Sheffield: JSOT Press, 1990. Pp. 221–56.

Tcherikover, V. A. "Was Jerusalem a 'Polis'?" *IEJ* 14 (1964): 61–78.

Teeple, Howard M. *The Mosaic Eschatological Prophet*. JBL Monograph Series, vol. 10. Philadelphia: SBL, 1957.

Temporini, H., and W. Haase, eds. *Aufstieg und Niedergang der römischen Welt: Geschichte und Kultur Roms im Spiegel der neueren Forschung*. Berlin and New York: Walter de Gruyter, 1972- .

Thackeray, H. St. John. *Josephus: The Man and the Historian*. With a Preface by George Foot Moore. New York: Jewish Institute of Religion, 1929.

Thackeray, H. St. John, and Ralph Marcus. *A Lexicon to Josephus*. 4 pts. (A–θεμφιλοχωρεῖν). Paris: Librairie Orientaliste Paul Geuthner, 1930–55.

Thackeray, H. St. John (vols. 1–5), Ralph Marcus (vols. 5–8), Allen Wikgren (vol. 8), and Louis H. Feldman (vols. 9–10), trans. and eds. *Josephus*. 10 vols. LCL. London: William Heinemann; Cambridge, Mass.: Harvard University Press, 1926–65.

Tiede, David Lenz. *The Charismatic Figure as Miracle Worker*. SBL Dissertation Series, no. 1. Missoula, Mont.: University of Montana Press, 1972.

Unnik, W. C. van "A Formula Describing Prophecy." *NTS* 9 (1962–63): 86–94.

———. "A Greek Characteristic of Prophecy in the Fourth Gospel." In *Text and Interpretation: Studies in the New Testament Presented to Matthew Black*, ed. E. Best and R. McL. Wilson. Cambridge: Cambridge University Press, 1979. Pp. 211–29.

———. "Die Prophetie bei Josephus." In his *Flavius Josephus als historischer Schriftsteller*. Heidelberg: Lambert Schneider, 1978. Pp. 41–54.

———. "Die rechte Bedeutung des Wortes treffen, Lukas 2, 19." In *Verbum: Essays on Some Aspects of the Religious Function of Words*, ed. H. W. Obbink, A. A. van Ruler, and W. C. van Unnik. Studia Theologica Rheno-Traiectina, vol. 6. Utrecht: Kemink and Zoon, 1964. Pp. 129–47.

Vaux, Roland de. *Ancient Israel: Its Life and Institutions*. Trans. John McHugh. 2d ed. London: Darton, Longman and Todd, 1965.

————. *Archaeology and the Dead Sea Scrolls*. The Schweich Lectures of the British Academy, 1959. Rev. English ed. London: Oxford University Press, 1973.

Vermes, Geza. *The Dead Sea Scrolls in English*. 3d ed. Harmondsworth: Penguin, 1987.

————. *The Dead Sea Scrolls: Qumran in Perspective*. 2d ed. London: SCM, 1982.

————. "The Etymology of 'Essenes.'" In his *Post-Biblical Jewish Studies*. SJLA 8. Leiden: E. J. Brill, 1975. Pp. 8–29 (= *RQ* 2 [1960]: 427–43).

————. *Jesus the Jew: A Historian's Reading of the Gospels*. London: Collins, 1973; Philadelphia: Fortress, 1981.

————. "Josephus' Treatment of the Book of Daniel." *JJS* 42 (1991): 149–66.

Vermes, Geza, and Martin D. Goodman, eds. *The Essenes According to the Classical Sources*. Oxford Centre Textbooks, vol. 1. Sheffield: JSOT Press, 1989.

Walbank, F. W. *A Historical Commentary on Polybius*. 3 vols. Oxford: Oxford University Press, 1957–79.

White, Robert J., trans. and ed. *The Interpretation of Dreams (Oneirocritica) by Artemidorus*. Noyes Classical Studies. Park Ridge, N.J.: Noyes Press, 1975.

Wilson, Robert R. "Prophecy and Ecstasy: A Reexamination." *JBL* 98 (1979): 321–37.

Winter, Paul. *On the Trial of Jesus*. 2d ed., rev. and ed. T. A. Burkill and Geza Vermes. Studia Judaica, vol. 1. Berlin: Walter de Gruyter, 1974.

Wolff, Christian. *Jeremia im Frühjudentum und Urchristentum*. TU 118. Berlin: Akademie, 1976.

Yadin, Yigael. *The Temple Scroll*. 3 vols. Jerusalem: Israel Exploration Society, 1977–83.

Yavetz, Zvi. "Reflections on Titus and Josephus." *Greek, Roman, and Byzantine Studies* 16 (1975): 411–32.

Zeitlin, S. "The Account of the Essenes in Josephus and the Philosophumena." *JQR* 49 (1958–59): 292–300.

————. "Dreams and Their Interpretation from the Biblical Period to the Tannaitic Time: An Historical Study." *JQR* 66 (1975–76): 1–18.

Index of Passages

Author Index

Subject Index